Kant's Transcendental Imagination

Also by Gary Banham

KANT AND THE ENDS OF AESTHETICS

KANT'S PRACTICAL PHILOSOPHY: From Critique to Doctrine

HUSSERL AND THE LOGIC OF EXPERIENCE (*ed.*)

EVIL SPIRITS: Nihilism and the Fate of Modernity (*ed. with Charlie Blake*)

Kant's Transcendental Imagination

Gary Banham

First published 2006 by
PALGRAVE MACMILLAN
Houndmills, Basingstoke, Hampshire RG21 6XS and
175 Fifth Avenue, New York, N.Y. 10010
Companies and representatives throughout the world

PALGRAVE MACMILLAN is the global academic imprint of the Palgrave Macmillan division of St. Martin's Press, LLC and of Palgrave Macmillan Ltd. Macmillan® is a registered trademark in the United States, United Kingdom and other countries. Palgrave is a registered trademark in the European Union and other countries.

ISBN-13: 978–1–4039–1689–1 hardback
ISBN-10: 1–4039–1689–6 hardback

This book is printed on paper suitable for recycling and made from fully managed and sustained forest sources.

A catalogue record for this book is available from the British Library.

Library of Congress Cataloging-in-Publication Data
Banham, Gary, 1965–
    Kant's transcendental imagination / by Gary Banham.
        p.   cm.
    Includes bibliographical references and index.
    ISBN 1–4039–1689–6
    1. Kant, Immanuel, 1724–1804. Kritik der reinen Vernunft.
    2. Knowledge, Theory of.   3. Causation.   4. Reason.   5. Judgment.
    6. Neo-Kantianism.   I. Title.
    B2779.B34 2005
    121—dc22   2005050200

10   9   8   7   6   5   4   3   2   1
15   14   13   12   11   10   09   08   07   06

Printed and bound in Great Britain by
Antony Rowe Ltd, Chippenham and Eastbourne

For Jane Singleton—who introduced me to the Critique

We entitle the synthesis of the manifold in imagination transcendental, if without distinction of intuitions it is directed exclusively to the a priori *combination of the manifold; and the unity of this synthesis is called transcendental, if it is represented as* a priori *necessary in relation to the original unity of apperception. Since this unity of apperception underlies the possibility of all knowledge, the transcendental unity of imagination is the pure form of all possible knowledge; and by means of it all objects of possible experience must be represented* a priori.

– A118

I fear that the working out of Hume's problem in its widest extent (namely, my Critique of Pure Reason*) will fare as the problem itself fared when first proposed. It will be misjudged because it is misunderstood, and misunderstood because men choose to skim through the book and not to think through it—a disagreeable task, because the work is dry, obscure, opposed to all ordinary notions, and moreover long-winded.*

– Ak. 4: 261

Contents

Acknowledgements

The thoughts presented here have undergone transformation in the course of being worked out partly as a result of the input of colleagues and audiences to whom versions of parts of it have been delivered. Earlier versions of some of the thoughts here were presented to seminars at the University of Hertfordshire, the University of Lancaster and the University of Warwick and to a conference of the British Society for Phenomenology. I would like to thank participants on these occasions for helpful comments on certain points especially Paul Coates, Jane Singleton, Dan Hutto, Keith Ansell Pearson, Stephen Houlgate, Christine Battersby, Robin Durie, Veronique Foti, John Llewlyn, Fiona Hughes, Lillian Alweiss and Rachel Jones. I would also like to thank my colleagues at Manchester Metropolitan University for their support. Mike Garfield is particularly to be thanked for pointing me in the direction of some important references. The students who have attended my classes on the *Critique* have also always taught me a number of things. My thanks go to Howard Caygill for being a constant source of intellectual stimulation and to Nigel Hems for providing me with fresh vantages on problems. Jennifer Nelson and Daniel Bunyard gave important support to this project. As always, I am in the debt of Don Milligan whose love and care sustains me.

Introduction

This work is intended to provide a reading of the Transcendental Analytic of the *Critique of Pure Reason* that is focused on illuminating the connections between imagination, conceptuality and intuition in the Transcendental Deduction and the Analytic of Principles. Kant describes his enquiry as a transcendental one because that is *transcendental* which "is occupied not so much with objects as with the mode of our knowledge of objects in so far as this mode of knowledge is to be possible *a priori*" (A12/B25). What Kant has done in suggesting this point is to re-focus attention from the nature of things in general to how we must understand them if there is to be cognition of them at all. This re-focusing of attention is what, in my view, requires the setting out of a transcendental psychology. Hence I am understanding transcendental psychology as that part of transcendental philosophy that explicates the nature and possibility of the *a priori* elements of cognition themselves in order to show how these elements are what enable us to relate to objects. The claim that will be ventured here is that such notions as "the transcendental unity of apperception" and the "transcendental synthesis of imagination" are essential to demonstrating both *that* there are *a priori* elements of cognition of experience and *how* these *a priori* elements of experience cohere with each other.

What the basic argument of the work is intended to show is that Kant's conception of transcendental philosophy as based on the exposition of transcendental psychology is the basis for his re-foundation of metaphysics. Metaphysics, as Aristotle classically defined it, was concerned with the nature of being *as* being and its first causes (*Met*. IV. 1. 1003a 33). Hence on this definition it coalesced with what later came to be termed "ontology". Kant describes the notion of metaphysics in a number of places but two definitions of it will serve here. In one of his lecture courses on metaphysics he termed it "the system of pure philosophy" due to the fact that it was the description of the *a priori* principles on which all nature must depend (Ak. 28: 540–1). In the *Critique* he terms metaphysics "the system of pure reason" and that which comprehends the investigation of everything that can be known *a priori* (A841/B869). In accounting for the latter they provide the function of being what Aristotle thought of as "first causes" if we remember that what is often translated as "cause" in Aristotle is more appropriately thought of as ultimate explanation.

In this sense therefore Kant retains in his treatment of metaphysics an adherence to the traditional view of its domain. Where he departs from it concerns the connection of this enquiry to one into the limits of reason.

At the opening of the preface to the first edition of the *Critique* Kant makes clear that the presentation of questions that seem to us necessary to be asked and yet incapable of being answered is what motivates the enquiry he will give into the re-foundation of metaphysics (Avii). To address this tendency of thought is to inquire into the nature of cognition itself to find out what produces it and also what will enable us to claim that there are circumstances in which we have principles that do not arise *from* experience but are necessary *for* it. These principles are set out in the Analytic of Principles. The understanding of the Analytic of Principles is however, for reasons that will be described here in detail, not given to anyone who has not first grappled long and hard with the question of what we are told in the Transcendental Deduction about the nature of transcendental synthesis.

Chapter 1 sets out what is effectively a *short argument* for my view. Here I describe a central difficulty concerning the relationship between a statement Kant makes in the Metaphysical Deduction about the nature of synthesis and its relationship with a description in the B-Deduction of a synthesis that is one that is not determined by the *concepts* of understanding. The connection between these statements is used to indicate in this initial chapter a difficulty with understanding the structure of the Transcendental Analytic, a difficulty that I demonstrate here to create problems for the dominant models of interpretation provided by both Anglo-American and continental philosophers. I am aware that a simple statement to this effect is unlikely to be convincing and nor do I expect the argument of this initial chapter to be regarded as compelling to those who are wedded to more analytic and "austere" accounts of the *Critique*, accounts that effectively attempt to eschew all language of transcendental synthesis.

In deference to the view commonly current in Anglo-American reception of Kant that it is both possible and desirable to describe the strategy of justification of the pure concepts of understanding without recourse to the vocabulary of transcendental synthesis, I undertake in the second and third chapters of this work an extensive investigation of alternative deduction strategies. Chapter 2 is an investigation of the Strawsonian contention that it is possible to reconstruct the Kantian account of justification of fundamental judgments without engaging in an investigation of transcendental synthesis and this chapter includes a lengthy excursus into analytic ontology. The discussion of the nature and difficulties of this project leads in this chapter far away from an analysis of the *Critique* itself at many points in order to show that the logical inquiries that emerge from this investigation do have a transcendental structure but one that is insufficient to produce more than the meagre result that awareness of *quale* is necessarily complex.

The result of the failure of the deduction strategy promised from the most analytic and austere contemporary responses to Kant's transcendental philosophy has been the resurgence of interest in German Idealism, a resurgence that has focused on the description of the only viable deduction strategy as one founded on transcendental apperception.[1] The complications of this response to the Kantian view of philosophy already bring in considerations of transcendental psychology and in Chapter 3 I set out responses to some current views of what is meant by transcendental psychology arguing against Cartesian, functionalist and Idealist conceptions of it and demonstrating the impossibility of achieving, by primary concentration on transcendental apperception, a successful deduction strategy.

After having treated these alternative accounts of transcendental philosophy and transcendental psychology to lengthy consideration I proceed in Chapter 4 to a description of what I view as the only plausible deduction strategy, one that is based, as Kant himself thought it had to be, on a description of transcendental synthesis. The key form of this transcendental synthesis is here shown to be that of imagination and the nature and scope of the transcendental synthesis of imagination is dealt with here and a demonstration of the contention that this picture does not fundamentally alter in the reconstruction of the argument of the Transcendental Deduction in the second edition of the *Critique* is given. The defence of the centrality of transcendental synthesis aims also to show the connection of transcendental imagination to transcendental apperception and the structure of transcendental judgment.

Chapter 5 contains a brief summary account of the chapter on schematism. This chapter has two main points of contribution to the overall argument of this work. First, I aim to show here the types of schematism set out by Kant, namely the schematism of empirical concepts, the schematism of sensible concepts and the schematism of pure concepts. The discussion of these forms of schematism is accompanied with a defence of the very notion of schematism in response to some Wittgensteinian arguments against the possibility and desirability of it.

Chapter 6 connects the story concerning transcendental synthesis to the place of pure intuition in experience by showing the mereological nature of intuition. In this chapter I deal with the relationship between the form and matter of intuition and trace the genesis of the description of intuition in the argument of the Transcendental Aesthetic back through the "pre-Critical" inquiries into the nature of mathematics and geometry. The discussion of Kant's mathematical principles is here connected not merely, as has become standard, to a Kantian philosophy of mathematics but also to the Kantian picture of the nature of experience. The mathematical principles described in the treatment of the Axioms of Intuition and the Anticipations of Perception is here shown to be based on the exposition of transcendental synthesis, primarily that of imagination. The argument of this chapter is to the effect that the account of the mathematical principles in the Analytic of Principles is central to the understanding not merely of how Kant schematizes the categories of Quantity and Quality but also to comprehending the *material* principles of experience that are decisively important for grasping Kant's view of the nature of experience.

Chapter 7, like Chapter 6, provides a genetic description of how Kant arrives at the discussion of his principles. In Chapter 7 I focus on the dynamical principles that are described in the Analogies of Experience connecting the discussion of them to the "pre-Critical" inquiries into the nature of substance and to the arrival, after the composition of the Inaugural Dissertation, of Kant's central Critical problems, problems first described in the famous Herz letter. I argue in this chapter that Kant's construal of "Hume's problem" is through the lenses of the difficulty he describes in the letter to Herz and that this is key to comprehending what the nature of his response to "Hume's problem" was. The nature of the problem and the nature of Kant's response are some of the key questions that have always been important in the reception of the *Critique of Pure Reason* but on my analysis correct comprehension of them is only available once the nature and importance of transcendental synthesis has been understood. This chapter develops and defends a view of the three Analogies of Experience that describes them as constitutive of a distinctive renovation of metaphysical enquiry. The nature of Kant's metaphysics is unfortunately not one, however, that the reading of the *Critique* alone can resolve as the defence of the dynamical principles given in the *Critique* conforms to Kant's description of the *Critique* as only being "a treatise on the method" of metaphysics, not "a system of the science itself" (Bxxii). It will be the occasion for future work to describe the nature of Kant's *system* of metaphysics, a system almost lost from sight in contemporary readings of the *Critique* but some of the nature of which will at least be visible from the account of the mathematical and dynamical principles provided here.[2]

Notes

1. Whilst the most notable advocate of this approach is Dieter Henrich and it is his account that I will investigate at length in this chapter there are notable variants on this Idealist contention that I do not treat here and will investigate elsewhere. For one strong variant not here attended to, see Robert B. Pippin (1997) *Idealism As Modernism: Hegelian Variations*, Cambridge and New York: Cambridge University Press. Karl Ameriks has been the most notable advocate of a more "modest" conception of philosophy, one explicitly posed in opposition to the recent Idealist turn. For a lengthy account of the history of Idealist responses to Kant, see Karl Ameriks (2000) *Kant and the Fate of Autonomy: Problems in the Appropriation of the Critical Philosophy*, Cambridge and New York: Cambridge University Press, and for a different view that focuses primarily on the vicissitudes of the term "idealism", see Frederick C. Beiser (2002) *German Idealism: The Struggle Against Subjectivism 1781–1801*, Cambridge, Mass. and London: Harvard University Press.
2. Since the publication of my first book on Kant I have consistently argued for viewing him as providing a renovation, not a destruction, of metaphysics. See G. Banham (2000) *Kant and the Ends of Aesthetics*, London and New York: Macmillan, and G. Banham (2003) *Kant's Practical Philosophy: From Critique to Doctrine*, London and New York: Palgrave Macmillan. The completion of this project requires however an extensive investigation of Kant's metaphysics of nature, an investigation I hope to undertake in due course.

1
Synthesis and Intuition

The same function which gives unity to the different representations *in a judgment* also gives unity to the mere synthesis of
various representations *in an intuition*; and to this unity, in its
most general expression, we entitle the pure concept of the
understanding. The same understanding, through the same
operations by which in concept, by means of analytical unity,
it produced the logical form of a judgment, also introduces
a transcendental content into its representations, by means of
the synthetic unity of the manifold in intuition in general. On
this account we are entitled to call these representations pure
concepts of the understanding, and to regard them as applying
a priori to objects—a conclusion which general logic is not in a
position to establish.

(A79/B105)

Space, represented as *object* (as we are required to do in geometry), contains more than mere form of intuition; it also
contains *combination* of the manifold, given according to the
form of sensibility, in an *intuitive* representation, so that the
form of intuition gives only the manifold, but the *formal intuition* gives unity of the representation. In the Aesthetic I have
treated this unity as belonging merely to sensibility, simply in
order to emphasize that it precedes any concepts, although, as
a matter of fact, it presupposes a synthesis which does not
belong to the senses but through which all concepts of space
and time first become possible. For since by its means (in that
the understanding determines the sensibility) space or time
are first *given* as intuitions, the unity of this *a priori* intuition

1

belongs to space and time, and not to the concept of the understanding.

(cf. §24) (B160-1$_n$)

These two statements pose a fundamental problem for any interpretation of the nature of synthesis in the *Critique*. Whilst the first one given indicates that the unity of intuition is produced by the same function that gives unity to a judgment, the second indicates that the unity of intuition does not belong to the concept of the understanding. There would appear here to be a straight case of self-contradiction and if this impression is to be removed in the interest of a charitable reading of the *Critique* this would appear to require major hermeneutic work. In this chapter I will devote attention to some of the salient characteristics of what I take to be the most important ways of addressing this question of understanding the nature of the relationship between synthesis and intuition. The result of this will be to release the nature of the problem that has to be resolved by this work in terms of the account I will be giving of the transcendental psychology of the *Critique* and it should be the effect of the accounts offered here to persuade the reader that there is a problem that does need to be addressed.

Wilfrid Sellars on space and synthesis

In the first chapter of his book *Science and Metaphysics*[1] Wilfrid Sellars suggests that some types of intuitions are not as heterogeneous to concepts as Kant's "official" view would have us believe. The rationale for attempting to close the gap between concepts and intuitions is that Kant primarily thinks of concepts in terms of generality whilst Sellars argues that there is a ground for thinking of some intuitions as conceptual accounts of individuals. The model Sellars is here trading on is that of the demonstrative "this" so for him: "intuitions would be representations of *thises* and would be conceptual in that peculiar way in which to represent something as a *this* is conceptual" (Sellars, 1968, §7, p. 3). Sellars suggests that there are two types of intuitions as only some intuitions are a product of synthesis or, as Sellars also describes it, "that interesting meeting ground of receptivity with spontaneity which is the 'productive imagination'" (Sellars, 1968, §9, p. 4).[2] Sellars distinguishes the intuitions that are the result of synthesis from those that belong to what he terms "sheer receptivity".

This suggestion that there are two different senses to "intuition" in Kant is further described by Sellars as a difference between "the representations which are formed by the synthesizing activity of the productive imagination and the purely passive representations of receptivity which are the 'matter' (A86; B108) which the productive imagination takes into account" (Sellars, 1968, §18, p. 7). The indication that "intuition" is the name given both to the *product* of the synthesis of imagination and the basic element of what is worked on by this synthesis would indicate an important ambiguity in Kant's treatment. The rationale for Sellars' reading is his understanding of the structural bifurcation of cognition into receptivity and spontaneity. On the side of receptivity Sellars places the manifold of sense, understood as a "raw" manifold and aligned by him with Humean impressions. The reason for setting out a notion of "sheer receptivity", that is this "raw" manifold, is in order to satisfy a requirement Sellars takes from Wittgenstein, the requirement for representations to be *guided* by something beyond the conceptual.[3] Sellars takes this notion of *guidedness* to be necessary in order to avoid conceptual idealism. It makes clear, according to Sellars, the need for a primitive non-conceptual type of representation in order that states of consciousness' connection to the world can be grasped. However, such primitive non-conceptual representations would be necessarily simple and passive. This leads Sellars to suggest that there is a basic problem with Kant's account of space as an *a priori* intuition:

> If I am right, the idea that Space is the form of outer sense is incoherent. Space can scarcely be the form of the represent*ings* of outer sense; and if it is not the form of its represent*eds*, i.e. if nothing represented by outer sense as such is a spatial complex, the idea that Space is the form of outer sense threatens to disappear. (Sellars, 1968, §19, p. 8)

If *simple non-conceptual representations* are the ground of sheer receptivity and such a sheer receptivity is the basis of the synthesis of imagination then we would expect there to be an element of space that conformed to this presentation. So, on Sellars' interpretation, Kant is committed to the thesis that what the representations of outer sense are *of* is, at the level of sheer receptivity, non-complex or simple. But the manner of represent*ing* something in outer terms is *not* simple so it should be the case that the postulate that space is the form of outer sense involves a claim to the effect that nothing given *to* outer sense, at the level of sheer receptivity, is complex. But this claim would involve Kant in "the absurdity of saying that Space is a form of outer sense in that the manifold of outer sense is literally spatial" (Sellars, 1968, §77, p. 30).

Thus, Kant would seem to be involved in either committing himself to a transcendental realist claim about the nature of space, precisely the opposite position to that which he wishes to promote or, alternatively, will have to remove space from sheer receptivity altogether and think of it as only a product of the synthesis of productive imagination. So Sellars argues that Kant has a notion of intuition that is concept-involving and understands this concept-involving intuition to be the nature of the synthesis of imagination and this belief is the key to how he will interpret $B160-1_n$. But Sellars also argues for a notion of non-concept-involving intuition, characterized in broad terms as "sheer receptivity", a notion he suggests is transcendentally required in order for Kant to avoid conceptual idealism. But whilst Kant's systematic intent involves this requirement of sheer receptivity his argument allows no place for this as can be seen in the treatment of space, a treatment that fails to provide room for this requirement and hence leads Kant uncomfortably towards the position of conceptual idealism. Hence this reading of the passages that serve as twin epigraphs for this chapter indicates a systematic problem that Kant failed to resolve and which effectively marks his position as failing to grant the room required for the notion that is necessary for his position, the notion of "sheer receptivity" or of a unity that is not given conceptually.

The real problem that is pointed to by this reading is the nature of the relationship between spontaneity and receptivity and how this relationship is articulated in terms of synthesis. The basic response that Sellars wishes to articulate is the need for thinking of a process akin to concept formation in terms of intuitions, a notion that, in terms of space, would require some account not of "outer sense" in the sense that Sellars believes himself to have shown impossible but instead "a form of inner states or episodes" that, states John McDowell, "would have to be constructed by analogical extension from our comprehension of space as the outer matrix in which intuitions on the first interpretation, shapings of sensibility by the understanding, locate objects".[4] This requirement would present a notion of transcendental psychology but one that is thought not to be Kant's. It is rather provided by Aristotle's argument that "the mind which is actively thinking is the objects which it thinks" (*De Anima* III. 8 431b18) or as Sellars puts it the "representations of *sheer* receptivity" (Sellars, 1968, p. 5) enable the arising of general concepts by a process of abstraction.[5]

McDowell, Sellars and immediacy

John McDowell presents a critical response to Sellars' reading of Kant. But despite the fact that this response is critical, there is important common ground between them. McDowell accepts Sellars' assimilation of synthetic intuitions to concepts and indeed extends it in important respects through his picture of a logical structure pertaining to intuitions, a structure that involves the use of capacities that require representations of *thises*. On this basis McDowell rewrites the statement from the Metaphysical Deduction that provides one of our epigraphs in the following manner:

> The function that gives unity to the various representations in a judgment whose content we can imagine capturing from the subject's viewpoint as that there is a red cube *there* (the function that unites the various conceptual capacities exercised in such a judgment), or (this comes to the same thing) the function that gives unity to the various representations in an ostensible seeing with that same content (the function that unites the various conceptual capacities actualised in such an ostensible seeing), is the same function that—in the sort of case in which there is an intuition; that is, in the sort of case in which the ostensible seeing is a seeing—gives unity to the mere synthesis of representations in an intuition of *the red cube there* or *that red cube*, to speak again from an imagined occupation of the subject's viewpoint. (McDowell, 1998, pp. 460–1)

McDowell's rewriting of this passage from the Metaphysical Deduction is in accord with Sellars' suggestion that some intuitions involve the capacity to represent *thises* and McDowell connects synthesis to the notion of a conceptual repertoire. However, unlike Sellars, McDowell stresses that the notion of an intuition involves "immediate" relation to objects and this notion of immediacy has a role in McDowell's account that is as transcendentally significant as the notion of "sheer receptivity" was for Sellars. The requirement of immediacy is meant however to cut directly against the suggestion that there is a transcendental requirement for receptivity. McDowell states the kernel of his alternative position when he writes:

> The transcendental requirement is that it must be intelligible that conceptual activity has a *subject matter*. And Kant's thought is that this is intelligible only because we can see how the very idea of a conceptual repertoire provides for conceptual states or episodes in which a subject matter for conceptual activity is sensibly present, plainly in view in actualisations of capacities that belong to this repertoire. (McDowell, 1998, p. 464)

The stress hence is moved from *guidedness* to *subject matter*. The notion of a "conceptual repertoire" is utilized to make this shift as the conceptual repertoire is understood by McDowell as the possession of capacities whose potentiality can be actualized when involved immediately with objects. Hence what McDowell's account will harmonize with is a different facet of Aristotle's approach, the one that emphasizes the nature of potentiality rather than that which is concerned with sheer receptivity. To follow through this reinterpretation of transcendental philosophy, McDowell indicates that rather than thinking that there has to be a manifold of sheer receptivity that enables the connection between mind and world to be given a grounding we should instead attend to the role of *objects* as making possible this connection.

> Objects come into view for us in actualisations of conceptual capacities in *sensory* consciousness, and Kant naturally connects sensibility with receptivity...If we conceive subjects as receptive with regard to objects, then, whatever else we suppose to be true of such subjects, it cannot undermine our entitlement to the thought that the objects stand over against them, independently there for them. (McDowell, 1998, p. 470)

On this view sensory consciousness is a kind of *medium* that enables the world to be presented to consciousness. The effect of this is to re-interpret receptivity so that it comes to be thought of as merely the capacity to be affected in a sensory manner so that the object makes contact with our conceptual capacities by triggering the medium in which these capacities are given their actualization. This does allow for a notion of receptivity that is not, as it is for Sellars, "sheer" as it allows for the sensory consciousness to be formed by conceptual capacities whilst also conceiving of such consciousness as a medium that is the arena of actualization of such capacities. However, this reply to Sellars requires a different picture of transcendental philosophy to that at work in Sellars' interpretation. McDowell is forthright about this:

> There is a temptation to suppose transcendental philosophy would have to be done at a standpoint external to that of the conceptual goings-on whose objective purport is to be vindicated—a standpoint at which one could contemplate the relation between those conceptual goings-on and their subject matter from sideways on. Sellars's move fits this conception; he undertakes to vindicate the objective purport of the conceptual occurrences from outside the conceptual order. I shall be taking issue with this conception of transcendental philosophy.

It is important to see that this is not to take issue with the very idea of transcendental philosophy. (McDowell, 1998, pp. 445–6)[6]

McDowell's reply to Sellars does succeed in suggesting that Kant is not caught in the bind of needing an appeal to sheer receptivity that the nature of his thought proves unable to supply. However, not only does McDowell fail to reply to Sellars' account of Space in any detail but he also accepts Sellars' assimilation of synthesized intuitions to concepts. This response to the notion of sheer receptivity seems to deprive receptivity of any transcendental status at all as this is now construed in terms of a merely empirical constraint. The interpretation of B160–1$_n$ is to suggest that the unity of intuition is understood as conceptual, just as with Sellars. Finally, McDowell's rescue of the notion of immediacy as a key requirement for intuition dovetails with a marginalization of the notion of singularity as this notion is invoked, as with Sellars, as an occasion for assimilating synthetic intuitions to concepts. Hence McDowell's response to Sellars is far from a comprehensive reply to the latter's account as it involves important agreements with it and the divergences from it themselves raise significant problems.

Kitcher's picture of intuition

A different response to the difficulty of how to interpret Kant's notion of intuition that focuses on B160–1$_n$ is given by Patricia Kitcher. Kitcher's view acknowledges the point that Kant, in our first epigraph, points to the understanding as the source of all unity whilst, in our second epigraph, seeming to contradict this but she suggests that conceptualization must be necessary for unity and describes an occasion in which a child sees a kite in the sky. She writes that in such an ordinary case of perception it seems appropriate, albeit *after the fact*, to describe the sensory information as adequate for the judgment to be made.

That is, the data delivered by his senses were sufficiently internally coherent and cohered sufficiently with other possible sensory information to make the judgment possible. Under these circumstances, I suggest that we describe the manifold of intuition, that is, the varied contents of our sensory representations, as possessing a 'unity-correlate' of the concept 'kite', or better, a 'kite-unity-correlate'. I prefer the latter expression because it emphasizes the fact that we can talk sensibly only about the unity-correlates of specific concepts; we cannot appeal to an unlimited capacity to be unified.[7]

Whilst these unity-correlates are meant to precede concepts, it is still the case that it is because we *possess* concepts that we can infer their existence. As with Sellars' interpretation, this account involves the view that Kant has in effect conflated two different senses of "intuition" together under a common term. On Kitcher's reading, it is "formal intuition" that has this ambiguity whilst for Sellars it was presented as a difference between intuitions that are and those that are not products of synthesis. However, since Kitcher views "formal intuition" as referring to both the "unity-correlates" and the unity of judgments this involves pretty much the same charge as that made by Sellars as the latter involves synthesis and the former does not.

Günter Zöeller has replied to Kitcher's account suggesting that whilst her interpretation does enable a view of formal intuition that distinguishes it from both the manifold and the unification of concepts and judgments, it does so by multiplying entities. Furthermore, he charges her with a violation of critical philosophy in presenting a view of synthesis that would not match Kant's transcendental idealism:

> It would require an altogether realist reading of Kant's epistemology to see him supposing that the *products* of apperceptive synthesis are essentially *reproductions* of configurations of intuitions that, in principle, antedate any conceptualisation.[8]

In taking this view Zöeller has to abandon the notion that the unity of formal intuition involves an appeal to something that is pre-conceptual, a reading that requires emphasis of a strange sort with regard to the note at B160–1.[9] Whilst Kitcher's reading is as dependent as Sellars' on a notion of an unjustified conflation on Kant's part, it does point to a genuine difficulty albeit resolving it in an artificial manner by gratuitous hypotheses not made by Kant himself.

Heidegger's account of synthesis and intuition

The publication and English translation of all of Martin Heidegger's writings on Kant has now been completed, including the original lecture course that provided the first version of his famous "Kant book".[10] Whilst the aspect of Heidegger's interpretation that has attracted most attention is his account of the significance of transcendental imagination, it is worth looking at how his interpretation deals with the two passages that are our epigraphs.

Heidegger interprets the citation from the Metaphysical Deduction in a manner that involves a distinction between two different types of unity:

> The same function of understanding which gives unity to various representations, *in one judgment*, also gives unity to pure synthesis *in one intuition*. But 'unity' and 'giving unity' do not have the same meaning in each case. To *give unity* to representations in one *judgment* means to constitute the form of judgment as *form*. To *give unity* to pure *synthesis* of various representations means to contribute to the content which corresponds to this synthesis a *further content-factor [Inhaltsmoment] belonging to it*. (Heidegger, 1927–8, p. 197)

Whilst Heidegger is right that there is a distinction between the *form* of the judgment and the *content* of the synthesis, he is ignoring here the stress clearly placed by Kant on the fact that it is the same understanding, by means of the very same actions, that produces both unities. In failing to discuss this Heidegger threatens to break the connection between judgments and intuitions that it is the clear purpose of the passage to assert.

Heidegger's response to the note from B160–1 is given at greater length than this re-casting of the statement from the Metaphysical Deduction. Before looking at it however it is worth reminding ourselves of the text that the note is attached to. The paragraph that includes the note is presented, up to the point the note is introduced, in the following manner:

> In the representations of space and time we have *a priori forms* of outer and inner sensible intuition; and to these the synthesis of apprehension of the manifold of appearance must always conform, because in no other way can the synthesis take place at all. But space and time are represented *a priori* not merely as *forms* of sensible intuition, but as themselves *intuitions* which contain a manifold [of their own], and therefore are represented with the determination of the *unity* of this manifold (*vide* the Transcendental Aesthetic). (B160)

Having mentioned again the fundamental point taken from the Aesthetic that there are forms of outer and inner intuition and that the inner intuition of time gives the form to all appearances, Kant here states that space and time are not just forms of intuition but that they are also intuitions themselves and hence that they have a manifold and a unity. Since the note emerges also in relation to the topic of unity the first question that Heidegger's account attempts to answer is the relationship between the unity mentioned here in the main text and that referred to in the note.

In preparing to address this problem, Heidegger makes a distinction between two uses of synthesis in Kant:

> The expression 'synthesis' is by itself not only ambiguous but it is also often used by Kant precisely when he does not mean a putting together and gathering together by the positing, thetic spontaneity, but rather when he means a *putting* together which he understands more as an *intuiting* together, i.e., as letting-be-encountered. By such a syn*thesis* he actually means a syn*opsis*—as he admittedly says too seldom—and by that he means an original giving-together, i.e., to let the together be encountered out of a unity. This letting-be-encountered already in advance out of a unity holds together more originally than any subsequent holding together of what was previously scattered about. (Heidegger, 1927–8, p. 93)

In invoking this distinction Heidegger cites a term Kant does use, the term "synopsis" in order to argue that it is the true sense of this term that is often meant by Kant when he mistakenly writes of synthesis in some places. Heidegger states here that Kant refers to synopsis rarely and in fact, in a footnote to this passage, gives only two instances of the use of the term in the *Critique*. The first place where Kant uses the term is at A94 where sense, imagination and apperception are distinguished from each other and Kant refers to "the *synopsis* of the manifold *a priori* through sense". This is amplified at A97 where Kant writes: "As sense contains a manifold in its intuition, I ascribe to it a synopsis. But to such synopsis a synthesis must always correspond; receptivity can make knowledge possible only when combined with spontaneity." This second citation restricts the use of the expression to a manifold in the intuition of sense but immediately points to a synthesis that must correspond to this manifold. The synthesis is necessary for cognition as only the combination of spontaneity (here aligned with the notion of synthesis) with receptivity (here aligned with the manifold of intuition) produces it.

Rather than move in the direction of a closer interpretation of Kant's notion of synopsis, Heidegger instead suggests that the expression "synopsis" is itself insufficient to describe Kant's thought as it still suggests an action similar to that of synthesis. Heidegger hence proposes to replace "synopsis" with "syndosis", meaning by the latter expression a manifold that is given as "an original togetherness from unity as wholeness" (Heidegger, 1927–8, p. 93). The point of this is to claim that there is an original unity that is not that of concepts, an "original, intuitive, syndotical unity" (Heidegger, 1927–8, p. 93). On this basis Heidegger subsequently claims that the unity of formal intuition is added to the unity of syndosis, a unity "which is given in intuition as such" (Heidegger, 1927–8, p. 94). This account then culminates in the claim that there are in fact three distinct senses of what Kant terms "synthesis":

> Under the title synthesis he brings together (1) the *syndotical unification*, unity as the original oneness [*Einigkeit*] of wholeness, (2) the *synthetic combination*, unity as categorical concept of possible connection in judgment, (3) the unification of *syndosis and synthesis* in knowledge as thinking intuition. (Heidegger, 1927–8, p. 95)

The basic suggestion of Heidegger's interpretation is thus that sensibility has its own spontaneity.[11] But the basis for this claim in relation to the passage in question is somewhat difficult to find. In claiming that the syndotical unity is something prior to the unity of formal intuition, Heidegger is imposing on the note to B160 something that is not found within it as there is no unity mentioned here other than the unity of formal intuition and this suggestion of two types of unity mirrors that at work in his interpretation of the statement from the Metaphysical Deduction. It would have been more plausible to directly identify the syndotical unity with the unity of formal intuition given that the latter is said to "precede all concepts" but for the fact that it presupposes a synthesis through which "the understanding determines the sensibility". Since this synthesis involves a relationship to the understanding, Heidegger's notion of a syndotical unity that belongs wholly to intuition and has no involvement with the understanding lacks textual support.

When we combine the text prior to the note with the note it seems clear that it is space and time that are spoken of in the note as formal intuitions.[12] This is an important clue to the question of how to think of a unity that presupposes a synthesis in which the understanding determines the sensibility but which precedes all concepts. Connecting this notion to the statement from the Metaphysical Deduction means we have to think the relationship between this synthesis and the argument that the same understanding, by means of the very same actions, brings about unity of synthesis and unity of judgment (albeit, as Heidegger recognizes, that these unities are distinct in terms of the former being a unity of content and the latter one of form). Heidegger's reading gives no basis for enabling this thought to work and hence his account, whilst ingenious in its attempt to describe an original unity that is prior to concepts, lacks connection with the comprehension of the synthesis of understanding that is taken to be pre-conceptual.[13]

Allison's "hybrid" view of formal intuition

By far one of the most influential interpretations of the *Critique* in recent times has been that advanced by Henry Allison. Allison's view of the note at B160 is worth comparing with those already given. It is conceptualist in the sense that, for Allison, the difference between a formal intuition and a form of intuition is that the former is a determinate and hence conceptualized intuition whilst the latter is indeterminate and unconceptualized. However, his position involves a further distinction:

> Not only must we contrast a 'form of intuition' (indeterminate pure intuition) with a 'formal intuition' (determinate pure intuition), but we must distinguish two senses of the former term. This can be taken to mean either the form or manner (*Art*) of *intuiting*, which can be characterized as an innate capacity or disposition to intuit things in a certain way, such as spatially or temporally, or the form, the essential structure, of that which is *intuited*.[14]

The notion of a form of the intuited is introduced by Allison to characterize the all-inclusive space that contains the manifold of spaces. Allison presents it as a "preintuited" framework and it is equivalent therefore to the Heideggerian notion of an original unity with the difference being that this framework is taken by Allison to be transcendentally ideal.

The key feature of this conceptualist view of formal intuition is however concisely stated by Allison as the notion that the formal intuition is "a hybrid" that requires "both the form of intuition and a concept by means of which this form is determined in a certain way". Allison does not however venture to discuss the passage from the Metaphysical Deduction although the notion of the "hybrid" formal intuition gives a clear clue as to how he might wish to think the connection between the "functions" of judgment and the synthesis there described.

The popularity of the notion of the "hybrid" is recurrent and this reading seems so general in its appeal as to almost be the automatic response to the statement at B160n. There is however a clear problem with this interpretation which is that it simply ignores the point made in the note that there is a unity that "precedes all concepts" and that it is this unity, not a "hybrid" unity, that involves a connection between concepts and intuitions that is being spoken of as being the "formal intuition". It would, as hinted above, be much easier to make the notion of the "hybrid" fit the statement from the Metaphysical Deduction as there it is clear that the very same understanding, and by means of the same acts, produces the unity of judgment and the unity of synthesis whereas in the statement from B160n by contrast it is the unity that, whilst arising from the determination of sensibility by the understanding, does not involve the concepts of the understanding that is meant.

Hence Allison's "hybrid" view, showing an adherence to the Kantian official view that unity is a product of conceptuality, will not suffice as an account of the passage from the B-Deduction. The fact that this reading is not capable of grasping the statement from the text hence removes the possibility that the automatic reaction of so many readers is sufficient for an endorsement of a position.

Wayne Waxman on imagination, synthesis and intuition

Recent concentration on the role of transcendental imagination in the structure of the *Critique* has led to the posing of the problem that we have set out in this chapter in a sharper form than was given to Henry Allison. For the clearest statement of a view of the nature of synthesis that rests on an appeal to the transcendental imagination whilst avoiding Heideggerian appeals to a notion of "syndosis" is provided by Wayne Waxman. In interpreting the note at B160 however Waxman sides with Heidegger's view that it is not the notion of formal intuition that needs to be explained as he takes it that the unity that it provides has already been detailed and that it is rather the notion of forms of intuition that has to be explained. According to Waxman, the forms of intuition are "the *innate non-representational faculty ground* of space and time, the peculiar constitution of human receptivity that determines imagination to synthesize apprehended perceptions in conformity with the forms of synthesis, space and time".[15] This notion that the forms of intuition are to be understood in terms of an innate faculty ground refers to a statement made by Kant in his reply to Eberhard. In this late writing Kant described the "ground of the possibility of the sensible intuition" in a more detailed manner than is given in the *Critique*:

> It is the mere *receptivity* peculiar to the mind, when it is affected by something (in sensation), to receive a representation in accordance with its subjective constitution. Only this first formal ground, e.g., the possibility of an intuition of space, is innate, not the spatial representation itself. For impressions would always be required in order to determine the cognitive faculty to the representation of an object (which is always a specific act) in the first place. Thus arises the formal *intuition* called space, as an originally acquired representation (the form of outer objects in general), the ground of which (as mere receptivity) is nevertheless innate, and whose acquisition long precedes the determinate *concepts* of things that are in accordance with this form; the acquisition of the latter is an *acquisitio derivata*, as it already presupposes universal transcendental concepts of the understanding, which are likewise acquired and not innate, though their *acquisitio*, like that of space, is no less *originaria* and presupposes nothing innate except the subjective conditions of the spontaneity of thought (in conformity with the unity of apperception). (Ak. 8: 222–3)

In responding to the Leibnizian Eberhard, Kant argues that it is only the *capacity for receptivity* that is innate and not the representation of space that is so. Kant goes on to identify the formal intuition with space and states that the acquisition of space precedes concepts. This also indicates that if the unity being referred to in the note to B160 is that of formal intuition that this is, as Waxman suggests, the unity of space. Within the *Critique* itself, and again in reply to Leibnizian positions, Kant also states that the form of intuition is original and that the possibility of appearances "presupposes a formal intuition (of space and time) as given" (A268/B324). Since the Aesthetic opens with a statement about how things are "given" to us (A19/B33) and that is clearly through the pure intuitions then it would seem reasonable, as Waxman suggests, to connect pure intuition with formal intuition and hence to take it that it is forms of intuition that are the new element. Whilst this is the case however the note clearly is concerned more to state that the unity of representation that is given by the formal intuition is a product of synthesis and hence it is this unity and this synthesis that is really Kant's concern.

Waxman's argument will subsequently be that it is, in some sense, the transcendental synthesis of imagination that is to be understood as the basis of the unity of the formal intuition that we term space (and time). Hence, unlike the conceptualist view, this position takes seriously the basic text of the note and connects this to an unfolding account within the *Critique* of a transcendental psychology. However, whilst Waxman's view of the note at B160 is much clearer than that of others and better grounded in the text, there is no equivalent place in his work for an account of how it can be that the same understanding, *by means of the very same acts*, can produce unity of judgment and unity of intuition. Since this is missing from his account there is a basic problem about the relationship between the unity of formal intuition and the unity of judgment that is simply not addressed in his account. This entails that our question is no more addressed by Waxman's account than it is by any of the previous ones considered.

In attempting to come to a closer consideration of how our opening epigraphs can be brought together in the unitary framework of one interpretation, it will first be necessary to step back and ask some more basic questions than I have been concerned to set out thus far. These questions concern the manner in which Kant's criter- ion for intuitions are set out, how receptivity is to be characterized, the nature of the understanding in relation to unity and, on the basis of these questions, to conclude by re-posing the problem of the relationship between the unity of judgment and the unity of intuition such that it can serve as a guiding thread for us in the interpretation of the *Critique* and the exposition of the transcendental psychology it sets out.

Kantian intuition: Its characteristics

Whilst I have so far concentrated on the question of what interpret- ations of the two epigraphs to this chapter exist and whether there is an interpretation that can bring them together I wish now to turn to the logically prior question of how one can determine the criterion of an intuition. It is widely agreed that Kant adopts two criteria for an intuition and thought that these two criteria may not converge. The two that Kant mentions are singularity and immediacy but the debate concerns which of the two has priority. As we noted earlier Sellars and McDowell assimilate synthesized intuitions to concepts, albeit singular concepts. This position is also presented in the work of Jaako Hintikka.[16]

There are however a number of reasons not to adopt this view of intu- itions. Manley Thompson points out some of these, including the point that on Kant's argument, even singular concepts require support from intuition in order to have application in experience. As Thompson puts it:

> When a concept is used as the subject of a singular judgment it purports to represent exactly one object. But then in order to accomplish what it purports to accomplish in this use it must satisfy two conditions: it must represent an object and do so by means of characteristics that this object alone possesses. In other words, it must satisfy an existence condition and a uniqueness condition.[17]

Existence conditions cannot be met by concepts alone, as Kant makes clear in his critique of the ontological argument for the existence of God. Since this is the case, for the existence conditions of a singular conceptual term to be met we have to appeal to intuitions, an indication that intuitions cannot be identified with singular conceptual terms.[18]

Another way of putting Thompson's point is that intuitions cannot be presented, as they are by both Sellars and McDowell, as *thises* as to so present them is to erase the distinction between a demonstrative term and an intuition. This indicates that the notion of singularity involved in the determination of intuitions is not equivalent to that given in singular concepts so that if singularity is the cardinal criteria for an intuition then the notion of singularity involved here must be one that is in principle undetermined.

An important reason for thinking that the singularity of an intuition should be presented as undetermined is Kant's famous statement that "Thoughts without content are empty, intuitions without concepts are blind" (A51/B75). This statement of the interdependence of concepts and intuitions for cognition does not appear in the *Critique* until after the argument of the Transcendental Aesthetic has been concluded. This leads Lorne Falkenstein to argue, contrary to the position of Thompson, that it is immediacy that is the primary criteria of intuition, not singularity. The evidence for this view is that Kant, subsequent to the argument of the Aesthetic, presents his argument there as a "transcendental deduction" in which he has "traced the concepts of space and time to their sources" (A87/B120). This is taken by Falkenstein to suggest that the arguments of the Aesthetic are rightly understood as having a regressive quality designed to uncover the genetic basis of intuition. Falkenstein's suggestion thus amounts to the view that the arguments of the Aesthetic are investigations of intellectual representations of space and time in order to reveal the origin of such representations in something non-conceptual and one example of this interpretation concerns Kant's argument that Space is essentially unified, an argument Falkenstein restates as follows: "Were Space constructed by intellect out of sensations it would not be *essentially* united; it would be united only to the degree that the spaces defined by various groups of sensations are in fact synthesized, so that there could well be discrete spaces."[19]

Falkenstein's argument concurs with that of McDowell in emphasizing the criteria of immediacy above that of singularity, albeit following a different set of reasons. But what this stress on immediacy neglects is the problem pointed out by Howard Caygill, the problem that it would appear on Kant's argument that direct apprehension of objects requires formal principles to be given for it to take place, a paradox that suggests that unless the criteria of singularity is pre-given that there is no means for immediate apprehension to take place. As he puts it: "Intuition... seems both to provide the conditions *for* something to affect our sensibility, and to be conditioned *by* something affecting it." He also points to a further paradox when he notes that on Kant's account "we consider intuition both as direct knowledge of objects, namely 'the things we intuit', and as mediated appearance or 'what we intuit them as being' ".[20] Caygill traces these problems back to the reception of Aristotle's divergent accounts of the relationship between νοετα and αιεςθα in *De Anima* and elsewhere.

The presentation of these paradoxes suggests that the stress on singularity that follows from Thompson's argument is the right move but one that still requires some answer to the problem of how to understand the original possibility of this singular unification that is apparently prior to conceptual unification and yet produced by the same understanding, by means of the very same acts, as the unity of judgment. Whilst contemporary scholarship on the criteria for intuition has remained involved in a debate about the relative priority of the two types of criteria that Kant mentions, there is in fact a problem that is intertwined with this problem and that is the difficulty this chapter has set out to expose as the problem of the unification of intuition by means of a synthesis. This problem of the unification of intuition concerns the connection between the synthesis that unites intuition and the possibility of unification in judgment given that the former is both pre-conceptual and yet an act of the understanding.

Is receptivity a transcendental condition?

The interpretation of Sellars took its cue from a notion of "sheer receptivity" that was presented as a transcendental condition for concepts to connect with something beyond themselves, a condition Sellars describes as "guidedness". Whilst McDowell's response to Sellars involves a displacement of this notion in favour of an immediate appeal to the givenness of objects the vulnerable spot of this riposte is exposed by Caygill's paradox. Hence we need to visit again the problem of how, and in what manner, receptivity is a transcendental condition.

The citation from Kant's response to Eberhard that is used by Waxman in proposing his imaginative notion of the unity of intuition involves an appeal to receptivity as such a transcendental condition. In this response to Eberhard Kant argues that the original possibility of receptivity is what is innate. This would be a notion of receptivity quite distinct from the empirical capacity to be affected by objects. This innate ground is the receptivity of the mind to have a relationship to appearances at all. This capacity for receptivity is what enables objects to play the immediate role that they do play, the role emphasized by McDowell. This statement about receptivity in the response to Eberhard is however of the highest generality as what we really need an account of is the constitution of the receptive part of cognition, intuition. This is the area where there is a serious question but here again it must be the case that we have to provide an account of how it is possible for objects to immediately appeal to intuition rather than simply taking this immediacy as our ground for a coherentist account of cognition as McDowell does. On the basis of McDowell's position we cannot describe the *principles* of such immediacy, a fact that leaves them paradoxical in quite the manner pointed out by Caygill. For all dissatisfied with such a paradoxical situation there needs to be a deeper inquiry, than McDowell takes to be necessary, into the distinction of intuition from concepts, a distinction that is greater than is suggested by McDowell and which has to be accounted for in terms of both its genesis and structure. It is to provide this account that we need an investigation into Kant's transcendental psychology.

Understanding and unity: The guiding thread of our interpretation

What this chapter has revealed is that Kant's account of intuition is one that is the subject of extremely varied interpretations and that these interpretations express a central difficulty that they are unable to resolve. This difficulty can be stated in two distinct ways. On the one hand, there is the problem of how to reconcile our two epigraphs. Whilst Kant states in the Metaphysical Deduction that the same under-standing, by means of the same acts, produces a unity both in intuition and in judgment, he also elsewhere suggests that the unity of intuition is not a product of the concepts of understanding but rather of a synthesis that precedes all concepts. So how can there be a synthesis, prior to conceptuality, carried out by the understanding that produces unity in intuition when the unity of judgment, said to be carried out by the understanding, by means of the same acts of understanding, clearly involves concepts?

This way of stating the problem was my first account of the guiding difficulty that this work will attempt to resolve. However, in the course of reviewing the literature on Kantian intuition, we encountered another way of stating the problem. This is in the form of the paradox from Caygill. This paradox involves the fact that whilst intuition is taken, on one of Kant's criteria, to be "immediate", this immediate relationship involves formal principles. Since formal principles are, in the largest sense, products of understanding, this would seem another way of stating the problem of the relationship between intuition and understanding.

Both formulations share the same problem of how we are to understand the possibility of relationship between intuition and understanding and both point to the notion that such a relationship is in fact of primary significance for the very possibility of intuition as such. At this point we can therefore release the problem that will explicate the rationale for the structure of the rest of this work. The problem is how to articulate and explicate the transcendental synthesis of the imagination. It is surely this synthesis that is referred to in the note to B160–1. It is surely also this synthesis implicitly referred to in the statement from the Metaphysical Deduction, a section of the *Critique* otherwise described by Kant as providing "the clue to the discovery of all pure concepts of the understanding" (A66/B91).

What has emerged as the agenda for the interpretation of the central sections of the *Critique* is the requirement to think spontaneity and receptivity in such a way that their transcendental relationship can be understood. This requires re-thinking the accounts of matter and form, intuition and synthesis and making explicit the connection between imagination and apperception. On the basis of the combination of these connections being elucidated, the fundamental problem of the relationship between intuitions and concepts can be recast. What is however clear from the investigations of this chapter is that the shape of a viable picture of Kantian transcendental psychology will be connected, at least at the level of primary principles, to a reshaping of the Aristotelian tradition of philosophical psychology.

In investigating the reshaping of philosophical psychology we will need to place the comprehension of intuitions in relation to that of concepts. In order to think about this relationship however we need to enter the terrain of the interpretation of the Transcendental Deduction. There are two reasons why we need to do this. First, to show how Kant there brings together concepts and intuitions and secondly to address the concerns of those who would argue that the most viable deduction strategy Kant has is one that does not require recourse to the story concerning transcendental synthesis. In Chapter 2 we will address in some detail those, such as Strawson and, in one sense, Sellars, who argue for central reconstruction of the nature of deduction on the basis of a new assessment of the subject–predicate relationship and in Chapter 3 we will assess the chances of a viable deduction strategy based centrally on the transcendental unity of apperception. Only on the basis of these treatments will we be able to return, in Chapter 4, to showing how the transcendental story we wish to uphold is the one that provides Kant's only viable deduction strategy.

2
Judgment and Austerity

We can summarize the results of the first chapter now as follows: there are two fundamental problems in understanding Kant's account of cognition. These problems are: (a) how is intuition itself synthesized such that it is available for cognition at all; (b) what relationship does the synthesized unity of intuition have to the unity of concepts that Kant consistently describes as "judgment"? The citation from the Metaphysical Deduction asserts what I will from now on refer to as the *symmetry thesis*: The symmetry thesis is that there is a basic relation between the *forms of judgment* and the *content of empirical intuition*. Our question concerning this thesis would be what enables us to suggest that this symmetry holds? What, in other words, are the grounds for it? The citation from B160–1$_{n}$ by contrast suggests the following: the claim that there is a basic *intuitive unity* and that this unity is not brought about by concepts. However since this is a unity of pure intuition what we have to think is how it is connected to the unity of apperception (the vehicle of judgments).

So we can distinguish now *three* problems: (a) the problem concerning how intuition is unified as such since this is not brought about by concepts but in some sense *is* a product of a synthesis; (b) the relationship between the synthetic unity of intuition (which is a *formal unity* according to the statement from the Metaphysical Deduction) and the *content* of empirical intuition; (c) the relationship between the synthetic unity of intuition and the unity of apperception. If the synthesis that gives unity to intuition is what is often termed the "transcendental synthesis of imagination" then it is necessary to connect this synthesis to that which relates the content of empirical intuition to the form of judgment. It would also be necessary to think through how the unity of pure intuition connects to the unity of conceptuality (which we think in general as the transcendental unity of apperception).

The relationships between these elements are what have to be understood for the argument of the deduction to be comprehended. Officially Kant's main task in the Transcendental Deduction is to describe the justification for thinking that the pure concepts of understanding (or categories) are what give our perceptions the unitary status of presenting us with objects. Kant describes this task in a number of different ways but it is one that is often thought of as *the* task of the deduction. The reason for this is not hard to seek. In the preface to the first edition of the *Critique* Kant described the enquiry of the Transcendental Deduction as having two sides, one of which concerned the "objects of pure understanding" and was concerned to validate the *a priori* concepts of understanding (Axvi) and the other being a concern to investigate the possibility of the understanding itself, including a display of the faculties upon which it rests (Axvi–xvii). Kant goes on to add here that whilst the first of these tasks is "essential" to his purposes, the second, whilst being of "great importance", is *not* essential. I will be suggesting however that this division cannot be maintained. These two aspects of the investigation have become known as the "objective" and the "subjective" deduction respectively with the latter being thought to have a special prominence in the first or A version of the deduction and the former, by contrast, taken to be particularly important for the second or B version of the deduction.

However the line-up of questions and difficulties that have been generated thus far is likely to meet with a certain type of philosophical resistance. This could broadly be defined as arising from an analytical cast of mind that insists on finding in the structure of Kant's works the outline of an *argument* that need not draw on the subject of transcendental psychology or would at the very least insist on maintaining a subordinate role for it in comprehending the philosophical motivation for comprehending how *objective judgments* arise. This requires however two forms of analysis, one that connects the examination of judgment to the understanding of the atomic elements of experience and one that examines the properties of judgment in connection with the arguments presented in published forms of Kant's writings and is thus more strictly exegetical. The first kind of analysis is pioneered by Dieter Henrich but draws substantially on the account of particulars that was set out by Wilfrid Sellars. In order to uncover the nature of this analysis we will require a lengthy excursus in this chapter into analytic ontology, an excursus that will take us some way from the description of Kant's texts in order that the analytic argument here being considered be assessed as constitutively independent of any specifically "Kantian" terminology.

The Strawsonian and Sellarsian interpretations of Kantian synthesis and Kantian imagination will be shown in Chapter 3 to differ precisely due to their distinctive treatments of analytic ontology. On closing the analytic excursus in this chapter we will address the attempt of Paul Guyer to describe certain elements of the Transcendental Deduction as dependent upon strong views about the nature of judgment.

I want to concentrate primarily in this chapter, however, on the attempt to construct an analytic argument that will basically adduce a consideration of judgment in regard to particulars and predication. The nature of this attempt and the reasons for thinking of it as not ultimately satisfactory will be important in motivating the return to the consideration of transcendental psychology. However we will also thereby have released, for the discussion of such a transcendental psychology, an understanding of the ways its accounts of synthesis will need to be connected to questions of substantive metaphysical import.

Judgment and particulars

In thinking about the thematic of judgment as connected to a question about particulars there are certain licences in the text of the deduction itself. One such is provided at A99 when Kant describes how representations are only absolute unities when considered in connection with single moments. The argument is here indicated to require an understanding of time in relation to the moment as moments will be treated as the elementary units of time. Whilst this is already of significance in itself (as will be clear to anyone who refers this characterization to its ultimate Aristotelian root) it also suggests that the combination of these elementary units together is required for anything like experience to become possible and hence that one fundamental sense of synthesis is given in this combination of elementary moments. But if this is one sense of synthesis then it requires us to connect synthesis to a basic condition of judgment: the condition of combining particulars in such a way that they generate something that is no longer particular. A final element to this consideration is that it would appear on this picture that *sensa* are to be understood as distinct from each other in a basic sense and thus this requires us to resolve the question as to how the distinction between them is overcome in order to describe something like a genesis of experience.

Now that these elements are painted in it becomes possible to understand the first focus of Dieter Henrich's reconstruction of the elements of the deduction in terms of a relationship between the analysis of judgment and the account of synthesis in which the forms of the former in some sense will become shown to be intimately linked to the transcendental conditions of the latter as asserted, after all, in the *symmetry thesis*. The form in which these complexes are tied together for Henrich is in terms of a historical reference to what he occasionally terms "data-sensualism" and which he explicates as involving the following conception: "the primary occurrences of the real for cognition are presentations of simple qualities in diffuse spatial juxtaposition".[1] Once this is set out as a prime element of what Kant needs to account for, the relationship between synthesis, judgment and sensibility is given an emphasis that requires a thought of the logical possibilities of cognition in relation to the understanding of particulars.

The nature of the particulars in question is that Kant specifies them as "sensations" as in the opening paragraphs of the Aesthetic (A20/B34). However the occurrence of "sensations" alone is not sufficient to give rise to the cognition of "objects" as these require not merely the event-occurrences that are so termed but also conditions in thought. One of the prime elements of such conditions is that recognition should literally include *re*-cognition, that is iteration. For this to take place there is required a conception that the *re*-cognition is literally *of* something that is constantly available, a particular that in some sense continues to be presented.[2] The fact is however that we need some kind of bridge between the "sensations" and the objective particulars that they are apparently produced by and *of* which we are informed by the latter. The need for this is described in the distinction between a "sensation" as literally something that informs only instants of time and the "object" which has to have the condition of endurance over time and be given in distinctly different relations to "sensation" in the sense of prompting many different types of sensations at different times. Thus the "sensations" in question are clearly not literal presentations of "objects" as the particularity of the former is different in kind to that of the latter. This creates a seminal problem however which is how, given that what appears to be "immediate" is after all described in such terms of simplicity, there can appear a relation to objects at all.[3]

In order to progress with this problem it is necessary to make a distinction between types of sensation. Some must be taken to be purely and simply atomistic, that is merely a relation of cognition to something "immediate" that we might term in general, "subjective". This type of "sensation" would, that is, be constitutively independent of relation to any "object" and not be informed by the latter. This would need to be distinguished therefore from the "sensation" that is connected to objects and would point to the fact that whereas the first type of sensation (which we could now term "sensation₁") is merely a response of the cognizer to something purely felt by them, the latter type of sensation ("sensation₂") would in some intrinsic sense be connected to "objects". The difference between the two types of "sensation" would be that whereas the former is simple, the latter is complex as the possibility of iteration would require more than can be given in the fleeting atomistic form of "sensation₁" and what this would require would be that "sensation₂" would have a durability that would permit being revisited. Hence the latter would be a phenomenal form of "substance".

The analytic exposition of these elements of consideration leaves untouched the question of how the combination that would be required for "sensation₂" to provide us with an objective correlate takes place. This is the point at which the notion of synthesis seems to be required. But if it is required to demonstrate how these particulars come together into complexes then the sense of synthesis that is initially required is described in the notion of "judgment" itself as Kant states in the famous footnote to the *Metaphysical Foundations of Natural Science* where he terms judgment in general as "an act by which given representations first become cognitions of an object" (Ak. 4: 475–6n). This licenses the attempt to construct, in the first instance, an *austere* argument that will begin by understanding "synthesis" on the model of "judgment" and hence will attempt to describe the problem of the objectivity of "sensation" through a connection of "sensation" to "judgment" as is required for the *symmetry thesis*. To the basic definition of judgment as given in the *Metaphysical Foundations* we can add the first description Kant gives of judgment in the Metaphysical Deduction where he describes the action of judgment as the collection of presentations under general headings so that: "a *higher* representation [than the immediate one of 'sensation₁'], which comprises the immediate representation and various others, is used in knowing the object" (A69/B94, my interpolation).

The connection between this "*higher* representation" that goes beyond the immediacy of "sensation₁" in order to make possible the action of combination that is required for "sensation₂" to be allied with the basic notion of "object" is what needs to be explicated for an austere argument to succeed in demonstrating the basis of the *symmetry thesis* to be analytically derived from properties of intuition on the one hand and the form of the judgment on the other. This requires a turn of attention now from the analysis of the "sensations" to the "judgment". In a sense this might be thought to simply replay the same problem that led us to distinguish between two senses of sensation because just as sensations can be either merely subjective or in relation to something "objective" so it would also appear that judgments asserting anything can be made but only some such would in fact refer correctly to something that is really the case and hence whilst the first sort would be subjective ("judgment$_1$"), the second would be objective ("judgment$_2$"). However, whilst this would seem to simply replicate the position already found problematic with regard to the matter of intuition, it does not really do so as the characteristic of judgments by which they correctly assert something to be the case would appear to be a property of their *form* irrespective of any existent "object" that they might be thought to describe. Thus judgments, unlike "sensations" can be "objective" without requiring the existence of "objects" that are taken to be present in the world.[4]

Since the objective validity of judgments is hence not bound to their capacity to describe correctly something thought presently to be taking place there is in fact a more complex structure in their case than we have so far disclosed to belong to sensation. This complexity touches on the nature of the *symmetry thesis* itself as we find that the *form* of the judgment gives it objective validity whereas it would appear to be part of the *content* of the empirical intuition that allows the latter to be termed "objective", *just as is asserted in the symmetry thesis*. However whilst this is an important and intuitively satisfying point it complicates the difficulty of how we are going to find any connection between the two elements of the *symmetry thesis* since it would appear that the possibility of objectivity in each part of the thesis is so strikingly different. What we have however found thus far to be an important point about the nature of the type of intuition that would allow connection to an object ("sensation$_2$") is that it requires conditions of iteration that allow for its re-cognition as without such there would appear only to be a transitory character to the matter of intuition. Therefore at this point we appear able to state that the connection of the austere argument would appear to be one between the form of an objectively valid judgment and the stability of presentation of the content of intuition. At this point we can turn to an elaboration of such an "austere" argument and assess its prospects for success as an account that will not require the resolution of the elaborate problems to which we were directed in Chapter 1.

Combination, predication and particulars

There are a number of possibilities for such an "austere" argument and one would involve a refinement of the attention to judgments such that we work out whether there is something like a basic form or mode of judgment on which the genus of judgment in general can be shown to rest. Philosophers who focused on the notion of predication classically followed this line of thought. Leibniz is perhaps the key modern exemplar of such an approach but in more recent philosophy a revival of it has been key to the considerations of Peter Strawson. He writes for example of concepts that enter into what he terms "fundamental judgments" that:

> They are what—special training apart—we *experience* the world *as* exemplifying, what we *see* things and situations *as* cases of. Correlatively, experience is awareness of the world as exemplifying *them*. We should not say that judgments at this level are made on the basis of experience. Rather we should say that at that this level judgment, concept and experience are merged; that seeing and believing really are, at this level, one.[5]

The basis of this connection includes an explicit suggestion that the ability of iteration with regard to objectively valid judgments is connected to the unification of the manifold by "the two great notions of Space and Time". Clearly to locate exemplars of a general concept in experience is to bring together spatially and temporally discrete particulars under the collective heading that the judgment is asserting. Furthermore, whilst particulars can be brought together under an almost infinite number of different collections, there is a limit to what can be shared by discreet particulars which is not given merely in the logical connection of particulars to general concepts but requires in addition the placing of particulars in locations with regard to each other. In other terms two particulars cannot be of exactly the same kind and be located in the same precise spatial position, a fact that suggests a first connection between judgments of distinction and spatial locations. As Strawson puts it: "Particulars, then, are ultimately differentiated by spatio-temporal difference" (Strawson, 1974a, p. 17).

However whilst this might be thought to indicate a first clue as to how we can bring together judgments and intuitions it is no more than that. After all, the judgment *as* judgment does not directly concern particulars but rather their manner of being collected, as Kant asserts. Concepts as set out in judgments are principles of such collection but, states Strawson, they are also "principles of distinction". How do concepts serve this latter function of enabling distinction between terms to take place? According to Strawson this occurs through the fact that concepts describe "ranges".[6] The nature of the ranges in question is that within them the concepts that belong to the given set cannot be co-descriptive of the same particular and hence these concepts are, as it were, in "competition" with each other. By contrast, the particulars that the range of concepts describes are *not* in "competition" with each other as there is nothing in the nature of the particulars to prevent two from being co-exemplificatory of the same concept. Hence, as Strawson puts it, "concepts of particulars come in incompatibility-groups in relation to particulars but particulars do not come in incompatibility groups *vis-à-vis* concepts" (Strawson, 1974a, p. 19).

So if particulars are differentiated in the first instance spatio-temporally they are subsequently distinguished from each other not according to their own characteristic ranges but rather according to the distinction of ranges that emerge from the basic nature of conceptual collections. Therefore we seem to have uncovered not a basis for arriving at the *symmetry thesis* but rather an important *asymmetry*. This result is used by Strawson to argue that there is indeed a "basic combination" at work in what we might term "atomic judgments" (not an expression used by Strawson himself). This is to the effect that the subject–predicate form of the proposition is basic to its ability to be truth-bearing. In these elementary or "atomic" judgments "objects" are understood as falling under subject-concepts and hence as describing the particular that is being judged. The predicative element of the proposition is the supplying to the subject of it a property that brings it into connection with other subjects thereby giving it commonality. However there are at least two problems with connecting this Strawsonian thesis concerning the "basic combination" of judgments with the Kantian question about the relationship between the form of judgments and the matter of intuition.

These two problems are that on the one hand it would appear to be anathema to Kant to relate to space and time as themselves predicates of judgments and yet Strawson's suggestion that particulars are ultimately differentiated by reference to these forms of intuition suggests a need to build the distinction that comes from the nature of intuition into logical form itself thus radically undercutting the heterogeneity thesis that is so important to Kant. On the other hand it is unclear, given the account of the "basic combination" that Strawson supplies, why we should take the individuation of particulars to require, as it must for Kant, reference to something more than relational conceptions. Hence, if propositional functions that tie together elements of judgments into distinctions can be fixed by such things as proper names and demonstratives (which seems to fit Strawson's model of the judgmental-form well) then there is no rationale within this logical structure for the Kantian demand. Thus whatever we think of Strawson's suggestion it is not able to generate the connection between judgments and intuitions that Kant requires precisely due to its assimilation of the matter of intuition with judgmental data. On this basis alone it would further appear that there is no clear route from the simplicity of the elementary matter of sensation, even given as a component of a judgment, and the complex construction we are wont to term "objects". As Dieter Henrich puts this: "If one is unable to discern more about the particular properties of synthesis in judgment, then judgment could remain restricted merely to the ascertainment of simple characterizing features and sequences of sensations" (Henrich, 1976, p. 142).[7]

However the next point worth making seems to point in the opposite direction to this assertion that we have yet to leave the ground of "data-sensualism". Just as judgments can collect together particulars in relation to determinations so also we can, in formulating a valid judgment, entirely leave aside the realm of particulars and simply assert relations between classes. Since classes can also be formed of attributes and predicates, not merely subjects, it follows that we can create a set of judgmental relations that do not require reference at all to "subjects" of propositional sort. However, whilst the importance of this part of the examination of judgment will be amply demonstrated in due course let us initially stick to the question of the simplicity of what can be involved in conceptual grasping. Leaving aside for the moment the questions that have thus far arisen about the nature of judgment we can also describe concepts as apparently having connection even to the simplest data of presentation in the form for example of the fleeting sensation if we grasp a basic name for these sensations such as Wilfrid Sellars' notion of "quale".[8] I do not simply mean by this that it is possible to give "sensations₁," a technical name that frees us from having to duplicate a term or that the capacity to grasp fleeting moments of experience under general terms is a conceptual possibility (albeit one that might be thought pale in comparison to the richness of the sensible data). Rather, I think it is necessary to investigate the possibility of such "quale" precisely due to the fact that if statements concerning them are logically possible at all and particularly if such statements can be expressed in logical connectives then this gives us reason to think that perhaps judgments with regard to them may be *more* basic than the ones Strawson has captured in his analysis of predication. The possibility of such "ultra-basic" judgment would then re-open the prospect for a different type of "austere" path towards establishment of a deduction of objects from the examination of judgment.

Bare particulars and logical form

Wilfrid Sellars examined over a number of years questions about the nature of logical form that are concerned with the ways in which distinctly different statements can be obscured by apparently having the same translation when set into logical formulae. So for example whilst $f(x)$ would appear to state a functional relationship between elements that does not officially require the introduction of class analysis, the necessity for this latter type of analysis can be soon found to undermine the apparent simplicity of this functional relation. The classic example provided by Sellars is how the following statements all seem to be characterizable by the form $f(x)$:

A.1. Fido is a dog.
A.2. It is a twinge.
B.1. Fido is angry.
B.2. It (a certain experience) is painful.

However whilst the same function seems adequate for all of the statements as given the fact is that there is a reason why we have, in our tabulation, treated them as describing different classes of statements. The reason for this is that the first pair, unlike the second, can be simply translated into giving a relation between classes (as in "A.12 Fido Dog") so that the words that previously were predicates become class terms but in the second case it would appear that by contrast the best that can be established is a reference to something that was not explicit in the original statement (as in "B.22 It Painful-*situation*"). This points, for Sellars, to the need to analyse the nature of the complexity of the B-statements that does not permit their simple translation into logical relations between classes.

In order to facilitate this analysis Sellars provides a question that will take the analysis as so far given a further stage. This is to the level of mereological analysis:

> Consider A.2, 'It is a twinge'. Would it not be reasonable to say that this statement asserts that its subject item *as a whole* is a *case* of, an *instance* of the concept Twinge. In 'Fido is a dog' is it not Fido *as a whole* that is said to be a *case* or *instance* of Dog?[9]

The questions initially appear very strange as it would appear, for the analyst of logical form, that there is here nothing being asked. If, as

Strawson apparently asserts, the subject–predicate relation is the "basic combination" of judgments then this is because in such cases we have revealed the simple elements that are being asserted in propositional functions. In these cases we are, are we not, simply asserting that one part is subject and the other predicate so that the subject is not a *part* of what can be being described by the predicate, something that rules out consideration of mereology. However if we turn to the B-statements and ask the same question in their cases then there does appear to be a problem that can be stated in mereological form. After all, in the statement that the experience is painful it would appear strange to say that the experience in question was a *case* or *instance* of pain and we would normally by contrast describe the experience as a complex, the important part of which we are singling out, as the inclusion within it of something painful. In such a situation we cannot say that the experience is not what the statement is concerned with but we can say that the experience is not itself an *instance* of the pain we are describing. Hence the experience is not *as a whole* characterized by the pain, we are stating it was an *occasion* of. If however we follow this hint and ask what then the relation is between the pain and the experience in the judgment it may seem necessary to state that the former is an *ingredient* of the latter.[10]

It seems necessary to suggest that instead of thinking of the *experience* as the *case* of pain the experience *regarded as a situation* be so thought. This requires us to attempt an investigation of what would be meant by this reference to situations. It is this notion that Sellars describes as requiring us to refer to "complex particulars" and the minute we see that the arrival of the description of the painful experience is part of a complex we are led to a term that designates this complex and that is what "situation" (or "thing" in the case of the other judgment) does. The logical peculiarity of these complex particulars is then substantiated by Sellars as follows: "They are concepts or universals which require for their analysis the use of existential operators" (Sellars, 1949, p. 315). This result is sufficiently peculiar for Sellars to argue that we should not view the relation $f(x)$ when applied to the difficult class of judgments we have been tracing in this way but instead as involving relations of *exemplification* between particulars and functions that are not linguistic. The basis of this claim is a departure from the analysis of incompatibility-relations of ranges that we took from Strawson. The argument here is that whilst incompatibility-relations tell us about the nature of particulars once they are *complexes*, we need first of all a description of how such complexes are arrived at that does not require us to specify them as necessarily requiring existential operators. The distinction of what we might term one basic particular from another is that the two are *different* to each other and this difference is a key element of the characterization of these particulars *qua* particulars.[11]

Recognition of this point requires analysis of what is occurring such that basic particulars can become ingredients of complex particulars. There would appear to be a set of relations between basic particulars that is established for the basic particulars to belong together in the complex particular. These relations are ones of co-ingredience and are specified in terms of a basic logic by Sellars.[12] The key characteristic feature of this logic that emerges from the analysis as a whole is that at the level of atomic judgment the identity conditions for the class of atomic particulars and the universals that exemplify such particulars are the same. Hence when dealing with such atomic elements of judgment we can assert an equivalence between universals and classes and this equivalence points to the fact that judgments concerning simples and judgments concerning that which appears to be the opposite of a simple (namely a universal) can be tied together. This implies, at the level of logical analysis, a connection between the ability of atomic judgments to capture the characteristics of simples *as such* and the characteristics of the latter as being transitory items that does not prevent them from being treated to iteration.

If however the simples that can be captured in even atomic judgments are capable of iteration then this implies that the basic particulars to which they refer are not *bare* particulars or, as we might otherwise term them, featureless substrata.[13] The argument as to whether it follows either from the nature of this analysis or from an understanding of ontology that such bare particulars are impossible forms an important point of contention between Sellars and William Alston. A survey of this dispute will finally bring us to the brink of an understanding of what is and what is not involved in acceptance of *quale*. Sellars' attempt to demonstrate the problem with "bare particulars" is conceived of by him as a response to a logical problem, the full point of which it will take some time yet to reveal. In order to motivate the riposte to the doctrine of "bare particulars" however he first postulates a source of belief in them that is distinct from what might be thought obvious.[14] This is through a conception of particulars as instances of only one simple non-relational universal.[15] The conceptual framework of this view is then supplied in some detail:

> It is to be a defining characteristic of the conceptual frame we are elaborating that no particular belonging to it *can* exemplify more

than one simple non-relational universal. Let us call these particulars *bare particulars*, and the simple non-relational universals they exemplify, *qualia*. Now the first step in removing the air of complete unreality which surrounds the above stipulation is to point out that even though the basic particulars of this universe each exemplify one and only one *quale*, it is nevertheless possible for this universe to contain complex objects exemplifying complex properties. To say this, of course, is not to assert that *over and above* basic particulars exemplifying *qualia*, the universe under consideration might contain additional particulars and universals, only this time, complex ones. For sentences attributing complex properties to complex particulars are logical shorthand for conjunctions of sentences each of which attributes a *quale* to a basic particular, or a simple dyadic (or triadic) relation to a pair (or trio) of basic particulars. In short, the fundamental principle of this conceptual frame is that what is ostensibly a single particular exemplifying a number of universals, is actually a number of particulars exemplifying simple universals.[16]

At this point we get a clear sense of what Sellars takes *quale* to be: namely the expression of what in the basic particular enables it to come to conceptual expression. Thus if we take our *quale* to be, as Sellars does, "Greenness" then it would follow that this *quale* is exemplified by a basic particular. The relation between the *quale* and the particular that exemplifies it would be one of class membership so that a member of the class of Greenness would be said to be a *grum*. The question then arises as to whether it is possible for a basic particular to be an instance of more than one *quale*? What gives this question edge is the fact that, in order for the particular in question to be basic in the appropriate sense, it would have to without internal complexity as if it included such complexity this would either be in the form of containing within itself further particulars (and hence would stamp it as non-basic) or universals (which would have the unfortunate consequence of treating Greemness as *part of* the grum). So can we think of a particular then as instancing more than one *quale* whilst being basic? The truth is that to think of such a bare particular as itself being either Greem or anything else (such as Veem) is in fact not plausible as this would be to say of the particular in question that it *is* greem whilst "the theory says that not *a* but the complex *a-instancing-Greemness* is greem" (Sellars, 1952, p. 290) which leads to the point that to attempt to think of this particular as instancing more than one *quale* reveals to us the fact that it cannot instance any at all as it is after all a bare particular.[17]

What this shows is in accord with the previous article of Sellars' that we described to the effect that only complex particulars are capable of instancing anything at all and that hence the subjects of logical language are sets and types of such complexes.[18] To instance is to have a relation to a *quality* which is what occurs in the case of complex particulars and not in that of bare particulars and thus it is false to state that qualities are themselves bare particulars. This hence frees the appearance of qualities of any sort (including "sensations$_1$") from being designated as logically singular. Does this therefore mean that Sellars' argument has introduced the notion of a *quale* only to demolish it as part of the programme of arguing against a role for "bare particulars" in ontology? No as if we transfer our talk of Greem into the world of sensations in which we are placed then the elements of any appearance of green is built out of parts that cover a surface. The parts of the green would appear to be divisible into simpler points and these latter could be termed "basic particulars" although to retain the notion of *quale* would be to suggest that the points that collectively produce a green expanse would themselves have to neither instance green nor extension.

It is the question as to why bare particulars are taken not to be capable of instancing relations with *quale* that is the centre of William Alston's reply to Sellars. According to Alston what the argument that a bare particular cannot instance two distinct *quale* really turns on is the assumption that instancing is not a relation in the case of bare particulars. The reason why Alston suggests this point is in the case of the bare particular exemplifying Greemness we were told by Sellars that it does not stand in a *relation* to Greemness as it is rather a grum. However if we instead took it that for the grum to exemplify Greemness it would have to include as part of its conception a relation to Greemness then what is there to prevent it from also having a relation to a different *quale* such as Veemness? The reason for thinking of the possession of instancing as requiring relationality by Alston is that it is unclear what other categorial connection could be being stated between Greemness and the grum in question if not one of relation. Alston then brings out the point of this when he raises the question of what the relata are in the relation between Greemness and grum. What, in other words, stands in the instancing relation to Greemness? Evidently not a complex (or, in Alston's term, qualified) particular so it must be a bare particular or a substratum.[19]

Alston's riposte to Sellars is based primarily therefore not on an assessment of the nature of the bare particular's internal structure but rather on its extrinsic properties and in him claiming that even such a particular has extrinsic *logical* properties. However in so pointing Alston's argument fails to register the point about the nature of bare particulars as incapable of internal complexity. The importance of this for Sellars was precisely that in the absence of such complexity instancing was impossible. Hence for Sellars the question turns on understanding intrinsic properties of bare particulars whilst for Alston the possibility of relations between bare particulars and *quale* is built on an extrinsic relation. If we take the bare particular to be capable of such an extrinsic relation this requires a conception of it as something that can instance many properties. For it to instance many properties however is for the bare particular to include within its internal structure complexity of connections whether through universals or particulars and this is precisely what Sellars' argument turns on as at this point the "bare particular" ceases to be bare and becomes complex. At this point however it becomes clear that the introduction of the substratum into Alston's reply has altered the nature of what is being discussed as this latter is apparently capable of underlying any number of particulars and not having identity conditions being given by any particular that it appears to underlie (Alston, 1954, p. 257). This indicates that in fact the nature of the substratum is not strictly capable of being identified at all, whether in relations of instancing or otherwise as no relation to any element of what it underlies can be securely shown to be necessary for it at which point its appearance in ontology becomes superfluous.[20]

The result of analysis of this exchange is to reveal what does emerge positively from Sellars' analysis of particulars. It is that whilst the notion of a particular instancing a *quale* is not in itself implausible what is shown to be so is that there could be a substratum that could perform the function of being the fundamental referent of atomic judgments whilst simultaneously lacking the complexity of structure needed for predication to in fact take place. This demonstrates in turn that predication does have requirements that are connected not merely to logical relations of compatibility but also to *ontological* relations of ingredience. This hence demonstrates part of what we need to understand the *symmetry thesis* which is that the nature of judgment is intrinsically tied in its elementary features to the nature of what can intrinsically be an object *of* judgment and that even "sensations$_1$" to be available for description have to display the complexity of structure that allows them to be distinguished from each other, a complexity that cannot be given to bare particulars and hence no form of sensation can be described as a bare particular even if the basic qualities of sensation can be termed *qualia*.

Logical individuals and spatio-temporal particulars

The relation between the positions outlined by Sellars in the writings devoted to an explication of the logic of complex particulars and those set out subsequently by Strawson as part of an analysis of the subject–predicate relation now needs to be drawn out. Fortunately this can be done both in regard to a further articulation of these positions in their own terms and, more pertinently, in relation to their distinctive interpretations of Kant. With regard to the first point the occasion of an exchange at Duke University in 1955 between Sellars and Strawson allowed for a comparison between their distinct accounts of the relationship between the analysis of logic and the description of the nature of spatio-temporal objects. Strawson initiates this exchange by describing the subjects of logical expressions as individuals whilst the "object" regarded as occupying a distinct spatio-temporal location is contrastively termed a "particular". On this construal "individuals" are taken to be whatever can replace the x in $F(x)$ or as whatever can be said to be *the* so-and-so in question. Individuals are, thus, it would appear, intrinsically complex as they must be capable of being identified, distinguished from other things both of similar and different type and describable as unities. The problem with the characterization that thus emerges is that it seems that, given appropriate nominalization, almost anything could thus fit the classification of "individual". Whatever does so appear however would be the subject of a judgment. To this corresponds a predicate which is represented by the F in $F(x)$ and which would have to be able to present us with a basis for collecting or classifying together things that appear as individuals. A first connection Strawson suggests here between subjects and predicates is that the former can in some cases supply of themselves a principle of collection and hence certain individuals carry, as it were, with them their predicates such that these predicates belong primarily to the individuals in question. This marks these predicates as *primary*.

These preliminary treatments of the nature of logical individuation are then followed by remarks on the nature of spatio-temporal particulars and the key here is that Strawson wants to distinguish these from what he terms "non-particulars" where it is characteristic of the particular that it is essential to its identification that it occupies a particular spatio-temporal position whilst it is not meaningful to speak of non-particulars in this way.[21]

Having brought out these terms Strawson reveals his agenda to be one that is close to the problem that it would appear must be given serious treatment for the *symmetry thesis* to be set out. The agenda for Strawson is set by a consideration of why it is that amongst the apparently infinite number of possible "fillers" for the position of individuals we have an almost universal tendency to select particulars for specific attention as being central exemplars of individuation. This points back to the classic philosophical problem of universals bringing out, however, an aspect of it that is elementary to our understanding of the linkage suggested in Kant's statement of symmetry. This would concern the ontological priority accorded to particulars that seems so insistent in philosophical thought.[22] The ontological priority accorded to particulars is connected to the doctrine that the basic individuals of logical form should correspond with this, an alleged requirement that provides a distinctly different form of required symmetry than is given in Kant's statement but which appears related to it. Strawson describes this in the following manner:

> This doctrine is expressed by saying that particulars can appear in discourse only as logical subjects, never as predicates, whereas non-particulars can appear both as subjects and as predicates. So particulars are unique among individuals in never appearing in any other role *but* that of individuals. (Strawson, 1957a, p. 446)

If it can be shown to be a requirement not merely of a satisfactory ontology but also of a logic that would display the basic structures of combination in a correct way that there is an intrinsic connection between individuation and particulars then we would have discovered a basis for the *symmetry thesis* that would not require for its assertion anything more than an "austere" exposition of the nature of logical form. However the claim may appear to have been won too easily if we recall the infinite variety of possibilities of what can serve as an individual. Given this variety and thus the capacity, after appropriate quantification, what is to prevent ultimate relativization of the distinction between subject and predicate?[23]

In response to this problem Strawson looks at the nature of how discourse in language appears to relate to logical structures and argues that we are primarily concerned not with all or even most so-and-so's but rather with a certain type of so-and-so that is our concern at the given time of the discourse. In other terms reference in what Strawson would characterize as "ordinary discourse" does not require strict identification conditions. Predicates of particulars would, by contrast, be the characterizing features by which what we refer to in such manner can be captured as the thing in question. The primary such predicates that allow relative fixing of the individuals that we think of when we speak of the so-and-so that we do in the indeterminate way that is normal are of course expressed for Strawson as the general notions of space and time. Hence the lack of fixity in general terms of the individuals of ordinary speech is given its relative dimension by the space/time nexus and this latter is what basically guarantees individuation in general. In other terms, what is primarily capable of nominalization and hence gives point to quantification is not the apparent "direct" referent of talk but rather the means of expression of such talk, the framing of which occurs in fundamental judgments through their reliance on the basic conditions of intuition.

Sellars' response to Strawson in this symposium is initiated by reference to a set of ontological distinctions. We found that Sellars' article on the nature of particulars demonstrated that belief in "bare particulars" was sustained according to him by two errors, one of which is the confusion of particulars with "facts". In his reply to Strawson Sellars is keen to make clear that "facts" are non-particulars along with "attributes". Facts are taken to be ontological categories that relate attributes to each other or connect particulars together such that one can express a true statement concerning the other. This notion of "facts" and its tie to the nature of "statements" is key to the reply assayed to Strawson by Sellars as what the latter wishes to deny is the potential ontological plasticity of the distinction between subject and predicate whatever the apparent grammatical infinity of possible individuals. The basis for this differentiation is that if "Socrates" is related to as not a *logical* subject but an *ontological* one then the point in ontological terms is that it is not possible to relate to "Socrates" as predicate.[24] Sellars want to state that this ontological point tells us something about the nature of what he terms "statement utterances" or "statement events". What these involve is what he terms a "dialectical distinction" between subject and predicate that is dissimilar to the logical distinction in that it describes the roles that are fulfilled in types of statements by the statement events that are possible in them. Statements are composed of term-events in such a manner that "Socrates: wisdom" can be a pairing that responds to the two alternative questions "Socrates: Ø?" and "x: wisdom?". The blank that requires filling in the questions is referred to in these cases by Sellars as the *old term* whilst the filler in the reply is the *new term* such that Socrates is old term in reply to one question and wisdom in reply to the other (and vice versa with new terms). This points to the rationale for the plasticity in Strawson's notion of an individual. However: "it would be puzzling in the extreme to say without further ado that *Socrates* is the (dialectical) *predicate* of 'Socrates: wisdom' even if we are considering this statement as an answer to the question 'x: wisdom?' "[25]

The reason for the oddity of the suggestion that Socrates is a *predicate* is what needs to be brought out for Sellars' reply to Strawson to be grasped. It concerns the fact that whilst we could logically analyse the answer to the question "Socrates: Ø" either by saying that the answer shows Socrates possesses an attribute or by saying that Socrates has had something predicated of him we could not state that Socrateness had itself been predicated of wisdom. The reason this latter cannot be said, however, is for Sellars not a remark about logical grammar but about the ontological commitments revealed to reside in statement-events. We can say that wisdom is exemplified by Socrates, a statement that attributes an event that demonstrates that Socrates can work as an exemplification of a type that he tokens. But we do this, on Sellars proposal, with regard to the dialectical events of Socrates and wisdom, not with the logical constructions of subject and predicate.[26]

The basic contention that Sellars makes against Strawson follows from this construction as when he states that Strawson has "confused viewing something as *belonging to the range of a variable*, with viewing something as *belonging to the set of items which satisfy a certain function*" (Sellars, 1957, p. 468). The importance of this is that whereas in the former case we are dealing with ontological *subjects*, in the latter we are dealing only with ontological *attributes* and *predicates*. Whilst a number of possibles can fit the realm of predication in this respect the number that fit that of subjects is rather curtailed. The suggestion to the contrary is, for Sellars, based on a misunderstanding of what "functions" might refer to in our discussion, such that we may be speaking of either "propositional" or "real" functions.

> For though an item cannot satisfy a real function without satisfying a propositional function, it is not the case that to satisfy a propositional function is necessarily to satisfy a real function. To satisfy a real function is *to be subject constituent in a fact*, and therefore the logical subject (in our sense) of the statement which formulates the fact; whereas merely satisfying a propositional function is compatible with playing either subject or attribute role in a fact belonging to the range of the function, and therefore with being either logical subject or predicate (in our sense) of the statement which formulates this fact. (Sellars, 1957, pp. 468–9)

All quantification over non-particulars requires bringing them into sets but this is not equivalent to revealing them as what Sellars thinks of as true (onto)logical subjects, that is, as what Strawson is terming "individuals". This produces the conclusion therefore that the shape of Strawson's account of the subject–predicate discussion does not match the structure of things and hence, for our purposes, is not sufficient therefore to point to a basic connection between judgments and the "matter" of experience. What would follow however from Sellar's account is a different way of bringing out the distinction between what things are and how they can be thought, a distinction which in its turn would still point to the capacity of judgmental form to reveal something significant about the nature of things.[27]

Strawson's reply to Sellars however can be given simply once we have seen that it turns fundamentally on the nature of statement-types and their relation to "facts". Strawson can simply say that the rationale for thinking of such things as Socrates only as ontological subjects and not as predicates is not disclosed simply by reiterating its provenance. Or, as he puts it: "why should I not say that this snub-nose is a member of the class *Socrates*, and Socrates a member of the class *mankind*?"[28] Whereas the latter conjunction of Socrates with a class that we can say he belongs to is not odd, the former inclusion of the snub-nose Socrates happens to possess as part of the class he is said to *be* certainly is. The rationale for its being odd points to what Strawson might think of as indicating a bias towards particularity as built into our construction of the logical relation of terms. This bias is based for him on how terms enter discourse referentially, which is basically through having in the first instance the capacity of direct designation, something lacking in the case of non-particulars.[29] Once we look at this as the basis of the distinction we are free to look at the nature of the formal logic of the difference between subject and predicate as something that may release for us a notion of "individual" that is not tied to the division of functions on which Sellars draws.

The debate between these positions is intrinsically difficult to evaluate. It is clear that the problem that Strawson is posing is not one that Sellars is facing as in a sense it is the point of Sellars' piece to suggest that the basic nature of concepts does not allow it to be put. However what is clear from the point of view of the problem of constructing an "austere" argument for the connection between judgment and intuition is that these positions present alternative ways of approaching such a task. For Strawson it appears that the structural nature of space and time turn out to be what is ontologically significant in itself whereas for Sellars it would appear that the Aristotelian notion of the subject of predication still has philosophical bite in it at the level of ontological analysis. This difference of view with regard to the ontological tradition will create the space between the two variants of an "austere" reading that they present. We will now go on to view these variants in relation to other considerations of Kant's view of judgment in order to be able to address fully the question of whether the attempt to build a view of forms of judgment that can connect with the matter of experience can be either recast in terms of contemporary logic or semantics or rather in its turn exerts pressure *upon* such contemporary movements in philosophy.

Quale and sounds: A minimalist ontology explored

Returning from the examination of the details of the contrast between individuals and particulars in the dispute between Strawson and Sellars to an investigation of how the distinct accounts they offer provide us with differing minimalist ontologies is necessary to prepare for a critical confrontation of differing austere constructions of the argument connecting the deduction of categories to a primary sense of "objectivity". In what must count as one of his key contributions to philosophy Strawson analyses the problem concerning the nature of objectivity as one in which basic particulars turn out to be *material* objects. However in attempting to justify the notion that this is the case he sets out at some length an account of a possible world in which the condition of spatiality was missing from experience and there was only given to us a sense of time. The condition for this is that there is consciousness of sounds but effectively of nothing else. This is a world composed only of what Sellars would term *quale*. The analysis of such a world is suggested, however, by Strawson to point to a fundamental distinction as necessary to be able to re-identify the particulars of which it is composed and this is the distinction between my own states and the states of things that are beyond me. However for this distinction itself to be given requires, he suggests, some kind of *analogy* to space since by hypothesis there is no experience of space itself in this world. The reason for this claim is that the condition of reidentification of objects is, in our world, one in which they can be placed *in relation* to each other according to a common grid. A notion of *distance* is the minimal concept required for spatiality and hence it is this that needs an analogical counterpart. The way in which he fills this out involves the distinction between what he terms a "master-sound" that was unique in the sound-world in having continuity of presence despite variation of pitch and other sounds that occur at varying times against its backdrop.

> The pitch of the master-sound at any moment would determine the auditory analogue of position in the sound-world at that moment. The sound-world is then conceived of as containing many particulars, unheard at any moment, but audible at other positions than the one occupied at that moment. There is a clear criterion for distinguishing the case of hearing a later part of a *particular* unitary sound-sequence of which the earlier part had been heard previously, from the more general case of merely hearing the later part of the same *universal* unitary sound-sequence of which an earlier part has been heard previously.[30]

The distinction between master-sound and sequences of transitory and variant duration allows for the analogy to take hold and hence something similar to the spatial conception to be described. The fact that this minimal type of world can be given this degree of filling such that something at least appreciably similar to our own ontological situation can be generated within its confines points to a question that has thus far been denied appropriate expression. This could be put in the following way: if empirical intuitions involve necessary relation to particulars but the conception of what they are particulars *of* requires not merely the form of intuition but the form of concepts as well then how do the generality of the latter relate to the matter of the former since the latter is different in kind from the form of intuition?

This is the basic problem that Kant is working at through the arguments of the Transcendental Deduction and the schematism. In thinking about our minimalist ontology we seem to have another clue for how an "austere" construction of this argument could go. It would appear that whilst the subject–predicate form of judgment has a basic connection to that between particulars and universals in ontology, the nature of this connection has to somehow be given shape in relation to forms of sensation if we are to get a conception of "experience". What the minimalist ontology of the above citation suggests however is that below the level of what we take to be objects such an ordering as that which is necessary to have anything as coherent as an "experience" is already at work in a pure relation to sensations themselves. For sensations to be related to in the auditory world as providing us with particulars at all requires the analogue of space to be in place to the extent that there is a constant presence (in the form of the master-sound) that guarantees a backdrop that allows for awareness of the transitory and variant sounds. Hence even sounds *qua* sounds are only coherently available to be experienced if there is something like an order that "places" them.

This austere argument for the notion of *a priori* intuitions needs to be connected now to our considerations concerning the nature of judgment. It does not follow from what we have taken from the Strawsonian imagination of a peculiarly auditory world that the sounds that we distinguish from the master-sound and are able to appreciate as distinguishable from it are anything other than *quale*. They are such in precisely being open to classification by reference to conjunctions of characteristics. This possibility of referential connection with the *quale* in question is opened by not merely their appearance as part of a common language (that of "sounds") but also in their conditions of iteration guaranteeing the appropriate level of classification of each particular in regard to what Strawson earlier termed "ranges". Since they are susceptible to such classification it is not the case that all that is given with the *quale* is the instancing of bare particulars and indeed this harmonizes with the argument of Sellars that such bare particulars are not themselves capable in any sense of *instancing*.[31]

From this minimalist description we already have a primitive notion of "object" as something that can be re-identified by reference to conditions of a logic that is supported by universal conditions of placement and which can be stated in the form of complex particulars. The articulation of such complex particulars requires however a developed logical understanding, two competing variations of which are offered by Sellars and Strawson. Either would in any event point to the necessity of even simple experience of a minimal world of referential statement having to include the possibility of a re-identification of particulars and the condition of this removes us from being able to continue to formulate the problem of objective validity of judgment of one that begins from an immediate data such as we were earlier assuming could be termed "sensation$_1$". What the consideration of *quale* and the logical discussions that emerged from it have shown is that there could be no experience *simpliciter* that was constituted as that of such bare particulars as we initially took purely subjective sensations to be *of*. Thus the "data-sensualism" that it appeared Kant began with could not itself describe even a possible world of experience. This is the meaning of Kant's statement in the introduction to the Second Analogy: "The appearances, in so far as they are objects of consciousness simply in virtue of being representations, are not in any way distinct from their apprehension, that is, from their reception in the synthesis of imagination; and we must therefore agree that the manifold of appearances is always generated in the mind successively" (A190/B235). This is, in a sense, a gloss on the statement from the A-Deduction which helped to generate our question in the first place. Whereas in the statement from the A-Deduction it at least appeared to be Kant's view that there are particular presentations that are each given to the mind as distinct and isolated presentations of discreet data, it is here made clear that without the connection of appearances to each other being given there is effectively no cognition at all taking place. Looking back at the statement from the A-Deduction anew after our excursus through the material we have reviewed in the interim it is also possible to read it differently. What was in fact stressed at A99 was that, looked at from the vantage point of only a *particular* moment all that we viewed the manifold as was something *unified* but since this isolation of the manifold would, in terms of locating its particularity, only be able to isolate the condition of the moment being identified as a moment at all then all that could be given within it would be what belongs essentially to the *form* of intuition. Comprehension of its *matter*, hence its nature as an *empirical* manifold, is precisely not capturable within the limits of a *particular* moment. All that emerges at that level is the logic of complex particulars, something that we can now state after this lengthy excursus. As Dieter Henrich correctly puts it: "What constitutes a particular is ... a product of construction; it is not something given. But in this respect it is also different from the sum of its properties, even though the construction that has this particular as its result can only be produced by properties combined in relation to it" (Henrich, 1976, p. 152).

Judgment and objectivity

We have uncovered the fact that the subject–predicate combination requires a relation to complex objects to be in place and cannot be stated with pure simples. We have also described the condition of even *quale* as requiring, for the most minimal notion of a world to be productive of the possibility of experience, a conception of particularity that cannot be "bare". The conjunction of these discoveries is the suggestion that the form of judgment is connected to the basic form of experience and this is without as yet having attempted to work through the complexity of the doctrine of synthesis which we have carefully eschewed commitment to for the purpose of constructing something like an "austere" deduction-strategy. However there is a clear problem with the results of our argument to date. This is that it only supplies us with the *form* of the thought of something that is real, it does not yet describe the manner in which the notion of "object" is capable of capturing for us the kind of relation to materiality that we take it conventionally to involve. The considerations from Strawson begin to point in this direction inasmuch as he describes material bodies as primary in cognition but the nature of his argument for this has not yet been fully uncovered. The reason for this is that to go into the nature of this argument will require expanding our horizon beyond an understanding of judgment towards that of the role of the transcendental unity of apperception, a notion that has a prominence and role in Strawson's account of objectivity that ensures his attempt to promote an "austere" reading of the deduction is effectively less distant than first appears from a description of transcendental psychology. In this chapter however we are venturing as far as we can, in deference to those suspicious of the need for transcendental psychology, to provide an argument that justifies at least to some degree the *symmetry thesis* without overtly relying on the language of synthesis that Kant actually employs in stating it. To go further along this road it is necessary to turn now to the ways in which Kant seeks to draw out considerations concerning judgment that purport to show how certain kinds of judgment lead us to the conviction that categories are required for experience to be made coherent. What we have found so far is much less than this as whilst something seems to have been uncovered about what must be minimally taken to be ontologically required in order for something like "experience" to happen at all what this has not told us to date is either what kinds of "objects" we need to have "experience" of or what kinds of judgments lead us towards a need for "categories" in explication of "experience".

Paul Guyer has suggested in a number of pieces addressing the structure and purpose of the deduction that there are two discreet sets of arguments presented by Kant that move from an understanding of certain properties of some judgments to the requirement that we need "categories" for experience to be coherently given to us. Guyer describes these arguments as being of two types, both of which he gives general formulation of separately from examining the exemplifications of them he argues he can find in Kant's text. The first general formulation is stated as follows: "Judgments about empirical objects are possible, and these assume some synthetic *a priori* knowledge (or a near relative), which implies the further *a priori* knowledge of the categories." The second formulation, by contrast, he states as: "Judgments about empirical objects are possible, and although these do not themselves assert any *a priori* knowledge, they do imply *a priori* knowledge of the categories."[32] I will now turn to assessing whether Kant does in fact give putative deduction arguments that have the forms of connection between judgments and categories that Guyer suggests.

First we will address the assumption that arguments of the first type, namely arguments that suggest judgments concerning empirical objects require a reference to some form of *a priori* knowledge, not itself involving the categories, but which effectively depend upon the assumption that categories do exist and are necessary for the coherent representations we term "experience" to be possible. The first example of such an argument is taken by Guyer from the A-Deduction, particularly in fact from the place where Kant argues that the possibility of re-identification of particulars requires synthesis. As such, it immediately becomes obvious that since Guyer's method of division of the deduction-strategies requires us to think not merely of the form of judgments in general but to work out what is required for synthetic *a priori* judgments to be necessary, we have here decisively moved on from the considerations of Strawson and Sellars. The importance of this move is that we are now relating judgment to synthesis and, indeed, thinking of certain types of judgments as requiring a notion of synthesis to be possible at all. This involves us therefore in considerations of complexity of a different nature to those we have tracked thus far in our attempt to trace a possible "austere" deduction-strategy and suggests that working out a relationship between the nature of judgment and consciousness of objects in a "weighty" sense requires bringing in the very considerations of synthesis that we have thus far been careful to leave out of our account. Hence to this degree Guyer's procedure *requires* the presence of the notion of synthesis to be part of the deduction-strategies he is considering as moving from judgment to objectivity. In this respect the nature of Guyer's considerations is *less* analytic than those we have followed so far.

Let us look at the first example given of the first argument-strategy. The example is from A101 where, interestingly, Kant is initially expounding the notion of the synthesis of reproduction in imagination:

> For if we show that even our purest *a priori* intuitions yield no knowledge, save in so far as they contain a combination of the manifold such as renders a thoroughgoing synthesis of representations possible, then this synthesis of imagination is likewise grounded,

antecendently to all experience, upon *a priori* principles; and we must assume a pure transcendental synthesis of imagination as conditioning the very possibility of all experience. (A101)

Analysing this citation in context what Kant is setting out is that if re-identification of particulars is possible then this requires two features that make it possible. The first line of the citation makes clear what one of these features is: the *a priori* intuitions of space and time. However these *a priori* intuitions are then stated to be in themselves incapable of providing us with knowledge unless there is something that is added to them that enables the cognition of particulars not merely to be mapped as part of a unitary space and captured as part of the series of moments we call the overarching temporality of experience but also related to in their particularity in such a way that the empirical intuition can be possible *of* them as the same particulars they were before, an intuition that enables the connection of them with further presentations as the latter arise. This possibility is one that Kant then states requires *a priori* principles to be possible and he relates to it as involving a synthesis that has *a priori* elements and the synthesis in question is named as that of "imagination". The analysis of the passage leads us to the conclusion that Kant does not here intend any reference to the properties of judgments. Nor is there here any reference to the categories.

The passage as given continues with a discussion of the *necessity* of reproduction for "experience" to arise. What this seems to mean is that the connection of appearances with each other requires a relationship of successive presentations with each other to be taken to be coherent as in lieu of this connection "a complete representation would never be obtained" (A102). The "complete representation" in question is exemplified by the capacity to draw a line in thought, to think the time from one noon to another and even to represent some particular number. These examples are interesting as in each case the reproduction required is something that allows succession to be mapped as part of a process of addition of moment to moment, that is as something that requires connection of *quantities* with each other. A complete representation of something hence appears to be conceived of here as the ability to give oneself something in such a way that it can be *measured*. The importance of this in Kant's exposition of objectivity generally will emerge from this point in the *Critique* as central to the whole conception of "experience" that it presents.

The argument of the passage hence appears to be that the synthesis that enables judgments of measurement to be given in relation to time, geometry and even basic mathematical presentation of units is one that is produced *a priori* by what is termed "imagination". This synthesis of "imagination" is based on *a priori* principles although Kant does not here state what these principles are, how they operate or why we should understand them to relate to anything we might term "imagination". Given that this passage is however part of the preliminary argument of the A-Deduction which Kant states is inserted in order to "prepare rather than to instruct" (A98) this is perhaps not surprising. Thus what the passage seems to us to state is simply some connections that can be shown to be required for the synthetic *a priori* judgments of measurement to be possible, requirements pointing to the ability to combine presentations together in an *a priori* manner according to as yet unspecified principles acting in an as yet unclear manner.

Paul Guyer however approaches this passage in quite a different way and it is worth evaluating the manner in which he approaches it to see whether it leads to a conception of possible deduction-strategies based in some way on a more demanding conception of judgment than we were able to extract from the considerations advanced earlier in this chapter. In one response to this passage Guyer raises the question: "Why should our *a priori* knowledge of, say, the geometry of empirical objects require any *a priori* rules *other* than those which geometry itself contains?" (Guyer, 1982a, p. 165). The question raised here suggests an odd understanding of the passage given. It would appear from it that what Guyer wanted from this passage was some indication as to what the *a priori* principles are that render for us the possibility of being aware of geometrical objects. It is clearly not the purport of the passage to provide this. All that is being suggested in it is that for the principles of geometry to be cognizable items for us is a requirement that we can connect together heterogeneous presentations over a period of time that does not prevent continuous re-identification of the particulars with which we began. This is a demanding requirement but since such reproduction would seem required for geometrical objects to be cognized at all it points directly to what *a priori* knowledge is needed *above* that stated within the geometrical rules themselves.[33]

This suggests that Guyer has effectively placed a requirement on the passage in question which it does not meet precisely because it was not constructed to meet it. A point that is connected to the one examined but in a sense builds on it to make a more pointed objection to the passage is made when Guyer writes that the argument fails to provide a basis for the assumption that the transcendental synthesis of imagination referred to need be guided by anything other than "purely mathematical axioms derivable from acquaintance with the pure forms of intuition alone" (Guyer, 1987, p. 93). This question however points to the problem as to *how* these purely mathematical axioms are available for cognition at all. The passage cited suggests that the forms of intuition alone could not provide cognition of them. Something is required in *addition* to the forms for such axioms to be given to us and this enables us to move from pure intuition to empirical intuitions. The latter require conditions of re-identification and also combination with each other in order to leave behind the postulate of "data-sensualism", a point we have already derived from our discussion as to why "bare particulars" cannot be a data for experience. Guyer's point here hence seems to require us to suppose that there are not *conditions* of being aware of mathematical axioms, that such axioms are rather in some way independent cognizable items that are sufficiently complete as to require no derivation from any transcendental genesis. This runs full tilt against Kant's account of mathematics but, even more importantly, it does not address even the requirements we have taken from an "austere" path of looking at the nature of judgment. Guyer's problems here therefore are not ones that either address the point of this passage or are such as to grasp the need for the transcendental account of "experience" itself.

The nature of the relationship between the discussions of judgment in the Metaphysical Deduction and the Transcendental Deduction is a large issue and one which Guyer closes in a rather presumptive manner when he states: "it would certainly seem natural to suppose that the transcendental deduction is intended to...demonstrate precisely that all of the objective categories correlated with the logical functions of judgment must be used if experience is to be possible at all" (Guyer, 1987, p. 99). Since there is no account in either version of the Transcendental Deduction of "all of the objective categories" it seems odd to us to assume that Kant could at any stage of development of his account of it have intended to show this.[34] It is arguable in fact that Kant's general argumentation in the Transcendental Deduction alone is not intended to present direct evidence for *any* of the categories, but merely to suggest that something like the categories is going to be needed to account for the coherent possibility that we find existent, namely an "experience" of "objects". This highly general strategy will be given particular flesh with regard to distinct categories in the Analytic of Principles, not within the pages of the Transcendental Deduction.[35]

Guyer points to a second passage as an alleged example of the first strategy to deduce categories from judgments. This second argument is not taken from the *Critique* itself. It is rather stated to be part of the discussion in the *Prolegomena* and of the distinction Kant offers there between "judgments of perception" and "judgments of experience".

In the *Prolegomena* discussion Kant presents a notion of what "experience" is when he writes that it consists in the "synthetic connection of appearances (perceptions) in consciousness", something that is unsurprising, given our discussion thus far but to which he adds that this connection is something we term "experience" only if it is *necessary* (Ak. 4: 305). Judgments of perception are however such as only involve "the logical connection of perception" whilst an objectively valid judgment is by contrast something that contains necessity and universal validity (Ak. 4: 298). The difference between them thus seems to be that whilst the judgment of perception is, as a judgment, formed through adoption of one of the structures of judgment Kant has set out in the Table of Judgments, it is not, *in its connection to the intuition*, something that involves necessity. However Kant seems here to tie necessity very closely together with universality as he goes on to argue that a judgment of perception is something that is valid only for a particular experiencer and does not disclose anything inter-subjectively valid whilst a judgment of experience by contrast is not limited to particular states of any given subject of experience (Ak. 4: 299). Thus necessity and universality appear here to yield together a publicly shared world and this seems to be what Kant requires for a notion of "experience" to be given.[36]

The key point of the contrast appears however in section 20 of the *Prolegomena* where Kant states that it is not enough to compare perceptions and connect them through judgment to get reference to an "object" (taken, as I think it here must be, in a "weighty" sense). This is hence a suggestion that the notion of judgments of perception is something like a portrayal of how other philosophers have described the nature of judgments and a demonstration of the most that can be taken from their account.[37] By contrast, a judgment that would provide us with the material that we need to say that we are "experiencing" would require a connection of empirical intuitions with "the form of judging in general" in such a way that the latter is related to the conditions of "consciousness in general", which can only mean that for judgments of experience to arise requires connection of the nature of judgment to the transcendental unity of apperception as is apparently repeated in §§19–20 of the B-Deduction.

To this general set of considerations Guyer raises the following objection: "Why should objective validity be taken to consist in universality and necessity of a sort so strong that they can be secured only by the application of *a priori* concepts to empirical objects?" (Guyer, 1982a, p. 170). In a sense this question is poorly formulated, as the argument of these sections of the *Prolegomena* appears to be that without universal and necessary conditions being met we do not have a relation to "empirical objects" at all, only to subjective states. Hence the real question is rather what it is that suggests to us the requirement that a relation to objects of experience needs inclusion of universal and necessary conditions. The answer appears to be that these conditions are what relate the "form of consciousness" in general to a conception of re-identifiable particulars in such a way as to generate "experience" and it is worth reiterating in making this response the fact that the contrast as drawn in the *Prolegomena* is one that clearly involves reference to the conditions of consciousness in general in its treatment of "judgments of experience".[38] If this is correct then in fact this argument, to be given real consideration, cannot be regarded as providing on its own some kind of knock-down rationale for use of the categories in experience. Rather it is intended to suggest that the notion of inter-subjective validity of judgments is one that is somehow connected to the very nature of what the conception of a subject of experience itself involves and hence requires completion through reference to transcendental psychology. As such it is a further example of an argument that does *not* turn on "austere" conditions of judgment but rather requires filling out of the notion of synthesis. Hence I do not take this passage to provide a form of "transcendental deduction" in the *Prolegomena* as Guyer does and not taking it this way do not regard it therefore as failing to validate a form of judgment-strategy in relation to the need for categories making "experience" possible. It merely suggests that the relation of perceptions to pure concepts of the understanding is going to be necessary for objectively valid judgments to be made but does not detail the manner of the latter other than through a connection to the notion of consciousness in general, the conditions of which are not here revealed.

The considerations that we are led to in considering this passage from the *Prolegomena* require some further investigation of the notion of "consciousness in general" itself and indeed it is to an argument that seems to involve this notion that Guyer turns in another example of an argument of the first type of consideration of judgment that he gives. This is again from the A-Deduction but now in connection not with the treatment of the synthesis of reproduction but rather with the synthesis of recognition in a concept. This section opens with a treatment of the relationship of consciousness to the conditions of reproduction that

Kant has just finished enumerating. Kant now adds the point that reproduction in the series would be without point unless it were connected to being conscious of re-identification of not merely the particulars that are being reproduced and connected but also of the connection of the same *thoughts* that we represent to ourselves in relation to the particulars. Hence, for example, the reproduction of a tree as part of a series that we call an avenue would be without point if the notion of "tree" was itself something that underwent change as we worked through the series. Thus what Kant has here added to the considerations of reproduction of the data of what is being perceived is a condition of re-identification of the nominal acts that allow us to form constant concepts of what is being given to us as "experience".

Hence to reach a "whole" would require a condition of unity in our presentations and this is necessary for us to be said to be *conscious* of what we are faced with. This is, as was the case with the account of the examples in the discussion of reproduction, then connected to a basic presentation, that of counting units. The point here is that for even basic arithmetic to take place this condition of re-identification of concepts of units has to be given as without it the nature of what is being counted could not be constant. This allows us to understand that there is a condition even for synthesis, which is "consciousness of unity" (A103). This notion of unity is then further related to the conception of an "object of representations" (A104) which must likewise have a notion of unity in it if it is to be something that is capable of being re-identified. Hence what I take it that the argument from A103–5 states is that if consciousness of unity is the condition of awareness of discrete particulars being re-cognized then this unity has two aspects: one that is a reference to the unity of the cognizer and the other which is a reference to the unity of what is being cognized.

In response to this passage's account of what I am taking to be a description of the conditions of awareness being shown to have an analytic element in them that is requisite for the synthesis to take place at all Guyer poses a question about the nature of what the concept of the object in question has to involve. Does it, he asks, have to be an *a priori* condition or could it not be the case that these conditions could be met by objects that are taken to be empirical? As he puts it: "there seems to be no reason why . . . the concept of my writing pad should not be thoroughly empirical and yet be the concept of the *same object* by which I connect my several representations of yellowness, rectangularity, and stubborn resistance to the motion of my pen as representations of one object" (Guyer, 1982a, p. 171). Here there is, in my view, confusion about the nature of this passage. Is Kant suggesting that the concept of the "object" in question is that of an *a priori* object? I do not think so. Rather, what he is suggesting is that empirical objects to be supplied to our awareness as "objects" have *a priori* conditions of being so given. Just as the previous point revealed the dependence that even *a priori* bodies of knowledge such as mathematics have on conditions of cognition so here it is being stated that whilst the "object" of which we are aware need not be conceived of as being itself *a priori* (as a number might be thought to be), it does nonetheless have *a priori* conditions of being available to our cognition *as* an object.[39]

We have not found that any of the arguments that Guyer presents as examples of the first type of construction of a rationale for the categories from a consideration of the nature of certain types of judgments is in fact intended to do service as a basic form of deduction-argument at all. What we have uncovered from them instead is a set of conditions that Kant takes it are required for us to be able to have awareness of objects, some of which point to the need for a certain kind of synthesis to take place and others of which point to analytic conditions of synthesis and this shows that one of the requirements of assessing the nature of Kant's arguments will be to demonstrate a relationship between analytic and synthetic claims in his account.

We can now turn to the second set of alleged arguments concerning the nature of judgment that Guyer takes Kant to be using in constructing a form of deduction-strategy. These arguments are distinguished by Guyer from the ones we have considered so far in that whilst they concern judgments about empirical objects they are not judgments that themselves are part of a claimed *a priori* knowledge (such as mathematics and geometry) but are taken to in some sense show the presupposition of knowledge of the categories in assessments concerning empirical objects. Somewhat oddly however the first such of these arguments is once again taken to be given in the account of the synthesis of reproduction in the A-Deduction albeit without citation here of the paragraph with which we began this discussion. It is now one of the central parts of the description of the transcendental synthesis of imagination that is aimed at by Guyer. Guyer exposes the nature of the argument in question as involving an illicit move between two distinct premises thus:

> Even if we concede that to be able to reproduce representations requires being aware of a regularity among these representations, Kant's argument still requires not just the conditional that

(1) it is necessary that if I am to experience an object, then I must be aware of a regularity among the representations of it, but the stronger claim that

(2) if I am to experience an object, then I must be aware of a necessary regularity among the representations of it. (Guyer, 1982a, p. 173)

Let us look at the conditions of regularity that Guyer refers to as the first premise in the argument. On my reading the passage is stating that it is necessary to do the following: (1) have a presentation of distinct particulars in relation to each other; (2) find the relation between these particulars constant through re-identification of each; (3) generate a succession through holding each in place so that "a complete representation" (A102) is given. This does not require a determinate order having to be given in one specific form for the representation to be in place and if this is what is meant by "necessary regularity" it cannot be what Kant is claiming as it is more than he needs to claim. What is involved is rather that reproduction has *necessary conditions of occurring*, not necessary ways of presenting any given manifold *as* the manifold that it is. Hence I do not think Kant's argument has here the structure Guyer is taking it to have.[40]

What we have uncovered is that Guyer's treatment of the arguments given has been in each case faulty, consisting in attributing to Kant a purpose that there is good reason to dispute with regard to the passages he cites. Therefore it appears that the view that there is a serious attempt on Kant's part to construct an account of judgment of the types suggested as part of his deduction-strategy is, at least, thus far not proven. This is not, of course, to dispute the evidence that is provided by the reference in the preface to the *Metaphysical Foundations of Natural Science* to the effect that Kant believed it was possible to construct an important argument that turned on the notion of judgment and which we may believe is part of the rationale for the reformulation of the argument of the deduction between the first and the second editions of the *Critique*. What we are left with after concluding this discussion however is a sense that there are more considerations at stake in the treatment of judgment than can be taken to be described by either the proponents of "austere" arguments or by Guyer in his treatment of passages that concern the nature of synthetic judgments. What has emerged for consideration is that the deduction seems to require the following: an attention to the nature of synthesis and its conditions; a discussion of the transcendental unity of apperception and a connection between the conditions of awareness of objects and the conditions of there being awareness at all.

The attempt to set out either an analytic or a synthetic justification of the categories from the nature of "judgment" has thus far not proven successful. Whilst the analytic justification revealed some important ontological results the nature of these is meagre with regard to our attempt to reach a justification of the cognition of "objects". What we will now assess is the attempt to argue that there are important and possibly even successful deduction-strategies based upon the notion of apperception. We will assess this notion of "apperception" initially in as "austere" a fashion as possible and only afterwards view it in a synthetic manner.

3
Apperception and Synthesis

The result of the investigations of the last two chapters has been to show that on the one hand there is a limit to "austere" constructions of an account of objectivity from the very nature of judgment alone but that once one admits to the need for an account of synthesis there are parallel difficulties with comprehending how "synthesis" is itself possible. What any cautious philosophical inquiry into the nature and possibilities of a transcendental description of experience would deduce from these outcomes is that we need, in the first instance, to describe how the description of apperception can reveal reciprocal connections between the nature of consciousness and the nature of its awareness of "objects". This requires us to think of the model of a form of "transcendental psychology" that can be based on an account of apperception that is still conceived of in an "austere" way, that is with minimal reference to the machinery of synthesis. The prime exemplar of such an approach is Strawson's description of the strategies for a transcendental argument that will justify the notion of objectivity from what seems to be required even to have a conception of consciousness itself. The nature and the limits of this approach will hence be our first quarry. The move towards a synthetic conception of judgment will hence be justified as necessary due to the limited nature of what can be revealed on a purely analytic approach. The question will in due course emerge however as to the nature and limits of a synthetic deduction-argument that will bring in such an expanded notion of transcendental psychology as to require not merely the reference to transcendental apperception (conceived of as synthetic and not merely analytic) but also the transcendental synthesis of imagination.

Apperception and objectivity: An "austere" approach

Peter Strawson first presented the notion of an "austere" account of the *Critique* that we have been tracking since the opening of Chapter 2. His project, one that continues to find adherents in the analytic literature on the *Critique*, was to set out an account of its central argument that would not require specific reference to the doctrines of transcendental idealism and, at least in his first and most ambitious reconstruction of Kant, to do this also without requiring recourse to the vocabulary of "transcendental psychology".[1] The nature of the problem of the deduction as conceived in such an "austere" idiom relates intimately to the problems with which we were concerned in Chapter 2. Strawson phrases the deduction-problem "austerely" as follows:

> abstracting from the forms of particularity, from the temporal and spatial ordering of particular items encountered in experience, what features can we find to be necessarily involved in any coherent conception of experience solely in virtue of the fact that the particular items of which we become aware must fall under (be brought under) general concepts?.[2]

Interestingly this formulation relates the formation of particulars through *a priori* intuition to their empirical presentation via general concepts as one that requires us to discover what it is about the connection between these two elements that shows us the necessary elements of experience. Since we discovered in Chapter 2 that the nature of the forms of particularity was understood on the basis of Strawson's own premises to refer to space and time, the question as to how these forms connect to the forms of concepts in order to provide us with a *coherent* manifold of experience is regarded as an identical question with that concerning which elements of such a manifold *necessarily* have to be present for us to have coherence at all.

What we can see from the investigations already conducted in Chapter 2 is that the notion of such a conception of "experience" will have to involve a view of "objects" that will be more demanding than any we have yet had occasion to justify, one that effectively will be in some sense synonymous with the notion of "material bodies". We have also noted from our response to Guyer above however that this conception in its turn requires some kind of analytic connection to consciousness itself. However we also found that the relationship between the form of judgment in general and our conception of "objects" revealed a rather minimal result to the effect that even the simplest conception of "matter" for us in fact involves a logic of complexity. On this basis it would appear that Strawson's conception of an "austere" argument cannot take us further than we reached in the last chapter if it is limited to considering the nature of judgment alone. Hence to this we need to add a minimal notion of what "synthesis" requires which would be the combination of particulars together such that they can be aligned in a stable enough manner to be re-identified and connected with each other. This effectively reprises what we have taken from the preliminary argument of the A-Deduction. To this we can add the point that whatever it is that enables awareness of particulars over time to be stably identified must be connected to whatever it is that enables such *consciousness* of particulars to itself be stabilized over time. The question of the weight to attach to this notion of the unity of consciousness hence emerges as the first problem to be addressed in furthering an "austere" argument. Since the construction in question is "austere", however, it necessarily eschews trying to give general sense to the elaborate descriptions of the transcendental unity of apperception in order to try to derive from such accounts a more sober and analytically grounded conception.

A minimal conception of such unity of consciousness can be given fuller elaboration by stating that for it to be taken to describe something is to ascribe the possibility of having experiences to that which is having them. We could add to this the point that relative stability of "objects" is necessary in any case even for awareness of that direct sort we might take to be involved in such momentary impressions as that of "this itch". However if this relative stability is such a requirement and hence part of the complexity of the logic of awareness of such momentary events then perhaps this is connected to the point that we are, in being aware of these events, aware *of being aware* of them? This contention has many ways of being understood and we will have to look at different shades of it as a notion in order to advance. But for now let us say no more than that for awareness to relate to the conception of what it is to be aware requires a sense of what it is to be aware taking place in the awareness of him in whom it is taking place. A more succinct way of phrasing this would be to state that if conditions of awareness of object-ivity are connected to conditions of *being*-aware then the latter will have to minimally include a notion of a series. Strawson elaborates carefully on this theme:

> it is a shining fact about such a series of experiences, whether self-ascribed or not, that its members collectively hold up or yield, though

not all of them contribute to, a picture of a unified objective world through which the experiences themselves collectively constitute a single, subjective, experiential route, one among other possible subjective routes through the same objective world. (Strawson, 1966, p. 104)

This indicates that the notion of the unity of consciousness requires us to think of the nature of objectivity as connected to the conception of the nature of a *person*. Persons would be those things that would in some sense have a *story* to tell about the nature of their experiences such that they could determine what in them belonged to a world that surpassed any "private" notion of "objects" and required therefore the notion of "objects" to be disclosive in some important sense of what it meant to be an experiencer at all.

The nature of the coherence-requirements that seems thus to be emergent is that they should lead to a conception of a world in which the experiences that are being had are understood as something that one *can* have due to the nature of the structure of what *allows* us to have them. This is what I take it is meant by a "unified objective world" in which a number of possible experiential routes are available. If these different routes are possible and mutually describable this is due to their co-belonging to the same "order of things". However if this notion of a "world" is in fact to be taken to be something so intimately involved with what it means to be one who can have experiences at all then it would follow that the complex notion of being a "subject of experience" is itself part of what has to be explicated in a detailed way for the nature of what is *being* experienced to be articulated. One of the conditions we can immediately see must be implied however, for such a series to be involved in our conception of the "experience" of a "world", is that this world be something that is temporally ordered.

This reference to temporal order brings in new questions since it would surely be necessary to distinguish in some sense the temporal connection that may be experienced between "objects" and that which we might say "objectively" holds between them at pains of otherwise collapsing the conception of "object" back into a phenomenalist register. Not only does this notion of a distinction between what I am *taking* to be temporal order and what *may be* the temporal order attaching to the objects itself require a certain articulation however but also it must be the case that these two orders have some form of dependency as otherwise the conception that there is a unitary temporality in experience will itself collapse and with it our hard-won attempt to articulate conditions of experiential coherence.

In addition to the articulation of the conditions of temporality as having the above-described double aspect we also naturally need to free the conception of what we are terming "personal consciousness" from reference to anything that empirically goes under this name. Hence what the reference to such consciousness really involves is the ability to distinguish between what occurs to the experiencer as a set of events that *is* the experience in question on the one hand and how things actually are said to belong in relation to each other on the other. As with the double aspect of temporality this distinction requires us to add a notion of clear dependence as without this we are again left adrift. This is why Strawson takes it that the notion of transcendental self-consciousness is not equivalent to that of empirical self-consciousness in range but is what gives the latter the basic possibility of taking place and having sense.

This is the core of Strawson's "austere" account of the deduction. What it provides us with is a rationale for the notion of transcendental self-consciousness and a suggestion as to how this notion is needed to fill out a story concerning "experience" that specifies why we might think it to be the case that the development of experiences into a range that we call our own is required for us to state that we relate to "objects" at all. This result is in its way a considerable advance on the relatively meagre results we found emerged from the conception of judgment alone. It is however one that has deliberately prescinded from the notion of synthesis and in doing so has left us without any compelling story as to what we might take to be happening in the development of the account of the "experience" it refers to. How can the development of a range of experiences be thought to give sense to transcendental self-consciousness or vice-versa? We have only the most general response here and the generality of it, whilst involving a concession to the centrality of the unity of temporality, is such as to provide only a very shadowy notion of what we might be doing in claiming that our experience is of "objects". Hence to fill out a strategy for the deduction that reveals more than this requires, it would seem, an account that will be less "austere" than Strawson's.

The scope and nature of the principle of the unity of apperception

What we have taken from our account of Strawson's skeletal reconstruction of the unity of consciousness is a sense of it as integrally connected to providing a story about what it would mean to "experience objects".

Two strands seem to emerge for further consideration: first, how to specify in more detail and sophistication the nature of this "unity" and its conditions of being given. Secondly, how to trace a relationship between this unified consciousness and the data of what it has experience *of* in such a way that the conception of "experience" gets more flesh than we found it to have on Strawson's excessively "austere" conception.[3] Taking these requirements in turn it would seem necessary to initially tease out the question of what can be taken to belong to the notion of the unity of consciousness, thinking for example of the senses in which this unity is "analytic" and the senses in which it requires us to think of a "synthesis".

Looking at the nature of the unity of consciousness requires us to collect together different parts of the *Critique* as it is necessary to outline a conception of what is occurring in the formulations of it in the two versions of the deduction that allows the harmonization of these accounts with that given in the Paralogisms. In the Paralogisms, part of Kant's argument with rationalist descriptions of the soul, concerns what can be stated concerning it, that requires more than a purely analytic conception of it. Here Kant takes from his investigation two conclusions that are purely analytic in import. First, he argues that the notion of the "subject" is something that is logically simple (A356), a fact that "concerns only the condition of our knowledge" and tells us nothing about any "object" that we might be tempted to claim awareness of in stating that we are ourselves conscious of being such a subject. If, as we have shown elaborately in Chapter 2, all thought is of its nature complex when it describes any kind of "object" of any sort, even that we could describe as a *quale*, then it would seem that this manifold nature of the possibility of thought is related to the simplicity of logical conception that we term being a thinker of such thoughts. Connected to this simplicity of representation of consciousness is the notion of the identity of what is being said to be simple such that if temporality can be shown to be formally the basis of the "matter" of all experience it is correlated with a formal identity of that which is aware of such matter. This notion of identity is again taken by Kant to be purely analytic and not to imply that I can state anything substantive about the nature of what is being claimed to be identical (A363–4).

The notion of identity that is described in this latter description is explicitly characterized as *numerical*. The importance of this numerical conception of identity is that unless we *add* this to the conception of simplicity then the nature of what is being asserted to *belong* to a "subject" could not be taken as so belonging over a duration. Numerical identity of the "subject" over time is however, whilst still a merely analytic criteria, something that allows this durational notion to be built in. However, whilst in some respects the problem of the nature of the connection between this claim and any synthetic one will occupy us for some time to come in this discussion, it is worthwhile now stating it as a problem. Kant clearly states, not just in the discussion of the Paralogisms, but also in the B-Deduction, the point that the principle of the necessary unity of apperception is "an identical, and therefore, analytic, proposition" (B135). However immediately after stating this point he adds that such an analytic proposition "reveals the necessity of a synthesis of the manifold given in intuition, *without which the thoroughgoing identity of self-consciousness cannot be thought*" (B135, my emphasis). Here the analytic proposition itself points to a condition of its being an element of awareness and this condition refers back to the synthesis of the manifold. Not only does this analytic unity of apperception have a synthetic condition but Kant also refers to a "synthetic unity" of apperception and seems to identify this latter with the "transcendental" unity of apperception (e.g. B134n). So two problems seem to initially emerge concerning the nature and scope of the principle of apperception, first, in what way does the analytic principle depend upon a synthesis of the manifold in order to be an element of awareness at all; and, secondly, how does this analytic unity relate to the synthetic unity? This second question could be further sharpened if the synthetic unity of apperception really is taken to be identical with the "transcendental" unity of apperception to lead to the question how logical unity of consciousness connects to transcendental unity of it.

These two questions arise from our preliminary attempt to further specify the nature of the principle of the unity of apperception which we did by relating statements from the Paralogisms with assertions made in the B-Deduction. However, in our account of Strawson earlier, we also found a further element of the principle of apperception that needs accounting for. This is the question of the understanding of our awareness of the very notion of a unity of consciousness as requiring in some sense a form of "second-order" or "reflexive" awareness, that is an awareness of being aware. As is well known, this reflexive interpretation of the principle of apperception was particularly significant for Kant's successors in the German Idealist tradition, particularly Fichte.[4] It will be important to assess versions of the apperception principle that bring Kant into close proximity to this tradition for the purpose of assessing the degree to which Kant can really be assimilated to it.[5] In pursuance of as "austere" a reading as we can propose initially as justifiable we will begin by assuming that such an assimilation will violate the safeguards of a close argument. However we need now to turn to assessing the passages in which Kant closely describes the nature of apperception, starting from the account in the B-Deduction. We will begin here for two reasons. First, the B-Deduction argument, in beginning by connecting the notion of apperception to the understanding of judgment in its first stage combines together the two elements we have austerely described to date. Hence its argument appears in the first instance better fitted to suit our austere assumptions. Secondly, if the argument that is given here requires reference to the synthetic apparatus that we have yet to adequately measure the range and purpose of then this will in its turn lead, by means of an argument couched in as minimal terms as we can set forth, towards the territory of transcendental psychology.

Analytic and synthetic unity of apperception and the nature of judgment

The question of the relationship between analytic and synthetic statements of the unity of apperception and their connection to the notion of reflexive awareness of conscious states leads us to turn now back to the nature of the structure of the argument of the B-Deduction. Ever since Dieter Henrich's classic article, this has been summarized as requiring attention to what is termed the problem of "the two-steps-in-one-proof".[6] The problem is that in §20 Kant appears to have completed the argument or, at least, an argument to the effect that the categories can be seen to be formative of our relationship to sensible intuitions and to connect these latter to the conditions of consciousness in general. However, since the deduction does not stop there and appears rather to reach another conclusion in §26 that also appears to justify the use of the categories to enable experience to be coherent, we appear to have two conclusions and this would suggest two lines of argument that need, in some sense, to be combined together. We will subsequently reach a conclusion of our own concerning this method of division of the B-Deduction argument but it is clearly *prima facie* plausible and we need in any case in order to develop the reading we have been following to this point to begin with an account of what appears to be happening in the celebrated first part of the argument running from §§15–20. This part of the argument opens with considerations about the nature of combination, moves from there to a discussion of apperception (which appears to run from §§16–18) to an account of judgment and after connecting apperception with judgment reaches its conclusion concerning the relationship between intuition and the categories.[7]

Section 15 of the argument of the B-Deduction tends to get overlooked in favour of detailed attention being paid to the nature of the introduction of the reference to apperception in §16. We should however open our consideration of the first stage of the argument with an account of what is stated here in order to test whether this account will impact on our response to readings of the role of the apperception principle in the argument of the B-Deduction. Kant here states that whilst the manifold can be given as intuitive only with the form of it being *a priori*, what he terms the "combination" of the manifold requires something more than reference to sense. This description of "combination" is explicitly connected to the spontaneous element of cognition and this latter is here named "understanding".[8] The nature of this part of cognition is also here connected to the story about synthesis that we have not yet retrieved due to our self-imposed "austere" requirements of reconstruction but Kant here relates such synthesis to the question of what elements of cognition can be taken to relate directly to something other than an outer affection suffered by the mode of cognition. Kant writes: "of all representations *combination* is the only one which cannot be given through objects" (B130). Hence the possibility of combination of presentations together is something that requires attention to the very possibility of having cognition at all. This is the basis of Kant's justification for turning to a description of the properties of "the subject" (B130) and, indeed, prime amongst these properties, that of "self-activity" (B130).

The second part of §15 then proceeds to add a further point, which is that for combination to take place requires three elements being brought together, namely the "concept" of the manifold and its synthesis but also the "concept" of the unity of such a manifold. The nature of these elements seems to provide in fact a provisional description of what might be here being meant by "synthesis", namely a combination of the form of cognition with the manifold of intuition via conceptuality with the latter being understood as requiring, in its turn, a notion of unity. The "unity" of conceptuality is what then has to be accounted for however pointing to a problem paralleling that dealt with in Chapter 1 about the nature of intuition. Just as we discovered there a question about how intuition was such as to be available for cognition as unified so the question raised here concerns how it is that the mode of consciousness itself is capable of reaching unification. Since we have already had the reference to "self-activity" it is perhaps not surprising that this immediately turns us towards a description of the understanding of this "self-activity" in the notion of what is termed in the title of §16 "the original synthetic unity of apperception". The basis for this move is that the unity involved in concepts of combination is something that has itself to be accounted for and this requires finding its source. It is important to be clear that Kant here states that the unity required to be discovered is one that is the condition even of the categories being elements of cognition (B131).

The result of the analysis of this first section of the argument of the B-Deduction is therefore significant. However it is open to question, as it has been, by Paul Guyer who writes:

Whence arises the requirement that some additional *concept* of unity is required which must precede such an act of synthetic reproduction and make it possible? Surely nothing in the first paragraph (§15) explains this inference; it is thus by no means apparent why the requirement of an *act* of combination should entail the existence of any special *rules* of combination which are known *a priori*.[9]

Implied in this question is a reference back to the A-Deduction discussion which begins its preliminary formulation *not* from the form of consciousness in general but rather from "the formal condition of inner sense" (A99). The discussion of the synthesis of reproduction indicates that for something to be re-identified as the particular that it is requires holding it in connection with what succeeds it. Guyer's question can therefore be re-phrased as asking why we should take it to be necessary that *concepts* are required for such elementary acts of re-cognition to take place. It is worth first of all pointing out however that this is not a novel principle of the B-Deduction as the discussion of reproduction in the A-Deduction was immediately followed by something stated to be a condition of its having any cognitive import, namely recognition which was said already there to be based upon *concepts*. Therefore the argument as reprised in §15 here effectively restates the dependence of reproduction on conceptuality for cognizability that was already the argument of the A-Deduction.

Guyer's question has not yet however been addressed. The notion that the *concept* of unity "precedes" reproduction cannot be taken in any other sense than logical precedence but effectively if what we are concerned with is how cognition of "objects" takes place at all the argument would here simply be that such *cognition* is not given by "reproduction" alone as, *in addition to reproduction*, we also need to *hold together* the elements of what has *been* reproduced and this points to something that enables that "holding-together", that re-cognition, to take place. What does this is here thought to be the "concept" of unity but, additionally to this suggestion, the point is made that for even such a "concept" to arise there must first be given an even higher condition of unification. Why should such an *act* of combination require reference to such an *a priori* condition or rule? The question once put in this form touches on the justification of the transcendental procedure as such. The reason why Kant's argument takes this tack is surely due to the preceding point having been made that combination cannot itself be given by reference to the "object" and hence cannot be thought of as empirical. If all combination that gives cognition of "objects" could be expressed in forms that are equivalent to statements of affection of the mode of cognition from without then we would be adopting the postulate that empiricism has been shown to be correct or at least that its principle is the one we should find the fall-back one. But this postulate faces a basic problem which is that it is unclear how, from the receipt of impressions alone, anything like a notion of an "object" could ever be formed, which is the reason why empiricism easily points one in the direction of phenomenalistic reduction of objects to sensible inputs. The precise difficulty with such an assumption from our point of view would be that it is simply insufficient *even* to describe how the most basic sensational component of cognition can be given due to the complexity we have found the latter to necessarily contain. Given this point it would appear that from our "austere" reconstruction we already have grounds to follow Kant's assumption here that we require a postulate distinct from that of empiricism and what such a postulate will clearly point us towards is the need for thinking of a "spontaneous" element or mode of cognition, a mode or element that if it cannot arise purely from "without" must therefore come from within. If however it must come from within it has not arisen from "experience" (using this term here in the standard empiricist sense) and so must have arisen "independently" of experience which is what we mean in the first instance by the *a priori*.[10]

A last point that can be made in response to Guyer's question is that whilst it would appear that Kant's argument does point to the need for an *a priori* condition of unification of presentations such that they can be cognized, it is not yet clear that these conditions will involve "rules" or, to put this point in another way, if there are "principles" or "rules" at issue in the formation of cognition any such have their own condition here revealed in the nature of consciousness itself and it is to that we have been led, not to any such "rules" themselves. The unity we need to describe is something that is required even for categories (which is why Kant demarcates it from the category *of* unity). If however there is a question raised about the understanding of this "unity" of consciousness it should now concentrate on its relationship to the "synthesis" of the manifold on the one hand, and to the comprehension of the analytic and synthetic understandings of this unity on the other.

As we have already stated the title of §16 refers us to an understanding of the unity of apperception as *synthetic*. The opening lines of this section help to illuminate the notion that we are here thinking of a synthetic principle as they mention a relationship between the notion "I think" and other presentations such that one "accompanies" the other. This notion of accompanying supposes an elementary addition and this is what we would mean by relating to it as something combined with the data that is given in the primary presentation of something I "sense". Put more simply, the notion of a "synthetic" principle of apperception concerns the relation between the condition of self-identification and the condition of awareness of the "matter" of intuition such that I can state that *I* am aware of the latter. This would be distinct from an analytic comprehension of the principle of apperception in the sense that whilst an analytic statement would simply be that if I am aware of something this clearly implies a relation of belonging (inherence) as is required by logical combination then the synthetic principle is one that is required for "experience" of any given particular to be stated to be occurring. The synthesis of awareness of experience as mine with the data given as occurring to me might well suggest the notion of reflexivity that we earlier reached in our account of Strawson and this suggests a need now to combine the hermeneutic task of reconstructing the argument of §§16–20 with the philosophical task of thinking the nature of the type of synthetic "experience" apparently being revealed in the synthetic principle of original apperception. In fact, considering the difficulties of this philosophical task will need to be given precedence *over* the hermeneutic problem.

Dieter Henrich gives one statement of this "experience" when he writes: "Only by thinking oneself in relation to an indefinite multiplicity of possible thoughts which are, or can be, one's own thoughts can one think of oneself as subject, and in this sense as 'I' " (Henrich, 1976, p. 165). This sounds at first disappointingly analytic in its rendition of the supposedly *synthetic* principle of apperception. However when Kant opens §16 he is initially prescending from the relationship to intuition to state a condition of thought itself as when he states that the "I think" is the condition under which anything can be "thought at all" (B132). Thus he begins from a statement that tells us that for thought to be had there must be someone that *is* thinking and to this degree he restates a basic notion such as we have in the Cartesian *cogito*.

It is after stating this truism about the nature of thought requiring a thinker that Kant goes on to re-introduce the notion of intuition stating that the manifold that it gives us is there in a manner that is prior to thought. For the manifold of intuition to be cognized however it has to be connected to the condition under which thought itself stands, that of the "I think". So we need to distinguish perceptions that relate cognition to "matter" from *apperceptions* which are something like the form of thoughts in general and whose original condition is nothing other than the simple and identical presentation we earlier discussed but can now characterize as the "I think". For the manifold of intuition to be such that we can re-identify elements within it sufficiently to generate awareness of a series requires not only that these elements themselves in their particularity be taken to be identical over time but that I also, in my representing of them, share this feature of identity over time. Hence for this to take place there needs to be a notion of consciousness that is different in kind from the empirical one that I know differs at different points as the nature, degree and quality of my attention diverges from centre to periphery in my quotidian concentration. This type of consciousness is what Kant is referring to as *transcendental* which requires the connection of one synthesis to another as part of a continuing awareness of combination. Stating this however seems to lead us to a question about the type of understanding of this unitary awareness that is possible, not least when Kant writes something such as the following: "I am conscious to myself *a priori* of a necessary synthesis of representations—to be entitled the original synthetic unity of apperception—under which all representations that are given to me must stand, but under which they have also first to be brought by means of a synthesis" (B135). How am I "conscious to myself" of this representation and how does the bringing of representations *under* this original synthesis take place?

The first question points us again in the direction of a reflexive conception of the transcendental unity of apperception. The nature of the consciousness that we can be said to have ourselves of the transcendental condition of statements of self-ascriptive sort and whether this has to be described as reflexive is the question to which we now need to turn in order subsequently to be able to raise the problem of how the original synthesis that brings presentations under the condition of such apperception itself takes place.

The nature of consciousness of apperception: Reflection, self-certainty and self-identity

Dieter Henrich has written concerning the nature of awareness that one can have of the possibility of conditions of awareness itself: "If it makes any sense at all to call the subject of thoughts that which comes to awareness in the consciousness of 'I think', then one must also consider this subject to be the initiator of that reflection. To suppose that every thought can be accompanied by the consciousness of 'I think' is tantamount to assuming that there is a subject of thoughts capable of reflection in relation to every thought" (Henrich, 1976, p. 165). The first reference to an initiator of the reflection that leads to the "I think" seems to be an echo of Kant's statement that there is a pure or original apperception that generates the "representation *'I think'*" (B132). However this immediately leads one to suppose that the thought "I think" is a product of reflection. It further suggests that awareness or consciousness of the transcendental unity of apperception must be consciousness of a reflective act, a notion that leads us in the direction of an Idealist rendition of Kant's principle.

However the first problem with such a reflexive interpretation of awareness of the transcendental unity of apperception is that it is not clear how simply reflecting upon my awareness of particulars will produce either a connection between two different particulars *of* which I am aware *or* a notion that the discrete acts *of being aware* are themselves acts that belong in some necessary sense to the same *subject* of awareness. Reflection in itself in other words does not seem sufficient to convey the *necessity* that seems to be involved in the notion that the unity of apperception is not merely *synthetic* but also *transcendental*. So reflection cannot itself be the basis of the unity that is claimed to be transcendental nor does it appear to be able to provide our awareness *of* awareness with any *content* other than a direction towards concentration on the nature of attending to one particular or another. Whilst this is a higher-level awareness than merely attending to the particular itself it is not conducive to showing me what it is that I can be said to be aware *of* in attending to a transcendental consciousness and seems therefore to substantiate a retreat back to a more "austere" form of argument when confronted with what Strawson, in regard to a similar matter, terms a "blank prospect".

Retreating in this way produces a difficulty of a different sort. We could claim that it is necessary to give the conception of what we are aware *of* in being aware of the unity of apperception only an analytic sense and that this will suffice on grounds similar to those advanced at one point by Henry Allison. He writes as follows:

> because of the contentlessness of the *I think*, there is literally nothing, apart from the consciousness of the identity of its action (in thinking a complex thought), through which the thinking subject, considered as such, could become aware of its own identity. Expressed schematically, the consciousness of the I that thinks *A* with the I that thinks *B* can only consist in the consciousness of the identity of its action in thinking together *A* and *B* as its representations. That is why a consciousness of synthesis (considered as activity as well as product) is a necessary condition of apperception, even though the latter requires merely the *possibility* of the self-ascription of one's representations.[11]

Taking his stand on the simplicity of the "I think" Allison indicates that all one could become aware of in becoming conscious *of* it could be the identity of the complex thought that is the "I think" itself. However to this claim Allison has added another that is importantly different, namely that in relating to the "I think" we are aware of the synthetic combination of elements of intuition with each other and that this latter is the condition of being aware of the *analytic* unity of apperception itself. However there are a number of problems with this attempted resolution of the difficulty we have been led to. First among these is the relationship between the awareness that lacks content of the "I think" and the awareness that is involved in connecting discrete elements together in one consciousness which latter is clearly synthetic. If the latter requires the *possibility*, as Allison emphasizes, of being related to the "I think" that is in some sense its condition then how can this *condition* also be *conditioned* by the awareness of synthesis? Secondly, how could the awareness of the act of identification of thinking a complex thought itself become an *object* of awareness if not via the very reflective process that we have already established is insufficient to guarantee continuity of reference over the thoughts that are apparently here combined? Thirdly, the notion that the unity of apperception *as a transcendental synthetic notion* is something of which we are aware precisely by becoming conscious of the ability to synthesize seems unpardonably regressive and lacking in explanatory power. It thus appears that we cannot rest satisfied with a description that just thinks of that *of* which we are aware in being confronted with the transcendental unity of apperception as being the simple and numerically identical notion that Kant mobilizes against the rationalist tradition. The reason for this is that Kant argues in the Paralogisms that if we take only the *cogito* as our text we cannot construct a viable notion of psychology as we also need intuition. This means we require an account of *how* the unification of intuition can be given as taking place and *what* awareness is of when we capture the condition of this awareness in the *transcendental unity*.

This points us back towards the need for an account of something that approaches a description of what makes the transcendental unity of apperception a *synthetic* unity. After all, it is also necessary to indicate how it is that such synthesis of the "matter" of intuition combines together particular sensible items *through concepts* (which was the kernel of Guyer's question concerning the argument of §15 that we have yet to conclusively address). The answer to the problem clearly has to do with the need for the elements of empirical intuition to be unified not merely by reference to the forms of intuition in general but also by reference to the categories and, indeed, to the suggestion that the reply to the problems we have pursued to this point requires some connection between synthesis, intuition, concepts and the matrix of considerations that describe cognition that we are terming "transcendental psychology". These considerations of the problem with Allison's account of what we are aware *of* in having the notion of the "transcendental unity of apperception" as something we are capable of cognizing show this notion to be closely connected, as Allison thinks, to the possibility of synthesis itself but also show we need some account of the nature of how synthesis itself is possible in order to become clearer about what our awareness of the unity of apperception is awareness *of*.

However rather than moving over to an immediate attempt to describe the nature of the synthetic process itself and how it apparently relates concepts to intuitions, I wish to attend to the nature of the principle of apperception itself a bit more fully, spelling out in more detail what here is meant by the distinction between analytic and synthetic unities of apperception and contrasting this with what can be analytically stated *concerning* the synthetic unity of apperception. The analytic unity of apperception is a statement to the effect that what is given to me as a representation is something that has been taken to require connection with other presentations "I" have. Thus the analytic principle is one that states simply a condition of being able to view anything as a particular given to one's states of cognition. The synthetic principle of the unity of apperception, by contrast, must be that which underlies *both* the ability to synthesize particulars together with each other *and supply* the rationale for thinking of this condition as something conceptual. As such, it must be possible to say that in grasping the transcendental unity of apperception as *a synthetic principle* that something has been grasped. It is *what* has been grasped and *how* it has been possible to grasp it that I am taking to be central problems.

Kant writes: "The synthetic unity of consciousness is...an objective condition of all knowledge. It is not merely a condition that I myself require in knowing an object, but is a condition under which every intuition must stand in order *to become an object for me*" (B138). This points to the tightness of connection between the transcendental unity of consciousness and the notion of objectivity in general. It is not merely that I have to have this notion in some, as yet unspecified, sense, but that unless it is present there is no way in which we can pass from intuitions to "objects". Hence the placing of the transcendental unity of apperception in connection with the synthesis of intuitions is the condition of discovering the basis under which we can relate to "objects" in "experience" at all and not be placed in the situation that the phenomenalist describes as ours. In the statement given at the top of this paragraph Kant states a "proposition" that he takes to be analytic. "For it says no more than that all *my* representations in any given intuition must be subject to that condition under which alone I can ascribe them to the identical self as *my* representations" (B138). This analytic proposition concerning synthetic unity restates the centrality of the synthetic principle of apperception as that which fundamentally enables us to pass into the condition of comprehending how intuitions can become for us the ground of an experience that transcends their particularity and thus enables us to have an "objective" relation to the world.

However, we have not yet left behind the problem we have taken from the citation of Allison above. It could still be pressed upon us that what we are aware *of* in comprehending the transcendental unity of apperception is no more than the condition that can be fulfilled in and only in the experience of relation between particular items of awareness itself. What else could Kant mean, it might be asked, in the following citation: "the mind could never think its identity in the manifoldness of its representations, and indeed think this identity *a priori*, if it did not have before its eyes the identity of its act" (A108)? This seems to support Allison's contention that what one is aware *of* in being aware of the transcendental unity of apperception is no more than the connection that is required for synthesis itself. In response to this suggestion it is possible to read this citation in the reverse way and resurrect again the notion of reflexivity as the act in question that is being referred to here by Kant. The question we have been pursuing in this discussion of the nature of what is occurring in this *awareness of the condition of awareness* can now be sharpened. It would appear that our real question is emerging as one concerning how the unity of the subject can be seen to be necessary for the unity of the "object" or put otherwise how does the unity of the synthesis of intuitions that gives us "objects" reveal to us the nature of that which is carrying out the synthesis?

Synthesis of intuitions and synthesis of apperception

We have reached the point at which consideration of the nature of the synthetic principle of apperception has been connected with the understanding of the synthesis of intuitions into "objects". The nature of the connection can be summarized as requiring us to show how awareness of discrete particulars enables them to be combined into the whole we term an "object" to be that which also reveals how the cognizer is able to come to awareness of their own ability so to cognize. A minimal description of these conditions would be one that showed how transition from one cognized item to another took place whilst maintaining some notion of unitary awareness of what it is that it is to *be* aware. What we took from the A-Deduction considerations we reviewed in Chapter 2 was a reference to the manifold being given in time so it would appear that what needs to be accounted for is the relationship between the awareness of the unity of apperception and the formal condition of cognition of intuition, namely, time.

When Kant moves in the preliminary argument of the A-Deduction from the discussion of reproduction to that of re-cognition he includes, as Guyer notes, a reference to concepts. The form of reference that seems primary in the description here of holding together the manifold through the conception of unification is what would have to be given for any form of unity to be described as grasped at all. This would be that the unity in question involves minimally a sense of quantitative accumulation. The reason why quantitative accumulation can be described as that which has this minimal sense of unity in it is that no comprehension of any two particulars, of whatever sort, held in relation *to* each other but distinguished *from* each other can be presented unless there is first of all a sense that one of the particulars in question is indeed something *different* from the other. This basic requirement of distinction already requires a basic counting to have taken place and we can think of this counting now as a nominalization of the particulars in question such that they become "intuition$_1$" and "intuition$_2$". This is why Kant states that "the consciousness of the number is nothing but the consciousness of the unity of the synthesis" (A103), but we could add to this the point that to be conscious of the unity of any type of synthetic process requires first of all the awareness that enables the counting of particulars sufficient to be able to distinguish them as exemplars of certain types.

If we now relate this point about the nature of quantitative accumulation to temporality we can think first of all of time as something that enables but is also in some sense "produced" by measurement.[12] The nature of measurement itself requires however the assumption that an act can be performed that permits the quantitative accumulation to take place, namely the act that I have been terming "nominalization". This is the act of fixing that which is being enumerated as the particular that we term it to be, the act that enables it to be stated to be a unit. This act is the basis of all enumeration itself and could not be related to as produced from sensuous impressions themselves as without it the distinction between these impressions is simply not given. Hence the first *a priori* act appears to be that of distinction itself, an *a priori* act that enables nominalized relation to the particulars distinguished and through which they are available to be counted. But what is this act of nominalization if not that of converting the "intuition" in question into a concept? The nature of the concept would thus be, as Kant first describes it, a "*unity of rule*" (A105). A first statement concerning it would be that it must involve a relationship of the moments of time to each other such that there is coherence of representation *across* these moments. This coherence *across* time requires then the relationship between the moments to be one which can be fixed by reference to the procedure of enumeration itself, which is why I spoke above of this process as *productive* of time.

We have come a long way with this consideration, reaching a point to which we will have to return subsequently since with this recognition we have moved within the range of understanding what is meant by the "transcendental synthesis of imagination". Something remains to be added to this however, which is the question of how the coherence condition that we have uncovered here relates to the possibility of ordering of experiences that are to-come. The question here concerns the manner in which the order given *across* time does not merely connect cognition of particulars from past to present but is also related to the notion of "futurity". We have disclosed the point that a way in which the empirical intuitions have to be related to the condition of cognition is via their incorporation into the conceptual requirements of distinction that permit nominal recognition to take place and this has given us a first clear sense of the *a priori* elements of experience. This needs now to be related to awareness of the consciousness of the condition of cognition in the most general sense, that is the formation of the notion of awareness as that which describes in some sense the conception that what one is aware *of* is, in some primary sense, that which makes one able to be a cognizer at all.

Identity and self-identity

If we have uncovered a basic reason for the use of quantitative notions in Kant's examples of synthetic combination in the A-Deduction then this points also to the key notion that is involved in even the transcendental unity of apperception which is no less than the conception of *unity* itself. If this notion is central to the conception of self-ascription such that we can state that certain distinctly different states are states of the same identical self then we need to look in some detail at the conditions of being able to formulate this notion of unity not merely with regard to items of awareness but for the notion of the "self" to be available to us at all. Kant writes of the conditions of awareness of the notion of "self" in the following passage: "as self-consciousness is a transcendental representation, numerical identity is inseparable from it, and is *a priori* certain" (A113). For "self-consciousness" to be grasped in terms of its possibility as such is to take it in a transcendental sense. In this respect, according to Kant, we cannot conceive of it in any other terms than as requiring *numerical* identity, one of the criteria we saw earlier that he mobilizes against rationalist descriptions of the nature of the soul. Kant elsewhere describes the transcendental conception of self-consciousness as *"necessarily"* represented as numerical identity (A107) and he connects this to the synthesis of intuitions by concepts as when he states: "The original and necessary consciousness of the identity of the self is thus *at the same time* a consciousness of an equally necessary unity of the synthesis of all appearances according to concepts" (A108, my emphasis). This latter citation indicates a kind of compresence of the consciousness of the numerical identity of self-consciousness with the capturing of the condition of the unity of appearances by concepts. This latter connection bears auspicious traces of an argument that will connect the synthesis that will produce "experience of objects" with the condition of awareness as such.

In order to articulate further this conception of the transcendental unity of apperception as a description of a *numerical identity* we need to distinguish between two different senses of the phrase "transcendental unity of apperception". James Van Cleve does this in the following way: "The phrase 'transcendental unity of apperception' names both a *property* and a *principle*—a principle attributing the property to certain collections of representations."[13] The *property* that is being attributed seems to involve some kind of consciousness that is one of numerical identity. However there are two things that we need now to add concerning this property. On the one hand, it is important to stress that Kant is not simply stating that the awareness of this numerical identity is one that relates to each particular given presentation in isolation from each other but rather that it is one that is taken to combine or, as he puts it, "*conjoin* one representation with another" (B133) and hence to require the distinction we will be taking as involved with any notion of quantity as such to be given in some sense as its condition. Kant explicitly states that this property is one that has such a synthetic condition:

> Only in so far...as I can unite a manifold of given representations in *one consciousness*, is it possible for me to represent to myself the *identity of the consciousness in* [*i.e. throughout*] *these representations*. In other words, the *analytic* unity of apperception is possible only under the presupposition of a certain *synthetic* unity. (B133)

The difference between two presentations is something that is in a sense taken to be prime data and on the basis of this difference we can arrive at a sense of the identity of the act of consciousness across this diversity of presentation. This importantly suggests the dependence of the analytic comprehension of the principle of apperception on the provision of such synthesis having first being taken as given. This gives a reason why it would appear that there is something intermediate between the capacity to state judgments in general logical form and to express these as categories that connect together "objects" of cognition. What this involves is a reference to the capacity for comparison of presentations to take place at all which requires a relation to subsist between the presentations such that any view of the logical nature of this relation can be expressed (whether categorical, hypothetical or problematic). This is what is expressed in the notions of identity and difference being taken by Kant to be "concepts of reflection" (B316), concepts that give to logic its possibility of connection, I am suggesting, to "categories of objects" at all (and, indeed, are key for the formulation of any logical judgments as such). This element of the notion of "concepts of reflection" would require us to view them not merely, as is cardinal for Kant, as enabling a transcendental distinction to take place but even as allowing the formulation of the notion of concepts that can connect to presentations in the first place.

The key such pair of "concepts of reflection" for our consideration is that of identity and difference. The question seems to be how the distinction between these concepts connects to the ability of self-consciousness to perform re-cognitive acts? The citation from B133 seems to state that the numerical identity of awareness of self-continuity is dependent upon the prior synthesis of manifold which latter hence seems to rely, I am suggesting, upon the operationalization of the distinction of the fundamental concepts of reflection. Kant does however seem to suggest a different pattern of reasoning at one point in the A-Deduction when he describes the unity of consciousness as preceding "all data of intuitions" stating that "even the purest objective unity, namely, that of the *a priori* concepts (space and time), is only possible through relation of the intuitions to such unity of consciousness" (A107). If the awareness of the unity of space and time is effectively treated as a product of the relation of intuitions to the unity of consciousness then it would appear that this unity precedes and brings about the synthesis of the manifold rather than being dependent upon this synthesis. This latter pattern of reasoning would take the "concepts of reflection" to arise, in Cartesian fashion, from the difference between self and other which difference is based then on the basic notion of the identity of self-consciousness being a primary data of cognition. The problem with this reading of the passage from A107 is that it seems to run full tilt against the natural understanding of the statement at A108 that consciousness of the identity of the self is "at the same time" consciousness of the unity of the synthesis of appearances according to concepts. This statement at A108 seems rather to support the view that identity of self-consciousness is not separable from the synthesis of the manifold and thus cannot be taken as logically prior to it. Since the two would thus be compresent conceptions they either are mutually entailing or co-dependent upon a further recognition which latter could simply be of the aforementioned "concepts of reflection". So a fuller look at the treatment in the A-Deduction of transcendental apperception seems to require either adoption of the thesis we were previously advocating or consideration of a mutual link of entailment between consciousness of self-identity and consciousness of the unity of synthesis of the manifold. The thesis of mutual entailment has the advantage that with it we have a basis, it would appear, for connecting the notion of transcendental unity of apperception with the synthesis of the manifold in a most direct fashion. However one significant problem that arises for such a mutual entailment thesis is that it seems to lead, once again, to modelling our understanding of apperception on that of reflection and hence brings Kant within the orbit of an Idealist account of the nature of "experience". Whilst this leads us away from Allison's "contentless" view of apperception it does so at the cost of requiring a reference of cognition at each point of comprehension *as* a cognition upon recognition of reflexivity and hence makes every act of awareness inclusive of consciousness of such acts, a conception that might well be thought to break the principle of parsimony, amongst other problems. This would however create a difficulty around any notion of compresence of awareness such as certainly appears to be suggested at A108 and might hence support the reversion to a simpler role for the "concepts of reflection" as initially suggested above.

We could begin to fill this suggestion out if we think of the "concepts of reflection" as *rules* that specify the nature of what it is to become an "object of representations" and indicate that conformity of representations *to* such rules would be what would enable the distinct presentations to be conjoined together for the cognizer and that such conjoinment could then be specified in its turn as being the only content of the cognition in question. This would retrieve Allison's notion of "contentless" reference to the identical act of synthesis in the sense of debarring thinking of the subject of synthesis as being anything other than a logical function. On this basis we could also bring together the diverse passages we have just contrasted with each other. B133 is clearly accounted for in this manner as now we can see that the formation of the analytic notion of apperception emerges from the possibility of combination of the elements of intuition by reference to conceptual unity whilst it also follows on this model that the account at A107–8 is no more than a statement to the effect that even the purest notion of intuition requires combination of a manifold in connection with the fundamental identity of logical functions. The problem with this line of argument however is that by means of it we seem to have reduced the notion of the synthetic principle of apperception to being no more than a statement of logical connection between presentations and we saw in Chapter 2 that such connection, whilst productive of a complex conception such as we have in *quale*, was insufficient to generate from "basic combination" anything like a "material body" and thus is not going to do the job of showing that we have anything like "experience" derived from its argument.

The other difficulty which such a modestly phrased argument involves is that even awareness of the "concepts of reflection" is, as their title suggests, itself something that requires a reflective act and that if such a reflective act is required for the identity of logical functions to relate to the differentia of "experience" then we *are* aware of something in becoming aware of the transcendental unity of apperception, namely such reflexive self-constitution, a fact that points again to the view of such constitution itself being further dependent upon other reflective acts. Hence even recourse to the "concepts of reflection" involves one in a reflexive circle of determination such as Fichte notoriously was unable to free himself from in any satisfactory sense.[14] However what motivates the understanding of the transcendental unity of apperception in a reflective way has not yet been sufficiently clarified such as to decisively be able to dismiss this view. Dieter Henrich expresses it in the statement that "Kant's transcendental subject is not merely a logical condition of possible self-consciousness. It is, rather, just that which real consciousness knows to be the subject of all possible real consciousness" and on this view has to be taken to be "the real ground of reflective acts" (Henrich, 1976, p. 184). If we depart from Allison's "contentless" conception of the numerical identity that we are terming "transcendental self-consciousness" then the move towards such a "ground" of synthesis seems required as it details a sense for us of what "the subject" of all the conscious states we are empirically aware of is. The cost of such a conception, on the other hand, would be that we have severely left behind any type of "austere" construction of the deduction-argument and seem to have become thereby committed to viewing the transcendental unity of apperception as what Henrich terms "a real particular" (Henrich, 1976, p. 184). To make this move at this point would however be premature without having tested in much greater detail the conception of the transcendental unity of apperception that treats it as a statement of functional unity.

Functionalist treatments of apperception

The conception of the transcendental unity of apperception as requiring comprehension of consciousness of a "real particular" has such substantive metaphysical implications and potential difficulties (particularly when this notion is combined with a reflective under-standing of the property of such awareness) that the alternative view of the principle as requiring only a "functional" unity has gained in popularity in recent accounts of the *Critique*. This is so much the case that it has become a commonplace to identify accounts of the transcen-dental psychology outlined in the *Critique* with an accommodation of it to central conceptions of cognitive science. Patricia Kitcher is the thinker most responsible for establishing this connection and her view of the nature of apperception needs to be addressed first before looking at variants of this reading. Kitcher views apperception as stating merely "a contentually interconnected system of states" due to the fact that acts of synthesis are for her "unconscious activities within agents that enable them to have cognitive capacities required for agency".[15] The difference between this view and the one repudiated as resting upon a merely logical understanding of the notion of "function" is that here it is taken to be a property of the distinct synthetic states that enables them to relate to each other in combination and hence produce a "system" of such states. Therefore it would appear, on this account, to be something that in a sense is built into the states themselves albeit at what is termed an "unconscious" level (hence avoiding the reflective account of apperception). There are however two clear problems with this reconstruction of Kant's position that are stated by Kitcher herself. On the one hand her construal of the principle as a reference to a system that operates in an unconscious fashion abstracts from all Kant's descriptions of the notion that what the principle allows is to state that my cognitive states are indeed *mine* as she admits in stating that on her reading Kant "has no idea of how we are conscious of our experiences or our cognitive states as our own" (Kitcher, 1990, p. 126).[16] On the other hand, there is a key passage in the *Critique* where Kant speaks about the nature of what is involved in the inference "I think" which he takes to express what he terms "an indeterminate empirical intuition" and which Kitcher acknowledges to state an understanding of the "I think" that is in conflict with her reading. Kant here describes this "indeterminate perception" as signifying "something real that is given, given indeed only to thought in general, and so not as appearance, nor as thing in itself (*noumenon*), but as something which actually exists, and which in the proposition, 'I think', is denoted as such" (B423n). This passage is taken by Kitcher to involve Kant in invoking a peculiar status for the transcendental unity of apperception as in some sense intermediate between phenomena and noumena, a status that she flatly denies can be the correct status of the principle as it must rather express the most general condition of empirical unification and thus can have no relation to the noumenal requirement of freedom.

In fact I do not think that Kant is here describing the status of the principle of apperception at all. What is being attempted in this passage is rather to connect the thought of thinking itself with the thought of existence due to the fact that in stating the "I think" a reference to existence does seem to follow (as Descartes famously observed). Kant's argument is that the existential referent is only to something whose actuality of existence is given to it by application to an event occurring for it that is distinct from simply its own self-representation. I am taking this passage hence to point to a view of the apperception principle that would more clearly support the logical conception of "function" than the systemic one to which Kitcher is committed.

What these twin points seem to me to bring out however is that Kitcher's reading fails to bring together the reference of apperception to the form of judgment that was clearly stated in the Metaphysical Deduction and appears to form the point of §19 of the B-Deduction with Kant's insistent use of personal terminology in description of the property the principle ascribes. In some sense the logical reading of the principle of apperception needs, that is, to be brought into connection with the account that recognizes Kant's reference to *self*-consciousness as the property ascribed in the principle. Without this connection what emerges is a systemic reading that can make no sense of how the notion of self-referentiality arises from the property ascribed by the principle as it deliberately prescinds from any such consideration. Since the reading in question is reconstructive it naturally need not account for all the detail of what is given in the *Critique*. It should however be thought through whether Kant has good reasons for thinking of the discussion of the property ascribed by the principle as requiring the reference to *self*-identity and *self*-consciousness that he consistently uses. In lieu of consideration of this question the vocabulary of Kant's account has not been given sufficient attention.

That Kitcher in fact recognized this latter gap is clear given her subsequent attempt to provide a defence of Kant's usage of such terminology. However her later understanding of the nature of Kant's usage has the same problems we noted in Chapter 1 that her description of intuitive unity suffers from, namely it is purely retrospective. She writes for example:

The conceptual and belief contents that made judgment possible must first be produced by spontaneous faculties. After those contents had been supplied, the remaining prerequisites for a cognitive self would be in place. *Once this has occurred*, consciousness of the activities that continue to create the needed contents is aptly called a '*Self-Consciousness*', because it is a consciousness of those activities that are essential to being a cognitive self and that continually create an ever more distinctive cognitive self.[17]

Since Kant's description of the transcendental unity of apperception is however itself set forth as an account of some notion of "self-consciousness" this description does not account for his discussion. In making the attribution of self-consciousness retrospective Kitcher collapses its conditions with empirical ones and reveals the cognitive science description of Kant to be no more than a generalization from experiential givens. This is not, in my view, sufficient to account for the transcendental description of experience itself. A prime reason for making this claim is that Kant does not, in any case, think of the problem that is being addressed as a unification of the manifold only in relation to how discrete items that are presented as particulars either at one time or even *over* time are connected to each other. He makes a much more ambitious claim, one that has to be *connected to* the problem of how discrete particulars are connected at one time and *over* time. This more ambitious claim is described in the following passage:

> There is one single experience in which all perceptions are repre-sented as in thoroughgoing and orderly connection, just as there is only one space and one time in which all modes of appearance and all relation of being or not being occur. When we speak of different experiences, we can refer only to the various perceptions, all of which, as such, belong to one and the same general experience. This thoroughgoing synthetic unity of perceptions is indeed the form of experience; it is nothing else than the synthetic unity of appearances in accordance with concepts. (A110)

In describing this notion of "one single experience" Kant raises the stakes concerning what the nature of a transcendental account needs to describe decisively beyond the level at which Kitcher's analysis is pitched. It is notable that he also in doing this makes a claim about the singularity of the notion of "experience" itself that is explicitly connected to the conception of the unity of intuition.[18]

The singular notion of "experience" that is at issue in the above citation is described as part of the "thoroughgoing synthetic unity of perceptions"

and this latter is connected here to the unity of appearances "in accordance with concepts". This suggests an implicit reference to the transcendental unity of apperception as that which is being described in the
unity of appearances into one "global" manifold. Some sense of what it
means to be aware of this "global manifold" needs to be built into any
account of the transcendental unity of apperception and this is singu-
larly lacking from Kitcher's description. It is however one of the
primary elements of Andrew Brook's description of the nature of the
property the principle of apperception ascribes to the subject of experience.
Brook distinguishes between what he terms "empirical self-awareness"
(ESA) and "apperceptive self-awareness" (ASA) in the following manner:

> It marks the difference between, for example, being aware, of
> desiring x, on the one hand, and being aware of myself having the
> desire, on the other. When I am aware of myself in this latter way, I
> am aware not just that I am the subject of this one desire; I am also
> aware of myself as the common subject of other psychological states;
> that I, a single unified being, believe that p, am seeing y, fear z, and
> so on. It seems fairly clear that being aware of myself in this way is
> something more than being aware of individual psychological states
> such as a desire or perception. If so, being aware of my desires,
> perceptions, and so on is not the same thing as being aware of myself
> as their subject and common subject.[19]

This adds the complexity required to recognize the reference to the
singularity of experience we have taken from A110. What Brook's
distinction involves is that the specifically *transcendental* conception of
unified apperceptive awareness has to incorporate more than just reference
to the combination of discrete particulars. The further move required is
the *recognition* that the combination of these particulars are indeed
related to me as their common cognizer. Without this extra level the
generalization that can be reached from the empirical possibility of
relation to given states of desire and perception is insufficient to
describe the nature of what makes this combination possible at all, and
is hence not a transcendental account.

Brook's account of the move towards the global represented object
from the combination that requires only connection of discrete particulars (even *across* time) is carefully related to accounts of both formulations of the transcendental deduction.[20] The place at which the
transition in the A-Deduction from the discussion of particulars to that
of global objects takes place is at A108, the same passage that concludes

with the description of the need for having before the "eyes" of the mind "the identity of its act". However whilst the transition seems to take place here Brook locates what he takes to be the principle that enables this transition later, at A116 when Kant refers to "the transcendental principle of the *unity* of all that is manifold in our representations". This principle also appears to be given a statement at A113 where Kant refers to "the totality of a possible self-consciousness". Brook however interprets these descriptions in a manner similar to that of Kitcher when he states that the reference to identity of self-consciousness is not to be understood as a reference to persons or minds but rather to a system of awareness. It is however important to realize that Brook's focus has brought out an ambiguity in the synthetic principle of apperception as it is "the name for both a unified recognitional ability and the unity of consciousness" (Brook, 1994, p. 137). The distinction he has drawn between the two is based on the suggestion that this ability to produce the consciousness of a global object is not equivalent to the unity of consciousness itself. The reason Brook suggests this is because, on his reading, Kant is concerned with "the conditions of a representation being recognizable, being something to someone, not its merely being someone's" (Brook, 1994, p. 138). Whilst these notions are importantly different and the burden of Kant's argument must be of the type Brook suggests primarily as otherwise he could never hope to produce an account of "objectivity" it is less clear that the possessive understanding of representation is something that Kant can so easily leave aside as of little concern.

Brook's reading of the A-Deduction discussion of transcendental apperception as not centrally concerned with a description of any type of possessive relation is due to his view that self-awareness is *not* what Kant is involved in explicating. As already stated, there is some reason to think that he is right about Kant's primary intent but what is the ground, on Brook's view, for separating this primary intent so sharply from any notion of self-awareness? Kant refers at A108 to "the identity of the self" in his description of transcendental apperception and again at A117n he states: "The synthetic proposition, that all the variety of *empirical consciousness* must be combined in one single self-consciousness, is the *absolutely* first and synthetic principle of our thought in general." Both these passages clearly tie the property ascribed by the principle to a possessive sense of awareness that is explicitly stated to reveal to us a transcendental notion of the "self". Brook denies that these passages should be taken to be conclusive arguing that they are unrepresentative of the general picture given in the A-Deduction.

However, if we look at A122, cited by Brook as evidence of a different conception, Kant here writes: "it is only because I ascribe all perceptions to one consciousness (original apperception) that I can say of all perceptions that I am conscious of them". It is true that this possessive specification of the principle of apperception as a property could be thought to imply a reference to the mere analytic unity of apperception. Even on these grounds however it is remarkable that the latter unity cannot be stated without possessive connotation being involved and in any case this response does not take account of the subsequent reference in this paragraph to "synthetic unity".

It is true that the entry of transcendental apperception into the argument of the A-Deduction does not involve a reference to any notion of "self", just to "pure original unchangeable consciousness" and subsequently to the bare notion of "numerical unity". But the moment that Kant goes on, at A108, to connect this notion to synthesis we get the reference to "identity of the self" that so perturbs Brook. Brook writes however: "If TA is our capacity to tie inner appearances together into one unified global object and, by extension (A107), our being the sort of fixed and abiding self that can do so, I cannot see that it either is or requires self-awareness, any more than apperception of a single object does" (Brook, 1994, p. 145). What does the property specified by the principle of apperception entail? As stated earlier, it states that there is the property in that which *exemplifies* the principle of being *able* to *combine* together presentations into an overall unity. If this combination is what occurs in the synthesis then the synthetic principle is simply given as the *ability* to perform the synthesis in question. This capacity has, as we have seen, two levels, that of combining discrete particulars together into representations either at one time or *over* time on the one hand and the ability to relate all these representations together into one experience on the other. However it is when this second element is explicitly stated in the A-Deduction that the reference to the identity of self appears as does the description of the mind needing to have "before its eyes the identity of its act" (A108). Thus it would appear that it is Kant's contention that the production of the "global object" that is unitary experience appears to have some dependence upon a reference to the "identity of the self" and the identity of its "acts". Whether this reference has to include some substantive sense of "self-awareness" is an importantly different question and if substantiated would seem to point us back in the direction of reflexive readings of the apperception principle. It would appear that it is this that Brook is resisting but in so doing he is also committed to viewing the reference to "identity of self" as merely an *extension* of the capacity to synthesize appearances at all whereas Kant here seems rather to be connecting it centrally to this ability.

Brook is aware of the problem that his account does not match Kant's text here and spends some time trying to puzzle out the nature of the connections Kant is making between transcendental apperception considered as a statement about "consciousness" alone and considered as a statement about "identity of the self" on the other. The reference to "consciousness" itself is complicated at A108 however as Kant here indicates that he thinks it necessary that the unity of it involves becoming conscious of "the identity of function" that enables synthetic combination to take place. If consciousness of this "identity of function" is in some sense part of the condition of unity of consciousness at all then the move towards "identity of the self" appears less odd than Brook is committed to thinking it to be. The question remains however what this notion of "identity of the self" involves and whether it is taken to have more content than reference to "numerical identity" or, as Brook and Kitcher would have it, a notion of a single unified system of awareness. The evidence of A108 is that it requires the thinking of the interconnection of presentations according to *a priori* rules and so these rules are in some sense part of the condition of the "identity of its act". Furthermore, for any object to be presented as a possible object of "appearance" is for it be governed by synthetic *a priori* rules and this is connected explicitly back by Kant to the statement about the rules of the "identity" of act taken from transcendental apperception when he writes: "appearances in experience must stand under the conditions of the necessary unity of apperception" (A110).

This point is subsequently repeated at A113 with reference to the notion of the "possibility of experience" requiring that appearances are subjected to *a priori* rules. Brook confesses himself at something of a loss as to why Kant should have thought this required reference to any notion of "self-awareness" asking why awareness alone would not be sufficient and the basic problem with this notion for him is it does not seem to allow for presentations of one which is unaware. This question about the nature and degree *of* what one is aware of when one is aware of transcendental apperception is here being pre-judged however so that Brook's complaints about this notion are simply that it does not seem to fit with his preconceptions about what should be stated by Kant. The account of the A-Deduction requires more attention than this reading suggests concerning the relationship between the transcendental unity of apperception and the transcendental synthesis. Not only is this required, as becomes evident from attending to the passages that Brook particularly concentrates on, but it is also necessary to work through these passages seeking the question as to what is meant by "awareness" and "self-awareness" as the objection Brook has to the latter is that it seems to imply Cartesian self-evidence and this needs to be tested.

Turning to the discussion in the B-Deduction Kant states at B134 that the condition of becoming aware of the identity of the consciousness in representations is that they are already united within one consciousness suggesting by this that the notion of "self-awareness" is a product of synthetic unity and he indeed concludes the paragraph here by saying that analytic unity (numerical identity) depends upon synthetic unity. Indeed he goes on to directly state this at B135: "Synthetic unity of the manifold of intuitions, as generated *a priori*, is thus the ground of the identity of apperception itself", making quite clear here that the unity of apperception is effectively a *product* of the synthesis of intuitions.[21] If this is correct then the generation of the transcendental unity of apperception *from the synthesis of intuitions* is what has to be accounted for in order for us to reach the point of understanding what it is that one is conscious *of* when one is aware of the synthetic unity of apperception. This would indicate that the notion of the transcendental unity of apperception is very far from a starting-point for the analysis and hence that Kant cannot here be proceeding in a Cartesian manner.

Brook does not, of course, want to view Kant's argument in a Cartesian way. He rather wants to argue that Kant's conception amounts to the following: "To be aware of the act *just is* to be aware of the action; the actor being a global representation, act and actor are two aspects of the same thing" (Brook, 1994, p. 241). On this basis Brook's reading advances over that of Kitcher's but this reading has a substantial problem which is that if being aware of the actor and the action is just the same thing then it would appear nothing at all is added in the notion of actor and this seems odd to say the least. Surely the "content" of the actor is not equivalent to that of the "action" even if the condition of the former being given is that the latter is? If the content of the two notions is different at least in sense then the notion that they may also differ in representational import has to be at least considered and not simply jettisoned on the basis that it does not fit with a view one has taken from elsewhere about the nature of what Kant may mean by referring to "function". Whilst Brook's reading is clearer and more sophisticated than Kitcher's, it neither succeeds in explaining the nature of the deduction-argument in relation to the unity of apperception nor does it demonstrate what could be meant by the "existence" of the transcendental subject.

Pierre Keller is the third important representative of a functionalist reading, one that opens by stating a disagreement with Brook precisely over whether the notion of transcendental apperception must include a reference to self-awareness with Keller taking it that the overwhelming evidence of the A-Deduction is in favour of this. However, whilst acknowledging this point Keller goes on to interpret the notion of "self-awareness" in a very unusual way as being meant by Kant in a manner that is "impersonal" or, as he also puts it, "transpersonal". Keller writes:

> The necessity of representing oneself as numerically identical does not commit Kant to the existence of a persistent bearer of my states of consciousness, but rather to a way of representing ourselves, a point of view from which what is represented by me and you at different times and places can be unified. Kant maintains that the self is necessarily *represented* as numerically identical; he does not argue that it is necessarily numerically identical over different states.[22]

So Keller is emphatic here in distancing the claim about numerical identity of self from one concerning an existent bearer of such claimed identity, demoting the notion to that of a mere "point of view". The peculiarity of this "point of view" however is that for each of us it has to be our *own* point of view whilst it is also for Keller a "shared" point of view that even permits communication between each holder of it. It is the notion that this "point of view" is required for communication that is used to reinforce the notion that it is an essentially *im*personal standpoint. This notion of the impersonality of the notion of the synthetic transcendental unity of apperception has the important advantage of providing some ground for the connection Kant makes between it and the unification of intuition itself. The basis of this connection is that the unification of intuition occurs only according to a function that permits concepts to select what is universally required for the representation of particulars in law-like manner and that this latter has its own "basic combination" that would be different from, as prior to, that of judgment itself. This "basic combination" would be what was being named by the impersonal capacity of combination termed the "synthetic unity of apperception".

A citation that gives some credence to this account of Keller's is the following:

> Every concept may be regarded as a point which, as the station for an observer, has its own horizon, that is, a variety of things which can

be represented, and, as it were, surveyed from that standpoint.... But for different horizons, that is, genera, each of which is determined by its own concept, there can be a common horizon, in reference to which, as from a common centre, they can all be surveyed... (A658/B686)

Here Kant seems to have a position that is on the lines that Keller has suggested. It is important to bring out, though, the fact that this passage is not from the Transcendental Analytic at all but from the "Appendix" to the Transcendental Dialectic. Hence what is being here described is not the transcendental unity of apperception but rather what Kant terms the "law of homogeneity" that brings all appearances together by reference to the rule under which they must fall. This regulative principle is one that soars beyond the principles that enable the connection of syntheses together to one that shows how what Brook was terming the "global object" that we can otherwise term "experience" is possible. It is true that this latter notion was *also* connected to transcendental apperception in the A-Deduction but it is worth pausing to wonder if there is nonetheless some measure of difference between the account there set out and the one described here. Keller himself does note a difference when he states that in the appendix to the Transcendental Dialectic "Kant regards the notion of affinity primarily as a property of concepts rather than as a property of their objects (that is, of the manifold itself) as he does in the Deduction" (Keller, 1998, p. 63). This difference is one he tries to bridge by noting that Kant presents the unification discussed in the "appendix" as one that is transcendental. This fact alone does not bridge the gap between these two considerations however as the unification of the *synthesis of intuition* is precisely what seems to be the key claimed role for the move towards a "global object" in the A-Deduction. Description even of the transcendental condition of conceptual unification cannot be stated to provide this as it would rather indicate something about what concepts have to be like to perform the synthesis that combines them with intuitions. Even in this latter role it may be that the citation from the "appendix" provides something that we need an analogue for in the deduction argument but still it is not equivalent to the role that the synthesis of apperception is primarily needed for.

Keller's impersonal account of transcendental apperception leads to the view that statements of self-ascriptive sort are effectively dependent upon the general capacity to refer presentations to what enables unification as such. This impersonal conception is hence the basis of any personal conception of identity. What is not accounted for on this reading however is the problem that Brook pointed to, which is that Kant appears to think of transcendental apperception (at for example A108) as involving descriptions of *self-identity* and *self-consciousness*. If the notion is as impersonal as Keller suggests whence comes this view of the *self* at all? At B157–8n Kant distinguishes between the possibility of self-intuition (which involves time) and the description of my existence that is not intuitive and states what is then available is the ability to represent the spontaneity of thought and that "it is owing to this spontaneity that I entitle myself an *intelligence*" and this might be thought to relate to the ability described at A108 of the self being able to present its self-identity to itself. On the basis of the latter claim it is often stated that in fact Kant's notion of the transcendental unity of apperception is Cartesian, not merely functional. Passages in support of this view include basic descriptions of what makes the reflective activity that is *Critique* itself possible as when Kant writes: "What reason produces entirely out of itself cannot be concealed, but is brought to light by reason itself immediately the common principle has been discovered" (Axx). Similarly, in his resolution of the antinomies Kant claims that the very concept that enables questions about the nature of reason to be asked "must also qualify us to answer it" since "the object is not to be met with outside the concept" (A477/B505). If however such self-knowledge is possible, some have alleged, this seems to suppose a certain possible self-transparency, and points in the direction of a Cartesian notion. These points certainly appear to cut against a purely functional view of Kant.

Apperception and subjectivity

The first rationale for presenting the notion of the transcendental unity of apperception as involving more than simply a reference to functional role concerned the possible Cartesian implications of reference to self-transparency. We will return to this consideration in due course. The notion that the transcendental unity of apperception should involve a more substantive discussion of transcendental subjectivity than is supplied by the functionalist account can however be justified more simply. It is possible to argue that if synthesis requires reference to the unity of apperception that the unity expressed in apperception must itself be conceivable separately from what it unites as otherwise it will not embody a separate principle from the heterogeneous elements supposedly being united and hence will not provide us with anything like a standard for how unity is possible. This would lead to support for the idea that the subject of unification is decidedly a particular in its own right and that it is only through this notion of such a particular that the functional role that is described in functionalist readings will be able to find a thematic representation in the transcendental account of experience. This particularity is what in some sense will be coming to self-consciousness when one is aware of the notion of the transcendental unity of apperception as expressive of an aspect of oneself.

Kant relates the possibility of the justification of the categories closely to the understanding of apperception when he states: "In original apperception everything must necessarily conform to the conditions of the thoroughgoing unity of self-consciousness, that is, to the universal functions of synthesis, namely, of that synthesis according to concepts in which alone apperception can demonstrate *a priori* its complete and necessary identity" (A111–12). At this point however it appears that Kant is presenting considerations that lend support to the functionalist reading as here the awareness of the identity of apperception seems to require first of all reference to the "universal functions of synthesis" so that these latter in some sense precede the awareness of identity and make it possible, as he also argues at B133. At B133, an almost parallel passage in the B-Deduction, he states clearly that the unity of the manifold in one consciousness is the condition of presentation of identity of consciousness through the presentations of the manifold. This seems to point us back to the notion that apperception is in some sense a *product* of the syntheses of apprehension and imagination. However this type of argument has the problem that it would appear, in making the identity of apperception *dependent* upon the prior performance of synthesis, that it does not enable understanding of how this identity can be maintained at all as on these grounds there would appear no guarantee of the basic continuance of identity of function since the manifold could become resistant to the attempt to constitute unity through it hence invalidating the functionality of apperception. So the arrival at a genetic account of apperception *from* synthesis would appear difficult to sustain unless this synthetic movement contains in itself something like an analogue to the unificatory notion of apperception itself. This analogue, if describable, would sustain the statement from the Metaphysical Deduction that gives the *symmetry thesis* but would require turning our attention from apperception towards an account of the syntheses of imagination and apprehension. To do this would be to take the decisive step in unfurling the necessity of transcendental psychology for the argument of the deduction to be sensibly expressed but it is part of our strategy not to move to this position until we have exhausted the argumentative possibilities that seem to be based primarily or principally upon apperception alone.

If the subject of apperception is related to, as seems necessary, as something simply identical then the nature of this identity has to be determined as primarily given via the consciousness of stability through the variety of presentations. This gives us a basic sense of what has to accrue to this subject independently of its connection with any particular synthetic combination and this is that there must be first of all a consciousness of the *ability* to preserve identity through the variety of presentations. This ability is what the notion of transcendental subjectivity primarily expresses and which is captured in Kant's notion of *vermögen*, variously translated as "capacity", "faculty" and "ability". This implies however that there is a *content* (*pace* Allison) to cognition of apperception itself, that is, something that must be contained in the notion of it independently of reference to the combination that is performed by and through it and this is the notion, separately from any such given combination, that the combination itself is possible. Would this not precisely after all be what is referred to in the crucial text at A108 of the ability to think identity *a priori* that appears "before the eyes" of cognition itself in "the identity of its act"?[23] This would, on this construal, refer us to the very possibility of such identity of act coming before the subject of cognition being comprehended as something that is not subsequent to the awareness of synthesis after all (despite the evidence of B133 and A111–12) but rather as what first has to be expressible in *a priori* form in order for subjectivity itself to emerge as a condition for cognition.

These considerations suggest two forms of *a priori* sense for the unity of apperception. There is the unity that is given through and in synthesis that relates apperception to the unity of intuition on the one hand, and the possibility of presentation of the very notion of the function of unification itself on the other which must precede and make possible the unity of synthesis. This would offer the rationale for taking the argument to require beginning from what appears to be a kind of Cartesian starting-point. However there is a problem with this pattern of reasoning. This is that to distinguish the notion of such combination from any particular way of being given needs to be filled out such that the notion of transition from one state to the next can be described in its own means of taking place. As Dieter Henrich puts this: "the knowledge of transition of a principle of identity that is known a priori is different from the knowledge of identical objects based on experience" (Henrich,

1976, p. 188). This way of expressing the difference is faulty as it suggests a knowledge of the identity of "objects" could ever be based on "experience" and this is false if by "experience" we mean a reference to the data of sense. Kant's fundamental postulate rather was that the data of sense alone give no credence to any such notion of the identity of their objects as this data can provide us with no such stability. We uncovered the rationale in Chapter 2 for thinking this false to the degree that we can stabilize a conception of *quale*, which is sufficient to give a notion of a thought of complexity that is a kind of analogue to the notion of material bodies. However Kant was surely right to think that the stability of the conception of such material embodiment is not itself based on the data of sense and hence something extra was required (apparently in the shape of the apperception principle) to give us the notion of "empirical intuition". Henrich's contrast was however intended, I take it, to state even the notion of "K-experience" does not allow for the view that the "objects" taken to preserve their identity through such "experience" can be made equivalent to the *a priori* principle of transition between states according to a notion of identity over these changes.

If however there is a distinction between two such principles of identity it emerges as a key problem to think their relationship. This points to the attempt to describe the distinction between synthetic and analytic unity as one means of specifying a distinction between principles of identity (B134n). However, all that Kant thinks when he states this is that the logical connections of function require prior dependence on something synthetic (which is perhaps all that is meant also by the statements at B133 and A111–12). What we are now trying to think however is how the *a priori* rules of transition are themselves expressible separately from their connection to the construction of a conception of identical objects being given. There is more to this question than would be described by setting out rules of temporal connection as the comprehension of the subject as identical over time is not the same as the ability of the subject to be comprehended via transitions of thought that seem not to require temporality as part of their condition (as in logic). This in fact threatens Kant's suggestion that the notion of functionality should be thought as dependent on that of synthesis.

What we are led to is a consideration of transcendental subjectivity as something that has to be presented in as complex a manner as we found the simplest conception of the notion of a basic state to be when we outlined in Chapter 2 the notion of *quale*. The reason for thinking of the transcendental subject in such a complex manner is eloquently described by Henrich: "Something is the representational state, and thus likewise the representational content, of *one* subject only when it is known as that to which advancement can be made starting from *every* representational content" (Henrich, 1976, p. 190). Each representational content must be connected to every other regardless of the mode of being given of any such content. This requirement is what indicates a complex logic of the notion of the subject of cognition as that which can be thought as the condition of such connection. In a sense the universality of connection is part of the identity of the notion but this universality has to not only span *across* temporal order but also first allow the notion of ordering itself to be manifested. Thus there must be something about the nature of any given content that allows it, as a content, to be connected with others that are radically different from it in terms of their modes of evidence and manifestation.

This has led us by thinking about the nature of the principles that must relate given cognitions to the transcendental unity of apperception to see that if these principles are not content-dependent and, as we have found from Chapter 2, that they cannot simply be identified with the functional unities provided by the subject–predicate relationship, that they must rather be ontological categories. Such categories would perform then the function of describing the shapes that must be attached to objects in general in order for them to be cognized at all. However if we can specify these categories as indeed the thoughts of objects in general and supplement this with the notion that for something to be cognized at all it must be presented as such an object we would then have a rationale for thinking of the transcendental subject as itself something thinkable only by reference to the unity of synthesis after all. This would indicate that the unity of subjectivity does not arise however, as Kant often suggests, from the unity of intuition but that rather both are products of the thought of unification of objectivity by reference to categories that permit us to think what "objects" in any sense have to be. The statement at A108 concerning the necessity of the "identity of its act" before its eyes would therefore be a description of the precise conditions of the *symmetry thesis*.[24]

The citation at A108 does however have the problem that it seems to require that the notion of identity is thought twice over or, as it might otherwise be put, described in two orders with the second order having an apparently reflexive sense that is nonetheless stated as also providing a condition of possibility for the first-order notion of identity. This might be thought to undercut the identification of the rules expressed by the categories with the conception that allows thinking the identity of the unity of apperception because, as Henrich puts it: "The act that is attributed an identity is manifestly supposed to derive from self-consciousness is spoken of only in the singular, whereas rules of synthesis are spoken of in the plural" (Henrich, 1976, p. 200). However the identity that arises at A108 is stated there to make possible the interconnection of all particular syntheses according to *a priori* rules so this identity, even given its singularity, is clearly taken to be centrally connected to the role of the categories. This suggests that there are certain conditions for any such rules to be applicable and that these conditions have something to do with the very conception of a transcendental subject. Henrich's question concerns whether the theory that is elaborated of the transcendental unity of apperception gives however such a decisive notion of a subject and he hence relapses back into taking it that the only means of providing such rules would be by reference to the argument which we explored so exhaustively in Chapter 2 concerning the structure of judgment.[25] In lieu of any such possibility however it would seem to us necessary to articulate here the relationship between the unity of apperception and the unity of the syntheses that are set out in the two versions of the deduction, thereby making room for a more elaborate conception of transcendental psychology than can be done by following the traces of transcendental apperception alone. This would clearly however require synthesis itself to have a structural complexity akin to that of both *quale* and the notion of transcendental subjectivity. This conception is also suggested by Paul Guyer who, in his analysis of the arguments thought to concern a deduction from transcendental apperception, focuses not on the passages that emerge as important for Henrich (such as A108) but rather more extended discussions such as A116–18 which, Guyer recognizes, rely on reference to the transcendental synthesis of imagination.[26] Hence if the discussion of a deduction proof that is based either on the logic of judgments concerning complex objects or on a view of transcendental subjectivity as foundation for cognition is incapable of providing a ground for the deduction of the categories it is now necessary to turn to the consideration of the deduction argument from the standpoint of the assumption that we can consider the nature of transcendental synthesis itself as articulating a theory of cognition by means of the notion of transcendental psychology. This is what we will turn to in the next chapter.

4
Synthesis and Imagination

The attempts to substantiate a deduction strategy beginning either from the form of judgment or from the transcendental unity of apperception have proven unsuccessful and this has led to a substantiation of our view that it is in fact requisite to articulate a conception of the deduction beginning from a discussion of *a priori* synthesis. Thus far, the argument to this effect has proceeded by a process of elimination of alternatives but now it is necessary to show that we can illuminate the nature of the Transcendental Deduction in our preferred manner. This will require articulating principally the notion of the transcendental synthesis of imagination. As with our previous chapters we will not proceed here by first setting out a general hermeneutic strategy with regard to the texts of the deduction but rather from a process of reconstruction that will respond to readings of it that have brought to our attention what we take to be particularly pertinent considerations. However, we can state a number of points at the initiation of this reading that will set out parameters that will be important for us in assessing both Kant's own discussions and reconstructions of them. These include the need to articulate the nature and point of the *symmetry thesis* hence connecting the complex notion of synthesis that will be required for a viable recon-struction of the deduction argument to the complex notions already articulated as those of judgment and transcendental subjectivity. The nature of this investigation will be connected then to a description of how the unity of intuition can be brought before cognition and a description of how the nature of perception itself can be articulated in a complex enough manner for a justification of the conception of material objects to emerge from it. An even more important criterion, and one unmentioned by us up to this point, is that the argument of the deduction be shown to have clear connection to that of the transcendental schematism. This certainly could not be done by a reconstruction centred on either judgment or the transcendental unity of apperception. Hence it will be the burden of our argument that not only is the reconstruction of a viable deduction strategy one that has to rely upon transcendental psychology but, furthermore, it is only such a strategy that can connect the deduction argument to the considerations of transcendental schematism. In conclusion, since the discussion of transcendental synthesis will naturally articulate intuition in relation to its *a priori* conditions, not least those of time, it will also be necessary to show the connection between the unity of intuition and the articulation of *a priori* identity that we have seen needs to be comprehensive enough in conception to extend to a thought of objects in general, even to their purest formality. Another way of putting this point is that we need to connect the unity of conceptual possibility, a unity that is part of a coherent conception of the notion of transcendental subjectivity, to that of the unity of intuition as provided for us in experience in empirical intuitions.

In order to execute this programme of research, however, it will first be necessary to look at some considerations that suggest that if the argument of the transcendental deduction does turn on considerations from transcendental psychology, particularly considerations that require an account of *a priori* synthesis, that this effectively counts against the very programme of the deduction. Two types of such argument exist at present, albeit, pointing in quite different directions. On the one hand, there are analytical arguments that view any presentation of transcendental psychology, particularly one that relies on the notion of *a priori* synthesis, as tantamount to an admission that the project of the Transcendental Deduction cannot be carried out. These arguments are presented in their firmest and most influential form in the works of Paul Guyer. By contrast, I will be arguing that the apparent opposition to the notion of transcendental psychology on the part of Strawson is not characteristic of his full position. On the other hand, the phenomenological reading of the Transcendental Deduction carried out by Martin Heidegger argues for a reinterpretation of the discussion of transcendental synthesis in a manner that effectively removes the suggestion of transcendental psychology. This reading will be considered subsequent to some of the basic characterizations of why a need for transcendental psychology can be seen to emerge from discussions of different aspects of Strawson's and Sellars' accounts of Kant than we have discussed thus far.

Guyer on transcendental synthesis and transcendental psychology

Paul Guyer rejects Henrich's suggestion that the notion of a comprehensive understanding of the nature of transcendental subjectivity must include a description of logical unifications that do not have temporal conditions. Guyer hence begins in a sense from a commitment to the view that Kant's reference at A99 to the necessity of all cognitions being subject to the formal condition of time, a commitment that means he *should* take the notion of synthesis to be of key importance.[1] This is also apparent in his emphasis, as against Henrich, on certain arguments of the Transcendental Deduction that connect the transcendental unity of apperception to the transcendental synthesis of imagination and suggest a dependence of the former on the latter, a dependence that Henrich's account cannot countenance. At A117, for example, Kant states that what Brook was referring to as the "global object" is unified by reference to the "principle of the synthetic unity of the manifold in all possible intuition". This principle is one of the ways in which the unity of apperception seems to manifest its effect upon the transcendental subject's possibility of having coherent representations. However the principle itself is subsequently stated to "presuppose" or include a synthesis that is as *a priori* as what it produces. This synthesis is subsequently termed by Kant the "pure synthesis of imagination" which is termed "an *a priori* condition of the possibility of all combination of the manifold in one knowledge" (A118). The passage in which the relationship between transcendental apperception and transcendental synthesis of imagination is set out here will require considerable attention and interpretative effort but what Guyer clearly takes from it is a reference on Kant's part to a type of synthesis that itself occurs *a priori*, a notion that he connects to a form of subjectivism manifest in the deduction as when Kant states that "the order and regularity in the appearances, which we entitle *nature*, we ourselves introduce" (A125).

Guyer's problem emerges from his objection to the subjectivism stated to appear in the latter passage as, like Brook, he objects to the move from understanding apperception as referring to consciousness in general to describing it as involving some conception of *self*-consciousness. This objection has, in a sense, been considered in Chapter 3 as it essentially creates the same difficulties as the functionalist reading given by Pierre Keller. On the grounds of attempting to rule out the subjectivist view of nature Guyer wants to move back to a comprehension of the unity of apperception considered in terms of functional rules of judgment, a strategy that either falls into the difficulties of functional-ism or resurrects the "austere" strategy of Strawson, the derivation of which we treated extensively earlier and the meagre results of which we have already amply demonstrated.[2] Later developments of Guyer's views however have shown him to have a view of transcendental psychology that are based on giving the transcendental unity of apper-ception the central role. This leads to Guyer producing against other conceptions variants on the arguments concerning "basic combination".[3] The distance between the two accounts is simply one of thinking in the earlier case that a functional sense can be given to judgmental arguments and in the latter case becoming convinced that such arguments are insufficient for a viable deduction strategy. In neither case, however, does Guyer give any extended consideration of transcendental psychology requiring a different approach to that of Henrich, namely one built on thinking through what seems to be involved in the notion of transcendental synthesis of imagination.

In objecting to the dependence of the deduction argument on transcendental apperception Guyer has two motivations, to distance Kant from what he takes to be an objectionable subjectivism and to move away from the Cartesian considerations that Henrich has intro-duced. The Cartesian considerations are taken to be a problem as it is unclear how the notion of self-certain identity can be connected to the claimed unification of a manifold over time. However, rather than investigate this claimed connection by means of thinking through the conditions of *a priori* synthesis, Guyer's tendency is simply to reject *a priori* synthesis as entirely dependent upon something taken to be *a priori* certain. This ensures that he attends only to the discussion of empirical intuition and thus rejects any place for *a priori* intuition, which is the reason why our opening problem as outlined in Chapter 1 does not even emerge on his reading. Not only is this the case, however, but these powerful motives have their ultimate root in a general convic-tion of empiricism as is clear when Guyer writes such typical sentences as the following: "it is not at all clear why *any* rules should be necessary for the act of combination to take place. Why cannot the mind collocate its several data as it chooses and call that the combination of the mani-fold?"[4] The reasons for the necessity of rules are clearly stated by Kant on a number of occasions which is that without stable rules governing representation of objects then the conditions of the appearance of objects is not given at all as anything other than a contingent property of them that could, at some point, perhaps the very next instant, dis-appear. Hume was clear enough that rules of association, such as he took it were all that could be justified on the grounds of appeal to "L-experience" could give no more than this. Furthermore, as we saw in Chapter 2, such a procedure is in fact insufficient even for the unity of *quale*. Guyer in fact recognizes essentially this point subsequently when he explicates the synthesis of recognition in a concept as stating that the reason that rule-less combination is not possible is because "apart from rules for the interpretation of the manifold its members do not exist to be combined" (Guyer, 1989, p. 63). However after reaching this point Guyer denies that such rules state anything about a notion of psychology as they could be applied to computational processes in general and hence are only "constraints on anything that would count as human cognitive psychology" indicating that, for him, an argument that could be said to relate to transcendental psychology would effect-ively have to state something more than this. Guyer's objections to transcendental psychology are hence effectively of two kinds. Either psychology is taken to be equivalent to the rational psychology Kant attacks in the Paralogisms or it is taken to be only empirical.[5] The notion of transcendental psychology is not even considered, let alone decisive arguments given against it. It is time therefore to turn instead to considerations of progressively increasing scope as to what such a notion as transcendental psychology could involve.

Strawson and transcendental psychology

Of all the interpretations that appear to abjure any reference to tran-scendental psychology the most famous is surely that of Strawson. However, as I will now set out, his response to transcendental psychology cannot be summarized by the reference that is often made to his dismissal of it as an "imaginary subject".[6] The first reason for thinking this to be the case is that in the very work in which Strawson makes this comment he also states that reconstruction of the notion of transcendental psychology would be "a profitable exercise in the philosophy of mind" (Strawson, 1966, p. 11). A statement accompanies this comment to the effect that such reconstruction has been abstracted from in the investigation Strawson was at this point primarily engaged with. Subsequently however he did in fact turn to investigation of it and when he did so he issued an apology for his previous neglect of the doctrine of synthesis.[7]

Kant gives two basic statements or definitions of what he means by imagination, in the two distinct versions he published of the Transcen-dental Deduction. In the first version he wrote:

Now, since every appearance contains a manifold, and since different perceptions therefore occur in the mind separately and singly, a combination of them, such as they cannot have in sense itself, is demanded. There must therefore exist in us an active faculty for the synthesis of this manifold. To this faculty I give the name, imagination. (A120)

Here the synthesis that is required to combine perceptions together is stated to be dependent upon a capacity that cannot belong to sensibility alone and the name of this capacity is stated to be "imagination". The description of this capacity as that of "imagination" is justified at this point by reference to what is required to bring the particular perceptions together which is said to bring them into "the form of an image" (A120). We will return to this notion soon. If we turn however to the B-Deduction there is given a different account of what "imagination" involves. At B151 Kant writes: "*Imagination* is the faculty of representing in intuition an object that is *not itself present.*" Here the capacity that is termed that of "imagination" is instantly connected to time as it is the capacity to present something to oneself even though it is not before one, even though, that is, it is *absent* due to, it would appear, it having been present at some point previously. This might also be thought to require production of images or, at any rate, of a relation to temporal objects that enables the capturing of a relation to something that once was but is presently not in front of one due to the trace, in some sense, of the absent object being capturable by the cognizer.

These two characterizations of "imagination" relate it to "images" on the one hand and combinations of intuitions and presentation of absent objects within intuition on the other. Hence both accounts connect imagination clearly to intuition and thus to a certain type of perception. Strawson's account of imagination is centrally concerned with illuminating this connection of it to perception and can all be taken to be a commentary on the passage from the *Critique* that Strawson uses as an epigraph, the passage from A120n:

Psychologists have hitherto failed to realise that imagination is a necessary ingredient in perception itself. This is due partly to the fact that that faculty has been limited to reproduction, partly to the belief that the senses not only supply impressions but also combine them so as to generate images of objects. For that purpose something more than the mere receptivity of impressions is undoubtedly required, namely a function for the synthesis of them.

This note supplies a number of important additional complications to our developing picture of what Kant means when he speaks about "imagination". It is clear here that he distinguishes between reproductive and productive types of capacity and that the capacity is one that involves not reference to just any type of "image" but rather to a very specific notion of image, that of "images of objects". This seems here to mean the capacity to form the very notion of an "object" as such. It is this capacity that I take it is indicated to require "a function" that enables synthesis of impressions. Strawson's first attempt to draw together these considerations is in presenting the capacity that Kant is terming that of "imagination", the ability to have "perceptual recognition", and this is hence connected by Strawson to the nature of our ability to ascribe to our presentations the nature of being *of* "objects".[8]

Since we are dealing here with perceptions, the account Strawson gives of what is involved in describing the recognition contained within them must articulate what we normally think of as being the prime property of our perceiving, namely that it is *of* what we term "physical" or "material" objects. So what Kant's notion of imagination involves is a description of something like an "image" where this notion is part of the additional element, over and above the data of sense, that enables cognition of "objects" to be given. Strawson suggests that this additional element that is named "imagination" involves the following two types of recognitions:

(a) that my recognizing the strange dog I see as a dog at all owes something to the imagination; and (b) that my taking what I continuously, or interruptedly, observe to be the same object, the same dog, throughout, also owes something to the imagination. (Strawson, 1970, p. 46)

The first type of recognition involves assimilation of something presently before one to a *type* so that it, as a particular item of awareness, can be related to a *kind* or general description. The second type of recognition, by contrast, appears to be related to the temporal conception referred to at B151 as here we have a relationship to the identity of the presentation in terms of concepts of the same notion having identical application over distant time periods as well or, as we might otherwise put it, in recognition of occurrent particulars.

At this point it becomes apparent that the discussion of imagination, even in a general and loose sense and with no more than the aim of arriving at a general picture of its possible role in Kant's overall account of cognition, must involve some type of connection of it to the doctrine of schematism. We shall review this connection from a number of angles in Chapter 5 but since it is clear that the recognition that is the ingredient element of perception Kant is terming "imagination" involves an essential temporal indexing then it is perhaps not surprising that schematism will be seen to have a great deal to do with this. But even before looking into this connection we can immediately see an important element of what this ingredient of perception seems to involve, namely at least with regard to (a) as Strawson has set it out: "Of a fleeting perception, a subjective event, I give a description involving the mention of something not fleeting at all, but lasting, not a subjective event at all, but a distinct object" (Strawson, 1970, p. 51).

This is what is involved in stating that my description of what I perceived when I perceived the strange dog of the example given was not merely the set of fleeting impressions I could enumerate but, over and above these and organizing them into a pattern, the conception that I could term the *intentional object* of my attention. I have gone beyond the impressions given to me in describing them as all containing and involving a reference to something that is not any of them but which is the holder of all of them. Not only does the intentional object involve this but it also would appear to be *this* "object" that can be presented even in the absence of any of the fleeting impressions in question. This takes us considerably further in our inquiries as to what Kant is naming by "imagination" as now we can see that this is, in effect, a description for the capacity to relate to intentional objects. This capacity would however seem to involve some kind of discussion of how individuals can be formed as occurrent particulars and how the nature of an object can be manifested for us as something conceptually available given that concepts would appear to be only terms for something like an ability to name whilst what we have before us in a "state of affairs" appears to be a pattern of reference to things in relations.

What we have taken thus far from Strawson is that the ability Kant is terming "imagination" seems to require a connection between concepts and percepts such that the latter have in them the ingredient that enables them not merely to be iterated (though this is important) but even presented as particulars to us in an intentional manner at all. This intentional manner of being presented is what we can now state must have been involved even in the complex conception of particulars that we articulated in Chapter 2 in isolation from description of any particular manifold. Now, the relationship of this notion to temporal objects needs spelling out in more detail. The presentation of any percept as an intentional object requires that it is possible to distinguish the given percept from others to the degree that the first percept can be said to be *of* something even if that something was only momentary and not what is termed a "material" object. It may only, for example, have been an itch. This-itch must be however distinguishable from that-yellow as that-yellow is distinct from that-softness. These elementary distinctions are one thing but another is that the softness and yellowness might, for example, be taken to be distinguishable aspects of the same object (say, the bath-duck). Further the same object could here be available in many different types of perceptual occasions and in fact unless it could it would not be identifiable clearly as a particular at any given occasion. For new perceptual experiences to occur is for them to be formed in relation to past ones such that the *kind* that the new experience possesses can be recognized as of the *sort* that it is. This reference to the past elements of perceptions also has to be related to the notion of possible perceptions which latter can form other notions that may never be realized in actuality but which still inform our relationship to it (as, for example, with notions such as those of angels and mermaids). As Strawson puts this: "The Kantian synthesis...is something necessarily involved in, a necessary condition of, actual occurrent reportable perceptions having the character they do have" (Strawson, 1970, p. 55).

In what sense is the synthesis in question necessary? Strawson's suggestion is that it is necessary in the sense that recognition of any *this* would require that whatever is being perceived at present as an example of what it is taken to be (so that this perception is, for example, of a woman) is dependent for its possibility on being able to take other particular perceptions as also being *of* the particular type of the *this* in question. If this is correct then part of the recognition of a particular is that it is an actual example of what a number of other perceptions could potentially be of. Only if the present perception actually does serve in this way in reference to the possibility in question can it be the case that perceptions involve necessary reference to types at all. However unless this reference to types is involved in perceptions then there is no clear story for how any particular becomes recognized not merely in terms of its specific characteristics (as a dog is a greyhound) but in terms of its very general modes of being given as what it is at all.

This description of the role of types in perception is the way in which Strawson accounts for the connection of the transcendental synthesis of imagination to the synthesis of recognition in a concept. This can be seen when, for example, he speaks of the perceptual experience as one that is *"irradiated* by, or *infused* with, the concept"* (Strawson, 1970, p. 57). This connection is important and is buttressed by the notion that what is involved in perceiving anything *as* what it is requires an intentional relation *to* it and hence that what is effectively being stated to be perceived is not the momentary stimuli that may be the occasion of the perception but rather the intentional object that we term the "chair" whilst what we have perceived has merely been a sensible set of certain sorts of perceptions. This is effectively as far as Strawson's account of imagination takes us. It is further than might have been thought from a thinker so generally associated with a negative attitude to the notion of transcendental psychology. Strawson can thus be shown to have a place for the notion of transcendental psychology as part of his more developed conception of how particulars are recognizable at all within the matrix of perceptions, a picture that shows that perception is necessarily intentional. If, however, perception has necessary features this is a basic notion of the transcendental conceded instantly and since what is being described is "perception" what is transcendental is the processes of significant cognitive referencing. The notion of the transcendental unity of apperception has however only been connected to transcendental imagination on this account in terms of a conceptually laden notion of perception having been set out. The problems of unification of synthesis by transcendental apperception are not touched on and nor are the substantive questions touching transcendental subjectivity addressed. These are the reasons why Strawson's account has to be taken to be minimal but in describing the necessary place of intentionality in perception as what must be meant by "transcendental imagination" Strawson has provided us with a significant beginning in our description of the nature of transcendental psychology.

Sellars on transcendental imagination

Sellars' account of transcendental imagination will now be considered with a key aim in view, namely to show a clear connection between the *symmetry thesis* announced in the Metaphysical Deduction and the argument centring on transcendental synthesis in the Transcendental Deduction. The articulation of Sellars' account of transcendental imagination will also enable a critical response to the description he gives of "intuition", a description we cast doubt on in Chapter 1.

Sellars devoted a specific article to describing his view of how imagination is important for Kant's account of "experience".[9] Sellars' account of "experience" begins as a discussion of the nature of perception and starts from the data we already saw to be important for Strawson, namely that the object seen at any moment has to be taken to be something distinct from the act of seeing that presents the object to us. A key reason for this difference between *content* of act of seeing and object of act of seeing is that whilst the former would clearly involve a reference to perspective the latter, due to its intentional nature, would not. To this distinction Sellars adds a second, namely that between the object that is presented as the occasion of the perceptual act and the description of it as the object that it is, which latter Strawson thought of as involving reference to *types* and *kinds*. Sellars, by contrast, here introduces the notion of "occurrent believing" (Sellars, 1978, §7). Such believing is expressed for the one who has the belief in question in a type of judgment that enables representation for the one who has the belief concerning the object in question that it is an example of the *thisness* it incarnates. This effectively still mirrors what we took to be Strawson's account of the process of formation of an understanding of the object in terms of its placing in a kind of logical universe. However at this point Sellars objects that the description of the act of "occurrent believing" only relates the belief in question to a kind of *bare* demonstrative and hence he here sets out a necessary complication that is of a piece with his objection, discussed in Chapter 2 against "bare particulars".

To understand the application of the argument against "bare particulars" to the consideration of perceptual judgments requires a step back as we need to grasp what Sellars would mean by a "bare demonstrative". This notion is that the *thisness* apparently presented by the believer in a given instance with regard to whatever content they are faced with is "sheer" or involving a form of complete immediacy such as we saw clearly demonstrated in Chapter 2 cannot be the manner in which even the merest fleeting impression of this-itch can be given to us at all. Hence the *thisness* that is involved in demonstrative pointing or simple taking of something to be something cannot *be* "sheer" at all. Sellars makes this point with a complexity that requires use of a lengthy citation:

> I submit, on the contrary, that *correctly represented*, a perceptual belief has the quite different form:
>
> > This brick with a red and rectangular facing surface
>
> Notice that this is not a sentence but a complex demonstrative phrase. In other words, I suggest that in such a perceptually grounded judgment as
>
> > This brick with a red and rectangular facing side is too large for the job at hand

the perceptual belief proper is that tokening of a complex Mentalese demonstrative which is the grammatical subject of the judgment as a whole. This can be rephrased as a distinction between a perceptual *taking* and *what is believed about* what is taken. What is *taken* or, if I may so put it, believed *in* is represented by the complex demonstrative phrase; while that which is believed *about* the object is represented by the explicitly predicative phrase which follows. Perceptual takings, thus construed, provide the perceiver with perceptual subject-terms for judgments proper. (Sellars, 1978, §10)

Demonstratives are here being taken, in accordance with the description of the logic of complex objects set out in Chapter 2, as necessarily *complex*. However, the interesting point that emerges from this is that whilst the intentional object strictly speaking is the referential correlate of the complex act of belief, that what is believed concerning this object connects it to particular modes of being given and this adds *content* to the formal complexity of objective representation. In a sense therefore the intentional object is composed both of a logic of complexity that attaches to the ability to represent objects as such, of any sort or generality on the one hand, and this is connected to the ability to present the particular on the other as having the particular contentual nature that it has.

Sellars turns now to examining the details of perceptual items judged in order to take his account forward and describes the visual perception of a red apple, a perception that has the redness as a vital element if the apple in question is before us and hence is being perceived now. The apple also contains, as we are well aware, an inside that is white. Sellars then argues that the white of the apple is not something we simply *believe* it to contain as he rather takes it to be the case that we *experience* the apple as an object that *contains* the colour that is not directly presented to us as the red was. The notion that the apple's whiteness is part of the *experience* of the apple when the whiteness is not present before us is what is meant by stating that we *imagine* the whiteness. This sense of "imagine" would, as with Strawson's discussion, take it that what occurs in imagining is in fact an ingredient of perceiving.

The discussion here is in a sense still revolving around the problem of the perspectival nature of perceiving as the presentation of the whiteness of the apple is not different in kind from the presentation of the side of the apple that is not presently given to our perceptual equipment. Seeing the back of the apple is not an act of present perceiving but, as with the whiteness, it seems nonetheless part of the *experience* of the apple and with the same reason that the seeing of the back is an ingredient of its perception in the sense that the back is *imagined*. Since the experience of the apple involves all these components but the relationship I have to the apple does not strike ordinary awareness as involving more than a direct relationship to what is given in acts of perceiving it is apparent that perceptual judgments, as we normally carry them out, are not thought in the act of their presentation as requiring reference to imagination. But further reflection can show how the presence of imagination in perceptual judgments is essential to the way in which definite objects are given to us as the objects we clearly take them to be. The relationship to something that is given in a film would provide an example here. In watching a scene that shows us characters in a desert we do not, in the viewing of the film that is required to relate seriously to it, simply *believe* in the heat being experienced by the characters as in that state all experience of presented scenery would only be a make-believe.[10] Rather the heat in the scene is part of the *experience* of the scene in the same way as the snow falling outside the window is experienced as containing the coldness that would be felt in walking out into it.

At this point we can get to the basic picture that has emerged of what imagining involves for Sellars. It is expressed well in the following statements:

> Thus, imagining a cool juicy red apple (*as* a cool juicy red apple) is a matter of (a) *imaging* a unified structure containing as aspects images of a volume of white, surrounded by red, and of mutually pervading volumes of juiciness and coolth, (b) *conceptualizing* this unified image-structure as a cool juicy red apple. (Sellars, 1978, §23)

So the act of imagination is a combination of a presentation of the object in question in terms of sets of items being given together (which Sellars is terming an "image") and then the structure that emerges from this combination being set forth in a nominal act that enables the recognition of the structured combination as being *of* what it is named by it. The fulfilment of this latter in completion requires an additional thought that fills out the picture completely by presenting the name and the image-structure as inhering in that which is named and structured and thus shows the requirement of substance to be that which finally describes for us the object as being intentionally provided to us.

Sellars sums up the account thus far provided with the lapidary statement that "perceptual consciousness involves the *constructing of sense-image models of external objects"* (Sellars, 1978, §25). The construction of such a model is what Sellars takes it that Kant has, with equal lapidary statement, characterized as the synthesis of transcendental (or productive) imagination. This image-model is connected by Sellars to a conception of self-hood. The perspectives that are always set out in the image-model are thus related to the position of the perceiver. However whilst this relation to a position is required for the perceiving of the object that is described in the perceptual judgment, the object that is *conceptualized* within this judgment (or subjected to nominalization which I am taking to be equivalent to conceptualization) is *not* given in positional form. Sellars describes this contrast thus: "we must distinguish carefully between objects, including oneself, as *conceived* by the productive imagination, on the one hand and the image-models *constructed* by the productive imagination, on the other" (Sellars, 1978, §29). This distinction between these levels of imagination is that the former action of the productive imagination, an action that involves conceptual-nominal positing, is a side of it that is essentially connected to the unity of apperception, whilst the latter action would rather be that which is essentially ingredient in acts of perception *qua* acts of perception. Hence we would need to account for imagination as that which brings the manifold *as* manifold together at all (second sense of productivity) as something that requires, for recognitional completion, a relation to the ability to stabilize objective reference through a supplementary act.

Once the account of imagination has reached this degree of complexity, however, it seems to be the case that we have already been moved to the position of thinking that the deduction argument that involves it is not completed until we have reached the discussion of schematism, a suggestion that, as we shall see, is capable of appreciation in a number of different ways. Sellars' form of statement of this suggestion is as follows: "the productive imagination is a unique blend of a capacity to form images *in accordance with* a recipe, and a capacity to conceive of objects in a way which *supplies* the relevant recipes" (Sellars, 1978, §31), a distinction that is connected to that between the *concept* of something and the *schema* of it. The concept would seem to be that which enables the formation of images by reference to a *type* or *sort* whilst the *schema* would be the means of carrying out the application to the given particular of the organization of its presentation through this conceptual recognition shaping the empirical intuition.

To understand this suggestion is to move towards an account of the place of temporality in the perceptual judgment. We can see that the formation of the conception of what the particular is taken to be requires some kind of connection between this particular and the nominal act of description of it as an exemplar of the *kind* it is said to belong to. This basic requirement of the perceptual judgment is one that immediately requires, however, that these *kinds* are available to cognition as a mode of organization. Sellars refers to this availability of kinds to cognition as part of a "proto-theory" that needs to be in place for material or physical objects to be grasped in their systematic patterns of organization. This pattern of organization of given particular perceptive experiences are what he terms the *family* of concepts that relate the sequences of perspectives to a common "object". The family is, however, itself also taken to be the "schema" by Sellars, which entails that the schema names such a multiplicity and so it must itself be a complex act in the sense of containing within itself a reference to the numerous possible states of perceiver and perceived.[11]

Whilst the investigation of the schema is a necessary development of the understanding of imagination it in turn points to the need to understand a distinction between two levels of imagination, marked by Kant as the difference between "productive" and "reproductive" imagination. The interesting thing about this distinction is that Kant's first discussion of synthesis of imagination in the A-Deduction is of a *reproductive* synthesis (A100). Kant here famously describes a set of examples of presentation of data that, to be experienced as what they are, cannot be such as to constantly change. Human beings could not, for example, change into all different kinds of animal forms and still be recognized *as* human beings. Kant derives from the examples he discusses the following key general point:

> Nor could there be an empirical synthesis of reproduction, if a certain name were sometimes given to this, sometimes to that object, or were one and the same thing named sometimes in one way, sometimes in another, independently of any rule to which appearances are in themselves subject. (A101)

The presentation of a stable nominal act requires that the object to which the nominalization is attached is capable of constant representation. The condition of this occurring is that appearances are themselves subject to the rule that has to attach to such nominal acts. Hence, not only is it the case that concepts cannot function as general names unless what they name is taken to include common and general characteristics but the *thing itself named* has to be capable of being *perceived* in accordance with this rule of conceptuality. The condition of the appearance being such that it meets in its perception the requirements of fitting the conceptual requirements of nominal acts is that it be given in accordance with the unification of the manifold after the pattern of *a priori* intuitions. Whilst Kant still in his first description describes this transcendental act as one of "reproductive synthesis of the imagination" (A102) it is clear that this synthesis is, as a transcendental act, the basis of the empirical synthesis of reproduction. Kant subsequently therefore changes the description of the name of the transcendental act to that of *productive* synthesis in order to make it easier to distinguish it from the empirical reproduction.[12]

Sellars correctly characterizes the empirical synthesis of reproduction as associative and it is the basis by which images and thoughts of objects are brought into loose connection. The transcendental synthesis is, by contrast, constitutive of the formation of objects as such. This transcendental synthesis is further understood by Sellars to be a kind of schema. In understanding it this way he is extending the term "schema" beyond Kant's usage in order to refer to the rules of transcendental synthesis of imagination. Effectively this notion of schema is equivalent to what Sellars means by "intuition" in the expanded sense that goes beyond that of "sheer receptivity". We can see this when we note that he now defines Kantian intuition in the following way: "for Kant intuitions are complex demonstrative thoughts which have implicit grammatical (and hence *categorial*) form" (Sellars, 1978, §48). The nature of intuition, as comprehended through the transcendental synthesis of imagination, is now set out as that which enables empirical presentation of an object as standing in conditions of temporal and spatial formation in relation to a perspectival positioning. Therefore the very form of empirical intuition is taken to embody for Sellars "a proto-theory of a world which contains perceivers of objects in that world" (Sellars, 1978, §50). An intuition is thus unlike a simple sensation in that whilst the simple form of the former already has the complexity of a *quale* the formation of this *quale* into that which we can term an "empirical acquaintance" with a perspectival object has undergone synthetic formation. As Sellars sums up his account: "Since intuitions *have* categorial form, we can *find* categorial form *in* them" (Sellars, 1978, §52).

Intuition, sheer receptivity and imagination: A reappraisal

In order to respond more fully to this account of Kantian imagination it is necessary to return to the questions we discussed in Chapter 1 concerning the nature of Kantian intuition. It is apparent that the description of transcendental imagination that Sellars has given is one that makes the nature of the description of empirical intuition as demonstrative thought much more compelling than seemed initially plausible. Sellars' analysis of the nature of receptivity is that it cannot be taken by Kant to be primarily a description of simple sensation (not least because this notion has by now been shown to itself be incoherent) and hence must instead be a description of something that is conceptually presented.[13] The nature of the connection between intuition, synthesis and conceptuality involved here is well brought out in the following statement of Sellars: "Space and time are 'forms of intuition', not by virtue of being attributes of or relations between things or events in nature, but by virtue of the fact that the logical powers distinctive of 'this' representings are specified in terms of concepts pertaining to relative location in space and time."[14] In other terms, the very possibility of presentation of *thisness* as such is that such thisness is a demonstrative that cannot be "bare" but that requires a logical complexity that, even in its greatest generality, is analogous to that given for the accounting of physical objects in spatio-temporal locations. No given intuition can emerge for us at all in fact except in relation to the formation of them by reference to a framework that cannot be derived from them and this framework is one that has to apply not merely to thought in general but to sensibility as such, as even the appearance of a sensible in the simplest form is the appearance of something according to the logic of complex thoughts. This is the heart of the *symmetry thesis*.

At this point, however, we might want to pursue this interpretation of the *symmetry thesis* a bit further and ask for how, on Sellars' reconstruction, we are to understand the connection stated by Kant to exist between the transcendental synthesis of imagination and the transcendental unity of apperception? A key passage to interpret here is the following one from the B-Deduction:

> But inasmuch as synthesis is an expression of spontaneity, which is determinative and not, like sense, determinable merely, and which is therefore able to determine sense *a priori* in accordance with the unity of apperception, imagination is to that extent a faculty which determines the sensibility *a priori*; and its synthesis of intuitions, conforming as it does to the *categories*, must be the transcendental synthesis of *imagination*. This synthesis is an action of the understanding on the sensibility; and is its first application—and thereby the ground of all its other applications—to the objects of our possible intuition. (B151–2)

If we connect this back to the discussion we described earlier of how the transcendental synthesis of imagination was distinguished from the empirical synthesis of reproduction in the A-Deduction then we can note there that the transcendental synthesis was connected to nominal-conceptual recognition. A doctrine that is stated throughout both versions of the deduction is that the basic form of conceptuality is provided in some sense by the transcendental unity of apperception. Hence it would appear that if the transcendental synthesis of imagination is connected to nominal acts that this would of itself bring it within the province of apperception.

The point at which the connection between conceptuality and the transcendental unity of apperception is made closest is in §19 of the B-Deduction. What Kant states here draws a contrast between the empirical reproduction of an association between two items by imagination and the connection of them together in a form of judgment. The description of the form of judgment is then stated to require bringing given modes together by reference to the unity of apperception. Kant goes as far as to state that it is the bringing of them together by reference to the unity of apperception which is precisely what is meant by ontological positing (B141). This suggests, in accordance with the heading of §19, that the logical form of judgment consists in a unification according to the principle of apperceptive unity. The reason for this can however be drawn out. Consciousness and concepts are connected together by Kant due to the nature of what possession of a concept involves and this was expounded at the opening of the Metaphysical Deduction. Kant wrote there that a concept is no more than a function and that meant "the unity of bringing various representations under one common representation" (A68/B93). This presentation of a concept accords with Sellars' description of Kant tending to understand them as *general* in character.[15] This is also why Kant thinks the concept as effectively incarnating nominal functions. If we pursue this then the cardinal nominal distinction is surely that between the self that ascribes presentations to itself and the presentations that are so ascribed so that the "I think" is that which must be able to accompany presentations in the sense of being able to articulate them in conscious form. Consciousness is hence the presentation in conceptual-nominal form of an awareness of relationship to given items such that these items are understandable in a fashion that both transcends their particularity and the perspectival mode of givenness that is essential to purely perceptual grasping.

If this enables us to comprehend in what sense the transcendental unity of apperception is a unification at all then what we can add to this is that the formation of the relationship to the object as being an item of intentional awareness requires *both* its fixing in spatio-temporal frameworks *and* its capacity to transcend these latter due to the judgmental framing accompanying the temporal one. If both are required for the object to be given as something that consciousness can become aware of at all then it follows that the transcendental synthesis of imagination has to be, as the citation from the B-Deduction has set it out as, an effect of "understanding" or "apperception" and cannot be considered separately from the latter. This can also be connected to the question of what one is aware *of* when one becomes of the transcendental unity of apperception. Whilst it is clear that in one sense it is merely consciousness of functionality (as the functionalist readers insist) it is also awareness of the very *ability* to perform combination that comes to awareness, and if this awareness itself can become an object of conceptual recognition this suggests that something is the *bearer* of this ability.

Intriguingly, it is precisely after the connection is made in the B-Deduction between the transcendental unity of apperception and the transcendental synthesis of imagination that Kant turns to describing the possibility of comprehending awareness of the self itself. In expounding this possibility he makes clear that the awareness that the subject has of itself is of something that is necessarily presented in time and that thought of the "I think" itself is thought *of* a line or pattern of thinking. Thus "self-affection" involves presentation the transcendental unity of apperception as an *effect* of the transcendental synthesis of imagination despite being what unifies this synthesis! There is only awareness of the transcendental unity of apperception according to the same conditions of reflexivity that bring anything to conceptual form with the additional point, however, that what one is aware of is something that points beyond the temporality that is its only means of being given. This is, at any rate, what seems to be being stated at B158n.[16]

By contrast with the generality of conceptuality, Sellars points out, intuitions have reference to individuals through their singularity. Such a singularity attaches in fact to the *a priori* form of intuitions as is clear from Kant's statements in the Aesthetic about the infinite given natures of time and space (A25/B40 and A32/B48). If we take this as the correct understanding, however, of the singularity of intuitions, that is, that it is their *a priori* form that is singular, then what this singularity of form allows is the presentation of *thises* to us, it is not, *pace* Sellars, *itself* a demonstrative presentation of an individual *this*.[17] So for the empirical intuition to be an intuition of the *this* in question is for the *this* in question to be formed as in a place at a time or to be perspectively given whilst also having the intentionality that enables it to take shape as part of a state of affairs. If this is right however then what does Sellars mean when he refers in Chapter 1 of *Science and Metaphysics* to "sheer receptivity"? This is apparently an individual intuition *prior to* formation by transcendental synthesis of imagination such that the original pre-synthetic intuition would be *of* a simple. This is the only sense that can be given to the description that Sellars gives of the notion of "sheer receptivity": "what the representations of sheer receptivity are *of* is in no sense complex" which leads him to state that "the representations of outer sense as such are not representations of spatial complexes".[18]

But whilst the non-conceptual nature of what is being presented is essential to the empirical reality of something's being sensible as such this non-conceptual nature of the sensible surely does not require that it be something that to be given as part of the whole nature of intuition has to be itself as simple as the intuition's *a priori* form? The confusion here is between what an intuition is *of* (an individual item given perspectivally and hence with reference to complexes) and what enables it to be presented to us at all (an *a priori* form that is singular). The form is simple but the content is complex and the simplicity of the form permits the variety of modes of givenness of the matter which is why the representation of spatial complexes *are* presentations of complexes of spaces despite the fact that space itself is a pure form and thus simple. Here Sellars has in effect confused the level of discussion that emerges from the Aesthetic with that required from the Axioms of Intuition despite his general picture of the transcendental synthesis of imagination helping us to comprehend the availability to cognition of the manifold of intuition.

If we reprise different aspects of Sellars' account, however, then what we could argue for instead of this conception of "sheer receptivity" is that the appearance to awareness of any sort of any item of sense is the relation to a *quale* so that the simplest awareness is itself necessarily *of* the same logical pattern as that of a complex thought even when it is not thought itself that we are referring to. [19]

Imagination, psychology and phenomenology

Strawson's description of transcendental imagination revealed it to be centrally connected to conceptual recognition and the formation of intentional objectivity. To this account Sellars has added the view that transcendental imagination is what forms intuitions as categorial presentations of particulars and hence Sellars has taken us to the heart of the conception of the role of transcendental imagination in the argument of the Transcendental Deduction. However, if the consideration of the discussions of Sellars and Strawson's readings of the argument concerning transcendental imagination has rendered plausible the notion that the deduction argument centrally turns on the consideration of transcendental psychology there are three potential criticisms of this view that we have yet to consider. The first would be that we have yet to show the connection of this argument in any detailed way with the justification of the categories. In order to do that we will need to review in more detail the manner in which Kant connects the whole discussion of transcendental synthesis with the account of how judgments as used in the experience of objects require reference to categories. This work has begun in the above but needs taking much further. However, there are two other critical objections that need to be considered in some detail before the response to this one can be set out. Henry Allison for example objects to the treatments of transcendental imagination provided by Strawson and Sellars arguing that they involve attributing too great an intellectual function to it.[20] As a second objection it requires filling out, however, with a different story about the nature of imagination to that given by Strawson and Sellars and we will need to turn to finding out in what ways such a different story can be set out in due course. A third objection is provided by the phenomenological tradition of interpretation of Kant, a tradition which describes a direct challenge to the view that transcendental imagination should be regarded as part of a story concerning transcendental psychology. There are two strands to this tradition of reading, strands which in part mesh together and in part pull apart.

The first strand comes from the founder of transcendental phenomenology, Edmund Husserl. As early as his seminal work of 1913 *Ideas I* Husserl argues that the A-Deduction "already moves strictly on phenomenological ground" adding however that Kant "misinterprets the same as psychological, and therefore eventually abandons it of his own accord".[21] The two claims made here will be important in the more developed responses to Kant that we will soon be reviewing so it is worth emphasizing their presence here. They are that, on the one hand, the A-Deduction is effectively already stating doctrines that phenomenology comes to rediscover. However to this is connected a disdain for the psychological vocabulary recognized to be Kant's so that it is suggested that the use of this prevented Kant from recognizing the nature of his own achievements and led to his subsequent abandonment of the discoveries made. This second point amounts to the suggestion that Kant's B-Deduction is philosophically inferior to the A-Deduction, a position diametrically opposed to the assumptions current in Anglo-American traditions of interpretation.

Husserl's suggestions require an articulation, however, of what the nature of phenomenological methods themselves consist in. Such a statement is subsequently given by him in a more extended comment concerning the argument of the Transcendental Deduction but this statement will present a particular conception of phenomenology that will be different from that described by other phenomenological interpreters of Kant. Hence the second strand of this interpretation is one that is not presented in the same manner by different philosophers. Husserl sets this position out in the following manner:

> It is of historical interest to recall here Kant's brilliant insights that are expressed in his profound but obscure doctrine of the synthesis of productive imagination, above all in his transcendental deduction from the first edition of the *Critique of Pure Reason*. When Kant in his great work speaks of an analytic synthesis, he means cognition deployed there in explicit forms of concepts and judgments, and this points back, for him, to a productive synthesis. But, in our view, that is nothing other than what we call passive constitution, nothing other than the team-work (disclosable by our phenomenological method) of the constantly higher developing intentionalities of passive consciousness in which an extremely multiform process of immanent and transcendent sense-giving is carried out passively and is organized into encompassing formations of sense and formations of being, as is the immanent unity of the stream of lived-experience, and with respect to transcendence, the unity of the world with its universal forms.[22]

Here Husserl again centres his understanding of the role of transcendental imagination in Kant's discussion squarely on the A-Deduction though with slightly more caution than in the statement from *Ideas I*. Now he identifies the synthesis of imagination with what he terms "passive constitution" suggesting with this notion the sense that there are forms of intentionality that are not explicitly described by the awareness that in some sense "has" them. This argument moves in the general direction of certain analytic readings of the transcendental unity of apperception that stress that it only has to be *possible* for the "I think" to accompany all representations. As with these readings of transcendental apperception so here Husserl is indicating a type of intentionality that enables formation of meaningful relationships to notions of "objects" (or, as Husserl puts it here, "beings") that are grasped without being articulated in explicit fashion. This notion requires Husserl to argue that there is a unity to the stream of lived-experience that transcends explicit awareness and yet involves in some way universal forms.[23] It suggests, in a manner reminiscent of Sellars' notion of "sheer receptivity", that there is some kind of analogue in sensibility itself to the logical forms and connections of conceptuality that enables the latter to emerge.[24] Following through this suggestion in Husserlian terms would take us far from our subject but we can point to the fact that, for Husserl, such an analogue would involve *a priori* associative combination and it would be the process of such associative connection that he would take to involve analogies.[25]

Husserl did not set out these considerations in such a way as to provide the ground for a phenomenological rather than psychological description of Kantian imagination.[26] The reasons for this seem partly to have been due to a lack of interest in the task of providing serious interpretations of the history of philosophy but, more importantly, to have centred on the fact that the notion of transcendental psychology was taken by Husserl to involve an intrinsic failure to reach the level of transcendental analysis of meaning-formation as such, a level at which the understanding of the nature of logic becomes a first problem.[27] This statement is of a general sort however and ensures that the question of how, in detail, the articulation of the argument of the Transcendental Deduction as involving transcendental psychology has impaired its enquiry is not seriously raised.

The same point cannot be made concerning the phenomenological interpretation of Kant provided by Martin Heidegger. Heidegger, rather, expounds in considerable detail a view of what Kant accomplished in phenomenological terms, what he *should* have added and where he went wrong in reverting to psychological vocabulary. It is hence to this account of the Transcendental Deduction that I will now turn.

Imagination, phenomenology and temporality

Heidegger's account of the transcendental imagination is fundamentally related to his discussion of the role of time. A key passage of the *Critique* in this respect is the description of self-affection in the B-Deduction at B157–9 that we have already described. Heidegger, in a lecture course on the interpretation of the *Critique*, points to this passage as containing what he calls "the most radical understanding of time", an understanding that "holds the key" to the core problem of the *Critique*.[28] The "core problem" is one that relates to questions that this chapter has posed with regard to issues discussed in the previous one. It is what the nature of subjectivity is such that it can involve a fundamental relationship between time and the "I think".[29]

To investigate this question Heidegger returns to analysing the notion of "synthesis". We described this in a preliminary manner in Chapter 1 as requiring Heidegger to argue that there is an immediate unity of intuition itself, which he terms *syndosis*. What we did not investigate in that preliminary discussion however was the manner in which Heidegger relates this notion to the exploration of imagination. At A50/B74 Kant distinguishes the two fundamental sources of cognition as being receptivity and spontaneity and here describes intuition as that which gives the object to us (in accord with the "immediacy" criterion of the Aesthetic). Heidegger contrasts this suggestion of the *giving* of the object by intuition with the capacity of imagination to give something to us even in the absence of what is given in order to make the claim that imagination is "an intuition without *affection*" (Heidegger, 1927–8, §21 d, p. 189). If imagination is taken to be that which presents something that is not itself present then it allows for a relationship of the cognizer to a temporal unity beyond the manifold's content or, in some sense, involves a relation to its form.

Heidegger's warrant for thinking of there being a relation to the form of intuition in imagination connects to the description in the Aesthetic of space and time as infinite *given* magnitudes (A25/B40 and A32/B48), a conception he relates to the notion of "largeness" that is treated by Kant in the *Critique of Aesthetic Judgment* (Ak. 5: 248–57). Due to the comprehensive manner in which space and time are given as wholes there is, in the pure intuition of them, no progressive accumulation and hence the whole lies in each part. As Heidegger puts this point:

> "Given" here obviously means 'intuited in a pure intuiting'. Space and time are thus each a mode of pure intuiting and at the same time something intuited. They are a pure intuiting which does not need any determination in terms of sensation. Rather this intuiting makes possible such determinations. But space and time are nevertheless an intuiting which intuits something given, not something which is to be produced by this intuiting. (Heidegger, 1927–8, §7, p. 84)

The pure intuition is hence something like an immediate unity that cannot be extracted from particulars like sensations as it is required for the very identification of something *as* a sensation. This argument connects Heidegger's view of pure intuitions to the Sellarsian thought of *quale*. Pure intuition is, on this reading, a kind of "advance view" of a type of space that makes possible the objective presentation of an empirical manifold. Heidegger here explicitly makes this stand for a *guiding* of the manifold of empirical intuition and hence draws out a connection between *quale* and *guidedness* that makes his account like that of "sheer receptivity".[30] This ensures however that these pure intuitions are independent of relation to spontaneity so that their connection with the "I think" becomes a problem.

At this point we can now turn again to understanding how Heidegger's description of pure intuition enables a phenomenological account of the epigraphs with which we began Chapter 1. Turning to §26 of the B-Deduction we discover a description of the synthesis of apprehension which is now explicated as "that combination of the manifold in an empirical intuition, whereby perception, that is, empirical consciousness of the intuition (as appearance) is possible" (B160). Hence Kant is here clearly stating that the synthesis of apprehension is that which enables us to say that we perceive anything at all. It is within the context of an account of this synthesis of apprehension that the note arises and we will now follow the exposition in §26 closely in order to see what Heidegger's reading of it produces and how he connects his reading of this to the passage from the Metaphysical Deduction.

After mentioning the synthesis of apprehension Kant moves to discussing the *a priori* forms of intuition stating that the synthesis of apprehension has to conform to these *a priori* forms. Kant then adds, in accordance with the argument that Heidegger has advanced concerning the infinite *given* manifold that: "space and time are represented *a priori* not merely as *forms* of sensible intuition, but as themselves *intuitions* which contain a manifold [of their own], and therefore are represented with the determination of the *unity* of this manifold (*vide* the Transcendental Aesthetic)" (B160). Kant here explicitly indicates then that space and time are *a priori* intuitions in two distinct senses. They are *a priori* intuitions in the sense of being the form of that which is sensible but they are also intuitions themselves, that is they have a manifold *of their own* and that this enables them to be *represented*. At this point the note is inserted that we cited as the epigraph to Chapter 1. The note opens by referring to the fact that for space to be *represented* as an *object*, as is required in geometry, requires that there is more than just the form of intuition, there is also combination of an intuitive representation so that "the *form of intuition* gives only a manifold, the *formal intuition* gives unity of representation" (B160n). Kant then adds that the unity of this representation was treated in the Aesthetic as something that belonged only to sensibility. The reason for this is now revealed which is that this unity precedes anything conceptual but it does presuppose a synthesis through which all concepts of space and time are made possible. The concluding all-important sentence then tells us something about this synthesis: "For since by its means (in that the understanding determines the sensibility) space and time are first *given* as intuitions, the unity of this *a priori* intuition belongs to space and time, and not to the concept of the understanding (cf. §24)" (B161n).

If the synthesis is that which first gives us space and time as intuitions then the urgent question arises: What is this synthesis? The note was introduced in the context of explication of a text that began from an account of the synthesis of apprehension and Kant stated of this at A99 that without it we should never have *a priori* representations of either space or time. However, if we follow the reference back to §24 with which the note ends then we discover in §24 not a discussion of the synthesis of apprehension but rather an account of the transcendental synthesis of imagination, an account that uses practically the same terms as the note has just given in its account of synthesis. In the note it is clearly stated that this synthesis is one whereby "understanding determines the sensibility" and at B152 the transcendental synthesis of imagination is stated to be "an action of the understanding on the sensibility". Furthermore, at B152, Kant states that the transcendental synthesis of imagination is the first application of understanding to the objects of possible intuition and hence the ground of all other applications of understanding to possible intuition. The peculiar thing is, though, that at B161n it is stated that the unity of *a priori* intuition belongs not to the *concepts* of understanding but to space and time, implying, despite the claim that by means of it the understanding determines sensibility, that this synthesis is an action that transcends that of Kantian categories. But at B152 Kant states that the synthesis of imagination is an expression of spontaneity "which is therefore able to determine sense *a priori* in respect of its form in accordance with the unity of apperception" and that it is due to this that it determines sensibility *a priori*. If it is however due to connecting the unity of apperception with the form of sensibility that the transcendental synthesis of imagination is an *a priori* synthesis then this would suggest that it is conducted according to the categories as Kant duly states (B152). But if it is conducted according to the categories how can the unity of intuition that results belong to space and time and not to the concepts of the understanding?

If we turn now to how Heidegger interprets these passages we find that the description of the note at B160–1 is set out as dependent upon the view that pure intuition has its own unity and this is what he now terms "syndosis" meaning thereby "original togetherness from unity as wholeness" (Heidegger, 1927–8, §9, p. 93). In accordance with this reading, and against the grain of the passage from B152, Heidegger therefore separates this unity from that given by the categories indicating that Kant's conception of categorial unity must be of something dependent upon this unity. Despite the fact that the footnote begins as an account of geometry, Heidegger indicates that the order of the note indicates that such unification of intuition as is presented in geometry is dependent on the original unity of intuition. As for the connection between the form of intuition and the formal intuition, Heidegger argues that the latter is what makes space into an explicit thematic object for the first time. Connected to this claim concerning space is an equivalent one about the nature of time as Heidegger refers to B155 where Kant speaks of a form of motion which is not a determination of an object but rather "an act of the subject" which is "a pure act of the successive synthesis of the manifold in outer intuition in general by means of the productive imagination" and hence belongs to transcendental philosophy (B155n). The strangeness of pointing to this citation as an indication of the pure intuition of time however is that here we have a synthesis necessarily of the *outer* manifold whereas time would be the form of "inner sense". Inner sense is the only manner in which I can confront myself as Kant states quite definitely in his treatment of self-affection so that it is only through time that I gain a sense of self. Not only is it the case that as the form of "inner sense" that time enables any representation I can have of myself (albeit such representation is not the function named by unity of apperception) but the representation of time itself is always in a form that is not exclusively one of its own intuitive nature as is made clear in the following passage from the Aesthetic:

> Time is nothing but the form of inner sense, that is, of the intuition of ourselves and of our inner state. It cannot be a determination of outer appearances; it has to do neither with shape nor position, but with the relation of representations in our inner state. And just because this inner intuition yields no shape, we endeavour to make up for this want by analogies. We represent the time-sequence by

a line progressing to infinity, in which the manifold constitutes a series of one dimension only; and we reason from the properties of this line to all the properties of time, with this one exception, that while the parts of the line are simultaneous the parts of time are always successive. From this fact also, that all the relations of time allow of being expressed in an outer intuition, it is evident that the representation is itself an intuition. (A33/B49–50)

What we can take from this passage is that if time is, like space, an infinite given magnitude, it is not given in the same way as space as the conditions of the representation of the infinite givenness of time include necessary connection to spatiality. The temporality of what we term *the present* is a vanishing moment as Kant recognizes when, in his account of the synthesis of apprehension in the A-Deduction, he refers to the moment as something absolutely unitary for the condition of such unity is that the moment be caught as something that describes a particular and yet particulars are not given in the grasp of the moment *qua* moment as this is merely an inner form. Hence for the synthesis of apprehension to unite its members together requires the combination that Kant speaks of from the passage at B155 when speaking of motion or the combination of what is needed "for the representation of space" at A99. In other words, *there is no pure representation of time qua time* as any representation of it requires spatialization. The "line of time" is the general way that time is represented: that is, as something that can be set out by reference to an infinity of spatial presentation with the great rival to the image of the line having always been that of a circle, another spatial representation.

We can now however give sense to Heidegger's description of self-affection as something that is an "intuition without affection" as what is meant here is that the self can *only* intuit itself through the presentation of time but what we need to add to this, on the basis of our treatment of the nature of the presentation of time itself, is that there is no self-presentation save through something like the pure form of motion. In other words, there is no self-presentation without the form of space being involved as well as that of time.

If we turn now, however, to Heidegger's interpretation of the passage from the Metaphysical Deduction that was the second epigraph of Chapter 1 we will need to proceed in such a way as to bring this together with the account of B160–1$_n$ and, as with the passage from the B-Deduction, to explicate the passage itself carefully before turning to how Heidegger treats it. At A79/B104–5 Kant begins by stating that what gives unity to judgmental representations is the same "function" that does this with the synthesis of intuitions. Having made this statement Kant then declares that the unity "in its most general expression" is termed the pure concept of the understanding, a clear reference to the categories as we found at B152. The understanding that connects together the one type of combination is the same understanding as that which connects together the other type. One form of combination, that of judgment, involves logical forms and analytical unity, hence concepts. The other form of combination, that of synthetic unity of the manifold of intuition, by contrast, involves transcendental contents. This description of the types of combination has two elements: on the one hand, it is the same understanding which produces the two unities "through the same operations". On the other hand, the two types of unity are distinguished as one involves logical form, the other synthetic content. Kant concludes however by stating: "On this account we are entitled to call these representations pure concepts of the understanding, and to regard them as applying *a priori* to objects— a conclusion which general logic is not in a position to establish" (A79/B105).

The passage seems to indicate a satisfactory conclusion has been reached although it would appear that there is a tension between the elements of what has been stated. Heidegger breaks the apparent unity of the passage by insisting on the fact that the unity of logical form is distinct from that of transcendental content and he takes the latter to be a unity of pure intuition on the grounds of the account we have expounded. However Heidegger has to admit the difficulty with this as an interpretation of the passage and this leads him to state that "the power of imagination and understanding" are battling with each other for priority in Kant's account (Heidegger, 1927–8, §21, p. 198). The ground of this battle is also taken to be Kant's casting of his inquiry into a psychological rather than a phenomenological idiom with the latter taken to be the only post-Critical way in which ontology can be articulated.[31]

It is clear that the passage from the Metaphysical Deduction has effectively to be responded to in a manner that empties it of its distinctive content by Heidegger and this point is connected to his emphatic presentation of his interpretation of Kant according to what he "should have said". This in itself cannot be taken as an objection to Heidegger alone, however, as we have seen the reconstructive model has been primary in analytic interpretations of the *Critique* also. It is rather fundamentally a question of the philosophical fertility of the recon-struction that should determine its acceptance or otherwise. If the passage from the Metaphysical Deduction does not fit Heidegger's interpretation then, it could be said, so much the worse for this passage if it really belongs to a deduction-strategy that requires starting from consider-ations either from the form of judgment or from reference to the supremacy of the principle of apperception, two strategies that the two previous chapters revealed could only have meagre results. Heidegger's interpretation manifestly, by contrast, is one based primarily on synthesis and should be judged as to whether it presents an account of synthesis that will reveal it to be the key notion for comprehending the deduction.

The nature of this treatment of synthesis is that it will have to advance from the suggestion that there is an immediate unity in intu-ition itself, the one that permits the presentation of space and time as infinite given manifolds. The treatment of this will require the elements of synthesis that are distinguished by Kant to be brought together and connected in some manner to this infinitely given manifold. The manner in which Heidegger attempts this is through articulation of the transcendental synthesis of imagination, despite the fact that at B152 this synthesis appears to be related centrally to the unity of appercep-tion and hence to the categories. The first evidence for treating imagin-ation as the basis of synthesis in general is the statement at A78/B103 that all synthesis is the result of the power of imagination, a statement buttressed by the claim at A102 that synthesis of apprehension and synthesis of imagination are "inseparably bound up" with each other. Similarly at A120 Kant describes the action of apprehension as the "immediate" action of imagination upon perceptions. Since we have already stated that the synthesis of apprehension requires combination of space with time in order for the latter to be represented at all (A99) then it would appear the first act of imagination is precisely this manner of representing time, the same manner that enables self-affection itself. This is why Kant states that all knowledge is subject to time at the beginning of the preliminary exposition of the A-Deduction (A99), meaning thereby, on our view, that it requires spatial representation of temporal process in order that anything be given to us at all.

Heidegger makes one of the moves that render his interpretation unique when he identifies imagination itself with "original time", also termed by him temporality (Heidegger, 1927–8, §24 b, p. 232). What this seems to mean is that the vocabulary of transcendental psychology can be translated as a description simply of pure intuitions themselves so that there is not a "power" producing the representation of time but that the original unification that is the infinite given magnitude is the time–space representation itself and that all synthesis is "guided" by this. The manner in which this enables an exposition of the synthesis of apprehension is in accord with our earlier portrayal of the necessity of spatiality as what Heidegger states is that for an absolute unity of the now to be given at all requires that there is "an already operative regard for a now" (Heidegger, §24 b, p. 234). This "operative regard" is the relation to the now as part of the time-line, that is the *representation of it*. This is the basis on which Henrich's suggestion of "data-sensualism", a suggestion that we thought through the consequences of in Chapter 2, needs radical modification. If Kant is committed to "data-sensualism" then what is meant by this is that consciousness of anything being given refers to a particular in the forms of space and time and this renders particulars in a universal form and thus as necessarily parts of a multiplicity.

However, due to the conception Heidegger has here of the original unity of intuition being something *given* to us according to the infinite magnitude he has to argue that the "synthesis" of apprehension is *not* a "synthesis" at all because this would be an act of spontaneity and Heidegger conceives of it instead as original receptivity. This requires Heidegger to argue for a synthesis that is not one of the empirical manifold and does not, in its purity, present such a manifold. This would be a type of "pure" synthesis which unifies the manifold *a priori*. In agreement with our modification of Henrich's notion of "data-sensualism" Heidegger writes: "the phenomenon of time called 'now' is as such never an absolute, isolated, simple element but is in itself a manifold" and the phenomenon of this being given to us is now characterized by Heidegger as "spontaneity of reception" in a deliberate crossing of Kant's terms (Heidegger, 1927–8, §24, p. 235). What this expression seems to mean for Heidegger is that it is due to the basic receptivity of the infinitely given magnitude that there is self-representation at all and so whilst it is receptive it is also that which makes spontaneity possible.

The relationship of this synthesis to imagination is connected however to the types of "pure" image that Strawson was also indicating as necessary in describing the place of imagination in perception. The pure image is effectively the image of time as given in a representation that must always be spatial. On the basis of this pure image something like objects are available to us. The extension of this account to the discussion of "reproduction" is a simple procedure as all reproduction presents is the iterable nature of impressions which must belong to them as without it they could not be presented to the infinite given magnitude that is temporal representation at all. The synthesis of recognition is not however so easy to deal with as we have noticed a number of times in treating it already that it requires nominal acts to take place and is that which supplies the sense of concepts as unificatory complex thoughts. It is mapped or should be mapped onto *quale* although Sellars and Henrich do not conceive of it in this way due to their respective allegiance to models of "sheer receptivity" and dependence on Cartesian self-certainty. Heidegger, like Sellars, requires here the view that there be a reference to that which *guides* synthesis as key for it and hence, like Sellars, requires a transcendental "sense-impression inference" albeit one that is related to the infinite given magnitude. Thus Heidegger explicitly discounts the manifest description of the synthesis of recognition in favour of an understanding of it as projective of futurity in terms of seeking the unity of the moments of time. This is due to his fundamental commitment to the view that the root form of synthesis is expressed simply in time and is hence not based on any conception of subjectivity, a fact that prevents concepts having any essential role in the articulation of experience for him and requires downgrading of the transcendental unity of apperception to little more than an accompaniment of the synthetic process.[32]

Critical problems with the phenomenological reading of Kant

Heidegger's account of Kant effectively relegates the descriptions of judgment, categories and apperception to a secondary level and is hence most emphatically based on the notion of transcendental imagination. It cannot however be said to provide the basis of a successful deduction strategy, as, on this account, it becomes difficult to see the categories as primarily required for experience. What rather seems to be thought of that way is the fundamental forms of intuition instead, in accord with the basic nature of phenomenological analysis. The fact that Heidegger's account has these radical consequences and leads away from central aspects of Kant's discussion entirely has led to its being subjected to a number of critical responses, some of which I want now to trace in order to work from them towards a more satisfactory description of the synthetic account that will provide us eventually with the outline of a successful deduction strategy.

The problems with aspects of Heidegger's account of the note at B160–1 have been set out to some degree in Chapter 1 but it is worth repeating the point that the unity that, according to Heidegger, is revealed in it is that of syndosis whilst Kant refers to the "formal intuition" as that which *gives* unity and hence that Heidegger's treatment, one that regards the formal intuition as applying only to geometry, precisely does not encounter the matter at issue in the note. This is evidently also the case with the failure to trace the note back to an account of §24 where Kant is clear about the transcendental synthesis of imagination being connected to categories and the transcendental unity of apperception. The note at B160–1 also refers to the unity in question as one that the understanding produces in sensibility albeit without making the unity of *a priori* intuition dependent upon concepts. Clearly understanding the note is difficult but there are a number of elements of it that do not fit Heidegger's account. If we return to the passage from the B-Deduction that the note is inserted into then we can see that the main text continues, after the note, by stating that unity of the synthesis of the manifold is given *a priori* as the condition of the synthesis of apprehension that Kant was initially there treating. The unity in question is now stated to be one that is given not "in" but *with* the intuitions and Kant writes: "This synthetic unity can be no other than the unity of the combination of the manifold of a given *intuition in general* in an original consciousness, in accordance with the categories, in so far as the combination is applied to our *sensible intuition*" (B161). So it would appear that the argument of §26 of the B-Deduction is that the condition of the synthesis of apprehension is provided by something that connects to it, namely original consciousness or the transcendental unity of apperception. This connects also to the reference back to B152 with which the note at B160–1 closed suggesting that the transcendental synthesis of imagination has to be thought as something that in some way connects the transcendental unity of apperception to the manifold and in performing this connection indicates the need for categories for perception to take place. This, at any rate, is the argument *around* the note at B160–1 and this argument is abstracted from by Heidegger's account. Further, the note itself here states that it is through the synthesis by which understanding determines sensibility that space and time are first *given* as intuitions and thus they are not given as pure unities merely from intuition itself.

The note at B160–1 begins with a discussion of how space is *represented* as an object and we need to progress in our response to

Heidegger's reading by thinking about the nature of this representation. At B136n Kant describes the representations of space and time as being of a particular sort as they are *singular* representations. This singularity is then distinguished from the unities that are conceptual, on the grounds of the argument from the Aesthetic distinguishing time and space as intuitions from concepts. Through a singular representation many elements are contained within *one* and Kant here refers to this as a form of *original consciousness* just as he goes on to state at B161. It is this reference to *original consciousness* that was abstracted from in the discussion of the Aesthetic which is why Kant states at B161n that the unity of intuition was, in the Aesthetic, treated as merely belonging to sensibility alone. But when we connect the form of intuition *to* original consciousness we get the means of presentation of intuition as intrinsically unified and yet also as divisible into parts, which are all parts of the whole. The synthesis in question seems to allow for both the differentiation and the identification of particulars within the manifold as one follows from the other with necessity. Indeed, the concepts of reflection would seem to be primitive for such representation. The question that arises for us therefore would be what the relationship is between the concepts of reflection and the unity of apperception such that the latter can be seen as part of the condition of perception. Cleary this is in some sense mediated by the transcendental synthesis of imagination, and the other step that needs elucidation here is the relationship between this synthesis and the categories, though this latter step also requires some clarification of how categories and concepts of reflection are connected.[33]

However the basic thread of Heidegger's interpretation of transcendental imagination has not yet been touched upon, let alone replied to. This is the suggestion that imagination is the "common root" of sensibility and understanding, which Kant mentions as something that may be that from which they both spring although such a root is unknown to us (A15/B29). It is however notable that the question as to whether there could be such a "common root" of all the powers of cognition was explicitly denied by Kant in the *Metaphysik L*$_1$ where he stated: "we certainly cannot derive effects which are actually different from one another from one basic power" going on to explicitly deny that imagination could be based upon understanding or vice versa (Ak. 28: 262). In the context of these lectures Kant also makes clear that the thinker who had the view of the "common root" from which he is distancing himself was Christian Wolff. Hence Kant associated the postulate of the "common root" with intellectualism. In the "Appendix" to the Transcendental Dialectic Kant treats the notion of "fundamental power" as only a regulative principle of reason that is "purely hypothetical" (A649/B677).

If we turn next to the question of where imagination fits in the structure of Kant's account it is worth stating that Heidegger's description of it is one that appears to be confirmed by the statement at A118: "the principle of the necessary unity of pure (productive) synthesis of imagination, prior to apperception, is the ground of the possibility of all knowledge, especially of experience" although it is also clearly undercut by the statement at A114 that transcendental apperception, not transcendental imagination, is the "radical faculty of all our knowledge". The relationship between these two passages and between the synthesis of imagination and the unity of apperception is hence another issue of importance that Heidegger's reading raises even if it resolves the question in a manner that appears violent. Still, the violence of Heidegger's reading is not equivalent to that of the German Idealists, despite the fact that the latter, like Heidegger, place immense stress on the transcendental imagination and the reason why the two are far from making the same move with regard to Kant is that the Idealist position revolves around the principle of identity given in apperception whilst Heidegger effectively tries to derive this principle from that of temporality.[34] The Idealist position arises from a certain interpretation of the centrality of reflection and taking such reflection to be constitutive not just of apperception's identity but also of the actions of imagination itself whilst the Heideggerian position, by contrast, revokes the reference to reflection and centres instead upon the original unity of pure intuition. The difference between the two appeals to imagination is thus important, despite the centrality both accord to it. Having unravelled some of the questions that need to be addressed in order for Heidegger's interpretation to be responded to more fully I will now turn to thinking through these questions and pursuing them.

Intuition and concepts of reflection

In describing the nature of synthesis I suggested that it seemed to require, for its most basic operation (as in the case of apprehension and its relationship to imagination) a process of identification and differentiation to be built into it as without these notions being primary for synthesis then they could never be arrived at as its product. This suggestion would involve turning to the place of the distinction between identity and difference in Kant's account and fleshing out further the relationship it has to synthesis. The distinction between identity and difference is one of the four sets of "concepts of reflection" that Kant distinguishes in the argument against Leibniz in the Amphiboly. In Chapter 3 I made the initial suggestion that these "concepts of reflection" might turn out to be key for the articulation of categories but since this suggestion appeared there in the context of the consideration of possible deduction strategies beginning from the unity of apperception the stress on these concepts seemed to meet with resistance due to the fact that stress on reflection tends to bring Kant within the proximity of Idealism. If we turn again to considering these concepts of reflection here, however, it will be in the first instance not from their connection to apperception but rather from a possible linkage to the synthesis of intuition though the problem about their connection to apperception will need to again be reviewed in due course.

Kant describes the four headings of the "concepts of reflection" as involving "the comparison of the representations which is prior to the concept of things" (A269/B325). So these are not concepts like the categories as categories *are* "concepts of things" whereas these concepts are rather what enable comparisons and differentiations to occur from which the concepts of things can arise. In the Amphiboly the primary operation described is one of transcendental reflection by means of which the use of concepts in reference to sensibility and understanding can be discriminated. When Kant describes this use of reflection, however, it is clear that by means of it he includes no kind of notion of reflexivity as he terms "reflection" here the description only of "the subjective conditions under which [alone] we are able to arrive at concepts" (A260/B316). This reflection is not described there as something that belongs to a self-transparent consciousness and hence is dependent on a reflexive interpretation of apperception and therefore implies no type of introspective comparison at its root. This type of reflection works critically on concepts in order to specify how and in what way they connect to notions of "objects" but there would appear to be necessary, prior to it, a reflection that sets out the very formation of such concepts in the "comparison of representations" or rather as that which makes comparison itself possible at all. It seems to me that Longuenesse is making a point akin to this when she describes the argument of the deduction on the following lines:

> If one inquires, as the deduction does, into the formation or acquisi-
> tion both of 'rules for the determination of our intuition' and of
> concepts ('representing' these rules, which in turn 'present' them in

intuition: are their 'schemata'), it seems clear that the 'rules for the synthesis of intuition' must first have been *acquired* at the outcome of the operations described in the A Deduction (apprehension, reproduction, and recognition), in order to be *reflected* as discursive concepts, "universal or reflected representations".[35]

In order for the rules described as applicable within the syntheses in question to be ones that are part of the intuitive combination discussed they must be originally part of the intuition itself just as we noted in Chapter 2 that the conception of *quale* required the complexity of thought characteristic of basic combinations even without itself being more than the capturing of the universal process of distinction of particulars. This, it seems to me, is the point Kant is making when he claims at A99 that the manifold cannot be given *in a single presentation* save in virtue of synthesis. We can restate this: without synthesis the singulars that we term "pure intuitions" are not given to us at all and for these singulars to be set out as the product of synthesis requires that there is *distinction*, the distinction that enables "the sequence of one impression upon another" to be set out (A99). The unity that is required for the presentation of these singulars arises from the manner by which "understanding determines sensibility", something that occurs *a priori* "as the condition of apprehension" (B161). Kant in the B-Deduction passage that discusses apprehension misses the stage of articulation of reflection, however, passing straight from this discussion to the articulation of the synthesis as one involving categories and on the view presented here there needs to be inserted into the argument, as it is set out in §26 of the B-Deduction, another stage.

The stage that is missing is that which is being described when in the *Stufenleiter* Kant speaks of sensation as a perception "which relates solely to the subject as the modification of its state" (A320/B376), a description reminiscent also of the account of judgments of perception in the *Prolegomena*. Such types of relation are also set out at some length in the account of pure judgments of taste in the *Critique of Aesthetic Judgment*. The nature of these relations is that they only involve comparison of perceptions with regard to my own state and these do not yet suffice to give us a notion of the object (Ak. 4: 300). Whilst we will need to return in due course to considering the nature of this discussion in terms of how this tells us something about the relationship of judgment to intuition what we can state immediately concerning this point is that there would appear to be a need, even for a consciousness that is pre-objective, for an act of identification to occur for it to relate to anything as given in the manifold at all. This primary act of identification would require that universal representation is part of the condition of grasping any particular *qua* particular just as we discovered in Chapter 2. When describing the concepts of reflection that are identity and difference Kant draws out the fact that spaces are necessarily presented in a mereological fashion, despite the conception of them as infinite given magnitudes that Heidegger had argued was a formal intuition of the *a priori* condition of sense on the basis of the passages of the Aesthetic. What we suggested above, on the basis of B161, is that such a notion as the infinite given magnitude requires some connection of singularity to the form of consciousness in general, precisely the type of connection that seems to be involved in what Kant later terms "judgments of experience" as these latter are called such on the basis of their connection to consciousness in general (Ak. 4: 300). So the question becomes one of thinking, on the suggestion I am putting forward, how the primary concepts of reflection that are required for anything to be given in even the most minimal and subjective sense are connected to the thought of the transcendental unity of apperception. Thinking this connection will also require revisiting the notion of the unity of apperception as reflective.

Concepts of reflection, judgments of experience and the unity of apperception

In Chapter 2 we considered and rejected Paul Guyer's suggestion that the discussion of the distinction between judgments of perception and judgments of experience constituted an argument attempting to arrive at the deduction of the categories from the nature of judgment alone and thus rejected any assimilation of this passage to an "austere" conception of the deduction. In the course of articulating this response to Guyer we also indicated our conviction that understanding this passage required connecting it to Kant's transcendental psychology due to the reference in the discussion of judgments of experience to the notion of "one consciousness". We will now draw out the way in which this reference to transcendental psychology is made part of the argument given in the *Prolegomena* concerning this distinction between types of judgment, a distinction that has met with general rejection from commentators. The reason the distinction has met with general disfavour is due to the apparent contrast between it and the discussion of judgment in §19 of the B-Deduction so it will be necessary to treat the relationship between these passages here.

The first question that should be raised about the move from judgments of perception to judgments of experience is how it is to be justified as it appears that the latter type of judgment is arrived at by adding to the intuition's judgmental form a category that somehow synthesizes the manifold in some additional and apparently unexplained way and in the process converts the initial judgment into one that has necessary and universal validity. In §19 of the B-Deduction by contrast Kant distinguishes not two types of judgment but rather an association of empirical imagination with the notion of judgment as something that is connected to original apperception. The discussion in the B-Deduction hence appears to be indicating that the deduction requires that the form of judgment be intrinsically linked to the unity of apperception but if this is a property of the *form* of judgment as such then why does the *Prolegomena* treatment indicate that there are forms of judgment that do not have this link to apperception? This is the problem that leads many commentators to reject the distinction in the *Prolegomena* or at the very least to radically reinterpret it.[36]

The *Prolegomena* follows a different method of treatment of topics from that described in the *Critique* as in the former work the possession of synthetic *a priori* bodies of truths is taken for granted as existent and the conditions of possibility of these bodies of truths is examined. The contrast between judgments of perception and judgments of experience is part of the treatment of the body of synthetic *a priori* truths that Kant terms "pure natural science". "Pure natural science" is Kant's name for truths that science expresses but which cannot be discovered by its methods and what makes these truths unavailable to the discovery of the processes of the sciences themselves is that they involve concepts that are "pure and independent of empirical sources" (Ak. 4: 295) amongst which are included motion, impenetrability and inertia. On the basis of these concepts laws such as those of thermodynamics can be stated. So, if it is in the context of this discussion that Kant makes this distinction, then we should try to relate the distinction to the discussion. The distinction is in fact introduced as part of the description of what must be involved for the statements of pure natural science to be possible which is that such statements express a reference of perceptions to "*concepts originally generated in the understanding*" (Ak. 4: 298), and by this the categories are clearly meant.

So if judgments of experience are judgments that involve categories then the point that needs to be made about such judgments and which Kant goes on to make in the discussion of the distinction of judgments is that the judgments of experience do not arise in the same manner as the judgments of perception. Judgments of perception are characterized as based upon *comparison* whilst judgments of experience require the concepts of reflection to be subsumed under another type of concept, the concepts we term "categories". But in order to understand the contrast well we need to look again at what happens when judgments of perception are formed in order to see how we can move from such judgments to judgments of experience. The following passage sets out an important description of this:

> The judgment of experience must therefore add to the sensuous intuition and its logical connection in a judgment (*after it has been rendered universal by comparison*) something that determines the synthetic judgment as necessary and therefore as universally valid. This can be nothing but that concept which represents the intuition as determined in itself with regard to one form of judgment rather than another, viz., a concept of that synthetic unity of intuitions which can only be represented by a given logical function of judgments. (Ak. 4: 304, my emphasis)

This passage demonstrates that the logical connection of perceptions together requires reference to the matter judged to a comparative act and that this comparative act renders the judgment universal. So, even prior to the formation of a judgment of experience, the form of the judgment of perception includes within itself a *logical* universality. On the basis of this *logical* universality, one arrived at by reference to concepts of reflection, it is possible to advance towards the judgment of experience by describing the universality of the judgment as one that is required for the connection of perceptions with each other. That which permits advance from one perception to the next has to include the reflective notions, this is minimal for a judgment as such to be made and this element already accords to judgments universality. But for this universality to reach to the condition of inter-subjective validity requires the addition of concepts that bring perceptions together into the form of a world. This latter is that which describes to us the rules of formation of "experience" itself as defined in the rules of pure natural science.

This account of the transition from judgments of perception to judgments of experience is open to objection due to the fact that Kant seems to describe only the latter as involving universality as the former are purely subjective. My contention is that the former *also* involve universality, albeit what may appear a paradoxical kind of universality, that of *subjective* universality. Kant gives as an example of a judgment of perception the statement that the room is warm. This minimal sense of the judgment also involves a comparison as for it to be warm suggests that it could become different from this and that there are states distinct from its warmth. These universal elements are required even for the judgment to express a purely subjective state. Whilst Kant states that this judgment only tells us of a *present* state of perception it is key to see that for this *present* state of perception to be expressible at all requires these elements of differentiation of it from other states and that without this differentiation we would be able to make no statement at all. Therefore the logical act of comparison conveys to the judgment a universal element, the element of identification and differentiation which element enables even singular judgments to state something universal in their formal givenness.[37]

The distinction of judgments of perception from judgments of experience is intended by Kant to show that even formally subjective statements involve universal elements of reference to states of affairs and cannot be stated or comprehended otherwise. This again accords with the outcome of our discussions in Chapter 2. However the movement from such a type of judgment to that of judgments of experience has not really been explicated within the text of the *Prolegomena* for the simple reason that it is not the intention of this work to make this movement perspicuous. All the argument of the *Prolegomena* is intended to do is make manifest the transcendental regress required to account for the statements of pure natural science and this has been done by demonstrating that such statements cannot have arisen in the manner of mere logical comparison *despite* the fact that such comparison requires reference to universality in form. The reason this is insufficient for the statements of pure natural science is due to the fact that such judgments can only express observations about present states, not the endurance of the state or its necessary nature being one that belongs to the state itself rather than being a requirement of any expression of a state of affairs. Hence although judgments of perception are such as to further solidify our convictions concerning subjective states having complex logical form they are not sufficient to demonstrate that complex logical form belongs in a necessary way not merely to the expression of states of affairs but to the states apparently referenced *in* the statements concerning states of affairs. For the latter to have necessity requires, states Kant, the use of the categories. This is all the demonstration of the *Prolegomena* is intended to show but such a demonstration is perfectly good if we have begun with an assumption that the body of synthetic *a priori* truths that are called "pure natural science" exists.

However the relationship between this demonstration and the account in §19 of the B-Deduction still requires accounting for. The judgment of perception includes necessary logical complexity but the complexity of this judgment does not require that which is judged about to retain the status of endurance that the judgment itself must express for it to be formulated concerning any type of state of affairs. Put otherwise, for a state of affairs to be given *in* a judgment is for this judgment to have utilized universal elements such as comparison, differentiation and identification, which elements put together all involve use of concepts of reflection. However whilst the state of affairs that is then *expressed* in the judgment is universal in its mode of statement, what it expresses concerning the states it is describing may only be a transitory connection. Thus the room being warm is a statement of a state of affairs that, purely as a state of affairs, is enduring in its logical sense since the statement continues to mean something long after the given room being referred to has ceased to be warm. But for a judgment of experience to be given requires that the connections stated in the judgment have the same universal connection with reference to the things described in the judgment of them as they do in the state of affairs that the judgment itself expresses. This is what seems to require the judgment of experience to utilize the concepts we term "categories".

This distinction seems to be repeated in §19 of the B-Deduction as Kant here speaks about judgments asserting necessary unity even when they are connecting together matters that are only contingently related in experience. So Kant states here that "even if the judgment is itself empirical, and therefore contingent" its elements "belong to one another *in virtue of the necessary unity* of apperception in the synthesis of intuitions" (B142). To understand this statement we can look back to §18 where Kant distinguished empirical unity of consciousness from its original *a priori* unity. The empirical unity brings together perceptions through associations and the associations in question are purely contingent but for these associations to be given at all it is required that they be part of the *a priori* unity of intuition, that is they have to be given in time. The condition of anything being given to perception at all is that it conforms to the infinite given magnitude of which Heidegger makes so much. But this infinite given magnitude is not merely *given* as a data prior to or independent of reference to a cognizer as it has to be given *to* and *for* this cognizer who is therefore taken to be the original unifier of the intuition in question. The empirical association of perceptions is an association which, in itself contingent, thus has to follow necessary rules even if the association in question at some point appears only to be the association *of* that point it has to follow according to the manifest requirements of unification of experience as a whole. Thus the move from the particular presentation to what Brook referred to as the "global object" or to what Kant presents as parts of "one experience" is part of the comprehension of the sense of any particular being given in its particularity as such.

What I am suggesting here is that the judgment, as discussed in §19 of the B-Deduction, involves two minimal elements that enable it to express eventually the conception of objective validity that it is Kant's aim to explicate here. The first minimal element is that it must involve logical universality, the type that was described in the *Prolegomena* under the heading of judgments of perception. This element is necessary for the understanding of the most fleeting perception and illustrates the requirement we discussed in Chapter 2 for *quale*. Another element that is also required for the formation of objective validity is that the judgment of perception is connected to the requirements of *a priori* intuition. In the judgment of perception we have prescinded from the conditions of *a priori* intuition and treated sensations as if they were simply given in themselves without having a universal form of their own and have seen that even in this situation they have to have a universal form *for us*. The next stage however is to see that for sensations to be given at all is for them to be given in *a priori* forms that belong to them as part of their very nature; these are the forms of space and time and this is the argument of the Aesthetic in a nutshell. However the further requirement is that these forms of *a priori* intuition are capable not merely of being the forms of intuition but of being capable of presenting something *to us*. This capability of presentation requires that a judgment concerning them as forms is possible and this relates their universality to the universality of reflective concepts. The connection between the universality of intuition and the universality of reflection is stated in the "I think". This third element of the judgment permits the arrival of "a relation which is *objectively valid*" (B142), that is a combination that arrives as that of percepts that belong to *objects*. This third element however is only possible if the form of judgment is one that passes from that of merely logical universality to a universality of ontological positing. The universality of ontological positing has two conditions—that there is something that posits (the unity of subjectivity) and that what is posited is so posited in accordance with a description of *objects* that conforms to the universal conditions of judgmental forms. That which provides a judgment of objects that so conforms to conditions of judgments is the *categories* which allow assertion of combination "*in the object*, no matter what the state of the subject may be" (B142). Categories do not require any dependence on the state of the subject as is required for example to assert that a room is warm. Whilst a room being warm states a condition that requires connection to a formal subjectivity as warmth is warmth for someone and whilst this judgment, despite its singularity has the form of subjective universality, the judgment in question asserts nothing about what has to hold *of* the state of affairs being asserted as it is describing a connection that is purely contingent. Even such contingency does require reference to the unity of apperception but for such unity of apperception to assert something of objects requires the additional element of bringing in the categories of objects themselves. Thus what I am suggesting is that for judgments to be made "according to principles of the objective determination of all representations" (B142) is for them to involve the categories but that the argument of §19 is one that does not rule out the possibility of judgments of perceptions. What the argument of this section requires is that the judgments that combine perceptions together "in the object" move beyond reference to states only of the subject but the way of doing this is by use of what describes the object itself, that is, the categories that give the forms of all objective description. The properties of judgments are such that they always require connection by use of universal formations and in that sense have always a *necessary unity* and this necessary unity is the same unity as that which is given in the very notion of the transcendental unity of apperception but that for "judgments of experience" to arise requires connection of this unity to all three of the above distinguished conditions.[38] The question that arises now however is how to connect this argument, an argument that suggests a connection between the transcendental unity of apperception and the categories in forming judgments of experience to the discussion of synthesis of intuitions, a discussion that brings in the transcendental synthesis of imagination.

Imagination, concepts of reflection and apperception

What I want to describe now is the nature of the transition from concepts of reflection to categories as this is set out in the transcendental synthesis of imagination. I indicated above that the synthesis of imagination allowed the transition from concepts that are required for the formation of any type of relation to the manifold at all (which are the concepts of reflection) to those that permit the manifold to be conceived of as a manifold of objects (which latter are the categories).

The nature of this connection is what I will now set out. In the A-Deduction treatment of synthesis the first discussion of imagination follows immediately after that of apprehension. What the description of apprehension demonstrated is the necessity of *distinction* for any manifold to be given *as* a manifold at all. For even a singular representation to be given required synthesis but what we saw when we looked at this point is that this affects even the possibility of *a priori* intuition being available for cognition as what *a priori* intuition involves is precisely the infinite given magnitude which is singular. No singular presentation of anything can be given without synthesis and hence the infinite given magnitudes of space and time require synthesis if they are to be given. Kant makes this clear when he states that *unity* of intuition is required for space to be presented (A99) although he goes on to state that the type of synthesis in question here is one that "sensibility produces in its original receptivity" (A100).

For sensibility to have the capacity of presenting something at all is for it to be capable of such synthesis as is described as that of apprehension. However the synthesis of apprehension alone is insufficient for the relationship to elements of the manifold to be one that renders these elements iterable. For even "the purest representations of space and time" to arise (A102) requires such iteration. Without this iteration we could not represent time itself as, we have seen already, such presentation of time requires use of space. Therefore the relationship to any manifold whatsoever, the relationship that is accorded when we state that it belongs to "inner sense", is itself dependent upon the condition of representability as such which condition is that there is the unity of intuition that enables space to be given. If the unification of space is a condition of the givenness of temporality then the possibility of iteration requires that spatiality has been capable of such unification and this is why the transcendental synthesis of imagination would seem to need to include the synthesis of apprehension.

The synthesis of apprehension involved the concepts of reflection that are essential to comparison in general: identification and distinction. The condition of these terms having sense is subsequently spelled out in the discussion of imagination, which is that there is a series given and that this series can be represented. To represent the series is to enable distinction of its parts from each other in such a way that the parts can be re-identified over time and a line can be drawn between one particular and another that connects them together as parts of the same givenness. The conditions of the givenness of any particulars as such are hence here tightly connected to the *a priori* forms of intuition but these forms are also treated as being available to cognition only through combination of each with the other. This elementary combination of the forms is what enables each to be intuitable and the nature of the purest intuitions of time and space is set out for Kant in pure mathematics *which is the reason for the mathematical examples* here given. "When I seek to draw a line in thought, or think of the time from one noon to another, or even to represent to myself some particular number, obviously the various manifold representations that are involved must be apprehended by me in thought one after the other" (A102). For such pure presentations to be given requires that there is an apprehension of *succession* but that the succession is also one that is traced as occurring in a manifold such that its path can be demarcated or, as Kant sometimes puts it, *exhibited*. But for the succession to be set out for us as a description of what it gives requires the holding together of its parts to form "a complete representation" so that a whole is reached (as in the example of a number being described as what it is a number *of*).

The first two elements of synthesis as described in the A-Deduction clearly bring together concepts of reflection with *a priori* intuition. The third step connects these two elements together with apperception. The element stressed here is that for iteration to be successfully carried out requires a further act, an act that is necessary for the whole to be given *as a whole*. This is again described in terms of the purest intuition of space and time, that is, via mathematical demonstration as when Kant writes that: "the concept of the number is nothing but the consciousness of this unity of synthesis" (A103). The successive intuition that is at work in the description of combination that we term the formation of a number has to include the recognition that the elements given are all elements of a unitary conception. This reference to unity has, up to this point, been thought of only as that which has to apply to the intuition. However, not only does it have to *have* such unity but *grasping* it requires unity in the act of cognition.[39] This act of grasping is not one that has to be something one is always aware of performing and so whilst it is a condition that relates the combination of the manifold it does not require an Idealist notion of reflexivity. What it does require is the notion that the unity of apperception is, effectively, related to as the basic origin of concepts of reflection as the recognitional ability that is manifested in the use of any such concept is always involved with the action of generation of representation that is performed by the unity of apperception. In this minimal sense the unity of apperception *is* a "reflective" unity.[40]

What we have so far seen justified is therefore the connection between imagination, apperception and concepts of reflection. Concepts are always, as Kant goes on to remind us, universal in form and this universality of form of concepts enables them to provide rules for the apprehension of any particular as such (A106). Such concepts however, to describe objects, require additional modifications and amplifications. The nature of conceptual unity is that it is always connected to the unity of apperception as this unity is the reflective basis of all comparison, differentiation and identification. The nature of apperception is thus distinct from any temporal or spatial presentation as all such require reference to it as the fount of reflection. This is why Kant ties the unity of apperception tightly to the unity of the manifold as the unity of apperception ties together all the moments of the manifold. Emphasis on this point leads us to the key passage that is so important for Henrich's notion of a self-certain self-transparent subject, the passage at A108 where Kant refers to "the identity of the act" being before the eyes of transcendental apperception. What it requires is that the basis of the act of combination should be rooted in the primary act of identification itself, which requires that the subject distinguish itself from what it apprehends. The separation of cognizer from what is cognized is the first data of cognition itself and all distinction and identification begins here. On the basis of it the identification in nominal acts of the endurance of other elements is presentable but this identification of the subject is one with the infinite given manifold of space being the basis of permanence. This is why Kant states that: "appearances in experience must stand under the conditions of the necessary unity of apperception, just as in mere intuition they must be subject to the formal conditions of space and time" (A110). The combination of the *a priori* intuitions with the transcendental unity of apperception is required for experience to be set out as a unity.

The connection between the *a priori* intuitions and the unity of apperception is next asserted to require the categories as these are the forms of thought concerning objects. The perception of succession in accordance with a rule has already been stated to be the key to the transcendental synthesis of imagination but if this requires reference to concepts then the concept in question will have to be that which enables the connection of one "object" to another. This involves concepts of relation and this is where the reference to causation comes in the argument of the A-Deduction (A112). The argument here is that "without such unity, which has its *a priori* rule, and which subjects the appearances to itself" no unity of consciousness could be found with regard to the manifold. Hence what is suggested here is that for the unity of apperception to really bring the synthesis of intuitions to completion requires more than recognition of the parts of the successive elements, it also requires thinking the relationship between these parts that permits us to state that one *produces* the other. This conception of production is required *even for* empirical imagination to associate one impression with another. Just as therefore the concepts of reflection point us to elementary acts that have to be regarded as central to the very possibility of perception itself so also we can state that these acts themselves, in order to be part of "one experience" require something that cannot itself be regarded as a product of association as it is necessary for the very act of association to take place at all and this is described by Kant now as *necessary succession*. The synthesis of imagination is clearly the attempt to describe this necessary succession but since, for anything to come to knowledge is for it to be combined in accordance with the fundamental reflective rule of identity, it follows that this synthesis must be intrinsically related to the transcendental unity of apperception.

The nature of this connection is set out in the following passage:

> The transcendental unity of apperception thus relates to the pure synthesis of imagination, as an *a priori* condition of the possibility of all combination of the manifold in one knowledge. But only the *productive* synthesis of the imagination can take place *a priori*; the reproductive rests upon empirical conditions. Thus the principle of the necessary unity of pure (productive) synthesis of imagination, prior to apperception, is the ground of the possibility of all knowledge, especially of experience. (A118)

The transcendental synthesis of the imagination is here described as productive due to the fact that what is required for it to take place is that the nature of objectivity is itself produced by it. This is not a synthesis *of* objects, it is rather a synthesis that enables there to be any relation of "objects" to each other such that we can speak of there being a world as it produces the very notion of what an "objective representation" is. The notion that it takes place "prior to apperception" should however, in our view be interpreted as meaning that the "identity of its act" is given *before the eyes* of apperception or, to put this in less metaphorical language, that it is directed by the principle of unification that is derived from apperception. The tracing of this synthesis, as a synthesis that brings the unity of apperception to the manifold of intuition, is the subsequent primary work of the *Critique*. Such at any rate is our argument and hence the viable deduction strategy is one that shows that the basis of the claim that categories are needed for experience to be possible is that without the use of categories there could be no sustained conception of what it meant to experience anything either as successive or in space. Without the reference to these *a priori* conditions of intuition being given the form of experience as such has not been set out but once it has been given there are two questions that centrally have to be addressed, namely, how do these forms produce a conception of particulars and, how do the relations between particulars as presented in these forms, present to us the constellation we refer to as "our experience of a world"?

It is necessary that the transcendental synthesis of imagination be set out as the basic element of the articulation of experience as this synthesis is what shows the connection between concepts of reflection, the unity of apperception, the categories and the infinite given magnitudes of *a priori* intuition. The depth of these connections is not justified in either version of the deduction argument as setting them out is the work not just of the deduction but also of the Analytic of Principles as will be shown in detail subsequently. However that this claim is not one that is eccentric to the understanding of the *Critique* should be clear when we read Kant asserting that "the synthesis of imagination is the pure form of all possible knowledge" as "by means of it all objects of possible experience must be represented *a priori*" (A118).

If however all *objects* of possible experience are presented by means of the synthesis of imagination then this synthesis will have to be carried out in accordance with the categories as the categories describe for Kant the form of thoughts about objects in general. The unification of the synthesis of imagination by apperception will therefore need to be carried out by means of the categories, exactly as Kant goes on to state (A119). The means by which the synthesis of imagination combines the elements of intuition through the categories needs to be described in detail and the detail of this is supplied fundamentally in the Axioms of Intuition, the Anticipations of Perception and, most fundamentally of all, the Analogies of Experience. But what is clearly stated in the A- Deduction is that the forms of synthesis that were distinguished in the preliminary argument all have to be connected to the imagination as the notion of apprehension is merely the "immediate" relation of imagination to intuition (A120). But the basic recognition of the manifold requires its organization in accordance with the form of the categories as brought about by the imagination (A125).[41]

Imagination and apperception in the B-Deduction

Whilst the above reconstruction of the A-Deduction has shown the basic pattern of reasoning by which Kant there connects concepts of reflection to the synthesis of imagination and the synthesis of imagination to both apperception and the categories it could be argued that the basic line of argument as set out there was subsequently abandoned by Kant when he attempted, on the lines first suggested in the introduction to the *Metaphysical Foundations of Natural Science*, to instead base the deduction on the notion of judgment. Our account in Chapter 2 of the impossibility of any successful deduction argument being based on the notion of judgment has given reasons for doubting this to be the case, reasons that we have buttressed in our account of the argument of §19 of the B-Deduction. It is however undeniable that the focus of argument in the B-Deduction appears different from that in the A-Deduction, not least because at least the stage from §§15–20 proceeds not from the type of detailed consideration of synthesis that we find in the A-Deduction but rather from considerations concerning the relationship of the transcendental unity of apperception to judgment. It is necessary to provide our reading of the argument of the B-Deduction now in order to show that the recasting of the argument of the deduction in this second edition by Kant is not focused on a denial of the view set out at A118 that the synthesis of imagination provides us with the pure form of all possible knowledge and the *a priori* means of comprehending objects of experience.

The B-Deduction opens with an account of synthesis, just as the A-Deduction did with Kant stating that it indicates as a term that "we cannot represent to ourselves anything as combined in the object which we have not ourselves previously combined" (B130). The point of the B-Deduction could be stated briefly as being that in it, as in the A-Deduction, Kant wishes to specify the nature of this combination and its conditions. Since it requires that combination is something performed by the cognizer it is an action of "the self-activity of the subject" (B130), something that brings in reference to the transcendental unity of apperception. Kant indicates after suggesting this need to refer all cognition to the unity of apperception that the basic condition of anything being cognized is that there is *distinction*, and the most elementary notion of this is the distinction between cognizer and cognized (B131n). The nature of the unity that is at work in the most elementary relationship to the manifold at all is taken next to require the "I think" as that which can accompany all representations just as we saw it to be the case at A103 that reference to the reflective act of consciousness is something that, whilst not always given to consciousness as the generative act of awareness, is always present for something to *be* an act of awareness at all.

The notion of the "I think" is not however identified in Cartesian fashion with the transcendental unity of apperception itself as Kant speaks of the "I think" being generated *by* it since for the I and its thought to be distinguished requires that there has already been formed the notion of distinction itself. *The primary act is the formation of the conceptions of identification and differentiation which is given its fullest reflexive form in the notion of the identity of apperception.* Furthermore, the relationship of myself as an empirical subject to any given percept is one that is dependent upon the conjunction of presentations with each other, the conjunction that we named in the A-Deduction "the synthesis of imagination" but which is simply introduced in the B-Deduction at first without any name. The nature of it is however specified immediately: "Only in so far ... as I can unite a manifold of given representations in *one consciousness*, is it possible for me to represent to myself the *identity of the consciousness in [i.e. throughout] these representations*" (B133). The necessity of identification of the cognizer throughout their experiences is something that is itself based upon the notion that this cognizer has been able to bring together in their consciousness the manifold in a basic act of unification. Therefore being identical to oneself *over time* first requires that one is able *at any given time* to bring the manifold to awareness as something that falls under basic forms of cognitive comprehension. This refers us back, once more, to the need for the manifold to be presented under the *a priori* forms of intuition. It also however has the consequence that for the notion of analytic unity of apperception to have sense is for it to be the case that a synthesis of unification has rendered the notion of apperception as something that is part of the process and nature of "experience".

The amplification of this point about the dependence of the analytic conception of unity of consciousness upon the synthetic unity points to the manner in which concepts of reflection play a primary role in the recognition of the elements of the manifold. We can see this in the following passage:

A representation which is to be thought as common to *different* representations is regarded as belonging to such as have, in addition to it, also something *different*. Consequently it must previously be thought in synthetic unity with other (though, it may be, only possible) representations, before I can think in it the analytic unity of consciousness, which makes it a *conceptus communis*. (B133–4n)

The condition of self-identification is thus shown as dependent upon the differentiation of self from other presentations with which it is connected in some form of "experience" so that the possibility of synthesis is the first form of "awareness" as such which is why Kant earlier distinguished original apperception from the "I think". The formation of a notion of self-identity in terms that enable the self to be thought as that to which all logical formations are related first requires that the self has been able, by the primitive use of concepts of reflection, to think itself at all, which is to say, to distinguish itself. This passage hence provides further evidence for the primitive nature of such concepts of reflection.

The relation to the manifold is set out in §16 as one that requires grasping of it in a synthesis of intuition and this synthesis is one that requires bringing out the notion of original apperception as something that is capable itself of being a self-reflexive awareness only after and because of the *a priori* synthesis of the manifold. Section 17 then opens by reminding us that the *a priori* intuitions of space and time are the forms to which the entire manifold has to be subjected and adding that these *a priori* intuitions need to be connected to the original unity of apperception. This section then proceeds again to remind us that the *a priori* forms of intuition are not themselves sufficient for knowledge as it is further necessary that something be presented *in* and *through* them and that the condition of anything being so given is the recognitional act we are familiar with from the A-Deduction (B137–8). Section 18 next adds the distinction between the empirical unity of consciousness and the transcendental unity of consciousness that we discussed earlier which leads in §19 to the point about judgment requiring relationship to the unity of apperception for it to be objectively valid, a point that already implies use of the categories. This implication is then drawn out in §20. The argument from §§15–20 can be summarized as stating that without synthesis there would be no presentation of unity in the manifold of intuition and the condition of this synthesis is that there is a *capacity* to perform it that is based on the presence of concepts of reflection in perception. The conditions of unification are thus first of all the concepts of reflection, which however are presented, in *universal form* in the forms of judgment and yet the latter cannot themselves describe *objects* as only the categories can. So, on our reading, the synthesis of intuitions is the basis of self-reflexive awareness being possible, even in the form of the "I think". The occurrence of this synthesis is dependent on the connection of perceptions by reference to concepts of reflection and these latter cannot be given at all without the primary recognitional difference of self from other. This primary recognitional difference is not yet reflective but becomes so through reflective acts becoming themselves second-order elements of awareness.

The reason why the argument of the first five sections of the B-Deduction is not complete is that it has not been shown in it how the unity of empirical intuitions can be said to be "no other than that which the category" prescribes to the manifold (B144–5). Kant's argument has has not yet demonstrated the manner in which spatio-temporal form requires unification by the categories, it has merely argued for the connection of the form of the manifold with the form of apperception. The question of how these forms come together in such a way as to provide us with awareness of the *content* of the manifold has not yet been addressed.

Section 22 opens with a repetition of the point that the *a priori* form of intuition does not itself present any object for cognition and adds to this the point that the form of an object in general as described in the categories cannot give us any knowledge either without connection to the *a priori* form of intuition. In relating to pure intuition as something that *is* intuited, not just taken to be a *form* of intuition we can develop pure mathematics but we cannot in this combination present any solution to the question of whether there are objects that conform to the demonstrations of such figures in general. Therefore we can only be said to have knowledge when such pure figures are connected to empirical intuitions and this leads to the point that if the categories are to describe any objects for us this cannot be by connection only to the pure figures of mathematics it must rather be by connection with empirical intuitions (B147–8).

The relationship of the unity of apperception to the categories is one that enables the latter to enter into a purely intellectual notion of combination with the thought of *a priori* intuition albeit such a combination gives no more than the thought of objects in general. The synthesis of intuition when connected to the original unity of apperception is, by contrast, the transcendental synthesis of imagination (B151). The imagination relates to sensibility as the intuitions that we have are sensible in their form but since imagination is itself an operation of the cognizer in an active sense (it is, as was stated in the A-Deduction, *productive*) it has an *a priori* connection with sensibility.

Imagination has to be that which determines the manifold and this determination is what enables "objects" to arise from intuition. Section 24 begins by restating these points. Kant then sets out a discussion of the nature of the self as required in order to account for the difference between empirical and transcendental notions of subjectivity, a distinction already utilized in §18 but not fully explained there. Kant now talks about the nature of our thought under the heading of "understanding" stating that thought cannot itself be identified with intuition. The synthesis of understanding that he has until now described as the unity of apperception is then explicated in terms directly reminiscent of the description at A108 when Kant states it consists in nothing but "the unity of the act, of which, as an act, it is conscious to itself" (B153). This self-reflexive act of awareness by which we transcendentally identify ourselves *as* ourselves requires synthetic combination. The synthesis required for such self-identification to take place is now related to the very synthesis of the manifold that is required for intuitions to present anything to us:

> The understanding, that is to say, in respect of the manifold which may be given to it in accordance with the form of sensible intuition, is able to determine sensibility inwardly. Thus the understanding, under the title of a *transcendental synthesis of imagination*, performs this act upon the *passive* subject, whose *faculty* it is, and we are there-fore justified in saying that inner sense is affected thereby. (B153–4)

It is possible to determine the form of sense by synthesis as we can see by the fact that we can form pure figures from intuition. This formation of pure figures in the context of pure mathematics is one with the formation of an image of time itself, the very image of it that we saw demonstrated in the A-Deduction as requiring its combination with the form of space (A99–100). The possibility of time and space being given at all as infinite magnitudes requires first of all that there is a means of measuring magnitude and this means of measurement is what supplies the possibility of figuration itself. This is why in the B-Deduction Kant refers to the synthesis of imagination as a *figurative* synthesis as it is the synthesis whereby figures are formed. The formation of figures is the determination of time as providing us with an image of objects as such. Kant further describes this when he provides the account of motion that Heidegger referred to: "Motion, as an act of the subject (not as a determination of an object), and therefore the synthesis of the manifold in space, first produces the concept of succession" (B154–5). It is through the subject taking itself as in motion that there is a notion of succession at all although this notion of motion evidently is built upon the previous reflective acts of identification and differentiation.

Successive synthesis of the manifold requires that the intuition present something within space and that space hence be seen as containing temporality within itself just as temporality requires spatial representation to be given to us at all. The combination of space with time to give motion is the first act of transcendental synthesis, the same act that enables the re-identification of particulars within a comprehensive whole and hence in setting out the synthesis of imagination here what Kant has done is re-describe the relationship of apprehension and reproduction from the A-Deduction. However what Kant now connects this combination with is the awareness of ourselves as transcendental subjects as when he goes on to write that "we intuit ourselves only as we are inwardly affected *by ourselves*" (B156). In other terms, the possibility of awareness of self is one with the possibility of awareness of spatial manifolds. We are ourselves only given *to* ourselves through the very combination of spatiality that is the condition of the cognition of objects which ensures that we can know ourselves only after the pattern of objects whilst the thought of ourselves that is the basis of all reflective awareness as such shows that we are *not* the object of which we can make statements of knowledge. Self-affection is thus shown, *pace* Heidegger, to be the means by which the nature of objectivity and subjectivity are shown to be purely identical, which means purely distinguishable as such.[42]

Section 25 argues that the possibility of comprehension of the self as *intelligence* is based upon the nature of spontaneity and this section in a sense presents a promissory note for how the transcendental view of subjectivity could produce a conception of the self that would have other aspects available than the connection with perceptions. This point completes the discussion of the nature of transcendental self-awareness as a discrete part of the discussion in the B-Deduction.

Section 26 by contrast returns to the main theme of the deduction by stating that it is necessary to show that the categories are the condition of *a priori* knowledge of objects of sensibility in terms of the "laws of combination" of empirical intuition requiring them (B159). This leads to the description of the synthesis of apprehension as the means by which empirical manifolds are combined together but the discussion of this is interrupted by an account of pure figures which leads to the note at B160–1. The unity of *a priori* intuition is here stated, as we would by now expect on the basis of our reading of the A-Deduction, to not simply belong to sensibility (as was suggested in the Aesthetic) but a product of synthesis with this synthesis being a product of understanding though not a product of its concepts. This synthesis has to provide the unity of the intuitions of space and time, and the reference back to §24 that is inserted is clearly a reference to the production of figures *of* space and time as produced by the transcendental synthesis of imagination. These combinations are what enable the successive combination of space with time in forms of motion and hence underlie the rules of pure natural science and give the figures of pure mathematics. The unity of space and time with each other is formulated through the provision of these figures and belongs to intuition itself but whilst this intuitive unity is not governed by the categories the possibility of knowledge emerging from it requires the pure figures to be connected to the empirical manifold. The connection of the combination of space and time with the empirical manifold is what the figurative synthesis brings about by means of apprehension and reproduction.

In illustration of the argument Kant gives now some examples of how the process he is describing works. For something to be given in an empirical manifold requires that the figure of the object in question is drawn in accordance with pure figures. However the very possibility of such drawing requires that the manifold be related to under the form of a basic thought of an object in general, the thought of *quantity*. Thus for the pure intuition to effectively present to us in the empirical manifold a shape requires that the motion of production of this shape be given through the thought of objects as *measurable*. This conception of measurement, the conception that underlies quantitative categories as such, is what must be given for the reflective act here to differentiate what it differentiates as filling a certain amount of space. Hence what is here described is the movement from the concept of reflection to the concept of the object in the terms of a categorial movement. The category provides the rule by which the empirical manifold can present an example of a shape and such shapes are the basic means by which intuitive manifolds are given to us in the purest form at all. Thus what underlies the possibility of giving pure mathematics its form is the same as what enables objects as such to be presented in the purest manner. This is why Kant writes: "It is one and the same spontaneity, which in the one case, under the title of imagination, and in the other case, under the title of understanding, brings combination into the manifold of intuition" (B162n).

The second example is even clearer. Here Kant talks about the presentation of the perception of water freezing. For this perception to be possible requires that successive states of something are given as being states of the same thing and so we have here already the reflective awareness of identification and differentiation. The process in question, since it requires succession, is clearly perceived through the *a priori* intuition of time just as the presentation of the shape in the previous example required reference to the *a priori* intuition of space. But we can add that the perception of states in this latter example is one in which one state is taken to have *produced* the other and for this production to take place requires that there is a relationship between the states in question, a relationship that we can take to be one of causal type. The nature of this perception is thus one in which causal change has been noted as part of the temporal perception of the states given, a perception that requires the temporal succession to be seen as one of spatial presentation and in which the spatio-temporal unity is one that required productive combination of the objects with each other. The use of the pure category of cause in the connection of the empirical manifold accounted for it being the connection of the one state with the other and yet noticeable of change within the self-identical object. This points to the fact that causation as a notion is connected to the primary concepts of reflection and is a way of stating an identity-in-difference as part of perceptual experience. The nature and justification of this awareness is clearly something that requires much more consideration than is given here but once again it demonstrates that Kant has shown the connection of the concepts of reflection with the categories to reside in the movement within a synthetic manifold requiring the addition of the latter to the former for certain types of perception to be provided to us in a form that gives them meaningful sense.

Kant however subsequently reaffirms that this combination is one of imagination when he states that imagination connects the manifold of empirical intuition together by reference to unitary rules of understanding. How the categories work to make experience itself possible is not shown in the deduction argument but *that* they do can only viably be constructed from an argument that is based upon synthesis. This is the result of our demonstration which is that arguments based on apperception primarily on "austere" conceptions of judgmental combination are insufficient to provide even a first rationale for the view that we need categories in experience. What we discovered from consideration of these constructions of the deduction argument however is that the complexity of thought that is given in judgment is in fact a complexity that is given its due in the notion of concepts of reflection and that the reference to transcendental subjectivity is a necessary element of the deduction argument. When these consider-ations are brought into connection with the concentration on synthesis the basis of the deduction argument is at last laid bare. To travel further down the road of explication of Kant's view of experience it will now be necessary to turn to a discussion of the distinctive role provided by the chapter on schematism in order then to describe the role of the tran-scendental synthesis of imagination in the Analytic of Principles.

5
Schematism and Imagination

The chapter on schematism in the *Critique* forms the hinge between the discussion of the Transcendental Deduction and the actual principles themselves although it is also succeeded by an account of the nature of transcendental synthetic judgments in general that emerges on the basis of the treatment of schematism. The first question in treating the chapter on schematism, however, concerns how its purpose is distinct from that of the Transcendental Deduction. This question has persistently troubled philosophers writing on the *Critique*. Paul Guyer for example argues that it is in the schematism (and the Analytic of Principles) that Kant really provides the deduction of the categories.[1] In a fundamental sense Martin Heidegger agrees with this verdict writing: "the schematism grounds the transcendental deduction, although Kant did not understand schematism in this way" (Heidegger, 1927–8, p. 292). The rationale for this argument in Heidegger's case rests upon his conviction that Kant discovers the solution to the question of the ground of relational connection between substances in something that goes beyond the condition of substantiality and even that of the divine, namely temporality itself.[2] By contrast Béatrice Longuenesse suggests that a reason for the redrafting of the Transcendental Deduction in the B version may have been to reveal the connection between the deduction and the schematism: "the *synthesis speciosa* is specified in the different schemata of the concepts of the pure understanding, and the a priori conformity of appearances to the categories is explained in the System of Principles".[3]

Whilst Longuenesse's comment suggests a clear connection between the Schematism and the Transcendental Deduction it implies that within the A edition at least the move from one to the other was not carried out smoothly and hence that the connection between the two chapters was not so tight as Kant might have wished. I would like to suggest that the distinction between the two chapters is that whilst the Transcendental Deduction provides us with a *quid juris* for the use of the categories it is only with the argument of the Schematism that the manner of connection between the categories and appearances is made manifest.

The argument of the chapter on schematism

The reason why there is some confusion about the connection of the argument of the Schematism to that of the Transcendental Deduction is that there is considerable disagreement and confusion concerning what the argument of the Schematism consists in. The first point made in the chapter on schematism concerns the conditions under which what Kant terms a "subsumption" takes place. Here he addresses the question of how we bring the concept *of* an object into connection with that which is spoken of *by* the concept and he argues that the way in which this connection is achieved is through the concept "containing" within it something of what it represents as belonging to the object it describes. This reference to "containment" should alert us to the distinction between synthetic and analytic judgments, not least in a chapter that is the first part of a doctrine of transcendental judgment. In the "Introduction" to the *Critique* Kant initially distinguished between synthetic and analytic judgments precisely in terms of the relationship of subject and predicate in them.[4] Kant stated there that with a synthetic judgment a third thing was necessary for the subject and predicate to connect, as the predicate did not belong to the subject by definition (A6–9/B11–13). What he now suggests with regard to empirical concepts is a connection between the manner in which they are thought and the conditions of their intuition: "the empirical concept of a *plate* is homogeneous with the pure geometrical concept of a *circle*. The roundness which is thought in the latter can be intuited in the former" (A137/B176). In other words it is because pure intuition enables there to be pure geometry that we are able to speak of the empirical concept of a plate. Hence empirical concepts contain in them both elements of pure intuition and pure concepts and this is how they can describe their objects. This point is later extended to the empirical concept of "dog" which is said by Kant to signify a rule: "according to which my imagination can delineate the figure of a four-footed animal in a general manner, without limitation to any single determinate figure such as experience, or any possible image that I can represent *in concreto*, actually presents" (A141/B180). In stating that the empirical concept signifies the rule of imagination according to which the figure of the animal can be given to me independently of any particular example Kant is suggesting that what empirical concepts effectively do is prescribe the normative structure of objects in a pure fashion. This indicates that empirical concepts are to be always regarded as involving a referential capacity not to what the terms might be thought to naturally describe (as "dog" describes "Rex" or "girl" describes "Alice") but rather to the possibility of an infinite range of examples or in other terms to determine a *type*. The ability to determine this type is what is dependent upon the mutual interaction of pure concepts and pure intuitions such that empirical concepts cannot be separated from normative conditions of their use.[5]

However once the account of schematism is put in this form then a philosophical objection can be made to it that can even be given a Kantian pedigree. Wittgenstein famously argues that the activity of following a rule cannot be exhaustively determined by such normative considerations as we have alluded to precisely because there is always a measure implied in such rules that cannot itself be measured by them. Hence rules hit bedrock and justification has to come to an end with reference to a transcendental anthropological condition.[6] To this objection to the characterization as given above could be added some statements from Kant himself in the section immediately prior to the chapter on schematism where he reports that judgment is a fundamental talent that cannot be taught to one who lacks it (with the person lacking in judgment identified by Kant with the stupid person who has a failing for which there is no remedy (B173n)). As Kant writes concerning the suggestion that rules of judgment be provided: "to give general instruction how we are to subsume under . . . rules, that is, to distinguish whether something does or does not come under them, that could only be by means of another rule. This in turn, for the very reason that it is a rule, again demands guidance from judgment" (A133/B172).

However it is when we turn to the passage from Kant that we derive the basis of our answer to this criticism for when Kant makes the quoted remark he is speaking about the demand for a doctrine of judgment within general logic and agreeing that general logic would be incapable of being provided with such. But as he goes on to write: "the situation is entirely different in transcendental logic" (A135/B174) and the reason why is because it relies upon the findings of transcendental philosophy. Transcendental philosophy has a basic task: "It must formulate by means of universal but sufficient marks the conditions under which objects can be given in harmony with these concepts" (A136/B175), the concepts, that is, of pure understanding. This requires that the objects be described in such a way that they can be cognized by means of the pure concepts. A last form of the objection already stated kicks in at this point and still has Wittgensteinian pedigree: "if I can understand my rule, and so understand what my illustrative method is *for*, I have *already* 'applied the concept' ".[7]

For a transcendental philosopher concerned with pure concepts however the above objection will not work. It is plausible to isolate the notion of pure concepts (as is done in the Metaphysical Deduction) indicating that these concepts are ones we seem to possess without the possession of them determining the manner in which they can apply to objects. To take one example: the concept of causality describes something like a necessary relationship between two entities such that if A is present B will be constrained in some specifiable manner. However whilst we can state that this concept is one that we possess and indeed indicate what the concept would involve were it to have application (and *in this sense* we can agree that possession of the concept indicates a rule for its use) we cannot by this means indicate whether it *does* have this use as we have to be able to show what in the appearances is susceptible to description by means of this concept.

What this indicates is that the fundamental question concerning schematism is not in relation to the empirical concepts with which Kant begins the chapter but with regard to pure concepts. However, whilst the question of schematism is really philosophically urgent at this level, it would be false to deny that the schematism of empirical concepts also describe something. With regard to the empirical concept "dog" for example what is indicated in the account of its schematism is that the term requires for its effective use a reference not merely to examples (such as spaniels and poodles) or to descriptions but rather to a connection between the intuition of animals of a certain type and the rule that determines them as belonging to this type. Certainly with empirical concepts the rule of belonging to the type is not one that can be given justification for itself alone, as it must also refer us to the pure conditions of operation of concepts in general that permit concepts to apply to appearances. Hence whilst the empirical schema provides an account of empirical concepts it is ultimately based upon the transcendental schema.

Another type of schema worthy of description is that of pure sensible concepts. It is noteworthy how similar Kant's treatment of it is to that of empirical concepts: "No image could ever be adequate to the concept of a triangle in general. It would never attain that universality of the concept which renders it valid of all triangles, whether right-angled, obtuse-angled, or acute-angled; it would always be limited to a part only of this sphere. The schema of the triangle can exist nowhere but in thought. It is a rule of the synthesis of the imagination, in respect of pure figures in space" (A141/B180). It is clear with regard to pure sensible concepts such as triangles that Kant is of the view that there is no figure that could be given that would correspond to what is being spoken of when we construct something in accordance with the rule of them. In this respect pure sensible concepts and empirical concepts surely join hands. Just as "Rover" and "Rex" as Dalmatians and bulldogs respectively are not themselves correspondent with the purity of "dog" so an obtuse triangle and a right-angled one are only partially representative of what is meant by "triangle". Edmund Husserl however objected in one of his earliest writings to the account of pure sensible concepts given here. The implication of Kant's account, elsewhere made explicit, is that mathematical concepts are *constructed*, something that Husserl replies to in the following way: "this surely is the intent of all constructing: to take what is grasped only inauthentically, and indeed is grasped only *via* conceptual determinations, and to present it as an intuition; thus to 'intuitionalize' the concept. But to regard the inscribing of arithmetical symbolism as an act of construction is wholly inadmissible. The sign and what it designates are here totally different kinds of contents, and are only united by association. The sign thus does not render intuitive that which is thought of, but rather only *refers* to it. Moreover, in the case at hand, that of arithmetic, what is designated is almost always something which *cannot* be made intuitable at all."[8]

Here the objection is that mathematical concepts do not involve intuitions because what they describe could never be brought within the province of an intuition. The objection oscillates however between the two different senses of "intuition" in Kant. If by intuition we mean "empirical intuition" then what Kant is claiming in his account of the schema of pure sensible concepts is that we are given a particular triangle or number and that this figure or number has the property of representing the pure figure it stands in for. However if we are thinking about "pure intuition" then Kant is claiming that the figure is a pure property of space and that space itself is what we do have a pure intuition of. Hence at the level of pure intuition the mathematical concepts determine an aspect of that which is the condition of their being given at all. Husserl's objection only works if it is thought that Kant is of the view that figures of pure space can be captured in empirical intuition but that is precisely what he is denying. If however Husserl's objection is that even pure intuition cannot capture the triangle then this would seem to mean that for Husserl the triangle is an idea, not a pure intu-ition and this would give a distinctly Platonic turn to his account.[9] This could only be accepted however if space itself is understood to be a pure idea and this consequence is one few would be willing to embrace.

Hence we can see that the schema of empirical concepts points to the dependence of such concepts on both pure intuitions and pure concepts whilst that of pure sensible concepts determines the possibility of describing pure figures on the fact that there are pure intuitions which are their condition of possibility. What we have also discovered through our account of the schema of pure sensible concepts is that a schema is something distinct from an image as we can clearly give images of triangles to our empirical intuition without this indicating that our empirical intuition thereby has captured in the particular figure presented the schema of the pure sensible concept. I will turn now to the key question of the chapter on schematism, the question concerning the description of the schema of pure concepts.

The problem with the schema of pure concepts concerns the fact that the *homogeneity* that can be said to be involved in the schemas of empir-ical concepts and pure sensible concepts between concept and that which is described by the concept is not applicable in this case. With the empirical concept the roundness that is involved in the notion of a plate is a determination of intuition and this determination of intuition is part of the empirical concept so that this concept is not pure as it contains within it elements of intuition. With the pure sensible concept the reference to the pure intuition is embedded in the concept in question again. So in neither case is the concept a *pure* concept *simpliciter* (as is marked in the latter case by the reference to *sensible* conditions). With pure concepts we have only a determination of thought and hence they seem to be completely different in kind to pure intuitions with the question arising as to how therefore the two can have the combination in experience that must be necessary for empirical concepts to be usable.

The heterogeneity between pure concept and pure intuition hence has to be somehow bridged if the pure concepts are to be applied to intuitive conditions. This is the problem of transcendental judgment and since transcendental judgments are synthetic we would expect some third thing to be at work that brings together the pure concept and the pure intuition. This third thing is what Kant terms the *transcendental schema*. The schema bridges the divide between pure concept and pure intuition in including universality (a condition of pure concepts) and sensibility (the basic condition of intuitions): "an application of the category to appearances becomes possible by means of the transcendental determination of time, which, as the schema of the concepts of the understanding, mediates the subsumption of the appearances under the category" (A139/B178). Time is referred to as the condition of all connection (including that of inner sense in which space is lacking) and hence as a universal element of sensibility and the suggestion would thus be that in temporalizing the pure concepts we will retain their universality whilst sensibilizing them. So to comprehend the doctrine of schematism we need to show how the "transcendental determination of time" takes place.

Kant suggests that the schematism of pure understanding is a product of the imagination. At this point we need to look more carefully again at how Kant describes the imagination. Whilst the fundamental and most basic description of imagination is that it is the ability to represent an object that is not present (B151), this representation does not have to take the form of an image, as is conventionally thought in empiricist descriptions of imagination.[10] We saw with both empirical concepts and pure sensible concepts that an image would not be sufficient to describe the possibility of their possession. Kant now states that in fact the possession of images is dependent on "the universal procedure of imagination" (A140/B180) of describing concepts such that they are capable of being *represented* by images. However: "the schema of a *pure* concept of understanding can never be brought into any image whatsoever" (A142/B181). Thus whilst the concept of the triangle can be represented by an obtuse or right-angled, three-sided figure and the concept of "dog" can be represented by a terrier the pure concept of causality cannot be represented at all. The schema of the pure concept is now given its most general determination: "It is a transcendental product of imagination, a product which concerns the determination of inner sense in general according to conditions of its form (time), in respect of all representations, so far as these representations are to be connected *a priori* in one concept in conformity with the unity of apperception" (A142/B181).

So the transcendental schema would be that which would determine the temporal form of representations *a priori* in conformity with the transcendental unity of apperception. As such it would appear that what is described by it is virtually identical with the transcendental synthesis of imagination and Kant argues that it is at any rate *effected* by this synthesis (A145/B185). Subsequently Kant suggests that the transcendental schemata are "*a priori* determinations of time in accordance with rules" (A145/B184) and that these determinations will effectively give us "the phenomenon, or sensible concept, of an object in agreement with the category" (A146/B186). The determinations of time in accordance with rules are set out in accordance with the table of categories as four-fold relating to "the *time-series*, the *time-content*, the *time-order*, and lastly to the *scope of time*" (A145/B184). Finally the schematism is said to "realise" the categories by restricting them (A146/B186). The realization of the categories is the demonstration of their mode of operation within experience whilst the restriction of them is the determination of them as only giving conditions of cognition through connection with intuition. I wish to turn now from expounding the sense I have uncovered the chapter on schematism to have to some critical treatments of its argument.

The schematism as aporetic

A first problem to discuss with regard to the doctrine of schematism is whether it conceals an *aporia*. A reason for thinking this would be that the schema of pure concepts is not something that can be described. Kant makes the following remark concerning it: "This schematism of our understanding, in its application to appearances and their mere form, is an art concealed in the depths of the human soul, whose real modes of activity nature is hardly likely ever to allow us to discover, and to have open to our gaze" (A141/B180–1). This has led Howard Caygill to make the following judgment: "The principle of judgment then, which is called upon to found the possibility of objective knowledge, possesses contradictory properties and is unthinkable: in other words, the *Critique of Pure Reason* is founded upon an *aporia*."[11] To this argument is added a second according to which the conclusion of the chapter on schematism involves a "slippage" from a discussion of the relationship between concept and intuition to a description of something prior to this, namely the "realization through restriction of the understanding by the sensibility as a whole".[12]

Effectively these two points are interconnected as what is really described by Kant as the art that is hidden from us is the second type of realization and restriction that Caygill has identified. There is no way of bringing the mechanism of this ultimate schematism to light and it is this which prevents us from being able to state that there exists, *pace* Heidegger, a fundamental unification of receptivity and spontaneity in a ground that we could describe. If however we take the point about what is hidden in this way it is less obvious that Caygill has correctly identified an *aporia* at the heart of the doctrine of schematism. The judgments that bring together concepts and intuitions *can* be described (this is the work of the Analytic of Principles). So there is not an aporetic problem with the operation of the schematism of pure concepts although there is an ultimate inability to determine the union of the two stems. This inability once stressed prevents Caygill's account from converging with Heidegger's and is an argument against the latter's reading.[13]

Heidegger and the "schema-image"

If we turn now to Heidegger's account of schematism we should begin by noting that it takes off not from the schema of pure concepts but from that of pure sensible concepts. The latter schema involves the "monogram of pure *a priori* imagination" (A142/B181); a schema that allows for the provision of pure images and it supplies what Heidegger terms a "schema-image". Despite Kant's suggestion that pure concepts of understanding have no such image Heidegger extends this character-ization to them on the ground of the following statement made by Kant in the schematism chapter: "The pure image of all magnitudes (*quantorum*) for outer sense is space; that of all objects of the pure senses in general is time" (A142/B182). On this basis Heidegger argues that the fundamental meaning of schematism is articulated in terms of such a schema-image where it is interpreted as a way of speaking of what he terms "transcendence": "The letting-stand-against of that which is objective and which offers itself, of the being-in-opposition-to, occurs in transcendence due to the fact that ontological knowledge, as schematising intuition, makes the transcendental affinity of the unity of the rule in the image of time discernible a priori and therewith capable of being taken in stride... Hence the interpretation of the indi-vidual, pure schemata as transcendental determinations of time must point out this correspondence forming character."[14]

Heidegger's interpretation hence works by arguing that the ability to have relations at all is articulated first of all through and in the orient-ation towards things that he terms "transcendence", the standing-against that emerges from and in the schema-image. A first problem concerns the quotation from the schematism chapter with which we began the expos-ition of this aspect of Heidegger's interpretation. Whilst Kant in this citation presented space as the pure image of all magnitudes (and time as that of the pure image of all objects), he goes on to distinguish this from an account of the schema of magnitudes indicating that the pure image described is not equivalent to a schema.[15] Whilst the schema-image does describe the manner in which pure sensible concepts and the schema of empirical concepts operate it is not directly applicable to pure concepts of the understanding. What Kant describes rather is a process whereby the pure concept of quantity is schematized as a pure sensible concept or in other words the schematization of the pure concept is what creates the "schema-image" rather than itself being operated by means of it.

Not only is it the case that there is no real fit between Heidegger's description of "schema-image" and Kant's account of the schema of the pure concepts of understanding but furthermore there would be problems for Heidegger's overall philosophical account of Kant where this element of his interpretation is to be accepted. As Martin Weatherston states Heidegger elsewhere argues against the distinction between concepts and principles in favouring of having the categories determined as mere representations of the original unity of the twin stems. "Yet this distinction between the rule of the presentation in pure intuition and the actual intuitive presentation reinstates precisely the distinction between concepts and principles, since this rule is not identical with the application."[16] Put another way, Heidegger is here revealed to import a doctrine of judgment into his account of Kant at the same time as apparently advocating its abolition.

Space and the schematism

A different question but one that connects to the citation about space given above concerns the place of space in the chapter of schematism and a set of questions concerning why it is apparently subordinated to time in Kant's presentation.[17] The reason why this is taken to be a problem concerns the relationship between time and space as given in the Transcendental Aesthetic at A33/B50-1, which I discussed in Chapter 4 as showing the need to represent time spatially.

What this objection turns on then is the question of how his acknowledgement of the above necessity of space being required for outer appearances to be comprehended is reflected in the chapter on schematism? Put another way, surely what Kant is stating in this part of the Aesthetic is that time alone is insufficient to give us properties of objects and that in fact it is necessary to represent time itself spatially in order for it to successfully connect to experiences? The latter part of this question would also threaten to resurrect Heidegger's notion of a "schema-image". Caygill's point concerning the broader schematism of understanding in general by sensibility in general would necessarily incorporate a reference to space in addition to time and this is one implicit reference to space in the chapter on schematism. The schema of pure sensible concepts also clearly involves reference to space and the provision of a description of time as applicable to existential conditions requires, states the passage from the Aesthetic, a figuration of time by space. This is in fact given in the Analogies of Experience. What occurs with them is that the schematization of magnitude is utilized to make time representable. Hence the very notion of the schema of categories of relation cannot in fact avoid reference to space and this is where we do find it operative. Whilst the presence of it in the schematism chapter is only implied if we connect this chapter to the citation given from the Aesthetic then we can see that this is of necessity where space enters the field of the schema of pure concepts, as without it relations would not be conceivable. Returning to the question of the "schema-image" what we can see as operative in a manner akin to what Heidegger describes by this term is the provision of time as a way of figuring relational concepts.

Revisiting synthetic judgments

In opening the second chapter of the transcendental doctrine of judgment Kant addresses the question of how systematically to assemble the principles of pure understanding. The notion of such principles is here first introduced. *A priori* principles are the basic grounds of all judgments. Here, if anywhere, is the real place we would expect to find an *aporia* of judgment such as Caygill professes to discover to be the foundation of the *Critique*. Kant distinguishes here between "objective" proof (effectively meaning proof that can be given via the notion of an object and hence what can be provided *by* the principles) and "subjective" proof. The principles are to be accorded the latter, which means they will be proved "from the subjective sources of the possibility of knowledge of an object in general" (A149/B188). In the case of an objective proof we are dealing not with an object in general but with an object of experience. We also approach the object of experience in terms of *actuality*, not merely *possibility*. With a subjective proof such as we will now be given we have to appeal to what the conditions of our possibly being able to have any cognition of an object in the first place are and this entails that the description of the principles to be given will depend heavily on transcendental psychology.[18]

In the account that follows Kant restricts the *a priori* principles he will attempt to prove stating that the principles of space and time have already been given in the Aesthetic and that mathematical principles, as based on intuition only and not from pure concepts, will not be treated.[19] Prior to explicating the principles themselves however Kant first treats of the highest principle of them, contrasting this principle with that of the highest principle of analytic judgments. The highest principle of analytic judgments is determined as the principle of contradiction, a principle Kant carefully elaborates as having no reference to temporal conditions. In arguing this he corrects the view he had adopted earlier as both in the *New Elucidation* (Ak. 1: 391) and in the *Inaugural Dissertation* he asserted that the principle of contradiction only holds if A and not-A are said to be held simultaneously (Ak. 2: 401 and Ak. 2: 406). Now Kant argues that the synthetic condition of time is not required for the principle of contradiction, as the subject of such a judgment should of itself directly contradict the predicate in such a judgment hence removing the necessity of reference to temporal conditions.[20]

By contrast with the account of analytic judgments, Kant describes that of synthetic judgments as the most important of all questions for transcendental logic (A154/B193). A synthetic judgment evidently involves, as the basic distinction between synthetic and analytic judgments states, the addition of something to the subject that would not be predicated of it merely according to its concept and hence the reverse of a synthetic proposition is never a logical contradiction. If the opposite of a synthetic proposition is never in violation of the rules of general logic then what Kant has to disclose is that the opposite of a synthetic *a priori* principle is not conceivable rather for transcendental reasons. Since synthetic judgments necessarily bring in something that exceeds the given concept of what is being described then it must do so by invoking something that will tie the subject and predicate together according to a different rule and Kant thus invokes, as in the preceding chapter on schematism, a "third thing" and states: "There is only one whole in which all our representations are contained, namely, inner sense and it's a *priori* form, time" (A155/B194). If an analytic judgment indicates that the predicate of the concept is contained within its concept in the sense that the separation of the two would involve a contradiction what a synthetic judgment of the sort that we are attempting to prove possible in transcendental logic would do is connect the subject and the predicate according to a determination of time. This is of course exactly what was stressed in the chapter on schematism were even empirical concepts where shown to depend on this relationship to pure *a priori* intuition (and hence in a sense *all* synthetic judgments, not merely those that are *a priori*, involve this relation although it is of course only the synthetic *a priori* judgments with which transcendental logic is really concerned).

What the argument of the transcendental deduction has demonstrated is that the synthesis of representations is produced by transcendental imagination and that the condition of the unity of this synthesis is the transcendental unity of apperception. Hence the three "subjective" sources of all the principles that we will be subsequently dealing with are here given. "That an object be given (if this expression be taken, not as referring to some merely mediate process, but as signifying immediate present-ation in intuition), means merely that the representation through which the object is thought relates to actual or possible experience" (A156/B195). Even space and time, inasmuch as they describe the deter-mination of anything (and are hence conditions of the comprehension of any objects) have to connect to the conditions of experience. This entails that they have to be related to the synthesis of imagination and its unitary condition, the transcendental unity of apperception. "The *possibility of experience* is, then, what gives objective reality to all our *a priori* modes of knowledge" (A156/B195).

What the synthesis of imagination has to involve is some form of account of the requirements of all possibility of cognition of experience and this basically means a reference to temporality and spatiality that will enable them to become connected to conceptuality. "The highest principle of all synthetic judgments is therefore this: every object stands under the necessary conditions of synthetic unity of the manifold of intuition in a possible experience" (A158/B197). If this is the basic prin-ciple of synthetic judgments then what emerges from it is a depiction of the conditions of synthetic unity as what makes possible the judgments we express in transcendental logic. From these conditions the very notion of an "object" will emerge in fact. As Kant concludes: "the conditions of the *possibility of experience* in general are likewise condi-tions of the *possibility of the objects of experience*" (A158/B197).[21] The nature of the demonstration of this claim is what is set out in the central portion of the *Critique*, the Analytic of Principles, and I will now turn to presenting an interpretation over the next two chapters of the nature of this section of the *Critique* and the central arguments provided there.

6
Synthesis, Intuition and Mathematics

It is possible now, on the basis of the treatment I have provided of the nature of transcendental synthesis as expounded in the only viable deduction argument and extended in the account of schematism, to return to the questions about the nature of intuition that were canvassed in Chapter 1. It will be recalled that there is a major disagreement in the current literature on Kantian intuitions concerning the priority of the two criteria that Kant offers for the notion of an "intuition" with some favouring the view that the primary criteria is that of immediacy, others that of singularity. Provisionally in Chapter 1 we leaned to the view that the singularity criteria may well be the primary one due to the paradox that Caygill pointed to around the notion of "immediacy". A further rationale for favouring the criteria of singularity in the literature generally has been that it is often taken to be the case that it is this criteria that is most important in Kant's treatment of mathematics as a body of synthetic *a priori* truths.[1] The concentration on the philosophy of mathematics as central to the treatment of Kantian intuition has ensured however that the discussion of construction in the Doctrine of Method has been given primacy over the account of the Aesthetic and comparatively little attention has been paid, by contrast, to the treatment of intuition in the first part of the Analytic of Principles. It will be my aim in this chapter to redress this balance. Whilst it will prove important in doing so to present my own account of Kant's philosophy of mathematics I will show that this discussion is intertwined with considerations of a wider sort that are often neglected or minimized in the exclusive concentration on philosophy of mathematics. In order to enable a treatment of intuition in the context of the Analytic of Principles I will retrace how Kant arrives at the view that space and time are pure intuitions. The discussion of this point will be a preliminary to demonstrating how the treatment of the first half of the Analytic of Principles provides us with an account of the nature of empirical intuition. This latter account will be provided in two stages, first through the mereological account of the Axioms of Intuition and secondly through the central discussion of sensation and the *matter* of intuition in the Anticipations of Perception, the latter of which I will argue to be central to an understanding of the synthetic argument of the *Critique*.

Kant's pre-Critical treatments of intuition and mathematics

In both this chapter and the succeeding one I will trace the pre-history of the accounts being provided in the Analytic of Principles and there will be some degree of overlap between these discussions. With regard to the accounts of mathematics it has, in fact, already proved conventional in the literature to refer back to Kant's early discussions though this has tended to mean an almost exclusive focus on the Prize Essay of 1764. This is far from the earliest treatment of mathematics by Kant however and it could be argued that the treatment of force in his very earliest works is already part of a contrast between mathematical and metaphysical procedures that Kant returned to insistently hereafter.[2] Since Kant also during the 1750s was capable of indulging in extended treatments of cosmogony it is clear that his early works raised serious questions concerning the connections between natural science, mathematics and metaphysics running through them in such a way that contemporary conceptions of which works were "purely philosophical" imposes a grid upon them that the author of these works would surely not have recognized.[3] In order to focus specifically upon the rationale for thinking of space and time eventually as being pure intuitions I will treat here only some aspects of a few of these very rich works.[4]

Given these constraints a natural place to start looking at Kant's treatment of space and time in connection with mathematics and the notion of intuition is the *Physical Monadology* (1756). The explicit aim of this work is to provide a reconciliation of the geometrical argument that space is infinitely divisible with the Leibnizian argument for the existence of monads or ultimate simples that do not have parts as parts are thought of as pluralizing.[5] Since the discussion turns on the consequences of infinite divisibility, it emerges partly from the Newtonian interpretation of the infinitesimal calculus which was based on a geometrical, not an algebraic interpretation.[6] This is manifest in Kant's opening statement of his problem which is cast as a mereological difficulty about the composition of bodies as composed of parts: "it is certainly of no little importance that it be clearly established of which parts, and in what way they are combined together, and whether they fill space merely by the co-presence of their primitive parts or by the reciprocal contact of forces" (Ak. 1: 475). Here there are three basic questions about the nature of bodies, namely of what parts they are constituted, how the composition of the parts takes place and whether the filling of space by bodies is a result only of the constitution of primitive parts or whether it requires some additional reference to forces. The third question points in the direction of the Leibnizian correction of the Cartesian conception of bodies as composed primarily of extension and geometrical qualities. Given the understanding of the geometrical qualities in a manner that is not described in algebraic terms we get an immediate question about the parts of bodies in terms of spatial qualities, not primary elements only.

If the parts of bodies are taken however to be spatial and yet space is infinitely divisible then there is no place for the Leibnizian conception of force, a factor pointing to a Cartesian interpretation of Newtonian physics.[7] In place of the notion of a force being required to relate the bodies to each other the Newtonian position points instead to the necessity to postulate space itself as absolute and thus the dependence of bodies on empty space emerges, a dependence that ensures that the filling of space would be a product of the way in which the inertia of bodies permits the exertion of action at a distance. Kant hints at a solution to the difficulty of combining the two conceptions at the close of the introduction to the work when he introduces what will be revealed to be primitive notions, the forces of attraction and repulsion (Ak. 1: 476).

The first part of the *Physical Monadology* opens with a brief argument for thinking that there must be monads. The argument has three parts. First, Kant maintains that parts of bodies are related to each other through composition. Secondly, he argues that the characteristic of all relations is that they are contingent. Thirdly, what any relation brings together are elements that must be in themselves free from plurality. Hence this is a very short argument for the existence of monads. This argument rests upon the basic distinction between substance and accidents and takes all relations of any substance to be accidents of the substance without which it would still subsist. Since space is then taken to be no more than a relation its existence is purely accidental and has no necessary connection to the elementary parts of anything so that these parts must be ultimately self-subsistent.[8]

Kant follows this argument with a conventional Euclidean demonstration of the infinite divisibility of spatial parts. The point of this demonstration is to show that space cannot be composed of primitive simple elements.[9] Since we have reached the point of asserting both the need for substances to be conceived as independent of space (as space is a mere set of relations) and that space is infinitely divisible it will follow that the divisibility of space does not produce a need to conceive of substantial wholes as divisible. This is frankly stated in the Theorem that Kant gives as Proposition IV of the *Physical Monadology* (Ak. 1: 479). Since bodies are composed of monads and yet apparently fill space in terms of their parts being composed within space the combination that they have is one that must only be that of an *aggregate* or what Kant now terms "a certain plurality or quantity in an external relation" (Ak. 1: 480). The filling of space by the monads cannot hence be a mere effect of their co-presence as this would not make the distinct monads different from each other any more than the ability to draw a line between parts of a monad would result in the monad being divided in itself. So the manner in which the filling of space takes place must rather be dynamical than mathematical.[10]

To further substantiate this claim Kant provides a subsequent demonstration of geometrical type to the effect that the division of space when applied to the monads merely gives us a division of "extensive quantity" (Ak. 1: 481). Since the internal quality of the monad is not spatial it provides us with a manner of thinking dynamically as all qualities of what is mathematical have their inherence finally within it (Ak. 1: 481). The extension of bodies is subsequently explained according to the clue vouchsafed in the introduction to this treatise with the notion of impenetrability exhibited as repulsive force to which an attractive force is co-ordinated. The key point about the relation between these forces, however, which prevents the understanding of them separately from quantitative conceptions is that it is mapped in terms of degree of effect, a mapping which shows the relation between the forces to be ultimately understood, separately from relation to space, as an exhibition of quantitative qualities (Ak. 1: 484).[11] The consequences of such a picture of the monads in terms of the understanding of the nature of substance and its connection to causality goes beyond the brief of this chapter. What we can see from this early account of the relationship between mathematics and metaphysics however is that the reconciliation between them being proposed turns on understanding that there are two kinds of part/whole relation being described, one that points to infinite divisibility of measurable quantities of space on the one hand

and one which suggests a combination of quantity with quality on the other in order to sketch a correlation of measurable forces which is not mathematical but dynamical.

In the *Physical Monadology* the treatment of mathematics was entirely set out as an account of geometry with the emphasis however on a physical interpretation of it as given in Newtonian physics. The nature of such mathematical demonstration was described as one of accidental combination giving an account of mathematics as a description of aggregates and hence extensive quantities. These aspects of the account of mathematics are tied to the description of space as being a network of relations as distinct from an account of substantial compounds. Leaving aside the nature of the metaphysics of substance in this treatise the account of space is set out entirely through the type of division that can be established in the mapping of space by geometrical combination and it is this that leads to the connection between space and mathematics in this work. Kant does not provide a parallel treatment of time despite the implications of his view of motion.

In the beginning of the 1760s Kant returns to the question of the relationship between mathematics and metaphysics in two parallel works, the essay on *Negative Magnitudes* and the Prize Essay.[12] The question in *Negative Magnitudes* is formally narrower than in the Prize Essay as here Kant only wishes to demonstrate that a concept that has proved useful in mathematics is also necessary in philosophy whilst the Prize Essay has the much larger task of demarcating the distinctive principles of metaphysics, a task partially accomplished by contrasting these principles with mathematical ones. It is worth noting however that the essay on *Negative Magnitudes* opens with a statement concerning the difference between mathematics and metaphysics arguing against the imitation of mathematical methods in philosophy but conjoining this with a plea that philosophers "acquire reliably established data...with a view to using them as the foundation" of its reflections (Ak. 2: 168). The nature of what has to be taken to be reliably established is connected however to precisely the demonstrations that were utilized in the *Physical Monadology* as Kant here refers again to the infinitesimal calculus and its use in the account of gravity (Ak. 2: 168). Proceeding to the introduction of the conception of negative magnitudes in physical terms Kant describes a classic case of such a magnitude as no other than the notion of repulsion, the notion by which he now explicates the Newtonian conception of "rest".

The conception of negative magnitudes on a physical interpretation leads Kant to begin this piece with an account of different ways of thinking opposition with "real opposition" being distinguished from merely "logical".[13] The key difference here is that whereas logical opposition of one predicate to another produces logical contradiction, a contradiction that ensures nothing is left for thought, real opposition of forces produces something, the something termed "rest" or repulsion. In explicating this conception of real opposition Kant reaches back to the source of the possibility of conceiving of negative magnitudes in physics, which is the description of negative quantities in mathematics. The exposition of the possibility of such quantities being mathematically presented points to a key comprehension of mathematical method which we will see to have important consequences:

> Since subtraction is a cancelling which occurs when opposed magnitudes are taken together, it is evident that the '−' cannot really be a sign of subtraction, as is commonly supposed; it is only the combination of '+' and '−' together which signifies subtraction. Hence the proposition '−4 −5 = −9' is not a subtraction at all, but a genuine increase and addition of magnitudes of the same kind. On the other hand, the proposition '+9 −5 = 4' does signify a subtraction, for the signs of opposition indicate that the one cancels as much in the other as is equal to itself. (Ak. 2: 173)

This demonstration is then extended in obvious fashion to the treatment of the sign "+" to indicate that it is only the presentation of the signs as different from each other that gives subtraction, if the signs are equivalent there is always addition, with the type of magnitude being here strictly irrelevant. This implicitly algebraic understanding of arithmetic demonstrates that the outcome of a sum of two magnitudes is dependent upon the assumption of equivalences between them. This requires a reciprocal relation between the magnitudes in question to be implicitly or explicitly stated. On this conception it follows that no magnitude is negative in itself, its negative comprehension is rather a function of its being placed in a relation of opposition to a different magnitude which has to be "added in thought" (Ak. 2: 174). Whilst Kant does not here use the expression it is apparent that he has uncovered the basis of a *synthetic* comprehension of mathematics and that this comprehension has no necessary connection to any particular way in which quantities are represented (whether by means of strokes, figures, points, etc.). The relation of opposition that is required for genuine combination of quantities together in a manner that permits their representation in a sum is one that has to be *brought to* the combination: it is not contained in the figures themselves but is the product of an arbitrary presentation of their relation, just as was implied in the *Physical Monadology*. That this account is centrally connected to that of the earlier piece is confirmed when Kant states that the discussion of negative quantities "only ever signifies the relation of certain things to each other" and thus that it does not imply the existence of negative things (Ak. 2: 174–5). But what it does permit, and this is the secret of its utility in physical description, is an understanding of real opposition as real opposition states the relation of things to each other such that the effect of one upon the other is to produce a cancellation of something in either or both.[14]

On the basis of this understanding we can map an algebraic account of physical things as involved in addition and diminution through contact of opposites that are measured by connection of inverse symbolizations. So for purposes of calculation "rest" has to be proposed as being repulsion or impenetrability as in this way we capture the means by which a real opposition is at work.[15] The exploration of examples that follows in the work are merely extrapolations from these central principles.

The Prize Essay opens by laying bare the account of mathematics that we have found to underlie both the *Physical Monadology* and *Negative Magnitudes* and opens with a description of a contrast between mathematical and philosophical procedures that we will need to compare with later Critical treatments. The Essay opens with a frank declaration:

> There are two ways in which one can arrive at a general concept: either by the *arbitrary combination* of concepts, or by *separating out* that cognition which has been rendered distinct by means of analysis. Mathematics only ever draws up its definitions in the first way. (Ak. 2: 276)

Mathematical concepts are here, consistently with the description of *aggregates* in the *Physical Monadology*, understood to involve arbitrary combination, a combination that permits, according to the rules expounded in *Negative Magnitudes*, the expression of real opposition of quantities. To the account set out is added the point that enables Kant to arrive at the description of this procedure as a *construction* which is that the mathematical demonstration of a term, such as that which occurs when shapes are defined in geometrical demonstrations, is one that emerges from the demonstration itself and is not given prior to it. Since mathematics thus constitutes its "objects" the objects with which it deals are produced in the manner of being symbolized, just as a quantity is in itself neither positive or negative but the presentation of it in a sum makes it so. Philosophical method is contrasted with this as the concepts dealt with in philosophy are not taken by Kant to be produced by it but rather to pre-exist its treatment and the treatment provided by philosophy thus consists in a clarification of this pre-given term through examination of what enables it to be utilized.

The account of philosophy as engaged in analysis of concepts is one that gives Kant some trouble as when he addresses the question how terms such as "monad" arise in philosophy. The point made in reply to this question is that the description of such things as monads is not accomplished by means of definitions and thus Kant states that Leibniz did not define this term but instead "invented it" (Ak. 2: 277) where this appears to mean something different from mathematical definition. The difference would be that the mathematical definition emerges from a procedure in which the definition demonstrates the "object" it describes through its method whereas the "invention" of such notions as a monad gives not an arbitrary combination that describes an "object" but rather accomplishes the provision of an arbitrary concept instead that has to be fitted into an analytic exposition of other terms that are pre-given as being something taken to be required for the latter's explanation.

The mathematician merely combines and compares magnitudes and in the process "constructs" space.[16] Kant moves on from this point to discussion of arithmetic, both in terms of indeterminate magnitudes (which must mean algebra) and with regard to numbers. In accord with the point made about the nature of magnitudes in *Negative Magnitudes* the key point is that the combination that is brought about in arithmetic does not concern things but rather "signs" or, as we might term it, a functional system of enumerable connections. Rules of combination of these signs can be set out in clear and systematic forms permitting addition, subtraction and substitution until we reach the point, even with numbers, that is recognizably a situation in which all admit that "the things signified are completely forgotten in the process" (Ak. 2: 278). Having set out this consideration of arithmetic Kant contrasts it with the situation in geometry in which the presentation *in concreto* of a particular set of lines is presented according to general rules and that these rules hold for all combinations of the same sort.[17]

It is after the accounts of both arithmetic and geometry have been given that Kant returns to the contrast between philosophy and arithmetic. Philosophy requires the use of *words*, not *figures* and thus does not permit the expression of arbitrary presentation of quantities. There is a significant difference canvassed between the symbols we term "words" in contrast to those set out in the forms of mathematical demonstration by reference to either specific figures or arbitrary signs. The difference is mereological, which is that words "can neither show in their composition the constituent concepts of which the whole idea, indicated by the word, consists; nor are they capable of indicating in their combinations the relations of the philosophical thoughts to each other" (Ak. 2: 278). The "word" is not thus an arbitrary symbol in the sense in which the letters or numerals of arithmetic are and nor is it a representation of a universal procedure in a particular instance as we can find in geometrical demonstration. The arbitrary symbols of arithmetic have a mereology that demonstrates the comprehension of the parts through the functional rule systems of the whole whilst the geometrical constructions have combinations that demonstrate the right relations of each part to every other. When dealing, as one is in philosophy, with words, there is no similar use of wholes as words lack the holistic properties of the symbols utilized in construction. Hence philosophy cannot engage in construction, unlike mathematics.

If geometry deals with the universal in a concrete form through its demonstrations, philosophy by contrast has to deal with *abstractions* and what this means is that a word is a type of universal sign. This naturally points to Kant's comprehension of the logic of thought by contrast to what we can here primitively see to be an understanding of the singular nature of mathematical constructions. Hence it would seem that in the Prize Essay Kant arrives at a criteria for what is being dealt with in mathematics that is based not on immediacy but on singularity.[18] It is the contrast between two kinds of certainty that Kant here has in mind however, rather than an explicit contrast between intuition and concept, as the former term is not yet in use in Kant's description. The difference in certainty is illustrated by the manner in which the geometer can show that space is infinitely divisible, using a demonstration of the same type as was described in the *Physical Monadology*. In contrasting this demonstration with the metaphysical conviction that there are simple substances Kant's point is here different from in the *Physical Monadology* as now he does not wish himself to bring these demonstrations into alignment but rather to point out the nature of the different procedures at issue in working towards the apparently disparate conclusions.

The nature of the difference in procedure is further accented when Kant states that effectively mathematics does not deal with concepts at all but merely with arbitrary combinations, which is another way of stating that it produces its "objects" in the process of conducting its demonstrations. The case in philosophy is different as not merely does philosophy of its nature depend upon concepts but it must have a number of primitive concepts at its base that it cannot possibly treat to analysis. There are stated to be some fundamental propositions presupposed in mathematics and indemonstrable within it although the examples here given are taken from Euclidean geometry and Kant makes no similar assertions about arithmetic here (Ak. 2: 281) but given the earlier statements about the nature of arbitrary combination within arithmetic it is possible he thought this point scarcely worth labouring. The basic point about geometry in contrast to philosophy is that if the latter begins with statements concerning, for example, space, it cannot treat the primary propositions it may wish to enunciate about space as capable of proof but must rather view them as indemonstrable fundamental judgments (Ak. 2: 282). This indicates that certain judgments are in a sense primitive for philosophy and that attempting, in Cartesian fashion, to begin *ab initio* must be impossible.

At this point Kant demonstrates in a simple statement what has become by this time a clear element of his conception of mathematics when he states that in his view its "object" is nothing other than magnitude (Ak. 2: 282) and he aligns algebra with the general theory of magnitude in accord with the treatment set out in *Negative Magnitudes*. This illustrates the clear sense of *pure* mathematics that is being formed at this stage of Kant's reflection and that will remain hereafter. Kant thinks of *pure* mathematics as deserving of its title simply by being unconcerned with what its magnitude apparently represents unlike applied mathematics for which the particular being counted is constantly held in mind.

Arithmetical concepts can contain reference to enormous quantities with great ease. Philosophy has a task that is quite different and lacks the ability to present its fundamental notions with the simplicity that arises from arbitrary combination. This is why the attainment of cognition in philosophy is so difficult, however easy some find it to memorize what is stated in certain works that present themselves as containing philosophical insights. This points to the moral of the contrast between mathematics and philosophy that Kant draws in the Prize Essay to the effect that if definition is an appropriate starting-point in mathematics it is not in philosophy, rather the nature of fundamental indemonstrable judgments should first be laid out and on the basis of these we should begin our inquiry from them and in accordance with what they point to. This requires that certain types of concepts be found and shown to have the completeness of these primitives and the demonstration be founded upon them. An example of such a fundamental judgment remains at this stage for Kant that bodies have parts that would continue to exist even if their composition into the integral whole which they presently belong to were dissolved. Since these parts of bodies are given within space and yet not divisible by means of this the same solution to the conflict between the demonstrations of geometry and metaphysics is apparently being offered as was given in the *Physical Monadology*. Kant refines the solution to this extent which is that he now thinks of the simples of substances as being "in" space even though they do not "occupy" space but once again points to impenetrability as central and now draws the anti-Cartesian conclusion that if bodies are extended this is not due to their occupation of space (Ak. 2: 287).

The clarity of the impression produced by attention to singular demonstrations is always greater than emerges from consideration of abstract representations according to Kant so that philosophy has a naturally more difficult task in impressing its conclusions on the mind than mathematics. This description of the methods of philosophy and mathematics is hence in accord with the treatment of the nature of mathematical demonstration given in the *Negative Magnitudes* yet also still shows adherence to the arguments presented in the *Physical Monadology*.

Four years after the Prize Essay was formally awarded recognition by the Royal Academy Kant turned again to questions concerning space in the short but crucial piece on regions (or, as the contemporary translator has it, "directions") of space. The intervening years produced a shift in outlook that is important for arriving at the critical view of space. Whereas the earlier pieces passed in review involve acceptance that the contrast between mathematics and metaphysics should involve recognition of the claims of the latter to acceptance of simple monadic substances and attempt only to describe a conception of space that permits monads a presence within it, the essay of 1768 turns instead to an account of the parts of space that will create problems for any such claimed reconciliation. What Kant here is concerned with is an analysis of how the parts of space are related to each other but he maps this against a view of the notion that there is an "absolute space" (Ak. 2: 377), the Newtonian position against which the earlier pieces had protested. The rationale for this alteration is first presented in this work in terms of the necessity for treating space itself as a unity but Kant is clear that the question that concerns him here is whether the demonstrations of geometry are sufficient to convince one that space has absolute reality.

In keeping with this concentration on geometry Kant here presents the three dimensions of space in terms of planes and mentions the connection of these planes to our bodies. In treating our bodies in this way Kant moves away from the abstract treatment of body in general that marked the earlier works towards the condition of cognition that is at work for us in our occupation of space. Our bodies are presented here not only in terms of occupation of heights but also as being split into sides that we can term "right and left" and "front and back". A number of observations relative to this fundamental description are enumerated and then Kant moves to the importance we all attach to the difference between right and left, pointing to the general advantage of the right side in terms of movement and capacity to enable us to effect purposes whilst by comparison the left side reveals our sensitivity to being affected (so that right and left are almost mapped on to the distinction between the types of cognition that emerges for Kant after establishing the transcendental distinction). This leads to the key point in the essay, the treatment of incongruent counterparts, which is illustrated precisely by reference to the difference between right and left hands. The nature of the difference is then expressed philosophically as a consequence of an argument that has been developed in the first instance from a physical application of geometrical properties:

> It is apparent from the ordinary example of the two hands that the shape of the one body may be perfectly similar to the shape of the other, and the magnitudes of their extensions may be exactly equal, and yet there remain an inner difference between the two, this difference consisting in the fact, namely, that the surface which encloses the one cannot possibly enclose the other. Since the surface which limits the physical space of the one body cannot serve as a boundary to limit the other, no matter how that surface be twisted and turned, it follows that the difference must be one which rests upon an inner ground. (Ak. 2: 382)

Here we see how the difference between the treatment of this essay and that of the earlier ones is part of an underlying continuity of approach. Just as in the earlier pieces Kant takes the differences between parts of the bodies, as given in space, to reside in a property that cannot itself have arisen merely from space itself but must be internal to it and yet, that its internal properties must be responsible for something fundamental to its spatial qualities. The difference is that whereas previously the argument was conducted at a high level of generality in order to distinguish two forms of mereological relation now Kant sets out instead a highly specific contrast to point to a property of bodies that we can all see to be basic to them and which can even be described in straightforward geometrical notions such as "boundary", "surface" and "limit". The relation of the parts of the discrete hands to each other appears to indicate that they are clear counterparts but the nature of the difference between a left and a right side is so evident that these counterparts are also *incongruent*. So the determinations of space are not a consequence of the determination of parts of matter. Kant therefore concludes that there is an original and absolute space that cannot be derived from the matter of sensation but rather provides the properties of the latter. In stating this he neglects however to consider the relation of such space to the internal difference within the parts of the bodies and thus moves to a smooth conclusion in favour of the absolute reality of space which the argument of the piece is far from having clearly grounded. With this piece we reach however a turning point in Kant's early treatment of space and mathematics. Whereas initially Kant approaches the question of the treatment of space as something which requires reconciliation of the demonstration of the infinite qualities of space as set out in geometry with the arguments for simple substances provided by metaphysicians, the turn is taken in two stages away from this. First, in the essays of 1762–4 Kant describes the methodology of mathematics in detail and separates it from metaphysics more clearly than initially with the result that the procedure of mathematics is revealed to involve a different mereology than can occur within cognition by means of language as is required for philosophy. Secondly, the 1768 essay demonstrates that there are properties of space that cannot be deduced from matter and seem to be internal to bodies. This latter demonstration could have pointed Kant back to the Leibnizian notion that the nature of the body is not described by the spatial conception and the intimation of this possibility still links this essay with the earlier ones but Kant's understanding of the argument from incongruent counterparts is rather towards showing the dependence of matter on space, a dependence interpreted here as requiring the adoption of the Newtonian position that space is an independent and absolute reality.

The Inaugural Dissertation on intuition and mathematics

It has traditionally been conventional to treat the argument of the Inaugural Dissertation separately from Kant's "pre-Critical" works due to the general acceptance of the view that it is, at least in broad outline, a work that presents substantially the same position as the *Critique*. This has particularly been held to be the case due to the evident overlap of a central part of its discussion with the account of space and time in the Transcendental Aesthetic. This general view has, however, in recent years, been subjected to some challenge, precisely on the ground that the treatment of space and time in the Dissertation has been alleged to be importantly different from that in the Aesthetic.[19] The difference, it is alleged, concerns precisely the criteria for intuition advanced in the Dissertation being different from that in the Aesthetic and the argument of the earlier work incorporating a flaw that is at least partially removed from the Aesthetic. I will in due course examine the arguments to this effect. It is also worth pointing out however that the treatments of space and time in the Dissertation have a number of distinctive qualities. Unlike in the Aesthetic, Kant treats time ahead of space in the Dissertation and provides the first extended treatment of time prior to the *Critique* here. The arguments for treating space and time as *a priori* intuitions are not presented with the same degree of parallel as often been noted to hold in the *Critique*, the number of arguments for time being greater than those for space. The first two parts of the Dissertation also have no parallel in the Aesthetic as here Kant discusses anew the contrast between mathematics and philosophy and considerably enriches the contrast above that provided in the Prize Essay. For all these reasons it is worth providing the treatment of space and time in the Dissertation to an extended consideration, one that will necessarily culminate in a discussion of the nature of the differences between its account and that provided in the *Critique*, both in the Aesthetic and in the Analytic of Principles treatment of intuition.

The Dissertation announces in its title that it will be an inquiry into the relationship between the forms and the principles of the sensible and the intelligible worlds and in accordance with this concentration Kant opens it with a treatment of what is involved in the concept of a world in general such that we will be able to distinguish between sensible and intelligible conceptions of one. In describing it we find an immediate allusion to the methodological distinction that we encountered in the Prize Essay as a description of the difference between philosophy and mathematics. The opening sentence refer us yet again to the central difficulty of thinking the nature of substantial compounds:

> In the case of a substantial compound, just as analysis does not come to an end until a part is reached which is not a whole, that is to say a SIMPLE, so likewise synthesis does not come to an end until we reach a whole which is not a part, that is say a WORLD. (Ak. 2: 387)

We note again the concentration on treatment of compounds in terms of their mereological properties and the different types of mereological treatment are here correlated with analytic and synthetic methods. Since the Prize Essay argued for a conception of philosophy as analysis by contrast to the synthetic or arbitrary combination at work in arithmetic it would appear that something akin to the latter is at work in the formation of the concept of a world whereas something like the former describes to us the properties of simples. Since the treatment of simples has been consistently correlated with Leibnizian analysis it would appear yet again that this latter is being thought to provide us with a model for a type of part that is not assimilable to the whole that may depend upon it. The suspicion that the contrast provided in the Prize Essay is still guiding the treatment here is furthered by noting that Kant goes on to speak of the account of the whole that emerges from a notion of the parts as either supplied by abstract concepts or by reference to the representation of concrete properties although this latter is now explicitly characterized as requiring "intuition".

The conditions of presentation of the concrete properties are now indicated to require a reference to time as that which enables the "successive addition of part to part" and this addition to be what is meant by synthesis. Kant now connects the notion of synthesis for the first time to progressive connection in formation of a composition whilst determining analysis by contrast as requiring regressive uncovering of the conditions of something being given. A footnote added here further explicates two senses of "synthesis" stating it can be either a movement from ground to grounded (which, he states, would be a qualitative movement) or in connection with things that are co-ordinate with each other. In this latter case we have a quantitative connection that progresses "from a given part, through parts complementary to it, to the whole" (Ak. 2: 388n). Analysis is stated to have the same two senses, proceeding merely in the opposite direction, that is, regressively, but in quantitative terms revealing the composition of wholes. Kant further adds that it is only the quantitative senses of "synthesis" and "analysis" that interest him. To reach the notions of simple or whole requires however that the respective syntheses and analyses can be completed and this requires time, a condition not previously mentioned in Kant's earlier discussions. Hence whilst we have seen him to be continuously interested in space and to have thought consistently about the relationship between mathematics and philosophy as a relationship between different thoughts of divisibility, thoughts that need to be connected to the comprehension of space, it is the condition of such thoughts that brings in time. So, conversely to what we discovered in the account of the schematism and the Transcendental Deduction, where the condition for apprehension of time was shown to be spatial, here we are given a reason to think that the condition for presentation of spatial conditions is temporal. Furthermore, this concentration on temporality as a condition for conceiving spatiality, demonstrates that Kant's concern with time emerges from an inquiry into space.

Having revealed temporality to be the condition for conceiving both the simple and the general concept of world Kant concludes that both these notions, in requiring unlimited movement of composition or decomposition, cannot be formed so that the complete analyses and syntheses they require are impossible. But just as Kant in the *Physical Monadology* did not derive from a demonstration of the infinite divisibility of space the expected conclusion that monads have to be rejected so here he does not take this notion of impossibility of representation of the notions of simplicity and worldhood the conclusion that there are no such "objects" as "simples" or "worlds", a conclusion that would, indeed, at least with regard to "worlds" be somewhat difficult to sustain. Rather he derives the consequence, important for his subsequent conception of Ideas in the *Critique*, that there are some thoughts that lack intuitional correlates and hence have what he here terms "*subjective* resistance" (Ak. 2: 389). This leads him to deny that the demonstration of such subjective resistance supports one in rejecting the conceptions in question simply because of their failing to meet conditions of intuition. If it is however the case that concepts that lack intuitional correlates, such as is the case with the notion of the "world" do still have some sense, this fact of their sense would help to explain the basis of what Kant will in the *Critique* describe as the mathematical antinomies.

In the Dissertation Kant goes on to describe the conditions under which the concept of "world" is given as this is required for us to give the concept philosophical and not merely mathematical credence as if we took the combination that produces this conception to be a purely arbitrary one, as might result from our understanding of its lack of intuitional correlate we might think it could be produced by some form of "arbitrary" combination akin to that given in algebra. Arguing for the place of the notion of "world" in philosophy requires demonstrating what conditions are given for thinking the combination that will produce it and this is what Kant goes on to do describing three elements of its notion, the third of which is effectively the combination of the first two, just as Kant will go on to argue is as required for the categories in the Metaphysical Deduction (B110).

The three elements of the concept of world are then expounded as being matter, form and entirety. Considered philosophically, or as Kant puts it "transcendentally", the *parts* of the world are what we are naming in the thought of matter although as philosophers what we mean by such parts are substances. The notion of the parts of world-hood as substances is essential as any other notion of parthood would describe only accidental predicates such as for example we can take successive states to be.[20] If the matter of the world is understood substantially what the form of the world will describe will be how these essential parts are co-ordinated with each other though in describing such co-ordination Kant is clearly not thinking about the nature of causality as this would require introduction of a notion of dependence and that would entail that some of the parts could not be taken to be substances in the strict sense here being used. Rather if the parts of world are essential to it then they must be complements of the whole of which they are part or related in a pattern of mutual determination. For this pattern of mutual determination to be described however requires that the whole that is composed from these essential parts be given in the principle of "possible influences" of the substances (Ak. 2: 390) where this entails a description of the basis in which the actual connections we might assume to be taking place between these parts is given a formulation in terms of what enables these connections to be given. Thus if the analysis of the "matter" of the world points us to one sense of its quantity, the description of "form" by contrast leads us to describe the principle of the "world" as one of immutability (Ak. 2: 390). As Kant puts this: "in any world there is a certain constant and invariable form, which, as the perennial principle of each contingent and transitory form belonging to the state of that world, must be regarded as belonging to its nature" (Ak. 2: 391). The combination of these two products of analysis of the concept of "world" together produces "entirety" or "totality" but since this is a conception of the combination of all parts together after the pattern of the principle of immutable form it would have to describe a condition that would exceed, as already stated, any intuitive correlate and thus be produced only by an intellectual synthesis. The notion of the unity of world is what gives the notion of world that we have taken to be basic in our description of matter and form however and hence in a sense Kant has here moved in a circle from the description of the conditions of thought of world back to the combination of the elements thus provided according to some further non-intuitive condition, the nature and possibility of which he appears not to have described but merely stated as something we can, in some sense, *think* as possible. Kant cannot be said to have shown in the first part of the Dissertation that the concept of "world" is a philosophical as opposed to a mathematical notion. The alternative way of viewing the result of this part of the Dissertation would be to state that since "world" is a description like "experience" itself that has to apply to all conditions in which things are given that it cannot be demonstrated to *exist* as existence conditions cannot emerge from concepts so, in this sense, philosophy cannot demonstrate existence in the way in which mathematics can construct its "objects". This second response to the argument of the section would point in the direction of Kant requiring further demonstration of the manner in which the "world" is given to us being somewhat different to the Cartesian notion of "proof" by means of concepts. This would point ultimately in the direction of the Refutation of Idealism.

Kant turns next to the distinction between sensitive and intelligible things, a distinction described, as was the concept of "world" in the opening section, in the most general terms and aligns sensibility with receptivity as the most general determination of it. Since sensibility is understood this way it describes a capacity for modification and hence belongs, in its particular determinations, under the category of accidents. The distinction of matter and form that was applied to the conception of world in the first section is repeated here and the matter of sense unsurprisingly identified as sensation. The *form* of sense refers to a certain law that governs the capacity to receive sensory impressions by means of which the cognitive power of the one receiving the impressions co-ordinates the sensory elements together. The discussion of understanding, by contrast, relates back to the distinction first clearly outlined in *Negative Magnitudes* between the real and logical use of concepts with the former taken to refer here to how concepts are given whilst the logical use is the means of subordinating these given concepts under rules of genera. The logical use thus appears here to have central importance as enabling the concepts to relate to each other in an ordered fashion and thus to have an appearance of being the correlate of the *form* of sense (whilst the "real use" here appears to mean that the concepts have a grasp of some *matter*). The logical use enables the concepts to be *compared* and this comparison is important for what appears to cognition to be given to us as a possible *experience* (Ak. 2: 394). The "real use" of concepts here correspondingly appears less clearly defined than was the case in *Negative Magnitudes* as now the "real use" refers to certain "pure ideas" and these to be potentially classifiable in terms of either what the *Critique* terms "forms of judgments" or categories or ideas of reason.

Whilst the contrast opens in a manner that ensures that the treatment of sensitive cognition is elaborated in a way that is more compelling than the corresponding treatment of intelligible concepts it is plausible to contend that Kant intends this. The reason for thinking this is that Kant goes on to display reasons for mistrusting the standard rationalist view that states that the difference between sensible and intelligible conceptions can be summarized in terms of the latter being clearer and more distinct than the former. The evidence of geometry is once again here referred to suggesting that sensible conceptions are capable of being very distinct whilst the evidence from metaphysics suggests that intelligible conceptions can be very confused. Here Kant reiterates the point made in the Prize Essay that metaphysics has yet to reach the stage of having attained a clear method of procedure. The Dissertation is in fact justified as a propaedeutic to the undertaking of metaphysics, just as the *Critique* will subsequently be (Bxxii). The fundamental concepts of metaphysics are then explicated as arising from the attention of the mind to itself.[21]

Kant then describes the difference between sensible and intelligible concepts in terms of the former being bound to the principle of form that enables them to be both singular and immediate. Hence here Kant views these criteria of intuition as derivative from the basic sense of the form that it is tied to, not as having a particular priority of one over the other. The intelligible is defined negatively as that which is not based on the given intuition. But the form of the intuition is here tied directly to the types of intuition that we have, namely temporal and spatial. The concepts that are described as emergent from the pure intuitions of space and time are accounted for as the basis of a connection between them. Such concepts are effectively those of *number* or, as we might more generally put it, of enumeration. This points to the fact that the provision of cognition from intuition is precisely comprehended as given through this combination in arithmetic.

Thus, pure mathematics, which explains the form of all our sensitive cognition, is the organon of each and every intuitive and distinct cognition. And since its objects themselves are not only the formal principles of every intuition, but are *originary intuitions*, it provides us with a cognition which is in the highest degree true, and at the same time, it provides us with a paradigm of the highest kind of evidence in other cases. (Ak. 2: 398)

The suggestion that the form of all sensitive cognition is accounted for by reference to the way in which enumeration works in the most general terms indicates a dependence of sensibility upon such enumerative operations so that the formality of the systems that can be captured in such enquiries as mathematicians pursue would be a description of the nature of the form of the sensible world for us. This remarkable claim is one that we might take it that this declaration here has not yet established.

Section 3 of the Dissertation turns to description of the nature of the form of the sensible in more detail. It is evident that the form of the sensible, as a description of modifications, presents us with a set of accidental determinations and this is what Kant is meaning in terming them *subjective*. But in arguing for the view that there are clear *principles* to such subjective organization Kant describes the outlines here of an enquiry that is cardinal to the whole critical philosophy and whose innovative character can be mapped on to the ancient division of essence and accident by saying that the revolution being proposed in metaphysics is one that moves it from being an essential enquiry into substance to *an essential enquiry into accidents*.[22] The accidents that are to be revealed as formally central for experience are space and time.

The third section of the Dissertation is the central part in which the passages that are correlated to the Transcendental Aesthetic of the *Critique* are set out. I now want to look at these in terms of working through the account provided in them prior to going on later to setting out a serious comparison between this discussion and that given in the Transcendental Aesthetic. The discussion of time begins by stating that our conception of time is not one we derive from the senses as empiricist positions might lead us to think as this conception is one that is presupposed in all use of the senses. The point in favour of this simply asserts that notions of succession and simultaneity cannot lead us to the concept of time as they presuppose it.[23] It is only after stating this first argument for thinking time to be an *a priori* concept that Kant turns to providing reasons for thinking it to be an intuition but noticeably although the second argument states reasons for taking it be singular it is only the third argument that directly argues that the consequence of singularity is that time is an intuition. The second argument states that time is a singular and not a general representation due to the condition of infinite representation of time or in other words that all parts of time are thought to be connected together as parts of the whole and can only be given *through* this whole. On this ground Kant subsequently reaches, in the third argument, the consequence that this infinite nature of the given representation leads to the view that time is an intuition and, indeed, because of the first argument showing that it is *a priori* derives the conclusion that it is a *pure* intuition.

The structure of the connection between these first three points about time in the third section of the Dissertation and the argument in the second section that the forms of sensibility do not allow us to have intellectual intuitions seems to be misstated by Lorne Falkenstein. Falkenstein states the second and third sections of the Dissertation are caught in a circular argument as the rationale for our intuition being only sensible and not intellectual in the second section is that our conception of singular cognitions is tied to space and time and yet the reason for thinking that space and time are not intellectual conceptions at all is not provided until the third section at which point it is simply based on the notion of singularity.[24] In fact the statement in the second section of the Dissertation to the effect that we do not have intellectual intuition merely states that the formal principle of intuitions is a singular condition of apprehension and does not here provide an *argument* to this effect. Thus whilst Kant does there state a distinction between the sensitive and the intellectual parts of cognition and provides in the process a distinguishing mark of the sensitive part thereof he does not provide us with a reason for accepting his claim to this effect in paragraph 10 of section 2. This argument is not given until he turns to examining the nature of sensible cognition in the third section. The ground for thinking of sensible cognition as singular is then revealed in the infinite given character of it or, in other terms, the fact that no part of time can be comprehended as distinct from the other parts as there is at any point of use of temporal markers the necessary connection of them all with each other. The basis of this is to argue that it cannot be the case, as Hume for example thinks, that we could first note a successive process of some sort and subsequently generalize it to the idea of temporality in some general way as without the inter-connection of temporal markers the specific process under observation could be distinct from all others and then there would be no formal unity to temporal statements. The argument is that the notion of "earlier" or "later" in any specific setting always requires that the marks in question are related to as elements of the same general process as without this there would be no possibility of allocating these notions within the description of experience at all, there would only be a local notice which would have no ground of connection with any other. So Falkenstein is wrong to think that Kant has here merely argued in a circle as the grounds for the distinction that are simply *stated* in paragraph 10 are revealed in the rationale for understanding intuitions to give us singular representations.

The nature of the infinite presentation of time is further examined in the fourth argument where Kant treats time as presenting continuous magnitudes before us. If there is a continuous magnitude *in* time, as we have seen to be a necessary consequence of singularity of representation then this has to be connected to the accidental nature of determination *by means of time.* Since all that is described in time as a subjective condition is a set of modifications it cannot be anything other than a way of demarcating relations and to this extent the Leibnizian conception is correct. But the point is then made that if time is hence the way in which representations of modifications are presented then what has to be built into this is a recognition that this representation is a universal condition of awareness of sensible objects and whilst itself singular is thus *a priori* in a positive sense as without it no sensible representation would be given. Thus time is a necessary condition of sensible awareness and as such the way in which sensibility is composed for us. Whilst it is a term for relations between sensible objects what we can state about it is that without it these objects would not be given to us at all. But if this is the case then there cannot be included in the presentation of sensibility reference to simples as what Kant has reiterated since the writing of the *Physical Monadology* about simples is that the nature of them is that they are what would exist even in the absence of composition as their essential character leaves them independent of relations. *So nothing sensible can be simple due to the continuous nature of the composition of time and hence if we have an idea of simples this cannot be an idea of something sensible.*

Kant then connects this description of continuous magnitude to the notion of negative magnitudes that he unearthed in the essay devoted to this subject. The flow that is at work in experience is one in which states can be viewed as opposed to each other as belonging to different moments of time as we speak of the present as a different point to the past due to the latter having lapsed and the former having begun.

The movement of annulment of one by the other is what we term "a process of real opposition" in process where the comparison of the magnitudes in motion is describable as an aspect of the connection of each to the same experiencer who hence provides them with the necessary common element that we can see to be necessary for a sum to be produced on the grounds of explanation of the terms for addition and subtraction Kant set out in *Negative Magnitudes*. As he puts it now: "between two moments there will always be an intervening time, and, in the infinite series of the moments of that time, the substance is not in one of the given states, nor in the other, and yet it is not in no state either" (Ak. 2: 399). The substance is thus rather in the infinite given magnitude that is meant by "time" in general but which can only be represented, as we are aware after the treatments of the Transcendental Deduction and Schematism, through space.

Nor is this point irrelevant here as Kant goes on to reply to a request on the part of the mathematician Kästner for a demonstration of the law of continuity as originally formulated as a condition for experience by Leibniz in terms of what is involved in tracing motion in a triangular figure. The demonstration that Kant provides argues for the impossibility of movement along the parts of a triangle without points of angles having to be distinguished from each other in the manner that we can conceive of as "rest" and which Kant applies to the understanding of motion as requiring curvature of bodies (Ak. 2: 400). The representation of motion along planes hence cannot be conceived of as uniformly straight due to the nature of motion being dependent on the difference between moments, a difference that is one of alignment along figures, an alignment not plausible without reference to rest.

The fifth point then undertakes a certain reduction of the fourth as now Kant suggests that whilst we have treated time there as a relation (in accordance with Leibniz's conception) it is not in fact one as relation is expressed as what is at work between substances and accidents. However what we have described is that neither substance nor accident are comprehensible in connection with anything sensible unless time is already given and this leads to the result that time is not a determination of "reality" if we mean by this a connection of essential elements to modifications as neither the modification nor the essential element can be given without time. Time is prior to anything being given *in* it as we in fact demonstrated in the description of composition that it forms. The effect of that description should however have been to render the way it was presented suspicious as if the removal of the composition of time would leave no simple behind then it must follow not just that there are no sensible simples but that effectively there are also no sensible substances despite the attempt Kant made in the 1750s and 1760s to defend a physical monadology. On these grounds Kant reaches the conclusion that time is not itself something that we can term "real" and means by this that it does not describe a substantial notion despite the fact that all sensible cognitions are dependent upon it. But in viewing it as "the immutable law of sensible things" he takes it to fit the description of the form of the world that he set out in the first section of the Dissertation, an alignment that shows him to be thinking of it as *empirically real*, just as will be defended in the Aesthetic.

The arguments concerning space, as in the Aesthetic, largely parallel those concerning time. The first anti-empiricist argument is to the effect that all presentations of place presuppose space, a reiteration of the rationale set out in the 1768 essay for taking space to be absolute. The singularity of space follows from its infinite givenness as with time but, unlike with time, the demonstration of the nature of it as an intuition which follows from its singularity is described in some detail from characteristics of geometry, a science that can only be apprehended *concretely* as was argued in the Prize Essay. The incongruent counterparts argument is here used again and the point on this occasion is to show that since the difference between right and left is one that cannot be derived from concepts (since the concepts of the two hands does not describe a universal difference due to the difference always requiring concrete presentation in singulars) therefore space is an intuition. Whilst the 1768 essay thus derived from the incongruent counterparts argument the conclusion that matter is dependent on space, a view in fact maintained here, it is the main point that since the incongruence in question cannot be derived from concepts alone of the things that are determined as left and right these determinations must describe something non-conceptual.

Kant dwells on the nature of geometry in a manner that does not have a correlate in his account of time despite the evident consequence he draws concerning the concept of motion. Geometry has a form of evidence, he states here, that is utilized in all the sciences and he declares its evidence to be the paradigm and means of all scientific evidence as such (Ak. 2: 403). The reason for this is that geometry states rules concerning the nature of the relations of space and such rules must be at the root of all sciences of nature since there is no nature without space. In a sense this is an extension of the argument from incongruent counterparts to the effect that just as left and right do not describe conceptual differences of bodies so also the properties of figure set out in geometrical demonstrations are not conceptual but are, like the difference between left and right, descriptions of the basic relations of spatiality. As we will see in due course an argument of basically the same type as this is still at work in the Axioms of Intuition and the challenges that can be made to it will be reviewed there.

Space is, like time, not "real" and, as with the treatment of time, Kant argues after having treated it as a description of relations that it is not in *the philosophical sense* an account of relations. Kant does however align space with a conception of the "entirety" of sensibility when he describes it as "a principle of a whole which cannot be a part of another whole" (Ak. 2: 405).[25] All points and moments belong however within the original representations that are time and space so taken together they provide the elements of what we can state to be the complete conception of the sensible world.

Intuition, mathematics and the synthetic *a priori*

It will be worth some attention in due course how the arguments of the Dissertation are altered in being re-presented in the Aesthetic. Prior to this treatment however I wish to pass under review the rationale Kant gives in the "Introduction" to the *Critique* and the preliminary part of the *Prolegomena* for thinking that pure mathematics is a body of synthetic *a priori* truths and how this is connected to the development of his view of intuition. In both places Kant gives a basic argument for taking mathematical propositions to be synthetic *a priori* with the real point for us being to explore the rationale for taking them to be synthetic given the general tendency of twentieth-century philosophers to think of them as analytic.[26] The argument in these parts of the *Critique* and the *Prolegomena* whilst simply put contains a conception of mathematics that is not, as was often thought, crude.[27]

The discussion in the "Introduction" of the *Critique* famously centres on a simple proposition of arithmetic, namely "$7+5=12$". Kant's point is that the concepts of "7" and "5" even when placed in connection with unification do not produce the outcome of the sum. As he puts it: "We have to go outside these concepts, and call in the aid of the intuition which corresponds to one of them" (B15). The intuition that corresponds to either of these numerals is something that has to be presented to us although in so doing it is not the case that we require a simple demonstration of counting despite Kant's reference here (derived from a textbook) to the procedure of presenting fingers before the eyes. The conversion of these quantitative measures into algebraic equations is clearly possible, as with any other quantitative measure. The combination of such figures would require intuition as much as does the combination of the numerals in question. So what is meant by bringing them before intuition is the conversion of the quantities in question into equivalents as was suggested in *Negative Magnitudes*. This conversion into equivalents is not however an effect of the analysis of the concepts in question as their equivalence cannot be conceptually demonstrated. This is what Kant means by stating that the thought of the outcome of the sum cannot be conceptually presented (B16). That this is his point here can be further shown by his subsequent reference to the geometrical demonstration that the shortest line between two points is a straight one. Here he simply states that "my concept of *straight* contains nothing of quantity, only of quality" (B16), which shows that the *concept* of straight alone cannot yield the demonstration required, a demonstration that needs a measurement of straight to be performed and hence converts straightness into a distantial term. This conversion is what is brought about by relating to straightness as a concrete singular rather than an abstract general term.

Production of the outcome of the sum in the case of arithmetic or the construction of the line to meet the requirement of brevity in the geometrical demonstration are normative requirements of engaging in the types of mathematics in question but the point Kant wishes to make here is that thought alone in such cases does not permit producing such results. Hence the appeal to intuition is the appeal to the reference to the ground of what permits the mathematical connection to be made at all, a connection that requires substitutivity to occur through provision of rules of equivalence.[28] It is this requirement that Kant is referring to in the *Prolegomena* treatment of the same point as requiring an addition that he terms "a need for succession" (Ak. 4: 269). This reference to succession is not a suggestion that there is a temporal notion included in the arithmetical combination but merely a reminder of the fact that the combination itself has a condition which is not that of the concepts alone or the thought of the concepts as involved in a sum but what enables the sum to occur and this condition is the provision of the rule for the combination being given as a description of the conversion of terms into equivalences.

This preliminary treatment of mathematics as a body of synthetic *a priori* truths thus points again to the need for intuition to be distinguished from concepts in terms of *enabling* and *providing* a singular form that allows rules of connection by reference to a different notion to that of the law of contradiction. This element of the notion of intuition shows the demonstration of the need for cognition to have rules that supplement those of analytic sort, an argument that in a sense goes back to the suggestion of the *New Elucidation* that there cannot be only one fundamental rule for cognition.

The argument of the Aesthetic and its connection to the Dissertation

What our enquiry into the "pre-Critical" writings and the Inaugural Dissertation has found is that Kant's initial concentration on space was motivated by a desire to demonstrate a possible reconciliation between the claims of Newtonian physics and Leibnizian metaphysics, a desire that led in turn to a considered inquiry into the specific methods of mathematics, particularly geometry and also arithmetic and algebra. This inquiry produced a description of mathematical inquiry as engaged in arbitrary combination of homogeneous quantities and demonstrated that the nature of such combination required conversion of quantities into equivalents. The post-rationalist element of Kant's enquiry reinforced the findings of the earlier writings with regard to the specific claims of spatial investigation showing that there are basic notions of spatial type that cannot be derived from general considerations concerning bodies and that these notions require formation of a distinct notion of space. The turn towards connecting space with time only really emerges in the argument of the Dissertation. In the argument of it we also finally reach the notion of "intuition", a notion introduced here not with reference to immediate cognition but rather through the notion of singularity.

Since we have noted in Chapter 1 that there has been a recurrent dispute concerning the criteria for intuition with regard to the determination of intuitions as having the distinct characteristics of immediacy and singularity what our inquiry has revealed is that Kant's investigations *chronologically* demonstrate a prior commitment to thinking of intuitions via the notion of singularity. This fact in itself suggests that those who argue for the *logical* priority of the criteria of singularity over immediacy can point to the pre-history of the Critical doctrine in their support and, furthermore, the account of mathematics in the introductory treatments of the *Critique* and the *Prolegomena* make no reference to immediacy.

The opening of the Transcendental Aesthetic give however a description of "intuition" in terms of immediacy (A19/B33). Kant introduces "intuition" here in the context of an account of how cognition relates to objects and in describing "intuition" as the immediate relation to objects Kant is outlining that this immediate relation is one of receptivity. The question is therefore whether the notion of immediacy points to anything more than the receptive condition of sensibility. Kant goes on to discuss the *matter* of sensibility as sensation and to describe the intuition that relates to objects through sensation as empirical. The nature of empirical intuition will be of some subsequent importance to us, not least concerning the question of how sensation and intuition are connected to each other since here we have the statement that empirical intuition is a form of relation to an object. How does this relation take place? Clearly, as suggested here, by "affection" but the meaning of this term is capable of considerable dispute.[29]

The opening of the Aesthetic speaks of "undetermined" objects by which Kant seems to mean a general description prior to any account of the means by which objects are presented to us as distinct from each other in experience. These "undetermined" objects are appearances, not yet phenomena. If the *matter* of them is given as sensation, the *form* of them, in accord with the arguments of the Dissertation, is understood to be *a priori* and the notion of such intuition is described as involving "extension and figure" (A21/B35).[30] The basic conception of Transcendental Aesthetic is then described as the enquiry into the pure elements of intuition. These elements we find to be space and time and now we can turn to the question of how the treatment of them in the Aesthetic relates to that in the Dissertation.

The reversal of order of the accounts from that provided in the Dissertation is the first noticeable difference, one that is not provided with any justification. The rationale for treating space first now would appear merely to be that Kant can argue that the treatment of space as an *a priori* intuition has a clear advantage over the treatments of it in Newtonian and Leibnizian accounts due to the ability of this discussion to describe the connection between geometry and physics without requiring the production of the view that something not itself a substance is treated as absolutely real. The initial negative argument for distinguishing space from empirical concepts is the same as was provided in the Dissertation though the second argument for positively describing it as *a priori* was not given there. Whilst the Dissertation demonstration that time is a continuous magnitude was a key part of the treatment of time the discussion that space is such was there passed over as "easy" (Ak. 2: 403n). The retrieval of this demonstration in the Aesthetic is presented in terms of a contrast between thinking about objects, which requires their presentation in space and thinking about space, which does not require the connection of it to objects. This argument could easily be understood as describing a form of thought-experiment but I take it that what Kant is here doing is arguing, in the vein of the 1768 essay, for the dependence of matter on space. This fact of dependence of matter on space is what makes space a *necessary* presentation as he now puts it. Hence whilst the negative demonstration that space cannot have arisen from abstraction from empirical events points to the universal use of the notion of space in experience the argument about the dependence of matter on space is meant to add the condition of necessity to the condition of universality to bolster the understanding that space is *a priori*. The care with which this demonstration is thus undertaken is connected to the delineation of the *a priori* as having these two criteria, a conception of it presented in the "Introduction" to the *Critique* but not described in the Dissertation.

The third point in the discussion of space in the second edition of the *Critique* (which departs in ordering from the first edition due to the inclusion in the first edition of the geometrical argument within the initial "metaphysical" treatment of space) refers us to the reason why it is not a description of "relations of things in general" (A24/B39). This wording also brings out clearly what was at issue in denying that space is a relation in the Dissertation. It is not a relational *concept* is what is meant, which it would be if it was essentially tied to the metaphysical notions of substance and accident. It is at this point that the reference to singularity is introduced in explicitly mereological terms as being a type of representation in which the parts cannot logically precede the description of the whole. The subsidiary element of this point that is made here about geometry is a repetition effectively of the argument of the introduction concerning the notion of straightness.

The fourth point about space is treated with slight variation of wording in the two editions of the *Critique* but in both cases the point is to argue for the treatment of the magnitude of space as something that is given infinitely. In the first edition Kant re-emphasizes with regard to this point that concepts are not sufficient to determine magnitude and this reiterates the reason for not treating space as a concept of relation (A25). In the second edition by contrast Kant makes the difference between concepts and intuitions vivid by distinguishing between types of mereological connection and the distinction fits that which underlay the treatment of the Prize Essay between the "signs" of mathematicians and the "words" of philosophers. The former can capture what is described *in* the formula whilst the latter can only, through the linguistic form of symbol, account for something *through* themselves. This difference ensures that the former gives a whole at once whilst the latter can only build up to one, which is what was described in the Prize Essay as the difference between *synthesis* and *analysis*.

Prior to presenting in the transcendental exposition arguments that suggest that this account of space as an *a priori* intuition is what will permit a description of the possibility of geometrical construction Kant has given four distinct arguments for his view of space. The first two arguments provide negative and positive reasons for taking space to be *a priori* focusing on first the rationale for thinking of space as universal and secondly for taking it to be a necessary condition of representation of any matter. The following two arguments then focus on the reasons for thinking of space as an intuition and in these arguments Kant aligns the notion of intuition with singularity. The first argument described the unity of space as given prior to the presentation of its parts, a unity that is here connected to the argument of the "Introduction" for thinking that a synthesis is required for a geometrical construction to be performed. The second argument then adds to this point the fact that the representation of space *qua* space is unlimited and argues that this is due to the fact that intuitions are mereologically distinct from concepts. By contrast to this treatment there were five arguments in the Dissertation concerning space. The arrangement of these arguments was much less symmetrical than is the case in the Aesthetic. The first argument is the same as the negative reason for thinking space to be *a priori* in the Aesthetic. But, rather than following this with a positive ground for thinking space to be *a priori* as is done in the Aesthetic, the second argument of the Dissertation moves instead directly to what is the fourth argument of the Aesthetic, the suggestion that the mereological nature of space requires singularity of representation and hence Kant moves directly from the suggestion that space is *a priori* to the view that it is an intuition. The third argument treating space in the Dissertation is a lengthy statement showing that geometrical construction depends on the singularity of space and really parallels the Transcendental Exposition of the Aesthetic though the first edition treatment of the Aesthetic here follows the Dissertation. The fourth argument in the Dissertation argues for the ideality of space, something treated only in the "conclusions" of the Aesthetic and not given in the specific arguments for thinking it to be an *a priori* intuition but the argument for this turns on not treating space as a relation, something defined more clearly in the Aesthetic where it is denied not that space is a relation *as such* but that it is a relational *concept* which is a more direct response to the Leibnizian picture of space. The final point in the

Dissertation is that space gives the notion of "entirety" to the conception of the sensible world which parallels the argument that space is an infinite given magnitude. In treating space as presenting an infinite given magnitude Kant is preparing for the distinction set out in the Antinomies between world and nature (A418–19/B446–7). The lack of description of this distinction in the Dissertation led to the puzzle we posed above concerning whether the Dissertation arguments allowed for any other combination in the conception of world than the arbitrary one that is mathematical.

Thus when we compare the treatment of space in the Aesthetic with that of the Dissertation it becomes apparent that the former treatment has a number of advantages comparative to the latter. Kant has moved to clarify the notion of the *a priori* and shown that space fits both notions of *a priori*. Subsequently he has then provided two distinct reasons for thinking of space as an intuition, both of which turn on the conditions of representation of space and thinking of space as singular. It is apparent that nothing in these arguments requires the assumption of immediacy to be given. Nor was immediacy even mentioned in the Dissertation so its insertion at the opening of the Aesthetic has yet to be justified.

The Transcendental Exposition of space is an argument inserted to show that only if space is an *a priori* intuition can it be the case that geometry is, as Kant takes it to be, a body of synthetic *a priori* truths. What we have seen from the treatment of *a priori* intuition is that if there are intuitions that give form to the sensible then these intuitions must be capable of being presented in a way that is distinct from that of concepts and what this is taken to mean is that they require singular representation. Here Kant simply relies on the argument provided in the "Introduction" of the *Critique* that the notion of straightness does not in itself describe anything quantitative despite the fact that such a use of it is required in geometrical construction. Kant now goes on to ask the question how there can exist for cognition an intuition that must, given its nature, precede all *matter* of representation as that which enables such matter to be represented? Kant is here drawing on the second argument for taking space to be *a priori* which showed the dependence of matter's representation on space and hence demonstrated that space is a necessary condition of sensible cognition. From this argument Kant now derives immediacy. The *formal* character of subjective representation is what *immediately* renders objects possible as cognizable. This argument is only given in this form in the second edition of the *Critique* (B41) as in the first edition Kant concentrated instead on asserting that unless spatial representation had necessary conditions it would present nothing other than the character of perceptions or, in other terms, empirical intuitions (A24). The first edition argument thus closely followed the argument in the Dissertation that Leibnizian treatments of space are insufficient to guarantee the universality of geometrical propositions justifying only comparative universality (Ak. 2: 404).

In departing from the treatment of the Dissertation in the second edition of the *Critique* Kant does more than distinguish metaphysical and transcendental expositions as the point of the latter is not merely to guarantee the status of geometry as a body of synthetic *a priori* truths. Rather, in addition to this Kant here wishes to give a reason for taking the intuition of space to be immediate. Immediacy is taken to follow however from necessity and necessity to be demonstrated by the fact that space has been shown to meet the classical condition of substantiality as being that on which all representation depends without itself depending on anything further. It is because in this sense that space is "substantial" that it is that which is immediately given.

Howard Caygill mentions two paradoxes concerning intuition, first that without formal singular principles there is no immediacy of apprehension and secondly that whilst immediacy suggests direct knowledge that the notion of appearance indicates a certain mediate apprehension.[31] To the first of these paradoxes we can respond now by stating that what is here described as immediacy is a presentation within experience that is *original* but that this original condition of experience is, in fact, as is subsequently demonstrated at great length in the Transcendental Deduction, a product of a synthetic process. Thus Kant cannot be taken to mean by immediacy a reference to a pure givenness that does not require investigation. Rather, the fact that objects are given to us at all is due to the presence of formal principles.

However once we make this move of stating that the reading of the Aesthetic with regard to the notion of immediacy can only arise *after* the description of the synthetic processes outlined in the Transcendental Deduction then we have to state that the criteria of immediacy is not merely a product of singularity, which is what Kant states in the Transcendental Exposition of space but that what is meant by immediacy is a condition without which no other element of sensibility can be given. Thus immediacy is not something of which we are "directly" aware as the second paradox from Cagyill would lead us to think. The fact that the immediate condition of apprehension is not something directly given in it is fact evident from Kant's repeated statements in the

Analogies that time is not perceived and the argument that we will see to be important in the Anticipations of Perception that sensation, the matter of intuition, is something that in a certain sense even "precedes" that which makes it apprehensible. This latter point in fact brings out the true nature of Caygill's paradoxes concerning intuition which concentrate really not on immediacy as such but on the nature of the relationship between form, matter and affection in the treatment of intuition. This will be treated below as a result of our subsequent outlining of the relationship between the arguments of the Aesthetic and the arguments of the Axioms and Anticipations.

Returning to the account of space in the Aesthetic Kant follows the Transcendental Exposition with a series of "conclusions" from the discussion. These conclusions have no direct correlate in the discussion of space in the Dissertation though some of them make more explicit the standpoint already adopted in the earlier work. Thus in reiterating the point that space does not describe relations Kant now makes clear that this means relations of "things in themselves" by which we can see from our treatment thus far he must mean things treated as substances, just as has been his constant motif since the writing of the *Physical Monadology*, as he refers here to what remains "even when abstraction has been made of all the subjective conditions of intuition" (A26/B42). These conditions are the way in which affection is given in appearances and the notion of substances was meant to describe reality itself separately from such appearances but taken that way space is not an account of either absolute or relative relations between substances and thus the Newtonian/Leibnizian disagreement centred on an assimilation of space to substances, an assimilation that we can now see to be based on the fact that it is only really space that, for us, *acts as* the substantial element of sensibility.

The second conclusion that is stated is that space, as the *transcendental* condition of receptivity is that which must necessarily be given to cognition as an original condition the principles of which determine how objects must be related in our experience. This produces the key conclusion concerning the dual status of space as empirically real and yet transcendentally ideal by which Kant simply means that there can be criterion for reality in experience that does not involve space but that considered metaphysically there can be described a view of what is real (substances) that does not require reference to space, just as he argued originally in the *Physical Monadology*. If however, as is now being stated, the conditions of cognition are equivalent to the description of what the Dissertation termed merely "sensitive cognition" then the thoughts that were there protected as describing an intelligible world will now be revealed to provide us with no form of knowledge as it on this that the Critical revolution in philosophy depends. The justification for stating that cognition is only of the sensible and cannot be of the intelligible would reside in the discussion of why only the former can supply us with any relation to "objects" and thus will only be justified once the condition of concepts describing objects has been shown to be that they must first be schematized.

The discussion of time here in the arguments of the Aesthetic is frequently relegated to the margins as a simple repetition of the arguments concerning space. The symmetry of these arguments is indeed impressive and worth attention but the degree of connection between the treatment of time in the Aesthetic and the Dissertation by comparison with that of space should also be given consideration, not least due to the fact that we have discovered Kant's interest in space to have substantial connection to the continued inquiry into the distinction between metaphysics and mathematics whilst time was not treated in this regard prior to the writing of the Dissertation.

The first two arguments concerning time, like the first two concerning space, aim to show that time is *a priori*. As with space, Kant presents both the negative contention that time does not derive from the senses as all temporal markers within sensory events presuppose it already and the argument stating that time is a necessary representation. The argument concerning necessity states that time is both a necessary and a universal condition and seems to suggest that the universality of time is a product of its necessity, an intimation lacking in the case of space. The third argument concerning time overlaps with the Transcendental Exposition of it but despite this was not removed from the Metaphysical Exposition in the second edition of the *Critique*, a point that is at variance with the treatment of space. The argument refers to what are termed "axioms of time" and argues that the universality of them is grounded upon the necessary nature of time as a form of sensory representation. The nature of these axioms is not however discussed. The final two arguments present the reasons for thinking that time is an intuition and, as with space, depend upon taking intuitions to be singular representations. The first such argument points to the mereological nature of temporal representation as distinct from that of conceptuality and the final point outlines the infinite givenness of temporality.

The connection of these arguments to the treatment of time in the Dissertation is again one in which we can see the arguments of the

Aesthetic as having a clearer division and justification. The first argument for time being *a priori* repeats the first treatment of time in the Dissertation but the argument that time is a necessary condition of sensory representations is not explicitly stated in the Dissertation. The second argument in the Dissertation instead moves directly to reasons for thinking time to be singular, a point not raised until the fourth argument of the Aesthetic. The description of the "axioms of time" is given however in the Dissertation but merely mentioned in the Metaphysical Exposition of the Aesthetic without there being spelt out. The Dissertation reveals that these axioms concern the laws of continuous magnitude, laws which underpin the infinity of representation that time presents. In the Dissertation this was argued for in terms of the discussion of the movement around a triangle, a demonstration dropped from the Aesthetic. The statement concerning time not being "real" is not included in the Metaphysical Exposition but given treatment in the "conclusions", a division not present in the Dissertation treatment. There are thus more differences in the treatment of time between the two works than there are in the treatments of space. The Transcendental Exposition of time, unlike that of space, does not derive immediacy from necessity and points to the notion of an undefined "doctrine of motion" as the body of synthetic *a priori* truths that depends upon time, not any direct element of mathematics. In the "Introduction" to the *Critique* the nature of this doctrine is mentioned as part of what the *Prolegomena* will term "pure natural science" and the propositions that are stated to belong to it here concern conservation of matter and communication of motion according to rules of action and reaction (B17). The treatment of them here is brief indeed and the nature of the synthetic *a priori* truths that are dependent upon time will require further attention when we look at the Axioms and Anticipations.

The "conclusions" that are derived by Kant from his treatment of time begin with a parallel claim to the first one about space, namely that it does not describe the nature of things in themselves. The second conclusion however is inserted to distinguish time from space stating that time is not a determination of outer appearances as space is as it does not connect to the determination of shape or position. This is the reason why we need analogies of spatial type to be able to represent time itself, representations which are described in fact in geometrical terms. It is only after these two conclusions have been reached that Kant presents a reason for attaching the immediacy criterion of intuitions to time. It is the immediate condition of cognition in the sense that no cognition, even of the states of the one cognizing, can be given except under the form of time. This does not apply to space and thus, whilst time itself can only be spatially represented, the form of the states of cognition itself are not spatially given. There are thus two asymmetries between time and space and the fact that spatial representations are only mediately temporal shows the difference between two forms of immediacy and sharpens our concentration on this point. Whilst all presentation of "objects" of experience is within space and only medi- ately belongs to time, all presentation of the states of cognition itself is immediately temporal and only mediately understood to be spatial when constructed for the purposes of inter-subjective communication. Due to these asymmetries between time and space the body of synthetic *a priori* truths that depend upon time presuppose something that is a form of empirical datum as Kant subsequently admits (A41/B58).

Mathematics and intuition in the *Prolegomena*

Between the composition of the two editions of the *Critique* Kant set out in the *Prolegomena* a regressive argument to show that pure mathematics rested upon *a priori* intuitions. Kant here repeats his claims about mathematical method depending upon concrete representation as first set out in the Prize Essay and indicates briefly the view that arithmetic refers in some sense to time (Ak. 4: 283), a point best understood as a repetition of the notion of succession given in the "Introduction" to the *Critique*. However, more importantly than this reference to the nature of arithmetic, is the treatment here given of the nature of geometrical construction. Kant refers to the possibility of relating to figures as congruent, a possibility essential in geometrical proofs. This operation of equivalence is also, as we noted in our exposition of the "Introduction" to the *Critique*, essential in arithmetic and draws implicitly there upon the characterization of magnitudes set out in the essay on negative magnitudes. However with regard to geometry this operation of equivalence is connected to the dimensions of space, dimensions that are in fact revealed to us in such simple geometrical demonstrations as occur with the discussion of intersection of lines. Just as straightness cannot be conceptually connected to quantity so it is also true that the impossibility of intersection of more than three lines at any given point is due not to the concept of lines but to a basic property of space, namely that it has only three dimensions. This element of space is effectively revealed to us in the geometrical demonstration about intersection showing that what occurs in the geometrical account is a combination that cannot be one of empirical intuition due to the universality of its claim but must rather relate to *pure* intuition.

Similarly the characteristic of indefinite prolongation of any given line is connected to the "immediate" sense of the infinity of space (Ak. 4: 285). The key distinctive point made in the *Prolegomena* and not included in the *Critique* however concerns the new use made in it of the argument from incongruent counterparts that we have witnessed as important both within the discussion of space in the Dissertation and in the 1768 essay. Whilst the 1768 essay used this argument to demonstrate that space was "absolute" the true sense of the demonstration given there was to the effect that all thought of matter is dependent upon the representation of space, a point repeated in the *Critique* from the demonstration there of the necessity of space. In the Dissertation the use of this argument by contrast pointed to the dependence of the representation of space on intuition as no concepts of left and right could account for their incongruity. In the *Prolegomena*, by contrast, Kant uses this lack of conceptual comprehension of the incongruity between right and left not merely to state that notions of right and left are based on intuition but also to bolster the contention that intuitions are not therefore relations of things in themselves. The point follows from the lack of conceptual distinction between right and left once we understand that things in themselves are conceptual relations taken from metaphysics, not synthetic ones derived from construction (Ak. 4: 286). Subsequent discussion of the nature of space, as revealed within the propositions of geometry, concentrates on the question as to what reason we have for being confident that what is described in them is actually an account of the world we inhabit. This reference in fact shows that the treatment of the *Prolegomena* combines here an element from the discussion of intuition in the Aesthetic with that of the mathematical principles in the *Critique*. It is the point at which Kant elaborates reasons for taking geometry to describe the nature of the space we inhabit that the controversy over his philosophy of mathematics takes sharp form. To respond to this controversy we must review how Kant moves from the treatment given in the Aesthetic to that described in the Axioms and discuss the relationship between these two essential parts of the *Critique*.

The division between mathematical and dynamical principles in the *Critique*

In order to move to an understanding of the relation between the Aesthetic and the mathematical principles of the *Critique* we need to establish what Kant means by these principles. Kant describes these principles as supplying "the concept which contains the condition, and as it were the exponent, of a rule in general" (A159/B198) and hence as being the rules on which all laws of nature are based. However, if there are such *a priori* principles some of them are based, as we have seen in the discussions of both the Dissertation and the Aesthetic, on pure intuitions. This might tempt one to think that the nature of pure mathematics having been justified in the Aesthetic that all we have to show in the Axioms is how such mathematics is applied.[32] In truth, what Kant has demonstrated in the Aesthetic is that it is because space and time are pure intuitions that the sciences of geometry and motion must tell us of something intuitive but when we add to this the point made in the "Introduction" about the nature of "7 + 5" and we question the basis of how the quality of straightness can be summarized in a system as a quantity we realize the need for these intuitions to be subject to a *synthesis* and the nature of this synthesis has not itself been described in the arguments of the Aesthetic. Hence it is necessary in introducing and defending the principle of the Axioms to demonstrate the *synthetic* nature of pure mathematics as it is this synthetic nature of it that *enables* it to be subsequently *applied* to specific enumerations.

The principles in question thus have to be connected to the concepts whose very possibility we have treated in the Analytic of Concepts. What we can state as a result of our enquiry into the Transcendental Deduction is that Kant is justified in the view that the only viable deduction strategy is one based on an account of transcendental synthesis. Hence, if pure mathematics is to be connected to experience in order to yield applied mathematics, this must be due to a form of synthesis that connects intuitions to concepts and will involve the transcendental imagination. Since pure mathematics involves pure intuition the connection of its principle to the concepts of pure understanding must yield a necessary condition of any possible experience and this is what Kant sets out in the Axioms and the Anticipations, the dynamical principles being by contrast connected to the *existence* of something and hence have a more conditional validity. The evidence Kant will wish to attach to the mathematical principles will be like the evidence of pure mathematics itself, an evidence he here states, following the Transcendental Exposition of space, to be "immediate" (A161/B200).

The kind of synthesis at work in the mathematical principles must be of the sort that the Prize Essay understood to be arbitrary. However, in accordance with the account of number in the schematism as a unity of the synthesis of the manifold of a homogeneous intuition (A143/B182), and which we explicated in our account of the treatment of "7 + 5" in the "Introduction" to the *Critique* this must be a synthesis that *creates* equivalence of measurement. Kant now argues that there are two kinds of such mathematical synthesis, meaning by this, two kinds of principle underlying the possibility of pure mathematics. These two kinds of synthesis are thus two forms of arbitrary combination and are described by Kant as that of either an "aggregate" or a "coalition" (B202n). The difference between these two forms of mathematical principle is a difference between two forms of quantification and the nature of this difference will be accounted for in distinguishing the Axioms from the Anticipations.

The principle of the Axioms

In accordance with the treatment of the mathematical principles as not being themselves principles *of* mathematics but rather what underlies these principles the account of the Axioms is not itself a justification of any particular axioms but of the principle that all such must presuppose. This principle is treated slightly differently in the two editions of the *Critique*. The first edition gives the following principle: "All appearances are, in their intuition, extensive magnitudes" (A162) whilst the second edition alters this to: "All intuitions are extensive magnitudes" (B202). Both versions have the merit of stating universal conditions but the first edition describes a universal condition of appearances through the notion of intuition whilst the second edition version simply treats the principle as a universal condition of intuitions. The problem with the version of the principle given in the first edition is that it does not make clear the point that we are here setting out a principle that must apply to the pure intuitions of pure mathematics whilst the extension of the second edition principle incorporates this. This would describe a reason for altering the wording of the principle in accord with what I here, following Daniel Sutherland, take to be the dual purpose of the description of the principle of the Axioms, namely to "establish both a principle of experience and a principle concerning the nature of any mathematical cognition whatsoever".[33]

The argument for the principle of the Axioms

The opening of the argument for the principle underlying the axioms of intuition is added to in the second edition of the *Critique* with a paragraph that immediately follows the statement of the principle.

What this adds to the account that was lacking in the first edition treatment of the principle is the point that appearances cannot be given to empirical awareness except in a manner that presents the synthesis of the manifold such that we have a representation of space and time in the first place. The nature of this synthesis was described in the Transcendental Deduction as requiring synthesis to connect to consciousness of unity. To this point Kant now reverts to the earlier statement, taken from the Schematism, concerning the schema of sensible concepts in the form of number. The description of the synthesis of recognition in the A-Deduction stated that the concept of number is "nothing but the consciousness of the unity of synthesis" (A103) but, as is pointed out in the B-Deduction at B158–9, the condition for such consciousness of unity is that I am aware of the combination of thought as a successive awareness in inner intuition. If we combine these points we can then state that identity of cognition of subjective combination is the original consciousness of myself as a numerical identity and this consciousness of numerical identity is likewise the original awareness of number itself. The schematization of the concept of quantity is the means by which magnitude, as given in pure mathematics, becomes number as an account of homogeneous intuition. "Thus even the perception of an object, as appearance, is only possible through the same synthetic unity of the manifold of the given sensible intuition as that whereby the unity of combination of the manifold [and] homogeneous is thought in the concept of a *magnitude*" (B203). In other words, without the presentation of number as something that enumerates the distinction of moments from each other and thus the representation of myself as identical, there could be no measurement of equivalents in experience either. This measurement of equivalents in experience is essential to the conception that what is before one is the same "object" across time as was already expounded in the treatment of reproduction (A100–102). So if there are "objects" of appearance what these must be are magnitudes that are given as enumerable and hence to be such must conform to the conditions described by the systems that we have encountered as transforming heterogeneous elements into common equivalents. Such common equivalents are given in experience as parts of the *same* time and space and it is this that renders discretely different "objects" capable of being captured under the generic homogeneous characterization that is objectivity.

It is after stating this point that we reach the beginning of the treatment of the principle of the Axioms as described in the first edition of the *Critique*, which is where Kant defines the notion of "extensive magnitudes". This definition is cast in mereological terms as a magnitude is termed extensive "when the representation of the parts makes possible and therefore necessarily precedes, the representation of the whole" (A162/B203). This description of the mereology of extensive magnitudes seems to assimilate them to concepts and has been the cause of some commentators detecting a conflict between the account here and that provided in the Aesthetic.[34] The conflict between the Axioms and the Aesthetic is alleged to arise in the difference between the mereologies of these two passages. In the Aesthetic Kant argues that intuitions are singular representations on the basis of the kind of part/whole combination they possess being different from that of concepts as with intuitions wholes are given at once and not built up from parts. The Aesthetic was concerned however to describe the nature of *pure* intuitions and to distinguish them from pure concepts. In the Axioms, by contrast, we have an account of the way in which empirical intuitions provide us with *determinate* wholes. Determinate wholes are distinguished from each other *within* the pre-given wholes of pure intuition. However, it is also the case that representation of temporality can only occur through spatial mapping as in the drawing of a line as a way of capturing the difference of moments, a point already conceded as we have seen above in the treatment of time in the Transcendental Aesthetic (A33–4/B49–50) and which was reiterated in the synthetic treatment of time in the analyses of the Transcendental Deduction. So, if anything is given as a determinate whole for empirical intuition, it is so given in the same manner in which conditions of representation of time itself are given, namely by "successive advance" of parts (A163/B203). Thus appearances are intuited as aggregates, that is, as "complexes of previously given parts" (A163/B204).

The possibility of such combination of parts together is what was described in the argument of the Transcendental Deduction as the transcendental synthesis of imagination, a point here expressly stated to be the basis of geometry (A163/B204). Given the transcendental synthesis of imagination as a construction of the form of the whole of experience we can generate figures as such. It is the possibility of such arbitrary combination as occurs in geometrical construction that is expressed in the axioms of geometry, axioms which the principle under discussion underlies. Thus to describe the conditions of pure mathematics of geometry as intuitive, as was done in the argument of the Aesthetic, is only to relate the demonstrations of geometry to the pure intuition that is space but for this intuition of space to describe the nature of experience itself to us is for geometry to be taken not just as an account of pure figures alone but for these to be schematically understood as describing the nature of any space that we can determinately experience. Thus what the transcendental synthesis of productive imagination generates is the nature of space as not merely the *form* of experience in general terms but as a space that is presented to us in *determinate* experience according to principles of exposition. The space of experience is not merely homogeneous but its condition is that it allows of description by reference to the notion of extensive magnitudes. This point is made even firmer and more explicit in the *Prolegomena* where Kant writes: "The principle that a straight line is the shortest distance between two points presupposes that the line is subsumed under the concept of quantity, which certainly is no mere intuition but has its seat in the understanding alone and serves to determine the intuition (of the line) with regard to the judgments which may be made about it in respect to the quantity, that is, to plurality" (Ak. 4: 302).

The pure concepts are, as Kant goes on to state, "nothing more than concepts of intuitions in general" as is here indicated in the *Critique* by reference to the axioms of geometry such as this one concerning the straight line. What has here been done is that the pure intuitions of space have been connected to the pure concepts in order for the synthesis to emerge from pure imagination as a statement about the substantial form of experience in general. The pure figures of geometry are "pure" in that they do not relate to any given specific region of space but the application of them to experience follows automatically from the realization that the successive synthesis of their generation is the same process as the successive generation of objects of sensibility as such. The principle of the axioms points to the nature of their application as from the statement that intuitions in general are extensive magnitudes it follows that appearances must all follow this rule.

By contrast to this treatment of geometry Kant denies that arithmetic has axioms and states that it possesses only numerical formulae. The reason for this is that arithmetic does not treat *quanta* but *quantitas*, that is, not an *object* of intuition but only, as Kant subsequently put in a letter to Johann Schultz, "*quantity as such*" or "the concept of the thing in general by means of quantitative determination" (Ak. 10: 556). That the thing in general is what Kant takes to be the "object" of arithmetic points to the reason why he thinks that in assessing arithmetic we have to address problems about the magnitude of a thing (A163/B204). This notion of the "thing" that is the "object" of arithmetic is explicated further in the Doctrine of Method when Kant discusses algebra. In describing algebra in the Doctrine of Method Kant states that its operations involve abstraction "from the properties of the object that is to be thought" (A717/B745) which produces indeterminate magnitudes. In expounding the treatment of algebra Kant argues that it simply requires the production of notation for construction as descriptions of relations that have universal rules hence producing "the various operations through which the magnitudes are produced and modified" (A717/B745). This account is of a piece with the description of the operation of equivalence by means of adoption of unity of signification given in *Negative Magnitudes*.

Arithmetic is either completely indeterminate (as in the case of algebra) or provided with numbers. In either case, on Kant's view, it has no axioms as an axiom has the purpose of formulating "the conditions of sensible *a priori* intuition under which alone the schema of a pure concept of outer appearance can arise" (A163/B204). What this entails is that the axioms therefore describe the conditions of spatial apprehension and since the symbolism of arithmetic requires no reference to *objects* of intuition it does not require construction of the *form* of outer appearances to be given. If this is the case however we might now ask what arithmetic has to do with intuition? This question is one that Kant was subsequently forced to return to in the previously cited letter to Schultz. Schultz was a mathematician who set out to provide a popular guide to the views of the *Critique* but who, on the basis of this problem, was led to initially viewing arithmetical connections as analytic. Kant's reply to Schultz and its significance have generated much debate.[35] The first point Kant makes here is that arithmetic is an ampliative science, a point introduced to persuade Schultz that it is synthetic and not analytic. This in a sense reiterates the point concerning arithmetical combination that was at issue in the discussion of "7 + 5" in the "Introduction" to the *Critique*. If the outcome of the sum cannot be regarded as the product of analysis however then not only must there be a synthesis at work in arithmetic but the nature of this synthesis can, Kant thinks, be stated. It is one that requires, as he puts it to Schultz, "successive addition" (Ak. 10: 556) which requires a construction through "a single counting up" (Ak. 10: 556). However, in accordance with the distinction in the Transcendental Deduction (B151–2) Kant refers to this as a "pure intellectual synthesis" (Ak. 10: 557). The description of it as such seems however to confirm that *synthetic* as arithmetical combinations may be they are not *intuitive*. However, as Kant puts it in his letter to Schultz: "insofar as specific magnitudes (quanta) are to be determined in accordance with this, they must be given to us in such a way that we can apprehend their intuition successively" (Ak. 10: 557) so arithmetic cannot determine any "object" except under the condition of time so all the "objects" it describes must be sensible.[36]

Since Kant thinks of arithmetic in relation to calculation as requiring a process of counting (Ak. 10: 556) in order to have "objects" the nature of this process is what gives its connection to intuition and since the process is, as is required for all construction for Kant, temporal, the intuition to which it is connected is that of time. Time is itself only spatially representable however so it is no surprise that the nature of the demonstration of arithmetic's intuitive status is as indirect as is time's representability. The manner of presentation of arithmetical propositions is itself not set out in axiomatic fashion as it does not provide a schema of outer appearances. The nature of the principles of arithmetic is correspondingly more complicated than is the case with geometry as Kant states that they are "immediately certain" and yet only "formulas" or, as he puts it in the letter to Schultz, "postulates" (Ak. 10: 556). What this entails is that the expression of a sum sets what he terms a "problem" or "task" that has only one way of being presented according to the systematic nature of the use of the symbols such as "+" and this can only be accomplished through a general operation of making numerals equivalent.

Space is constituted as an object by the synthesis of imagination at work in geometry whilst time is necessarily required for arithmetic to have any "objects" given to it at all. On the basis of the demonstration of this principle Kant takes it that pure mathematics is not only thus justified but also shown to connect to experience. Prior to describing the nature of Kant's treatment of the Anticipations of Perception it is worth reviewing some critical problems that have been raised concerning the argument for the principle of the Axioms of Intuition and, indeed, Kant's philosophy of mathematics in contemporary philosophy.

Difficulties with the argument for the principle of the Axioms

Paul Guyer raises a number of problems with the defence of the principle of the Axioms. The first concerns the relationship of the discussion of this principle with Kant's account of the process of schematization. Since the description of the connection of the categories with experience in the chapter on schematism was by reference to time, it might be thought that the account of the principles of the axioms would reveal a clear dependence upon time but in fact the nature of the principle is one that applies rather more clearly to space than time. Furthermore, we might have expected the "schematization" that has been undertaken to be one that applies to all of the three categories of quantity (unity, plurality and totality) rather than to "quantity" in general.[37]

The first point about schematization ignores the fact that the schema of sensible concepts was described within the chapter on schematism as necessarily involving space and it is difficult to see what the justification of the principles of geometry would be if it was not a schematization of sensible concepts. To the objection that what is supposedly being given here is a *transcendental schema of the pure concepts of quantity* it is I think necessary to reply that this schema of quantity is effectively what enables us to describe the nature of pure sensible concepts so that these two kinds of schematism are linked together. The schematism of quantity attaches, as Kant suggested in the chapter on schematism to the time-series (A145/B185) which was described there as the generation of time itself. This statement is surely connected to the point that space gives the condition of representation of time. The generation of time is a generation of *moments* but moments, to be figured, have to be given as *points*, as in the generation of a line. Thus it is no objection to Kant's procedure that he necessarily brings in space in his account of time. It is nonetheless incidentally important that the generation of arithmetic is connected not to space, but to time only and that due to the condition of successive apprehension being all that is required for numerals to be given.

The objection concerning the fact that only the category of "quantity" in general is justified and not the specific categories of unity, plurality and totality indicates a failure to attend to how extensive magnitudes are described. Since an extensive magnitude is a mereological combination it clearly has to involve the representation of plurality *as* unity. In a sense this point was already made in the chapter on schematism when Kant described number there (A143/B182). The nature of geometry is an application of quantitative measurement to the pure intuition in order to further describe the nature of the latter. The emergence of figures that are wholes from a combination of parts within an infinite givenness points to the generation of multiplicity *as* unity which is the combination of the first two parts of the category of quantity. The notion of totality was described in the Dissertation as the relationship of matter and form but in the Axioms we can see it to be revealed in the universal nature of the principle of extensive magnitude. It is because this principle applies universally that the whole of experience can be connected to the formal intuitions we justified in the Aesthetic.

Guyer's central objection to the argument of the axioms resides precisely however in his conviction that the relationship of pure intuition and empirical intuition has not here been justified but simply declared established "by fiat".[38] If the nature of the pure intuition of space has been described in the arguments of the Aesthetic then what follows from them is that space, as the universal form of sensibility, will be an essential element of all experience. In the discussion of space the argument that it is an intuition turned out to depend on the view that it is given in singular representation. Since geometry is taken by Kant to have the same nature it will supply formal principles to any possible spatial experience. Thus it is not a matter of fiat to declare that the properties of pure intuition will also be those of empirical intuition as if this is not true we would have no reason to take pure intuitions to describe necessary and universal conditions.

The core of this objection would hence turn on the question as to whether Kant's description of geometry is one that demonstrates it to have the necessary and universal properties he claims for it. The nature of the challenge to this assumption is, in my view, what underlies Guyer's concluding objection and it can be summarized very simply as the suggestion that the emergence of non-Euclidean geometries after Kant demonstrated that there are not universal properties of space *as* space describable in any systematic investigation of spatial relations as there are now divergent descriptions of the character of geometry.[39] At this point it is useful to address this question as the argument that there are competing ways of describing necessary features of space has much more bite as a criticism of Kant's philosophy of mathematics than references to axiomatization of arithmetic. The reason for this is that it is clearly central to Kant's justification of the axioms that the geometry he has described is one that the features of empirical space can be said to demonstrate.

There are ways of stating this objection to Kant's view of geometry that will decidedly not work. For example one could argue that the mere *conceivability* of other geometries than the Euclidean removes the connection between geometry and experience.[40] This is a bad objection, as Kant nowhere denies that it is conceivable that space could have different properties than are stated in such propositions as a straight line always being the shortest between two points. In his earliest publication, *Thoughts on the True Estimation of Living Forces*, Kant even set out this conceivability himself and even in the

Critique is quite clear that there is no *logical* impossibility in the notion of the axioms of Euclidean thought being contradicted (A220/B268). So the real objection should not be made on these grounds and since this is so it also follows that Kant would have no reason in principle to think of non-Euclidean geometries as having inconsistent elements.

The second line of objection to Kant's position is more promising in referring to the distinction between pure and applied geometry. The way this distinction has been viewed since non-Euclidean geometries have been formulated is in terms of pure geometry being a logical theory that does not describe space and applied geometry being something that does describe space but whose truth is contingent and not necessary. Since Kant's view of geometry does not fit either of these pictures he not only does not have this distinction but could not recognize it and hence, as Guyer pertinently puts it, simply by "fiat" declares that one of the systems of geometry applies to space due to its contingent characteristics of being codified.[41] Whilst the notion of "pure" geometry on this construal can be given variant interpretations it is clear that this picture will allow for a number of different geometrical systems and gives no cardinal rationale for priority of any given one.[42] The notion of "applied" geometry by contrast would involve an interpretation of what is being described as "straight" when we make the statement concerning the shortest line and would, in aligning such "straightness" with an empirical quality, reveal the statement concerning it not to be necessary but simply contingently applicable under certain conditions.[43]

The formulation of this contemporary disjunction would naturally prevent any contemporary disciplines that are described by it from fitting the role that Kant takes geometry to have and this is itself generally taken to be fatal to his treatment.[44] However, Stephen Barker's response to the dilemma set by the distinction between "pure" and "applied" geometry has more force in stating that the notion of the latter only demonstrates contingent application of the formulas of Euclidean geometry on certain assumptions concerning what it describes. Thus the notion of "straightness" is for example given an empirical correlate *and then this correlate is shown to be only occasionally applicable.* However, this simply begs the question as to what the correlate of the notion of "straightness" consists in. If "straightness" is a constant account of brevity of distance then to find that certain apparent correlates of it only occasionally so correlate would seem to indicate that these correlates are not what they have been said to be.

The notion of "straightness" hence first requires definition but if it simply is taken to be that which does always describe distance in the way stated then it has to be shown whether or not there is *anything* capable of so doing and modern critics have not shown that nothing could fill this role.[45] Without such a demonstration it has to remain at least open whether Kant is right about the nature of empirical space conforming to what he has described as the properties of pure intuitions.

However the argument from incongruent counterparts goes further than this. Since it is the case that it is not just "straightness" that requires definition for the distinction between pure and applied geometries to make sense but also notions of direction as described in terms of "right" and "left" the defender of the contemporary conception is in a position similar to that of the Leibnizian view attacked in the 1768 essay. The upholder of the contemporary view needs to account for the nature of space as given to us as including differences such as that between "right" and "left" that belong clearly to a three-dimensional view of space and whose difference is not deductively described according to patterns of concepts. Thus the conception that space as experienced by us conforms to the system of a particular geometry would appear correct in lieu of alternative convincing explanations of our experienced space.[46] The contemporary conceptions of geometry seem to require a different account than has been given by those who use them to attack Kant's view and since the evidence of non-Euclidean geometry *cannot* in itself invalidate Kant's conception and Kantians *can* point to evidence of spatial experience as demonstrating the constructive notion of geometry as in conformity with Euclidean assumptions it does not appear to me correct to think that Kant here simply argues by fiat.

It would be another task to argue that Kant's philosophy of arithmetic should be accepted, a task that would require attention to the contemporary arguments favouring its analyticity. But whilst this project would be of interest it is less necessary to Kant's story about the nature of experience.[47]

The principle of the anticipations of perception

After the treatment of the principle of the axioms Kant turns to providing a principle of anticipations of perception. As with the axioms, so with the anticipations, Kant alters the formulation between the two editions of the *Critique* and, as with the alteration of the principle of the axioms, so with the alteration of the principle of the anticipations it is worth assessing whether there is philosophical substance to this alteration. The formulation of the principle in the first edition is as follows: "The principle which anticipates all perceptions, as such, is as follows: In all appearances sensation, and the *real* which corresponds to it in the object (*realitas phaenomenon*), has an *intensive magnitude*, that is, a degree" (A166). The principle states a universal condition of appearances and in doing so describes the nature of both sensation and that which produces sensations in us, the "objects" of experience. The version of the principle in the second edition of the *Critique* is commendable by its brevity by contrast to that in the first edition stating merely: "In all appearances, the real that is an object of sensation has intensive magnitude, that is, a degree" (B207). Here Kant once again states a universal condition of appearances and attaches this universal condition here to that which is the "object" of sensation which seems to remove the universal condition from the sensation itself and locate it rather only within that which the sensation is *of*. This could either be interpreted to be a dilution of the principle or a reinforcement of its point as applying to the intentional object. It is the second reading of the alteration of the principle that appears to be favoured for example by Heidegger who states the wording of the principle in the first edition suggests a "misconception" namely that "sensation has, first of all, a degree and then in addition the reality which corresponds to it, differing from it in its thingness and standing behind it" whereas it should be stating that "the real has first and properly as *quale* a quantity of degree—and therefore also does sensation".[48] This preference for the second edition wording on Heidegger's part is effectively seconded by Caygill's claim that both principles are attempting to state that it is the "object" of sensation that possesses the intensive magnitude and not thus sensation itself.[49] Guyer concurs with these assessments and his view of the first edition formulation mirrors that of Heidegger.[50] The preference for the second edition formulation is shared by Kemp Smith for whom it points to a "phenomenalist" element of Kant's work whilst Paton alone argues that there is only the advantage of brevity to commend the second edition formula.[51] The general tendency of commentators who have addressed the principle is hence to favour the second edition formulation, a verdict we will assess *after* we have looked at the nature of the proof of the principle as the principle as stated includes a number of terms that require treatment for it be understood, treatment given in the proof of it.

The argument for the principle of the anticipations

The section on the anticipations of perception is one of the least discussed in the whole *Critique* despite the fact that those commentators who devote attention to it are generally disposed to viewing it as central to the argument about the nature of experience.[52] It is particularly strange that the treatment of the principle of the axioms should have attracted much more philosophical attention than the principle of the anticipations when Kant himself spends much more time treating the latter than the former. Since the anticipations also concern *perception* it would be reasonable to assume that we will discover more about the nature of experience from it than from the discussion of the principle of the axioms. Kant described perception at B160 as "empirical conscious-ness of the intuition" and the beginning of the second edition proof of the principle of the anticipations also describes perception as "empirical consciousness". Hence the discussion of the anticipations will lead to a greater degree of clarity concerning the relationship between pure and empirical intuitions.

The formulations of the principle in both editions also make clear that we are dealing here, as we would expect from the fact that it concerns empirical intuition, with appearances. This enables Kant to make clear that he is moving from the treatment of the "form" of sensitive cognition as the Dissertation put it to the "matter" of it. Appearances are here being directly considered as including such "matter" which is here understood in the most basic sense as "the consciousness that the subject is affected" (B207). This consciousness of affection is what is most generally at work in awareness of relationship to an object and this points to the fact that it is this consciousness that Kant is analysing in the treatment of the principle of the anticipations. The nature of consciousness of affection is described summarily as being whatever exercises "a degree of influence" on cognition (B208). If there is any type of sensation given of anything then this "degree of influence" has to be stated to be recognized but the important point that emerges from this is that this degree is met with *even prior to an "object" being given* as it occurs already in sensation alone. Kant is clear about this point stating that "sensation is not in itself an objective representation" (B208) and does *not* include the intuitions of space and time (B208 and compare Ak. 4: 306). This startling statement makes clear the importance of attending to this section of the *Critique*.

The claim of the principle of the anticipations is hence uncovered as requiring that *quale* are taken to have the complexity that is termed "degree" even though there is within their reception no intuition of space and time. "Corresponding to this intensity of sensation, an *intensive magnitude*, that is, a degree of influence on the sense... must be ascribed to all objects of perception, in so far as the perception contains sensation" (B208). The fact that Kant makes this claim in the context of the second edition proof of the principle of the anticipations suggests that Heidegger's reasons for favouring this version of the principle do not reflect the nature of what the principle itself involves. Heidegger's argument in favour of the second edition version of the principle turned, it will be recalled, precisely on the suggestion that this formulation was taken to state that intensive magnitude first of all belonged to the "real object" and only secondarily to the sensation so that the *quale* being treated was not thought of on his model as belonging to the sensation itself. This puts Heidegger's reading directly at odds with that of Kemp Smith who clearly aligns the proof of the second edition principle with the first edition formulation of the principle as giving a "phenomalist" orientation to the section in terms of precisely suggesting that the *quale* belongs to sensation itself primarily.[53]

In our description of *quale* in Chapter 2 we demonstrated at length that the notion of the most fleeting sensation does have to be taken to have precisely the degree of structural complexity that seems to be being here suggested. This has not prevented the text of this section of the *Critique* from being approached in such a manner as to involve denial that it can be stating a doctrine of this sort and reasons for this denial will subsequently be addressed but can be readily summarized in Kemp Smith's reference to the notion of "phenomenalism". Since phenomenalism as a doctrine about the nature of perception suggests that what is experienced is not "objects" at all but only sense-data it would appear that if Kant is suggesting that the "real" is that which is sensible then he is committing himself to this view, a view that would be at variance with the stated aim of the *Critique* to justify the notion that we are, in experience, engaged with objects. Hence the resistance to the conception we are here suggesting can be seen to have the creditable motive of both rescuing the central point of the *Critique* and saving Kant from an egregious self-contradiction in the account of the principle of the anticipations.

Despite these creditable motivations it is clear that Kant is here stating that because sensation does not include intuitions of time and space and thus that the "matter" of intuition has not got the form of it as an ingredient part, it has a specific quantity of its own that has to be distinguished from the extensive quantity that does belong to intuition as demonstrated in the principle of the axioms. The "matter" of sensation is here stated to be the means whereby something existing in time and space is represented and this "means" is by reference to affection and least this be thought in contradiction with the opening statements of the Aesthetic concerning immediacy it is worth pointing to Kant's statement shortly after the reference to immediacy in which he writes: "Objects are *given* to us by means of sensibility, and it alone yields us *intuitions*" (A19/B33). If sensibility *yields us intuitions* then the understanding of sensibility is requisite for the nature of "objects" to be understood. That this is the view of the *Critique* is what I will seek now to show in assessing the argument for the principle of the anticipations and in the process seek to demonstrate that this does not lead, as critics of such an emphasis have generally supposed, to phenomenalism.

In treating sensation Kant reverts to the point we developed initially in Chapter 2 as one of the rationales for the notion of *quale*, which is the statement in the A-Deduction that apprehension relates to what Henrich described as "data-sensualism". Sensation is taken in the account of the synthesis of apprehension in the A-Deduction to be first of all something given only in an instant and it is that that Kant reprises in the account of the principle of the anticipations (A167/ B209). It is due to the fact that sensation "occupies only an instant" that Kant can separate apprehension of it from the principle of the axioms as the occupation of an instant is something distinct from successive synthesis and thus does not involve an *extensive* magnitude. Kant now makes the connection between sensation and empirical intuition vivid through his schematization of the notion of reality stating that in empirical intuition the real is that which corresponds to sensation and thus is, in the case of empirical intuition, that which occupies only an instant.[54] What was also stated in the account of apprehension in the A-Deduction is that what occupies only an instant cannot be apprehended in that moment except as a unity and this fact of being only apprehended as a unity is, in the treatment of the proof of the principle of the anticipations, taken to reveal a particular form of magnitude. A magnitude that is given only as unity but which can be comprehended as having degrees of affect is an *intensive* magnitude. The reason for describing magnitudes at all here is stated by Kant in the following manner:

> Every sensation . . . is capable of diminution, so that it can decrease and gradually vanish. Between reality in the [field of] appearance

and negation there is therefore a continuity of many possible intermediate sensations, the difference between any two of which is always smaller than the difference between the given sensation and zero or complete negation. In other words, the real in the [field of] appearance has always a magnitude. But since its apprehension by means of mere sensation takes place in an instant and not through successive synthesis of different sensations, and therefore does not proceed from parts to the whole, the magnitude is to be met with only in the apprehension. (A168/B210)

A universal condition of sensations is that since they have degrees they can be experienced more or less intensively. So a pain, to take a classic example, can be sharp or dull, the feel of something be smooth or rough, the sound of something loud or quiet. This degree of being given involves a notion of comparison even though the particular in question may be given only in the most fleeting manner and this comparison involved as part of the reception of the affect in question suggests the complexity of the *quale* that we spent such time treating in Chapter 2. The complexity is here shown to have reference to magnitude as the ability to make the comparisons set out here is the ability to compare degrees of intensity. This comparison and hence measurement is thus freed from the requirement that what is being measured be enduring and what can be measured in such a manner is precisely what Kant means by "degree" (A169/B210).

If all sensations possess a degree this is what enables them to be measured, even if the degree in question is almost at vanishing point.[55] Therefore it follows that sensation cannot as such melt into nothingness without experience itself ceasing entirely so we can now say that if there are sensations then it cannot be true of them that they could be completely simple or incapable of being measured and so they are not monadic properties. If they cannot be described in such a manner but must always have complexity then the relationship we have to them must be one of continuity of connection between the different sensations being experienced. Thus although the *particular* sensation can be apprehended separately from the intuition of time the *relationship* between the sensations that has to be posited for anyone of them to be received as the complex "object" that it *is* points to the need for continuity between each moment of receptivity. Such continuity has, as we cannot fail to be aware after the demonstrations of the Aesthetic and, indeed, the argument of the *Critique* up to this point, one way of being described and this is by reference to the forms of intuition. The forms of intuition are, as Kant now puts it in a re-play of the point from the Aesthetic about infinite givenness, *quanta continua* (A169/B211). Since neither space nor time can be decomposed into anything else it is not possible to decompose them into sensations. This connection of the matter of intuition to its form hence does not require the form to be given as *ingredient perception* of any particular sensibilia but rather to be that which enables the sensibilia to come together for us in terms of the complexity that requires their continuity.

If perception requires as its condition that there is some form of degree of affection being given then it is only by means of this that there is the receipt of "objects" if what we mean by "objects" is the understanding that there is something given before us and independently of us. Thus the cognition of "objects" is dependent on the notion of "reality" where the latter is a way of speaking of the filling of time by *quale*. On these grounds Kant also shows that we could therefore never have *experience* of an empty space even though the conceivability of such a thing helped in the argument of the Aesthetic to show that the correlate of "substance" in experience is in fact space. This anti-Newtonian conclusion is a product of the transcendental demonstration and points to the rationale for challenging the assumption of empty space as part of any doctrine of pure natural science (A173–5/B214–16).

What the argument for the principle of the anticipations presents is the schematization of quality demonstrating thereby what the notion of reality refers to when applied to experience. Whilst the quality of given sensations is not capable of *a priori* demonstration in the case of such matters as sweetness or sourness, sharpness or brittleness, nonetheless there is a general statement that can be made about all sensation and the real that it presents to us which is that it cannot be otherwise given than as having a degree and this provides us with the single statement about quality that describes it in a quantitative manner (A176/B218).

Different approaches to the principle of the anticipations

The reading provided here of the argument for the principle of the anticipations is at variance with others that have been given and not merely by those who treat this section of the *Critique* dismissively. Heidegger for example was cited as indicating a problem with the formulation of the principle of the anticipations in the first edition of the *Critique*. The difference in wording between the two formulations can now be revisited. The first edition formulation suggests that sensation always has a degree and therefore the "objects" that are producing in us the affections we are feeling must always have them. This is a reasonable presentation of a deduction but does have the drawback of making the reference to the object appear to be the product of an inference and thus tilt towards a Cartesian notion of the existence of the world being something that is inferred. That Kant is not committed to this view is precisely the burden of the Refutation of Idealism. However, at this stage of the *Critique*, Kant cannot be taken to have established yet that there are "objects" separately from the sensation. What Kant has shown up to this point is that there can be no thought which is not that of objects precisely as phenomenology would lead one to suppose but what he wishes to show and which is not the province of phenomenology is that necessary "objectivity" of thought is correlated in experience with the notion of *empirical* objects so that experience is a whole in which *intentional objects and the conditions of sensibility are correlated into the notion of empirical objects*.

The alteration in the formulation of the principle of the anticipations removes the reference to "correspondence" that the first edition formulation inserts between the sensation and its "object" in order to move towards a straight statement about the real *as* an object of sensation. Whilst Heidegger is right to note that the "object" is not intended by Kant to be something distinct from the sensation in terms of what is deduced concerning it there is nonetheless a clear difference between a sensation of the sweetness of the ice cream and the ice cream "itself" so that if the continuity of sensational awareness of the sweetness belongs within the unity of experience so also does the "object" that produces it and yet it is also the case that what we have first of all demonstrated is not a quality of "objects" as such but rather of what must be given to the matter of any one of them in general. This was, in my view, the rationale for the distinction between "sensation" and its "object" in the first edition formulation.

Robert Paul Wolff, by contrast, argues that since it has been demonstrated that intensive quantity is a quantity that is not generated by successive synthesis then it is not clear how the discussion of it fits into the general story about transcendental synthesis, the very story on which our account of the *Critique* has been based.[56] Kant refers in the treatment of intensive quantities to a synthesis however which is that involved in generating "the magnitude of a sensation" (A166/B208). What is meant by this synthesis? I take it what this means is that for consciousness of awareness of anything to be given is for there to be the relationship termed "affection" and that affection presupposes connection between consciousness and the quality of the "object". For such connection to take place however requires that the "object" be sensed in terms of the degrees we have noted to be their condition. For degrees to be ascribed to the fleeting sensation is for them to have the complexity of connection we have witnessed to be their due. Such complexity requires that the matter of sensation have *determination* through the concepts of reflection, as these concepts are the basis of comparison taking place. The connection of the sensation to the concepts of reflection is what enables qualities to be comparable such that they can be assessed according to a level of homogeneity that makes them equivalents. However not only is this the case but since we discover in the course of the exposition of the principle of the anticipations that the result of the principle is that sensations hence have to be understood continuously this connection of them to the conditions of continuity renders them subsequently part of the transcendental synthesis of imagination even though they also in a sense provoke the operation of this synthesis. As Paton writes: "The transcendental synthesis of imagination by which we construct our phenomenal world in space and time is not merely a synthesis of empty times and spaces, but a filling of time and space with what is given to us in sensation, or a synthesis of sensation with time and space."[57]

A different question about the nature of the argument for the principle of the anticipations has been stated by Gordon Nagel who challenges Kemp Smith's translation of parts of this section of the *Critique*.[58] The central point at which Nagel challenges Kemp Smith is at A168/B210 where Kemp Smith follows Wille in reading *welche aber nur in der Apprehension* for *welche aber nicht in der Apprehension* hence producing the sentence: "apprehension by means of mere sensation takes place in an instant and not through successive synthesis of different sensations, and therefore does not proceed from the parts, the magnitude is to be with *only in* the apprehension" (my emphasis). If Wille's emendation were not followed by Kemp Smith the sentence would instead move from the standard point about the mereological succession of presentation as given in the treatment of the principle of the axioms to stating that the magnitude is *not* to be met with in the apprehension. The rationale for challenging the emendation of Kemp Smith and Wille here is made as follows by Nagel:

> It is because intensive magnitude is not to be met with in apprehension that it requires proof and explanation. It is the reason too that the argument for the principle of intensive magnitude requires us to

consider the mind's own contribution in the act of apprehension; for, if we did sense degrees of intensity, no account would need to be taken by the mind of its own capacity to respond to the effects of things to varying degrees.[59]

The first argument of this citation is weak as on this basis it could be claimed that there is no need to "prove" anything that is given is as it appears to be. The second point that we do not "sense" the degree indicates that Nagel views the inclusion of the degree within the apprehension to be equivalent to taking it to be part of the "sense". This rests on a misunderstanding, one worth attending to in order to further account for Kant's proof of this principle. Apprehension was clearly described in the A-Deduction as involving a synthesis and the discussion of the principle of the anticipations in a sense is a way of showing the nature of this synthesis so to state that the magnitude was "only" in the apprehension would be to state it belonged not to the "sense" as Nagel thinks but rather to the way in which the "sense" is taken up by the act of cognition. This further points to the question as to what the demonstration of the principle of the anticipations really means by "sensation". Paton addressed this question arguing that by this term what Kant means to refer to is the "sensum" considered as a modification of the cognitive act.[60]

Paton's reading seems to me right on this point but if that is what Kant means by "sensation" that it cannot be defined simply as something occurring to a sense but also involves a reference of this sense to the general nature of cognition itself and if it did not we would not have, as Wolff thinks we have not, a reference to synthesis at all. Therefore to claim that the magnitude is "in" the apprehension is as much as to say that it belongs within the subjective state. This prompts a different possible challenge to the alteration of the text by Wille and Kemp Smith to the effect that on those grounds Kant becomes committed not, as Kemp Smith himself feared, to phenomenalism but rather to "subjectivism" or the view that the affection has no referent outside the subject at all. But whilst the notion of "subjectivism" would have difficulties being accepted as a correct description of a number of Kant's views this is hardly the case here. The degree of sweetness of the ice cream can and does differ between distinct recipients as does the view of a texture as smooth or rough simply because such qualities cannot be anticipated in this respect *a priori*. It is only the fact of the degree in general that can be given *a priori* and this is irrespective of what the degree is taken as being and hence it is a condition of the experience of any object of sensibility that it has to have such a degree but, and this is the point of transcendental idealism, not necessarily the condition of objects *as such* and this is why there is a good sense to the emendation of Kemp Smith and Wille. Nagel is right to stress that the point of the principle is to show how we can make comparisons such as we do in understanding a sound to be loud and this is the ground of his complaint against finding the comparison or the specific degree *in the apprehension* but this does not mean that the condition of relating to a degree *as such* is not precisely found "only" in the apprehension. If, as our reading has suggested, it is sensation itself that is demonstrated to have the complexity of *quale* for us as we relate to sensation by means of synthesis then there is no need to challenge here the emendation of Kant's text by Kemp Smith and Wille.

A last objection to be considered is stated by Paul Guyer who argues that the principle of continuity is only a potential element of awareness of *quale* and, in any case, merely empirical and not *a priori*.[61] Both these points seem to me faulty. The problem with the first is that Kant's demonstration of continuity is to the effect that absence of sensation would entail that there was nothing at all given but for nothing at all to be given would ensure that there was no experience or, what is tantamount to the same thing, only forms would exist and no matter! The demonstration that there always is some *quale* given is the point of the argument that any *quale* has a degree. If any *quale* that is given has a degree there can be no experience of it without affection and this affection cannot cease without experience being at an end so to state that the continuity of sensibilia is only potential is false. The argument to the effect that the degree of continuity always being given, even with regard to the smallest degrees of affection imaginable is merely empirical, is false as this suggests that it is purely contingent.

The mathematical principles reviewed

The result of the treatment of the mathematical principles is that appearances can be shown to be have a formal condition in terms of being extensive quantities as there is no intuition which is not an extensive quantity and also intensive quantities as even prior to the forms being given any degree of attention the merest notion of sensation has to include the complexity we have discovered to characterize that of a *quale*. The description of the principle of the anticipations of perception has further justified the conclusions derived from the consideration of a hypothesis of "data-sensualism" in Chapter 2 and located the ground for the discussion there having the conclusion it did in terms not of a deduction strategy as was there assayed but rather in terms of a schematization of the category of quality.

To have a quantitative view of quality is to have given a principle which Kant rightly understands to be particularly unusual as it involves a description not of a formal principle but of a *material* one.[62] The tendency to relate this to Kant's dynamical theory fails however to deal with the division between mathematical and dynamical principles as only the latter deal with the nature of existent things, the former describing merely the relationship to such things as Kant states in introducing the division at A160/B199. Paul Guyer however objects to this division on the grounds that this statement refers to "the mere *intuition* of an appearance in general" as the concern of the mathematical principles whilst the principle of the anticipations explicitly deals instead with the matter of appearances.[63] However whilst the principle of the anticipations *is* a formulation about the *matter*, not the *form* of appearances and hence is something separate from the considerations of intuition, what the argument for the principle shows is that since it requires synthesis to generate relation to sensation that such synthesis effectively generates the forms of intuition as the means by which the continuity of sensation must be given. It hence touches on the means by which the form of intuition connects to its matter in empirical intuition. The suggestion Guyer makes that the statement of the principle requires or at least suggests the "existence" of the object of sensation fails to attend to the fact that what Kant means in denying connection to "existence" in the case of the mathematical principles is a dependence of them on something being given as existing. In this sense the principles can be read hypothetically, that is, as stating that *if* there is sensation *then* the following must be the case for it.

It is hence to analysis of the arguments for the principles of the Analogies of Experience that we now need to turn, the analogies whose nature was promised as early as the Transcendental Aesthetic (A33/B50) and which has been at the centre of the repeated designations of time by means of a line. It is hence with the dynamical principles that we will finally uncover the connection of the synthesis of intuitions with pure concepts that describes the nature of law-governed experience.

7

Substance, Causality and Community

In Chapter 6 I treated the mathematical principles to both a genetic consideration, showing how Kant arrived at them from a treatment of his pre-Critical works, and to a structural justification connecting them to the prior discussion of intuition in the Aesthetic. In this chapter I will treat the dynamical principles in both these respects, showing how they connect to Kant's discussions of dynamical questions in his "pre-Critical" writings and also how the arguments of the Analogies build on the discussions of the transcendental synthesis of imagination in the Transcendental Deduction and the chapter on schematism.

Substance, succession and co-existence in the *New Elucidation*

In 1755 Kant submitted as part of the qualification for the position of *Privatdozent* a writing that promised to provide a "new elucidation" of the first principles of metaphysical cognition. The statement of purpose that precedes the work carefully states the independence of the young thinker. Kant states that in the work he will critically assess the view that the principle of contradiction is the prime standard of truth as well as attending to an improvement of both the formulation of the principle of sufficient reason and its proof. Finally, he will also develop some subsidiary principles of metaphysics. The first section of the work in which Kant argues that the principle of contradiction is not the first principle of truth is connected to an overall argument to the effect that there is in fact *no* single principle of truth (Ak. 1: 388). The argument here foreshadows the distinction in *Negative Magnitudes* between real and logical opposition stating that affirmative truths and negative truths are different from each other and rest upon distinct principles just as the later work presents an argument for stating that only equivalent quantities can produce a sum.

The second section of the work is where Kant begins the discussion that is important for our purposes as here he treats the principle of sufficient reason, a principle he re-describes as a principle of determining ground. The reason for the re-description of the principle is connected to Kant's discussion of it as part of an account of truth. The opening of the second section is with a proposition that connects determination to predication and effectively states that to posit something is to exclude something that is opposed to that posited. Kant then states that determination of a subject, in respect of any predicates, is provision of a ground for the subject. On the one hand there is an "antecedently determining ground" that provides a concept which precedes that which it determines whilst, on the other hand, there is a consequentially determining ground which follows from what has been determined. The difference between the two is that the former is ontological whilst the latter is epistemological (Ak. 1: 392).[1] In giving a justification of his distinction Kant argues that the consequentially determining ground can in many cases be identified simply with experience (Ak. 1: 392) whilst the antecedently determining ground "converts things which are indeterminate into things which are determinate" (Ak. 1: 392) and is the *real* source of truth, not the formal principles that were treated in the first section of the work. This *real* source is one that does not simply set out what follows from something being the case but shows *why* it is the case. However the reference to such a *why* is not to be included in the statement of the principle of the ground as it presupposes the notion of ground so the key is simply to think of the antecedently determining ground as that which converts the indeterminate into something determinate whilst in so doing describing for us the necessity of its being as it is. The reason for Kant's redefining the principle as one of determining ground is given superficially in his treatise as based on Crusius' argument that the notion of sufficient reason involves an assumption as to what *is* sufficient. The real reason for Kant's alteration of formula is surely that the consideration of determination shows the treatment to be one that connects truth to real existence and is thus part of an understanding of predication, something not evidently true of the principle of sufficient reason.

In specifying the connection of this principle to the understanding of existence Kant argues that the ground of something cannot lie in the thing itself as where it to do so it would violate a key element of the understanding of causality, namely that it is temporally marked.

As Kant puts it: "the concept of a cause is by nature prior to the concept of that which is caused" so if the thing were to be its own cause then "it would follow that the same thing would be simultaneously both earlier and later than itself" (Ak. 1: 394). This connection of causality to succession, it is important to note, is part of the proof of Proposition VI of the work. This is important for understanding the key propositions concerning which there has been recent philosophical discussion, namely the Principles of Succession and Co-existence, which are propositions XII and XIII and are not treated until the third section of the work. From the point that the conditions of temporal succession rule out the view that something could be its own cause, Kant points out that if therefore there exists a necessary being the proof of it cannot be based on an understanding of grounds, but must instead reside in the conditions of thought.

The conditions of thought that are here being referred to are the conditions under which anything is possible although, given our account of the argument of the Transcendental Deduction, it is important to point out that the concept of possibility is already here conceived of by Kant as the product of comparison (Ak. 1: 395).[2] The central point of this contention is to state that God is "identical with possibility" (Ak. 1: 396) an identification which already connects the possibility of things with a statement about necessary conditions albeit here with the necessary conditions taken to be ones that rely upon a consideration of super-essentiality. The argument to the effect that the Supreme Being is not included within the pattern of determining grounds enables this being to provide a basis for these grounds. Kant subsequently gives a proof for why all contingent things require such determining grounds, a proof that turns on his account of determination as essential to the positing of a thing as without such determination there would be no way of stating what the thing was. Hence to describe something is to describe its *differentia* from other things and this positing of the thing leads to the question concerning why it is the thing it is and not otherwise, a problem that does not arise for God due to the identification of God with possibility.

The description of contingent existences as all requiring determining grounds already raises questions about the connection between such grounds and the freedom of the will (Ak. 1: 398–406) hence pointing in the direction of the consideration of the Third Antinomy which arises precisely on the grounds of the Second Analogy being taken to hold.[3] However, more important for the problems we are treating here is Kant's discussion of the corollaries from the principle of determining ground in Proposition X of the work. The first corollary is that there is nothing in what is grounded which was not in the ground itself. Kant immediately detaches this statement from any suggestion that the divine nature includes within itself the limits that are part of all things created, which illustrates that this is not a mathematical point but a dynamical one. In other terms, if something contains a *power*, it does so by virtue of the power that has constituted it having transmitted this to it. The second corollary is a negative form of the first stating that if two things have nothing in common one cannot be the ground of the other. The importance of this point is that if there is reason to think that two things do stand in relation of grounded to ground then there must be something that they share, even if this is not manifest. The third corollary is that there is no more in that which is grounded than in the ground and the key point that emerges from this third corollary is that the "quantity of absolute reality in the world does not change *naturally*, neither increasing nor decreasing" (Ak. 1: 407), a statement that is connected to the second edition formulation of the Second Analogy. The importance of this point that is stated as an "implication" of the third corollary is that whatever is truly real does not alter *in quantity* and it is the fact that it is the true reality that is being referred to here that is important as this would have to underlie the changes in that which is given to us in appearances.[4]

The "elucidation" of this implication is a description of the nature of forces. Kant here argues for the interaction of repulsive and attractive forces and the constancy of quantity between them stating that "the sum total of the forces is calculated from the effects which operate in conjunction with each other and are thus viewed in general as a totality" (Ak. 1: 407). The explanation of this is that the formal element "which consists in the combination of concepts" changes in a variety of ways whilst the material element remains the same so that "It follows that all the reality to be found in the forces inherent in the phenomenon of motion is equal to that which already inheres in the body when it is at rest" (Ak. 1: 408). This remarkable argument from the nature of forces treats the appearances of motion as dependent upon constancy of what the forces are *expressive* of.

In the third section of the work Kant turns to a description of the two principles of metaphysical cognition on the basis of the treatment of sufficient reason in the second section. The first of these is the Principle of Succession. It is stated as Proposition XII: "No change can happen to substances except in so far as they are connected with other substances; their reciprocal dependency on each other determines their reciprocal changes of state" (Ak. 1: 410). Here Kant turns to connecting the understanding of determination to the nature of the real, that is, to substances, suggesting that if there is change in them it can only occur due to their action on each other. The importance of this principle is that it requires a repudiation of Leibniz's conception that substances are isolated from each other on the ground that such separation of substances would not permit even internal change to take place.[5] The basis of the claim that the isolation of substances would ensure the impossibility of change is developed easily from Kant's earlier treatment of determination as he can now state that for change to take place requires the determination of a ground that is distinct from that which is grounded. If all principles of a substance are internal to it then these principles exclude their opposite and thus do not permit the arrival of new states (Ak. 1: 410). The key rationale for this argument is however one that again brings out the temporal conditions of change just as occurred when Kant ruled out the concept of a self-caused being. In this case he states that "since change is the succession of determinations, that is to say, since a change occurs when a determination comes into being *which was not previously present*, and the being is thus determined to the opposite of a certain determination which belongs to it, it follows that the change cannot take place by means of those factors which are to be found within the substance" (Ak. 1: 411, my emphasis).

The argument to the effect that change requires a principle *external* to that which is changed emerges from an understanding of change as a temporal alteration of determinations. A determination emerges that did not previously manifest itself and this must point to something external to that which is changed as a purely isolated substance would have no internal grounds for alteration without its internal principles being simply self-contradictory (Ak. 1: 411). This requirement for the temporal notion of change to point to something external to that which is changed suggests an elementary connection between temporality and spatiality. Kant derives from his principle an argument against "idealism" meaning by this here what he will subsequently term "problematic" idealism stating that since the soul changes and it cannot do so due to internal principles alone it must be in reciprocal connection with something beyond itself and so the existence of things beyond it is not a mere probability. On the grounds that the existence of things external to the soul is thus shown to be required for the soul to change Kant repudiates pre-established harmony (Ak. 1: 412).

This attack on pre-established harmony is one that we will need to re-examine after treating the other major principle that Kant sets out in the third section of the *New Elucidation*. This is the Principle of Co-Existence, Proposition XIII of the work which is stated as follows: "Finite substances do not, in virtue of their existence alone, stand in a relationship with each other, nor are they linked together by any interaction at all, except in so far as the common principle of their existence, namely the divine understanding, maintains them in a state of harmony in their reciprocal relations" (Ak. 1: 412–13). This principle follows from the principle of succession in its first part as this gave grounds for denying that there could be connection simply by virtue of distinct things *existing*. But what we found to be a corollary of that principle was that without the existence of things beyond any given substance that substance would have no means of alteration. The principle of connection between substances there appeared to one of spatio-temporal connection but Kant here adds a reference to the "common principle" of the different substances as being the "divine understanding".

For reasons we described in Chapter 6 *relations* are not in themselves necessary for substances as they are determinations that depend on that which is substantial. So the relations of space and time in themselves will be insufficient for Kant at this point to bring together substances and hence there needs to be a principle that connects the substances together that is more than a simple relational conception. This is why Kant needs to bring in reference to God as a principle of the communality of causes but this principle also requires reference to what Kant calls a "schema" of the divine understanding by means of which it conceives the existence of substances as correlated with each other. This "schema" is one whereby the substances are brought into reciprocal connection *in their origin*. On the basis of this notion Kant safeguards the substances from having to manifest spatial position whilst allowing them to interact as the freedom from the former is part of their independence of determination by relations whilst the latter is what we have found to be necessary for change to occur. The nature of this proof allows Kant to argue that space is constituted by the interconnection of substances and to derive attraction and repulsion from it (Ak. 1: 415) but since the link between substances is due to the schema of the divine intelligence the effect of one on another cannot be by means of physical influx but must be according to a principle of harmony after all. Kant distinguishes this principle of harmony from the Leibnizian pre-established harmony on the grounds that his harmony is one of substantial dependence not substantial agreement as the divine act that brings them into being also establishes their interaction. This effectively means however that Kant has to abolish the distinction between internal and external principles of substance on which his entire demonstration has been built as he admits in conclusion: "one is equally justified both in saying that external changes may be produced in this way by efficient causes, and also in saying that the changes which occur within the substances are ascribed to an internal force of the substance" (Ak. 1: 415).

Assessments of the argument of the *New Elucidation*

The argument of the *New Elucidation* is worth discussion for three separate reasons, the first of which is the intrinsic interest of its argument, the second its connection with the subsequent Critical treatment of the connections between succession, co-existence and causality and the third its reception in contemporary philosophical debate. The most important element of this latter reason is provided in Rae Langton's innovative interpretation of the *New Elucidation*. The first element of this interpretation is that if the Principle of Succession indicates that change requires the existence of things distinct from what is changed this shows that what is changed has to be *receptive* in order to be changed (Langton, 1998, p. 106). The Principle of Succession alone does not show the means of such receptivity since that is revealed in the Principle of Co-Existence but it does show that this receptivity must be part of the nature of substance. The element of Langton's interpretation of the *New Elucidation* that has been more controversial is her view of the way that Kant in this work has described the relationship between relational properties of substances and their intrinsic properties. Langton argues that Kant has broken from Leibniz here in denying that relational properties of substances are dependent upon their intrinsic properties. As Langton is aware, other commentators on the *New Elucidation* have not been convinced that this is the outcome of its demonstrations. Michael Friedman, for example, whilst taking it that Kant's deduction of a universal principle of connection between substances in the Principle of Co-Existence leads to the view that interaction is a distinct reality from that of substances nonetheless states that space is, in this work, "*derivative* from or constituted by the underlying non-spatial reality of simple substances".[6] Guyer, even more strongly, takes the argument of the *New Elucidation* to require the assumption that relations are not real.[7]

Given these verdicts what persuades Langton of the view that Kant has, in the *New Elucidation*, provided grounds for denying that relational properties are reducible to substantial ones? Langton provides two distinct arguments that she generates from consideration of the *New Elucidation* and, whilst only one of the arguments given really supports the conclusion she wishes to suggest is Kant's, both are worth looking at for the insight they provide into questions about the nature of properties. Langton argues for a distinction between two kinds of relational properties, those she describes as "ordinary" relational properties and others she terms "dispositional" relational properties. An example of the former is that if John is warm then there is something that is warming him. An example of the latter however would be provided in stating that John is *warmable* which only requires that he could be warmed under the right conditions.

Neither type of property can be reduced to the internal properties of a substance, as they are, according to Langton, "existentially committed" properties. But whilst Langton takes this to point against *unilateral* reducibility of ordinary properties she states that it does not preclude *bilateral reducibility* as when the property of taller-than can be shown to merely supervene on the existence of two distinct existents. But I cannot see this argument is relevant to the discussion of the Principle of Co-Existence. The attribute of *taller-than* involves spatial measurement and for it to be applied to substances would be for substances to be at least correlative to phenomenal appearances and Langton gives no argument as to why Kant should have thought this at the time of writing the *New Elucidation* and Friedman has provided a case against it. A second attempt at reconstructing this line of argument is given by Langton in the following formulation: "for any given set of things, the relational properties of those things are not reducible to the intrinsic properties of those things, considered distributively; or, for any given set of things, the relational properties of those things are not reducible to the intrinsic properties of those things, considered collectively" (Langton, 1998, pp. 114–15). This argument is one that Langton confesses she cannot accept, as it would require a conflation between unilateral and bilateral reducibility. So this would not be Kant's argument on her view or, if it is, would again not rule out bilateral reducibility.

These considerations of the versions of the first argument are at some remove from the *New Elucidation* in any case as in this text Kant is concerned with *causal* properties. Regardless of whether causal properties are thought to be "ordinary" or "dispositional" properties they are relational properties that require specifications about interaction of forces. Langton's second view of the argument is based on taking Kant's

concentration on causal relations seriously as now she asks whether God could have created substances with the same intrinsic properties but with different dynamical ones stating that Kant's argument is to the affirmative and will be so whether substances are considered distributively or collectively and on this basis that he argues against reducibility of causal relations to substantial properties (Langton, 1998, pp. 119–20).

This account of Kant's argument provides a plausible reconstruction of its argument but the importance of it remains to be established. Langton takes it that the argument here uncovered is in the background of some key Kantian texts, including the Third Analogy. We will test this argument in due course but it is worth asking whether the argument, even should it be in the background of the Critical texts, is a good one? Lorne Falkenstein for one argues not stating that it rests upon pure stipulative definitions of such things as intrinsic properties.[8] On these grounds Falkenstein takes the argument to be "trivial" and Langton acknowledges, in her reply to Falkenstein, that she in fact expressed a version of this worry herself in her original exposition.[9] The version of this complaint that Langton described concerned the dependence of intrinsicness on modal properties where the two are alleged by her to be circularly co-dependent on her fullest reconstruction of Kant's argument against reducibility of relational properties (Langton, 1998, p. 121, n. 34). There is a case for stating this as Kant in the *New Elucidation* clearly specifies that causal powers are part of the same schema whereby God constitutes the substances in question hence the modality of the type of powers given is connected to the type of creative act that gives us substances at all. Therefore the intrinsic properties of the substances seem here to be integrally connected in their conception to the modal ones with different modal properties giving different notions of substances as such and hence the intrinsic properties would appear to be understood as connected in action with the modal properties. However, Langton also expresses a rationale for taking this conception of harmonious relation between substances to be one that Kant rightfully regards as distinct from the Leibnizian view of pre-established harmony, on the grounds that super-added forces would for Leibniz be *accidentally* connected to substances (Langton, 1998, p. 121). If it does follow that the super-added powers are only accidentally connected to the substances however it should not be the case that the intrinsic properties are defined as being what they are through their relationship to the modal properties the substances happen to possess. Since the intrinsic properties could in principle be connected to an infinite number of distinct modal properties the understanding of intrinsicness is not, as Langton's notion of triviality suggests, "parasitic" upon modal properties. It cannot be as if it were this would be tantamount to treating the possession of the modal properties as definitional for the substances in question and hence treating relational properties as essential for the definition of substances, precisely against Kant's express intention.

The problem with Langton's reconstruction is that the irreducibility of relational properties to substantial ones seems to be understood by her as implying that the substantial properties are dependent upon the relational ones actually possessed. This is why Langton has trouble with Friedman's point that spatial properties are derivative from other properties of substances. Whilst Langton acknowledges that spatial properties of substances may, on the conception of the *New Elucidation*, be dependent on dynamical properties she denies that these latter are dependent upon substantial properties, a denial she takes it to be required by the thesis of irreducibility. It is not the case however that the principle of irreducibility requires the rejection of the notion of dependence of non-substantial properties on substantial ones. According to the tradition within which the young Kant was working a substance is that on which all attributes depend whilst not itself being dependent on anything further except, if the substance is finite, God. The dependence relation here is that the substance could still exist without the possession of the relational properties, something nowhere denied in the *New Elucidation*. Thus, it follows that the relational properties are not in themselves substantial and are therefore *dependent* on the properties that are.

On my view there are good reasons to doubt that space has been clearly shown by Kant in this text to be something "real", a doubt I share here with Guyer. Kant has argued in this piece that the notion of space is super-added by God and this fact of its super-addition whilst ensuring that it is not reducible to the property of substances is also introduced to provide the understanding of the linkage between them. Where there to be one isolated substance it would follow from Kant's argument that it could not change but not that it was not *real* whilst space would have no reality unless substances were given. Thus whilst the argument of the *New Elucidation* is interesting as an early defence of the connection between substances and causality and as a response to Leibniz the notion of harmonious connection is surely one that cannot guarantee an ultimate metaphysical status for space.

What the argument of the *New Elucidation* does show is that change cannot occur for isolated substances. This is the key difference between the metaphysical position given within it and the Leibnizian view that it is responding to and is the ground of the argument that the notion of harmony defended within it is not equivalent to that of *pre-established* harmony. The harmony has to be part of the schema of the divine intelligence that produces the substances in their connection with each other and so has to be part of the nature of the *world* they belong to. Within the world in which substances are set out they have to have the connection they do. The difficulty of the conception of substance in the piece is that whilst the substances are characterized as having primary properties that are not relational that nonetheless the world to which they belong together is one in which the schema of them has to bring them *into* relation so the relation is *real* within the world but still not part of the ultimate primary properties of the substances. Maintaining this nuanced view is difficult for Kant to achieve but without it he will either lapse into the reducibility that Langton sees him as having escaped from or alternatively take relational properties to be primary to substances in themselves which latter would entail that substances were dependent *on* these relations, a view that would not merely produce the circularity that Langton worries about but also entail the impossibility of conceiving of isolated substances, something Kant certainly does not regard as an outcome of his position.

Kant's subsequent pre-Critical treatments of substance and causality

A year after publication of the *New Elucidation* Kant returned, in the *Physical Monadology*, to an account of substance and causality. We described in Chapter 6 the ways in which Kant sought in this work to safeguard the simplicity of substances whilst conceding the infinite divisibility of space, a demonstration that supports the view that in this work Kant does not accept the ultimate reality of spatial properties. The demonstration of the third proposition in this work reprises a Euclidean reason for taking space to be infinitely divisible and the fourth proposition then adds to this the point that since divisibility requires composition space cannot consist of simple parts. Kant proceeds to argue that since this is the case bodies *are* made of such simple parts and hence that the substantial properties of bodies *are not* spatial parts. The reason for this view, as mentioned in Chapter 6, is that space is only "a certain appearance of the external relation of substances".[10]

The argument that the external relation is an "appearance" of the substances maintains the simplicity of the substances despite the divisibility of the space that they are taken to fill. The "filling" of space cannot be an accomplishment of any particular substance since they possess simplicity but must rather be a product of the relations between substances. This is what leads Kant to the view that "the monad fills the space by the sphere of its activity" (Ak. 1: 481) and does so by being impenetrable which latter property prevents any two substances occupying the same space. Impenetrability is subsequently aligned by Kant with repulsive force (Ak. 1: 483) but he adds that if this force were the only force that existed there would be no means for bodies to cohere and hence he adds the conception of attractive force in a demonstration that subsequently turns into a description of the nature of both volume and inertia. The basic point of this discussion is to try to provide a physical interpretation of the forces that monads possess as the forces of attraction and repulsion are Kant's way of re-writing Leibniz's distinction between living and dead forces. By this means Kant maintains, in my view, the argument of the *New Elucidation* that not only spatial properties are a necessary part of the world that the substances in question belong to but also relational properties of substances are dependent upon non-relational ones.[11]

This dependence is still being asserted in the Prize Essay where Kant demonstrates that the ground for thinking of bodies as extended is *not* that they occupy space. The true ground for extension flows rather from impenetrability, the property that must be possessed by substances even though substances are simple (Ak. 2: 287). Despite asserting this point Kant could write in the *Metaphysik Herder* that the conception of a world requires real dependence of substances upon each other (Ak. 28: 44–5) but this follows from our distinction between what belongs to *a world* of necessity and what belongs *to substances* of necessity. Thus, if there is a world, substances must be really dependent upon each other within it *or exist alone*.

In the *Metaphysik Herder* Kant describes the ground of the dependence of substances on one another in the world as a special action of God, like the divine schema of the *New Elucidation*. Here however he presents the harmony of the substances as being pre-established and he explicates this as follows: "*no substance can contain the ground of the accident in the other, if it does not at the same time contain the ground of the substantial power and of the existence of the other*: I cannot become the ground of a thought in another if I am not at the same time the ground of the power that produces the thoughts: in this manner *God is the ground*" (Ak. 28: 52). In aligning the conception of harmony here with that of Leibniz, Kant shows that the real dependence of the substances is not on each other but on God but in so doing removes *from* the world the necessity of connection *within* it.

The dynamical conception of world in the Dissertation and in *Metaphysik L₁*

In Chapter 6 I showed how the general conception of world in the first section of the Dissertation seemed to justify nothing more than a mathematical combination. In the fourth section of this work Kant turns however to addressing the question of how to describe the world in a dynamical fashion. The arguments of the third section have led to the conclusion that space and time belong only to the sensible form of the world and in the fourth section he turns to providing the principle of the form of the intelligible world. To do this he asks a key question about substances: "what is the principle upon which this relation of all substances itself rests, and which, when seen intuitively, is called space?" (Ak. 2: 407). The problem of how it is that a plurality of substances comes together to form a world is thus identified with giving an intelligible form *to* the world.

The consideration of this question begins from the same point as the *New Elucidation* took to be basic which is that the interaction of substances is not a simple result of the principle of their existence but Kant is also here unhappy with viewing the principle of interaction as causation as causal relations are relations of dependence and a principle that describes the ways substances are dependent upon each other is distinct from a principle which shows how they interact. So if there is causal dependence we first need to establish what the principle of interaction is that allows it to manifest itself. Kant moves on to state that the whole of a world cannot be based on a relation between distinct necessary substances as no necessary substance would require dependence on any other and without such dependence being shown to be established no interaction would have any ground other than a contingent one. So if there is a ground of interaction it would have to belong necessarily to things but for it to do so it would have to belong to things that are, in their *existence*, contingent.

The world in question is thus a world of contingent beings. Since such a world would depend on a necessary being this being cannot be connected mereologically to the world that depends *on* it as such mathematical combination would not allow the necessary being to be distinct in principle from the contingent world. The necessary being on which the world would depend is therefore something distinct *from* it and must exist *beyond* it. By this means Kant hopes to show that the entirety of the world is based on the necessary being and that the form of the unity of the world is connected to the entirety of its dependence. This short argument is a variant on the classic cosmological argument for the existence of God and only works through the first assumption that there is a necessary being, a being that is justified in its conception by reference to the notion of possibility as in the *New Elucidation*. The demonstration that this is so follows from Kant's description of the fact that the existence of worlds outside each other is a real impossibility, not a logical one (Ak. 2: 408). The principle that enables causal connections to take place and provides the ground of interaction is thus still pictured, as was the case in the "pre-Critical" works, as one of externally established harmony, a harmony Kant again distinguishes from pre-established harmony despite the concession to the latter in *Metaphysik Herder* (Ak. 2: 409).

The conception that substances need to stand in real interaction with each other for a dynamical conception of world to be formed is equivalent to the statement that the whole they form is not arbitrary but based on the nature of the things themselves. This is why Kant is reported in the notes for *Metaphysik L_1* as stating that the interaction of substances is "the essential condition of the world" (Ak. 28: 196). The unity of the world in its entirety requires that the condition of connection of the substances in their interaction is one that will cohere them together and this is the function of the reference to God. Without God, to put this in the terms of the *New Elucidation*, there would be succession but no co-existence. This not only foreshadows the importance of the Third Analogy but also demonstrates that the Principle of Co-Existence has to be connected to that of succession, as the successive states have to be brought into continuous relation. The description of space and time in the Dissertation failed to provide the grounds for understanding this dynamical connection giving only the arbitrary combination that justifies mathematics. To give a dynamical account is to describe the possibility of substances relating to each other by means of forces. But in *Metaphysik L_1* and the Dissertation Kant can go no further than he did in the earlier works. The account of causal interaction continuously comes back to the need for a divine principle.

What we have discovered from our account of the early treatments Kant gives of the problem of causal interaction is that, starting from the conception of substance, Kant requires something in addition to the substances to bring them into relation. The substances can be considered in isolation due to their simplicity. Thus the relational nature that is attached to causal interaction requires reference to something beyond the conception of substance itself and cannot simply be grounded in a statement concerning the existence of substances. This *extra* element shows that Kant throughout this period has to think his problem in terms of what he will come to understand as requiring synthesis. The synthesis that underlies dynamical connection and allows it to have the form of unification that is required for it to be part of a world is hence the problem that he has to deal with in the Analogies. Prior to moving to this however I wish first to review the famed Herz letter for it does, in my view, relate to the development of Kant's understanding of this problem into its Critical form.

The Herz letter and "Hume's problem"

Subsequently to the writing of the Dissertation Kant was the recipient of important communications from Moses Mendelssohn and Johann Lambert concerning it, both of whom had difficulty accepting its central contentions and to whom Kant was still replying in the "Elucidation" of the account of time in the Transcendental Aesthetic (A36/B53–A41/B58). The problems that were raised by Mendelssohn and Lambert chiefly concerned the nature of time as both undertook to defend its reality. However in thinking about the questions they raised Kant was led to a set of formulations of problems of his own with the argument of the Dissertation, not least in the famous letter to Marcus Herz of 21 February 1772, the letter generally referred to as "the" Herz letter. In this letter Kant indicates his plan to write a work on *The Limits of Sensibility and Reason*, confirming a plan indicated in an earlier letter to Herz.[12] As in the earlier letter Kant has ambitious plans wishing to treat principles of feeling and morality as well as metaphysics. However in considering this plan Kant notices a difficulty:

> As I thought through the theoretical part, considering its whole scope and the reciprocal relation of all its parts, I noticed that I lacked something essential, something that in my long metaphysical studies I, as well as others, had failed to consider and which in fact constitutes the key to the whole secret of metaphysics, hitherto still hidden from itself. I asked myself this question: What is the ground of the relation of that in us which we call "representation" to the object? (Ak. 10: 130)

In raising the question that has been neglected as a question concerning "grounds" Kant suggests, as in the *New Elucidation*, a problem concerning determination but he now centrally connects this question, as he did not in the *New Elucidation,* with the nature of cognition itself. *This bringing of the question concerning determination into connection with the understanding of cognition marks the Critical turn.* The question is posed here not as a question about the determination of substances but rather as a problem concerning how our cognition of an "object" relates to that object. Kant immediately after raising this question demonstrates that if our cognitive power were purely receptive or purely spontaneous there would be no difficulty in accounting for its relationship to its "objects". The condition of pure receptivity would ensure that we were merely affected by objects and thus the validity of our cognitive acts would simply depend upon this. This would be sufficient to guarantee concepts that simply described sensible conditions. The condition of pure spontaneity would be one in which the constitution of objects by our intelligence would determine the properties of the objects in question much as in the arbitrary combinations of mathematics. However with regard to "pure concepts of the understanding" neither of these conditions will be sufficient as they are "neither caused by the object nor do they bring the object into being" (Ak. 10: 130). In the Dissertation as Kant reminds Herz here the difference between intellectual and sensitive cognition had been described as that between appearance and reality with the intellectual cognitions describing how things really are (Ak. 2: 392) and Kant now asks the question as to how these concepts are given to us, if not by means of affection? The simple answer would be that they are spontaneously produced but this creates the difficulty as to what leads us to think that they describe something. The difficulty here, as should be clear from Chapter 6, concerns qualitative relationships as quantitative ones are susceptible to the arbitrary combinations of mathematics. The problem, as it is now posed, points directly forwards to the Transcendental Deduction as Kant states that the difficulty is one of showing how the understanding can form concepts of *a priori* qualitative relations "with which concepts the facts should necessarily agree" and how the understanding can formulate real principles "with which experience must be in exact agreement and which nevertheless are independent of experience" (Ak. 10: 131).

What Kant brings out here is that the question about causal relations touches on the nature of cognition itself. This internalization of the problem of causal relations transforms the terrain for its consideration. Kant sets out the theories of causal interaction as descriptions of how cognition connects to its objects as for example provided by Plato, Crusius and Leibniz and he indicates to Herz that unlike these thinkers he will give an account that will not depend upon "all sorts of wild notions and every pious and speculative brainstorm" (Ak. 10: 131). The move away from addressing the questions about causality as questions just about the nature of things to also describing the origination in cognition of pure concepts has led Kant to distrust the appeal to divine principles with which he was seemingly content previously.

The problem that Kant has arrived at in the letter to Herz is, I would contend, *the Critical problem*. This problem is one of showing the rationale for taking concepts that do not arise from sensibility to correctly describe the nature of the sensible world. The pure concepts that have here been put into question are substance and causation. The principles that Kant was attempting to justify as early as the *New Elucidation* were these same concepts with the demonstration there showing the importance of thinking the relationship of these two notions to each other for change to be accounted for. In the light of the Dissertation it would appear that the intellectual concepts do not describe the conditions of sensibility as the nature of the form and matter of everything sensible seems only to be described by means of arbitrary combination. How is it that the sensible world seems then to be a world in which change can be discerned? It is clear that Kant does not arrive at this question merely from taking Hume seriously. In fact, it would appear that he could take Hume seriously only because he has arrived at this question independently of Hume.

This is apparent when we look at the formulation of "Hume's problem" that Kant gives in the "Preface" to the *Prolegomena*. Kant presents this problem as one concerning the justification there could be for thinking that "anything could be so constituted that if that thing be posited, something else also must necessarily be posited" (Ak. 4: 257). Kant identifies the concept of cause with this suggestion of mutual posited connection. The argument of the *New Elucidation* already suggested the necessity of this mutual connection as the ground for accounting for change. The Dissertation only describes the nature of causal connection as applying to substances and the relation between them is there, as it has been since the writing of the *New Elucidation*, connected to a divine principle. This requires synthesis to form the conception of a unified world by pointing beyond the world itself to something on which it must depend. But what Kant, in the Herz letter, has shown is that the connection of this argument to the principles of sensibility is entirely lacking and, in the "Preface" to the *Prolegomena*, he now accepts the Humean point that the mutual positing of substances is not something that can follow from the concept of any one of them but this is no other than a repetition of the point that it does not follow from the pure existence of the substance being given, the point from which he began his enquiry into the Principle of Co-Existence in the *New Elucidation*. As he reiterates this now: "We cannot at all see why, in consequence of the existence of one thing, another must necessarily exist, or how the concept of such a combination can arise *a priori*" (Ak. 4: 258).

What Kant is announcing in the Herz letter and repeating in the "Preface" to the *Prolegomena* is the failure of all the attempts from the *New Elucidation* to the Dissertation to provide a ground for a dynamical conception of the world, which is what he will identify in the *Critique* with "nature". The ground of this conception of a dynamical world would be one of *a priori* combination that shows the necessity of certain concepts connecting with the conditions of sensible cognition and this combination would have to belong in some way to the principles of the *existence* of the things in question. This latter property would ensure that the combination was really dynamical and not mathematical, not, that is, a product of arbitrary combination. To answer Hume, according to Kant, it is necessary to show that the *origin* of the concept of cause is *a priori* as if this can be demonstrated then "the conditions of its use and the sphere of its valid application would have been determined as a matter of course" (Ak. 4: 259).

The description of reasons for thinking the concept of causality to be *a priori* has in a sense been provided when the categories have been shown to be required for transcendental synthesis to take place. This is the demonstration we have unearthed from our reading of the Transcendental Deduction. What we have further found however is that the mathematical principles can be justified as the basis for our understanding of the form and matter of sensible cognition but *not* for comprehension of how the *relations* of things in our world is justified. It is for this that the dynamical principles are required. The justification of them, by reference to the Copernican turn in the "Preface" to the second edition of the *Critique*, is through showing that the *experience* of objects has to conform to the dynamical principles (Bxvii).

Dynamical principles

Prior to discussing the account of the Analogies I wish to first bring out some points about the nature of the dynamical principles by contrast with the mathematical ones treated in Chapter 6. The synthesis that is involved in these principles is what the Prize Essay described as philosophical and hence requiring representation of universals by abstraction as, unlike with mathematics, no figure can be given here, only words supplied. The Dissertation also spoke of qualitative synthesis as requiring a progression whereby a series of things are subordinated to each other (Ak. 2: 387n). The philosophical procedure has to connect to things, not merely to figures and thus it has to describe not merely *a priori* intuition and its combinations but empirical intuition and thus gives, as Kant puts it, "the character of *a priori* necessity" only under the condition of thought in some experience (A160/B200). Due to the need to describe the necessity in question under these conditions the method of proof of them will be difficult, as Kant pointed out in the Prize Essay would be the case for conceptual as opposed to mathematical-sensible demonstrations.

The demonstration of the dynamical principles, as with the mathematical ones, takes place through connection of these principles to the conditions of inner sense, as we would expect following the argument of the chapter on schematism. Since the principles we will be concerned with are those of substance and causality we would expect the demonstration of them to require the inter-connection of inner and outer sense to be shown. The synthesis involved with these principles is, according to an additional note Kant adds in the second edition of the *Critique*, one of "connection" not mere composition. The difference is that whilst the composition that was described in the mathematical synthesis was one of arbitrary combination this one has rather to show that its constituents are *necessarily* connected and thus brings together in *a priori* form heterogeneous elements that are combined according to the principles of *existence* (B201–2n).

The principle of all the analogies

The three analogies are all parts of a continuous argument. The first reason for thinking this to be the case is that Kant describes a common principle that underpins each of them, a principle that he also provides a proof of prior to treating the particular analogies individually. The formulation of the general principle of all the analogies is treated slightly differently in the two editions of the *Critique* with the first edition formula stating: "All appearances are, as regards their existence, subject *a priori* to rules determining their relation to one another in one time" (A176–7). This formulation indicates that the Analogies supply a universal condition of appearances. This condition is that the existence of appearances is determined by *a priori* temporal rules. The second edition formulation by contrast is as follows: "Experience is possible only through the representation of a necessary connection of perceptions" (B219). The second edition formulation describes a principle, which is not merely universal but also necessary and which states that perceptions themselves have principle of connection. The second edition formula refers us back to the Anticipations of Perception and makes clear the progressive movement of the argument of the Analytic of Principles as a whole and this is a reason for taking it to be superior to the first edition formulation. Kemp Smith takes the second edition formula to state what he terms "the central thesis of the transcendental deduction" and it is the case that a principle of this form was described at the conclusion of the B-Deduction (B164–5).[13] Paton points out a disadvantage of the second edition formula, which is that in it Kant does not refer to time as he does in the first edition formula.[14] Wolff, by contrast, points to an advantage of the second edition formula, namely its concentration on necessary connection, precisely the point that has commended it to us.[15]

The proof of the general principle of the Analogies

After stating the principle of all the analogies Kant discusses the nature of them in the process providing further clarification of how the dynamical principles are different from the mathematical. The second edition describes this discussion as containing a "proof" of the general principles and includes an additional paragraph that provides the outline of such a "proof" though it should be clear that the real proof of the general principle is provided in the argument that will run through all the separate analogies and bring them together. The nature of empirical knowledge is restated at the opening of this discussion as involving cognition of an object through the determination of our perceptions of it. This refers us back to the demonstration of the Antici-pations of Perception. Kant now describes perceptions as involving a synthesis that unifies the manifold in one consciousness stating that synthetic unity describes that which has to belong to the "objects" of the senses. But the perception of "objects" in experience refers us to contingent orders of arrangement so it would appear not to include the necessary element that we are seeking within experience. The connection between perceptions refers us to the *a priori* intuitions but, as we have seen in the arguments for the Anticipations, these intuitions are not perceived within the matter of experience itself and so require reference to pure concepts as the conditions of determination of perceptual moments. Therefore the point of the analogies in general will be to show that it is the pure concepts that provide this connection and in this sense the argument of the Analogies is the central part of the *Critique*.

The pure concepts will be justified here as necessary elements of experience and will stand in for the elements of time. What Kant will provide in the Analogies is the principles by which the pure concepts perform this function in relation to the three modes of time, duration, succession and co-existence. What the principles will supply is the description of the relational properties that all objects will have to possess to be objects of experience. This is why Kant terms these principles *regulative* and not, like the mathematical principles, *constitutive* as, following the arguments given by him as early as the *Only Possible Argument*, existence cannot be *constructed*.

Kant's rationale for speaking of the dynamical principles as "analogies" involves a reprisal of the contrast between philosophy and mathematics, as the types of analogy in these areas are distinct from each other. Whereas in mathematics analogies express an equivalence between quantities and in so doing construct this equivalence, in philosophy the analogies are rather expressive of an equivalence between qualities so that "from three given members we can obtain *a priori* knowledge only of the relation to a fourth" (A179/B222), not cognition of the fourth itself. So the analogy is one whereby a relation is justified, not the members of the relation constituted. Whilst the mathematical principles demonstrated to us the nature of the form and matter of intuition here we have merely a rule for how the "objects" of experience have to relate. "The principles can therefore have no other purpose save that of being the conditions of the unity of *empirical* knowledge in the synthesis of *appearances*. But such unity can be thought only in the *schema* of the pure concept of understanding" (A181–2/B223–4). The analogy referred to in the title of these principles is between the combination by which the synthesis of appearances has to take place and the combination whereby concepts have unity. The statement of the principles of the distinct analogies includes reference to the category being schematized but the schema is then applied to it in order to realize the category in the process of restricting it.

Let us look now at some of the key elements of the argument that have emerged from this "proof" of the general principle of the analogies. First, as Guyer nicely puts this, Kant's intention in the argument for the analogies has been shown to be one of establishing the principles that will be required "to judge that our representations represent objects at all".[16] If this is indeed the main point of the Analogies, as I agree with Guyer that it is, then it follows that the Analogies *will* provide the full answer to the question raised in the Herz letter. A second point that has emerged from the consideration of the "proof" of the general principle of the Analogies is that in responding to the question in the Herz letter Kant will also reply to "Hume's problem" concerning the grounds for thinking that there is *a priori* combination *between* objects hence finally justifying the principles first described in the *New Elucidation*. The third point is that Kant will demonstrate the connection between the three modes of time and the pure concepts of relation hence showing that relational properties are part of the necessary condition of objects of experience being given to us.

The principle of the First Analogy

Both the title and the formulation of the principle of the First Analogy are altered between the two editions of the *Critique*. The first edition formulation calls the principle simply one of permanence and gives it as follows: "All appearances contain the permanent (substance) as the object itself, and the transitory as its mere determination that is, as a way in which the object exists" (A182). This formulation states a universal condition of appearances, which is that in them there is a distinction between "objects" and states that conforms to the classic metaphysical distinction between substance and accidents. The substance in appearances is determined as that which is sempiternal in experience with the determinations of it being transitory. The second edition formulation by contrast is altered so that it is now entitled *the principle of permanence of substance* and its formulation is: "In all changes of appearances substance is permanent; its quantum in nature is neither increased nor diminished" (B224). This formulation again describes a universal condition of appearances but does not refer to existence, unlike the first edition formula and what it does, unlike the first edition formula, is describe the nature of permanence as something that does not alter in quantity. This reference should call to mind the implication of Proposition X from the *New Elucidation* where Kant stated that the quantity of reality in the world does not alter *naturally* (Ak. 1: 407).

The differences between these two versions of the formula of the First Analogy are striking and have caused wide comment and dispute. Paton mentions, as a possible problem with the second edition formulation, its connection to Newton's law of the conservation of matter.[17] This would mean that the proof of the First Analogy would have however a very peculiar character, that of being, as Allison puts it, "a transcendental proof of an empirical thesis".[18] The closeness of the formulation of the second edition version of this proof to that of the implication of Proposition X in the *New Elucidation* should further provide grounds for caution in attributing to Kant such a strange design, one that would not, in any case, conform to the stated purpose of the arguments of the Analogies. We will return to assessing the question of the formulations of the principle of the First Analogy after attending to its argument.

The argument for the First Analogy

Kant opens the argument for the principle of the First Analogy in the second edition by repeating points from the Transcendental Aesthetic pointing out that the universal condition of appearances is that they are in time and this is the condition under which co-existence and succession (the two notions that he sought to prove in the *New Elucidation*) are represented within it. This point about co-existence and succession was used in the Transcendental Aesthetic to show that time is the necessary presupposition of anything being perceived at different times or any two things being perceived to be co-existent (A30/B46). Kant then adds the point, defended in the argument for the Anticipations, that time itself is not perceived so that if time is the substratum of all appearances then it needs to be shown that something represents it in the "objects of perception" (A182/B225). The notion of a substratum of appearances is one of the ways in which "substance" can be characterized. So whatever is substantial in appearances would be "the real in appearance" and would have to remain constant.

At this point Kant refers back to the arguments of the Transcendental Deduction and the Anticipations of Perception both of which traded on the account of the synthesis of apprehension. But this synthesis alone is now stated to be insufficient to determine whether any given "object" in the manifold should be regarded as the same *over* time or co-existent with something given *in* one time. "For such determination we require an underlying ground which exists *at all times*, that is, something *abiding* and *permanent*, of which all change and co-existence are only so many ways (modes of time) in which the permanent exists" (A182/B225–6). So, if succession and simultaneity are to be given to us as states of anything, then these relations must be predicates of something permanent, which would make the permanent the basis of empirical presentations of temporal states. Hence the criterion for describing substance would also indicate that what possesses this criterion stands in for time itself. At this point Kant connects the notion of permanence to that of duration as that which endures is taken to be that which is permanent. The permanent would hence be the condition of the synthesis of perception having unity. Kant thus argues that if there are "objects" then they are substances and that change is something that belongs to the way in which these objects exist. The way in which these "objects" would exist then would be that they endure and only their states (or accidents) changed.

Kant cannot prove that substances *exist* as given a concept of something the existence condition of the thing does not follow from its determination in thought. This is why philosophy cannot construct its objects, unlike mathematics. So to show that there are substances is to show the necessity for them as *a condition* of the possibility of experience. The argument for the Anticipations of Perception already showed that the *matter* of intuition cannot cease to be without experience ceasing so the nature of this matter must be connected to the conditions of the representation of change itself for, as Kant writes, "all existence, whether in past or in future time" can be determined only with regard to the substrate of experience (A185/B228). So if the *matter* of intuition has the condition of endurance we discovered that it must have in the argument of the Anticipations then it would deserve the title of substance in a phenomenal sense. Alteration, in accord with the second edition formulation of the principle of the First Analogy, is not an expression of things that begin and end but rather "a way of existing which follows upon another way of existing of the same object" (A187/B230) as all that alters continues to be whilst its accidents change.

The perception of alteration is dependent on the fact that there are substances and absolute origination or termination of them could not be perceived as for this to occur would require a lapse of time. Within time we have continuity of perception which refers us to continuity of what is perceived and this requires that what is perceived belongs to that which is permanent but if something could absolutely come to be then it would be discontinuous with all else. This discontinuity would require time to lapse, as without this lapsing of time there would be no grounds for the discontinuity of appearances. Therefore if time is unified the condition of this unification is that what is presented within it is a set of determinations of what must remain constant. The argument concludes however by referring us forward for consideration of the "empirical criterion" of this necessary permanence which has been argued has to be part of the condition of the possibility of appearances.

Examining the argument for the First Analogy

A first point that needs attention is that the permanent is taken in this argument to be the expression of the empirical representation of time itself (A183/B226) due to the fact that temporal relations as descriptive of change must be connected to that which is not changing and provide a means of noticing change. Time itself cannot change as it is the means of expressing all change so, in a sense, it is permanent but, since it cannot be perceived, it needs to be represented within experience by the appearances we term "objects" as these latter are the grounds for notice of alterations but that which remains when alteration has taken place must be the *matter* of experience that we identify with the representative of time itself whilst the *form* of the appearances is one of constant alteration. Paton correctly represents this point when he writes that what Kant is dealing with here is the question of how we can perceive change at all, not how it is *measured*.[19] Or, as Longuenesse puts this point: "Kant's problem is not how we situate appearances in time, but how we generate our representation of a unified time in the first place."[20]

Paul Guyer has argued against the premise that the permanence of time is in some way represented in the "objects" of appearances and does so by reference to a citation from the "Preface" to the second edition of the *Critique*. To judge his objection it will be necessary to look closely at the passage he cites and to provide a different analysis of it to Guyer. The passage in question is very pertinent to this discussion as Guyer suggests but not in the way Guyer thinks. Kant writes the following in the "Preface" to the second edition:

> The representation of something *permanent* in existence is not the same as *permanent representation*. For though the representation of [something permanent] may be very transitory and variable like all our other representations, not excepting those of matter, it yet refers to something permanent. This latter must therefore be an external thing distinct from all my representations, and its existence must be included in the *determination* of my own existence, constituting with it but a single experience such as would not take place even inwardly if it were not also at the same time, in part, outer. (Bxliin)

The passage is clearly added to the "Preface" as part of the explication and extension of the "Refutation of Idealism". The argument can be restated as saying that if there is something that has to be represented as permanent in existence this does not require it to be the case that what is so understood is therefore constantly represented. Any particular representation is in fact transitory, as Kant opens the proof of the First Analogy by stating and this applies even to the representation of *matter* in general as what is represented to us is only a particular determination of it at any time. This does not prevent it from being the case however that what is presented in transitory fashion does not refer us after all to something permanent and what this would be, Kant here clearly states, is something external to me. That which is external to me is connected to the condition of determination of myself as the latter only occurs through time. Hence, in accord with the statement in the Aesthetic (A33/B50–1), time to be represented requires space and since my representation requires time, it also requires space, and the latter is the basis of the determination of anything permanent. In a sense this citation not only therefore supports the contentions of the First Analogy, it adds to their clarity.

Guyer however interprets this passage differently. Seizing on the statement that whatever is permanently required for representation is not by means of this shown to be itself permanently *present* in representations he writes: "This implies that there is no general principle that the temporal properties of what is represented must be mirrored by what represents them, *a fortiori* there is no general principle from which it can be inferred that if time is permanent, then what represents time, even what represents its permanence, must itself be permanent" (Guyer, 1987, pp. 219–20). Regarded as an interpretation of the passage it fails as within the passage what Kant is pointing out is that simply because nothing is permanently represented before us does not mean that there are *not* permanent conditions that attach to anything being represented to us. Guyer mangles this point and in the process confuses Kant's argument. Kant certainly does not advance the view that there is a general principle that what represents temporal properties must possess the properties of temporal properties and considered at this level of generality it is in any case unclear what "representation" of temporal properties means. If we draw a line in thought then this line is a way of representing succession but the awareness of the line, once it has been drawn, can be simply presented as a unity and not as a set of points, which does not preclude the line from continuing to "represent" succession. When we see this point it becomes clear that Kant could not have intended to advance the general principle that Guyer argues against here. What he did want to argue however is that time is the substratum of all change and that there is, within the appearances, a substratum also and that this substratum can thus be linked to the permanence of time. The substratum would be the *matter* of appearances.

The second point in Guyer's argument was to the effect that what "represents" time in appearances does not have to possess the characteristic of permanence that time itself possesses in order to "represent" time. The notion of representation can here be approached more clearly than when Guyer was thinking in terms of the "general principle". In these terms what Kant is stating is that the conditions of representation of anything at all include invariant elements and this invariance is what we mean by describing them as "permanent" but time itself is also an invariant condition of representation so given the linkage between these elements one can "represent", or serve as an analogy for, the other. This does not mean that what is an invariant condition *for* representation has to itself be an invariant presence *within* representation and it is the distinction between these two means of understanding invariance that Kant is making in the citation from the "Preface" to the second edition. This last point shows why Guyer's argument is not even independently good as it trades on exploiting precisely the ambiguity of "permanent representation" that Kant, in the citation, is intent on unmasking.[21]

Since the classic discussion of substance in Aristotle's *Metaphysics* the criterion for substances has tended to move between the notion of "substratum" and the subject of predication and independence, or that on which things depend without it being dependent on anything else. According to Jonathan Bennett the unschematized notion of substance is identified with the subject of predication whilst the schematization of this concept produces the notion of sempiternality as a way of expressing independence.[22] In assessing this view we should look back to the conclusion of the chapter on schematism. In closing this chapter Kant justifies the renunciation of the view expressed in the Dissertation that intelligible concepts describe things as they are whilst sensible concepts only tell us of how things appear. The schema is, we are here told, "only the phenomenon, or sensible concept, of an object in agreement with the category" (A146/B186). It thus imposes a restriction upon the category, namely that the category is presented in sensible form as related to time (and, as we have good reason to think, space). To the view that the renunciation of such sensible conditions would hence expand the province of the concept and enable it more fully to express reality Kant counterposes his Critical argument that removal of sensible conditions only gives a purely logical meaning to a concept so that it expresses merely "the bare unity of the representations"

(A147/B186). An example of this is then provided, namely the pure concept of substance. Such a pure concept, unconnected to sensible representations, is merely that of a subject of predication which "tells me nothing as to the nature of that which is thus to be viewed as a primary subject" (A147/B186–7).

Bennett is thus right to think of the pure, unschematized concept of substance as equivalent to the subject of predications, but what we can also note from this argument at the conclusion of the chapter on schematism is Kant's conviction that such a pure concept can describe no object. So considered merely as a pure concept the supposed intentional correlate of this concept is left undetermined and this is the rationale for the process of schematization, namely to *determine* the "object" that is the concept's correlate. In doing this Kant is led to the criteria of permanence as the mode of schematizing the concept of substance as that which is the subject of predication must be something that remains underneath all the alterations of accidents. This is what leads him to the view that what must perform this role in experience is the *matter* of it or, as Wolff puts this, "the stuff, rather than the form, of objects is the permanent in appearances".[23] Kant expresses this himself in the following statements from the First Analogy: "All existence and all change in time have...to be viewed as simply a mode of the existence of that which remains and persists. In all appearances the permanent is the object itself, that is, substance as phenomenon; everything, on the other hand, which changes or can change belongs only to the way in which substance or substances exist, and therefore to their determinations" (A183–4/B227).

If all change is a mode of that which remains so that the permanent is the *object itself* then it follows that this "object itself" is the *matter* of appearances that is constant within them as the form alone does not describe any type of "object" merely the modes in which "objects" are presented. It is precisely due to the fact that the forms do no more than this which led Kant in the Dissertation to think of the pure concepts by contrast as descriptive of the things that are real in contrast to the things that appear. What we can see after the discussion of the Anticipations of Perception is that there is necessary continuity in the *matter* of appearances, a continuity that provides us with a material principle in our comprehension of experience. This material principle is, in our view, further specified in the First Analogy as pointing to *matter* or, as Wolff puts it, "stuff" as that which has to remain constant whilst the basic *form* of experience, namely time, presents us only with that which changes. The matter of experience is the "ever-abiding existence" of the

"the subject proper" of all predication and that which must continue to be, not merely that which has always been. Another way of putting this, which is how Kant does develop this point, is that the unity of what is *being experienced* points to a condition of what supplies us with this unity, namely a *permanence of duration* of that which really exists. "All that alters *persists*, and only its *state changes*" (A187/B230). The argument thus centrally turns on the suggestion that it is only due to the continued existence of the *matter* of experience that the determination of transitory accidents can be said to point to "objects" at all. Without this permanence of existence of the *matter* of experience there would be nothing other than the "states" that are changing and on that basis no ground for postulating the existence of "objects" at all. So, if we are to be justified in our general assumption that our experience is *of objects* then the condition of such "objects" being given is that they have to be the substances that are sempiternal, not however in terms of their "form" of being given as that which occupies a certain temporal or spatial position but rather as that which *endures beyond any given spatial or temporal position*. This is why Kant states, "even in fire the matter (substance) does not vanish, but only suffers an alteration of form" (A185/B228).

The schematization of the category of substance reveals that there is a condition for experiencing time itself as unitary, which is that the matter of the objects that are presented within time endures as without this endurance the synthesis of imagination would not attach to appearances. The argument of the First Analogy is thus a response to the problem pointed to in the A-Deduction in the following passage:

> If cinnabar were sometimes red, sometimes black, sometimes light, sometimes heavy, if a man changed his form sometimes into this and sometimes into that animal form, if the country on the longest day were sometimes covered with fruit, sometimes with ice and snow, my empirical imagination would never find opportunity when representing red colour to bring to mind heavy cinnabar. Nor could there be an empirical synthesis of reproduction, if a certain name were sometimes given to this, sometimes to that object, or were one and the same thing named sometimes in one way, sometimes in another, *independently of any rule to which appearances are in themselves subject.* (A100–01, my emphasis)

The stability of the representation of objects *over* time is dependent on their conformity to the conditions of what "appearances are in themselves" subject to. What they have to be so subject to is *a rule* of their general determination and this *rule* is provided in the transcendental synthesis of imagination as Kant subsequently made clear in the passages after this one (A101–2) which is a rule of temporal continuity. The condition of such temporal continuity is the continuity of the objects that are described within it. The essential nature of these objects cannot alter as if they did it would follow that the condition of representation of these objects would also alter but since this condition of representation is not merely something that attaches to *particulars* but to what Andrew Brook spoke of as the "global object" that is *experience* in general such an alteration of essential qualities would break the unity of temporality itself.

James Van Cleve however echoes the views of many when he objects to this argument that the unity of temporality requires the unity of temporal objects *over* time to be expressive of a permanent nature within these objects. Van Cleve puts his objection in the following form: "I cannot myself see any reason why the absence of permanent things would lead to the disunity of time. You might as well say that unless there were some omnipresent or all-pervading object (the ether, perhaps), there would be a rupture in the unity of space—two items that were not spatially related to each other."[24] The connection between two items in a common space is in fact subsequently going to be treated to extended consideration, from two distinct points of view, in the Second and Third analogies, as is consistent with the view that in the arguments for them Kant finally arrives at the justification of the Principles of Succession and Co-Existence that he identified in the *New Elucidation* as being required for metaphysics to have any solid foundation. Van Cleve's apparent dismissal of the need for any such justification does not match the degree of attention Kant gave to these problems.[25] The suggestion that permanent things are not required for the unity óf time is one that fails to address the difficulty announced in the A-Deduction and which Kant is treating in the First Analogy. The difficulty is that without the existence of permanent *matter* the fundamental nature of things would, as Hume suggested, be susceptible of alteration *at any moment* but not only is this the case but if such fundamental change cannot be ruled out of contention then it follows, on Kant's argument, that there is therefore no guarantee that moments themselves have continuity of connection. In other terms, there is a dependence of description of moments as belonging *to* one time on the description of the events *within* this time being recounted as events occurring in a single nature. If a single nature is the precondition of the unity of time then the ultimate elements of this nature have to be constant as without this constancy there would be unity to the nature and hence no unity to the time within it. Van Cleve's failure to grasp this point is further revealed when he takes Kant's basic assumption to be that change takes place merely against a backdrop of something permanent rather than the changes that are noted being described as changes *in* the state of what remains. Unless the changes are alterations of determination of what remains they are not expressive of the unitary rules of nature in general and hence could at any moment change thus leading to the difficulties set out at A100–101. The reference at the conclusion of the argument of the First Analogy to the impossibility of substances beginning or ending is another way of specifying the continuity of essential properties within experience.

In conclusion the two formulations of the principle of the First Analogy are not, as they appear to be, significantly different and the second edition formulation neither presupposes nor attempts to justify Newton's law of conservation of mass. What they both point to is the necessity of permanence of substance within appearances with the first edition formulation emphasizing that what is permanent is the object itself and the second deriving a consequence from this which is that there cannot be an alteration in the number of substances as all alteration is only expressive of whatever substances exist. The dissatisfaction that can legitimately be expressed at the close of the consideration of the argument for the First Analogy is that the "empirical criterion" for substance is introduced only in its conclusion as a promissory note. We will find that it is subsequently delivered in the Third Analogy and in so finding it will substantiate our initial claim that the three analogies are three parts of a single argument. What we have found however is that the First Analogy conforms to our account of the three conditions each of the analogies has to meet. First, in accordance with Guyer's statement that the Analogies will show that the principles expressed in them are required for our representations to be *of* objects we have here demonstrated that the principle of the First Analogy is what permits us to comprehend the "objects" of experience to have the stability of representation required for time to fulfil its role of providing universal conditions of experience. Thus for our representations to be of "objects" that actually exist in the world is for them to be of permanent existents. Secondly, *a priori* combination is required for the representation of the *matter* of experience as receptive to the rule of combination that the principle of the First Analogy expresses and this refers us to the transcendental synthesis of imagination. It is true that in his proof of this principle Kant does not describe the "empirical correlate" of substances and in subsequently doing so we will need this synthesis of imagination to be described in its mode of operation with regard to empirical intuition. Thirdly, the relational properties expressed as those of substance and accident have been shown to be necessary for objects of experience to be represented to us at all.

The principle of the Second Analogy

The principle of the Second Analogy is again altered in terms of both its title and its formulation between the two editions of the *Critique*. The first edition principle calls it a principle of production and it is formulated as follows: "Everything that happens, that is, begins to be, presupposes something upon which it follows according to a rule" (A189). This formulation states a universal condition that is attached to the nature of events stating that for an event to take place is for it to succeed something previously given. Not only does an event require reference back to something previous but it also expresses this backward reference in a constant form, that is, by use of a rule. The second edition principle is, by contrast, entitled a "principle of succession of time", in accordance with the law of causality. It is formulated in the following way: "All alterations take place in conformity with the connection of cause and effect" (B232). This second formulation in its title expresses the fact that the Second Analogy is the schematization of the category of causal dependence, something missing from the first edition title of the principle. The formulation of the second edition principle is, as with the first edition formulation, expressive of a universal condition, stated here not to attach only to "events" but to alterations in general, a shift in scope. The difference between the two is that whilst an "event" requires, as the first edition formulation indicated, reference to distinction between the momentary presentations of some phenomena, that "alteration" may rather be of some simultaneously existing elements and so the second edition formula tells us that even under these conditions there is a rule attached to the change in question. Whilst the first edition formulation of the principle simply refers to a rule in general, like the first edition formulation of the First Analogy, the second edition formulation tells us what this rule is, the rule of casual connection. For all these reasons the second edition formulation of the principle of the Second Analogy is to be preferred to the first edition formulation.

The proof of the Second Analogy

In attending to the interpretation of the argument for the principle of the Second Analogy we have arrived at Kant's statement of his response to "Hume's problem", the problem we described earlier as decisively connected to the very project of the *Critique* but only due to the fact that Kant connected this problem, as we saw from consideration of the Herz letter, to the question of how it is that we have concepts of objects at all. Guyer has also rightly picked out this latter point as central to the argument of the Analogies. In this sense the Analogies provide us at last with the Kantian conception of experience and, on the burden of our interpretation, they must in so doing finally and decisively describe the nature of the transcendental synthesis of imagination. What will be original to our interpretation of the Second Analogy will be the description of it as giving the fullest treatment of the synthetic account of experience that is the point, on our view, of the *Critique*.

In assessing the Second Analogy in this way we will also, in working through its argument, show how it enables us to complete the consideration of the First Analogy and point towards the need for the Third. The first point we want to make concerning the interpretation of the Second Analogy concerns the connection of it to the schematization of the categories of relation. In the chapter on schematism Kant described the schema of the pure concepts as connected to different facets of time and in introducing the argument for the Second Analogy by reference to these we hope to prepare the way for the nature of our interpretation of the argument for the principle of the Second Analogy. Kant described the schema of magnitude that was given in the Axioms of Intuition as that which concerned "the generation (synthesis) of time itself in the successive apprehension of an object" and as thus relating to the time-series (A145–6/B184). By contrast the schema of the category of quality demonstrated the *filling* of time with the synthesis of sensation and thus described the *content* of time. The schema of relation however concerns the manner in which perceptions are connected together at "all times according to a rule of time-determination" and thus concerns the *order* of time. This description of the schema of relation as descriptive of the *rules of the order of time* is what Kant means by reference to the *determination* of time in empirical intuition. The burden of our interpretation will be that it is this disclosure of necessary characteristics of the order of time in empirical intuition that is the key to the argument for the Second Analogy and, indeed, for understanding how the three analogies are connected together.

Exposition of the nature of the argument of the Second Analogy will require division of it into parts. Kemp Smith and Paton classically approached the argument of the Second Analogy as made of distinct parts but in so doing viewed these parts as composed of discretely different arguments, only some of which were thought successful.[26] I will instead be treating the discussion as involving discrete parts of a *single* argument but will, like these writers, focus my discussion of this on close attention to the text as here, more than anywhere else in the whole *Critique*, it is essential to give a clear description of what Kant's argument actually states and what contentions can be given in its support. I will provide now an extended commentary on the stages of the argument demonstrating the separate steps and how they lead to Kant's desired conclusion.

Kant's introduction to the proof in the second edition (B233–4)

Kant added two paragraphs to the front of the discussion of the Second Analogy in the second edition and in so doing provided an "introduction" to its argument. These two paragraphs are not, I will suggest, themselves an argument but a promise of one to come. The first of these paragraphs refers back to the First Analogy reminding us that it has shown that the appearance of succession requires that what is being perceived at any time is change in the *form* of that which is enduring and restating the point that substances do not come to be or pass away. Kant then moves to an examination of perception, which is logical since perception was shown in the argument for the Anticipations to be *of* the matter of appearance, not of its form. Perception is, however, as we saw in the argument for the First Analogy, merely successive and this means that there is an appearance of what the Prize Essay described as "real opposition", that is, movement from one state to another where the latter state negates the former.

Since perception is successive and such succession requires that what *was, is,* no longer, there is a *connection* required within it between the discrete parts of it. Without this connection between the different elements of the perception there would be no way of stating that successive states were of the same "object". But this connection that is required for the perception to be of the same "object" is not itself a product of either sensa or even of intuitions alone, even pure ones. It requires rather a *synthesis*, the synthesis of imagination. This dependence of connection of the elements of perception on the synthesis of imagination was the key claim of the argument of the Transcendental Deduction on our interpretation and it is important to note that Kant here, in the preliminary part of the proof of the Second Analogy, refers to it.

The next point is that whilst the synthesis of imagination is required for the connection of perceptions together that this synthesis does not seem sufficient as, whilst imagination is the faculty by which we can represent an object which is not itself present (B152), we need to acknowledge that it would appear that the succession of any two states or events could, in principle, take any order. So if we are witnessing a succession of states it would appear that any part of the succession could have precedence in chronology over any other. Thus imagination alone does not seem sufficient for us to be able to say which state precedes which in the *object* of our perception. So if our perception is taken to be of an "object" then it would appear that "objects" must be something more than simply the *quale* of perceptions as these latter have no necessary order in them. This is what Kant is referring to as a lack of determination in perceptual representation of objects. For the succession of states we perceive to describe truly the succession of what is *being* perceived requires *determination* in the sense of describing an *order* that cannot be reversed. This determination of succession by reference to a necessary order in that which is being perceived is indicated to require, in addition to the synthesis of perception by imagination, the provision of something that unifies it in a necessary way. What would do this, Kant suggests, is the concept of a necessary relation which concept is equivalent to that of cause and effect. This section then concludes with a simple statement that experience requires that this law of causality govern the succession of appearances.

This discussion is clearly not intended as a distinct argument for the view that causality is essential to the experience of objects but merely as a preparation for this argument. What we have got from it are three essential opening points. First, the basic data of perception is succession of states. Secondly, for successive states to be taken to be successive representations of something they have to be combined together in the synthesis of imagination as neither the form nor the matter of intuition taken alone provide this combination and hence it is an effect of cognition itself. Thirdly and finally, the order of succession *in* perception does not reliably inform us of the order of the succession of what is *being* perceived and for us to have an understanding of the order as being one that belongs to the object we need the pure concept of causality. The assumption that what our perceptions are of in the first place is an "object" has not yet been justified and without this the whole discussion clearly fails to provide an argument for its conclusion which is why, in our view, it should instead be taken to be a promissory note for one once we have justified the conception of the "object" itself.

Objective and subjective succession (A190/B235–A194/B239)

The next section of the discussion probes more deeply the nature of the conditions of apprehension of succession. If we perceive succession then we have admitted that there are extensive magnitudes. Kant here reminds us of the principle of extensive magnitudes by referring to the mereological condition of successive representation: "representations of parts follow upon one another" (A190/B234), something stated in the discussion of the principle of the Axioms as requiring "successive advance from one moment to another" (A163/B203). So if we perceive succession we have, in this perception, *generated* time as was indicated would be the schema of quantity in the chapter on schematism. The apprehension of succession is not itself proof however that what is being apprehended in successive fashion *is* successive in the way in which our apprehension would suggest it to be. Kant puts this mereologically asking whether the parts of the "object" follow each other in the manner that the parts of our successive apprehension of it do.

Kant next makes a seemingly paradoxical move. Rather than instantly addressing the question concerning the reason for taking the "object" to possess the successive character our apprehension of it leads us to view it as having, he instead examines, what we might mean by an "object". This accords with our suggestion that the introductory paragraphs were making quite an assumption in determining successive appearances as being *of* an "object" at all. In doing so he points out that anything that we present to ourselves, such as, for example, a state of affairs, can be taken to be an "object". What he then does is ask what is occurring when by taking something to be an "object" we are asserting that it is something present before us in experience. The opening assumption of the discussion of the Second Analogy is then repeated which is that if anything is taken to be an "object" in experience it is something given to us successively. If the "objects" we encounter in experience were to conform to the classic metaphysical description of substances as something constitutively independent of their conditions of perception then it would follow that there would be no way of connecting such "objects" with our successive perception of them, no way, that is, of showing that the object itself was really successive in the way that our perception of it was. The fact that "objects" of experience are rather appearances gives us some reason to hope that they will conform to the condition of appearances and thus be given in relation to the *a priori* intuitions.

Even taking the objects of experience to be appearances there is still a difficulty. The difficulty is that since the apprehension of anything at all is successive then having successive representation does not mean that the "object" is itself successive *even as an appearance* in the way that the representation of it is. In illustration of this point Kant uses the example of a house, which is perceived successively, and yet which no one takes to itself be successive. Any "object" of experience that is described normally as stationary fits the same point. Looking at a chair is looking at something that I only perceive successively since the back and sides are not present simultaneously but this does not entail that the chair is itself successive. So even though this "object" is not taken to be a thing in itself it still seems to require distinction from my subjective means of receiving impressions from it. What is the condition then under which I can form a correct view of appearances if it would appear that all of them are successive for me without all being in themselves, even as appearances, successive? There must be, Kant states, a rule that enables us to distinguish one apprehension from another and which in so doing demonstrates the necessity of modes of connection between these apprehensions.

The argument up to this point has thus made two surprising turns. First, we began with a question about succession and were diverted into a discussion of the nature of what is meant by talking in terms of "objects". Then the resolution of the enquiry that opened up as to how we were to describe what an "object" of appearance was described the condition under which anything in appearances could be termed one. This second turn referred us back to the need for a rule concerning the nature of apprehension. So the argument has apparently so far stated that if there is apprehension it is successive but that succession in my apprehension of something does not permit me in itself to describe succession in what has been apprehended and then stated that to see something as successive requires me to have a rule to distinguish distinct apprehensions *from each other*. We seem to have got to the nub of the issue as one whereby something about the nature of what enables us in experience to distinguish objects *from each other* will tell also us the way in which we can distinguish between a purely subjective need for successive representation and a situation in which the succession is part of the true appearance of the object.

All of this discussion is part of the preparation for Kant's laying out of the argument. We can see this from the way he now proceeds to examine the nature of succession yet again emphasizing, as in the introductory paragraphs added in the second edition, that the occurrence of an event involves real opposition as it was described in the Prize Essay or, in other words, that something which was *not* comes to *be*. If something comes to be that was not then we know, following the argument of the First Analogy, that this is an alteration and, following the argument for the Anticipations of Perception, that it must be part of a continuity of temporal givenness as there can be no perception of empty time. It is the fact that there can be no apprehension of empty time that Kant insists on when he repeats that time is not itself perceived. So if there is no perception of time alone but it is rather always, in accordance with the demonstration of the argument of the Anticipations, perceived as *filled* then the appearance of any event is always part of the continuity of appearances of other events and so perceptions follow each other. This however is not yet sufficient for us to understand when a perception of succession is a perception of something that is really successive in its true appearance as the perception of succession occurs, as we have already noted, when we perceive even stationary objects.

Now Kant gets to the point that will prove crucial. If apprehension is not merely successive for me but descriptive of something that is truly successive itself then what is happening has a *determinate order*. We noted in our discussion of the introductory matter of the Second Analogy that this determinate order was not something that flowed merely from the combination of perceptions together into the synthesis of imagination. *What is occurring when the successive perception is of something that is successive is that the manner in which the elements of the perception are presented to me is not something capable of variation but must have the order that it does.* The famous example given of this is the perception of a ship moving downstream which can only be perceived in one order. Appearing downstream is an effect of the ship having been upstream and the movement cannot vary and be a description of the actual events involved. The events of happenings are thus distinguished from the subjective presentations of "objects" of experience in general in the sense that the latter can be given in any order whilst the events of happenings cannot.

If the mode in which the ship is given is one that requires a certain order then we are justified in treating this order as a *necessary* one, which means that the perception of it has to conform to a *rule* of apprehension. Without conformity of the apprehension of the ship to this necessary rule the distinction of it from the purely contingent ordering of apprehension of mountains and houses would not be given. If it is given to us as a distinction that no-one would deny as important *within* experience then the nature of this distinction is one that requires a formulation of its rule and this is one whereby happenings have a form of succession which is *objective* in being determined in their mode of being given. The determination of the order of the apprehension in this case is by provision of an invariant rule of irreversibility of perceptions if perceptions are of something that is itself truly moving. "The event, as the condition, thus affords reliable evidence of some condition, and this condition is what determines the event" (A194/B239).

This discussion is still far from conclusive with regard to showing that the causal principle is a necessary element of experience. What has been shown by these considerations is that for perception of succession to actually be a perception of successive states of the "object" being experienced is for the succession to have a necessary order. It still includes the major assumption that successive states are states *of* an "object", an assumption that has not yet been validated. Further, this discussion in introducing the distinction between subjective succession and objective succession has failed to demonstrate that the latter is not parasitic upon the former. Without this being established and without the notion of the "object" of experience being justified this discussion of the contrast between objective and subjective succession is, on its own, insufficient to show that we need the concept of causation if our perceptual states are to count as "experiences". What has been added in this discussion to the account thus far developed has been the attention to the *order* of temporal presentation of succession as a means for describing something as objectively successive. This reference to *order* is what we suggested would be necessary given the account of the schema of concepts of relation in the chapter on schematism.

Succession requires rules (A194–5/B239–40)

The development of the argument is now furthered by a short *reductio* proof that succession requires that apprehension be governed by rules. The argument for this is that without provision of this rule succession would only be given to apprehension subjectively and on these grounds we would never be able to tell when successive states were really states of the "object" being perceived rather than merely being part of my way of perceiving. This point is then presented in a sharpened form by Kant that shows that this element of his discussion is bringing us closer to the demonstration we need as Kant states that under these conditions "it would not be possible through our perception to distinguish one appearance from another as regards relations of time" (A194/B239). We discovered the emergence of this consideration in the discussion of the distinction between subjective and objective succession. What Kant was there getting at and here repeats is that the distinction of one temporal appearance from another has *conditions* and that these conditions point to a need for succession to be more than just how I have to present things in general. If succession were just the condition under which I have to present things in general and no more then there would be no way of making the distinction between moving and stationary objects. Since this distinction *is* made the conditions of its being made need to be made clear and these conditions, Kant is again suggesting, point to the need for a notion of succession as something that truly belongs to the appearance of the object as an object of experience and not merely to the nature of my "inner sense" of the object.

If succession were purely understood as the form of "inner sense" and not also something that justly attached to some forms of outer sense as expressive of the nature of the object of appearance in question then "the succession in our apprehension would always be one and the same" and the distinction we *do* make between stationary objects and moving ones would have no justification. So, given that we do experience happenings as taking place, the condition of this must be that these temporal occurrences are governed by a rule according to which the moments of their appearance have an order that is necessarily part of their apprehension. Without this rule we could not state that we experience happenings at all.

This short *reductio* is a much more important contribution to the exposition of the argument than the lengthier treatment of the distinction between objective and subjective succession that preceded it. If we did not have the distinction between objective and subjective succession there would be only arbitrary succession. Such a situation would be one of being in a world in which all combination was merely mathematical. All combination would be based, that is, only on construction without the construction referring us to anything real beyond ourselves and on these grounds we could never state that we had knowledge of "objects". Thus what this argument brings out is that *if there is knowledge of objects*

this is due to the fact that there are happenings, that is, objective successions.
This provides us with a condition for the cognition of "objects" meaning
by this the existence of real things beyond me even taking these things
to be appearances and not things in themselves. Whilst this argument is
important in demonstrating what the condition of "objects" thus involves
it does not show that we actually do have experience of "objects" and
thus does not yet meet the criteria for a successful demonstration of the
principle that we indicated earlier we shared with Guyer. But what this
does promise us is that in justifying the principle of the Second Analogy
Kant will simultaneously justify the notion that experience is necessarily
of objects beyond us.

The conditions of causal awareness and objective succession (A195–9/B240–4)

The development of the argument that is next presented opens through
a consideration of what Kant is suggesting is the nature of the causal
principle which includes a direct reply to Hume though not yet the
decisive answer to "Hume's problem". The opening response to Hume
occurs through a description of what Kant calls the "accepted view" of
how we arrive at the concept of cause, which is by means of comparing
perceptions with each other and thus arriving at an inductive generalization to the effect that "everything which happens has a cause" (A196/
B241).[27] Such inductive generalization would give only comparative
universality, not "genuine universality" as it would derive merely from
custom and association and thus be a form of arbitrary combination. By
contrast Kant wishes to show that the causal rule is *not* derived from
such inductive generalization by means of comparison, as this would
make it a purely mathematical combination and not a dynamical one.
So what Kant will wish to show, it is worth emphasizing yet again, is
that the causal principle does state a real *dynamical* connection as
necessary *within* experience.

After stating this intention, the nature of which will guide the reply
to "Hume's problem", Kant goes on to state that the provision of a rule
of determination of occurrences in succession is what "first makes
possible the representation of a succession in the object" (A197/B242).
In showing this he returns again to the problem of how we arrive at the
conception that our subjective representations are *of* an object, the very
problem that was stated in the Herz letter and that we linked earlier to
Kant's construal of "Hume's problem". This notion that our representations are *of* objects that exist beyond the representations themselves is

one that brings in the conception of a *relation* between the object in question and us. Kant then repeats his view that this very relation to an "object" as something existent beyond us requires that our representations be necessitated to occur in certain determinate time-relations.

The provision of the reason for this contention follows from attending again to the successive condition of apprehension. Succession of apprehension, simply taken alone, would provide us with no "object" of any kind, as nothing would be stable enough to qualify as an object. So succession alone does not appear sufficient for us to arrive at any conception of "objects". But succession is not simply given *tout court*, rather succession is attached as a determination to things that are described *as* having distinct states and for me to view them *as* having these distinct states requires the conception that these states occupy certain determinate temporal positions. The first such is that something previous to the present perception *was* given and, when it was given, it gave to me an impression that was *different* to the present one. So the present perception occurs *subsequent to* the previous one and this subsequent appearance requires that the present perception be taken to *follow from* the previous one. This *following-from* is the statement of a *rule* of temporal determination. The rule is that if one state has succeeded another then this succession is not one that I have any control over. I cannot, at will, suddenly reverse the order in which the states occurred. At this point Kant spells out the qualitative analogy that his argument up to this point has been building towards: "there is an order in our representations in which the present, so far as it has come to be, refers us to some preceding state as a correlate of the event which is given; and though this correlate is, indeed, indeterminate, it none the less stands in a determining relation to the event as its consequence, connecting the event in necessary relation with itself in the time-series" (A198–9/B244).

The time-series was described in the schema of quantity as requiring succession of moments but the schema of relation is suggesting that the elements of this succession cannot be given in just any arbitrary order as would be the case if the causal principle was a form of mathematical combination. As a dynamical relation it specifies a rule that shows that the order of connection between events is one in which the possibility of happenings taking place is dependent upon a *necessary* connection. What is necessary is not what the preceding state given prior to my present state was but that there had to be a preceding state. Furthermore, given that the preceding state was the one that it was, the succeeding state will be precisely the one that it is. The rule is indeterminate in being qualitative, that is what the correlates are in any given case is not described but the *relation of them* is what has a necessary *order*, the order of before and after, an order that shows that succession has to occur in a given form.

Succession thus has to follow the order of time, which demonstrates that the conditions that were set out in the Axioms of Intuition as indicating the presence of extensive magnitudes are now amplified through connection to the relation of cognition to an object that exists beyond the cognizer. For a cognizer to cognize an "object" is for them to relate to it in connection to the order of succession that follows from the nature of time. This will be expanded upon in the next element of the discussion. What we can see in this discussion is that "Hume's problem" has here been centrally connected to the problem posed in the Herz letter just as we initially suggested it would be. This is what this part of the discussion has decisively added to the development of Kant's account and, in the process, he has given grounds for thinking that the causal relation is not a mathematical arbitrary one but a philosophical, qualitative one that has to attach to the existence of what it describes, not arise as a construction of a figure.[28]

The possibility of objects and the nature of time (A199–201/B244–6)

The next section of the argument builds on the previous display of connection between "Hume's problem" and the difficulty stated in the Herz letter. Kant points out that the formal condition of perceptions is that preceding times necessarily determine succeeding ones and that this in fact gives the condition of representation of all temporal objects. It is therefore a condition of the empirical intuition of objects as it is only in this intuition that the continuity of times is apprehended. Next Kant returns to the question about the nature of our understanding of "objects" again and makes a decisively important statement:

> Understanding is required for all experience and for its possibility. Its primary contribution does not consist in making the representation of objects distinct, *but in making the representation of an object possible at all*. (A199/B244–5)

This points to what we, in agreement here with Guyer and in accordance with our interpretation of the connection between Kant's construal of "Hume's problem" and the difficulty stated in the Herz letter, have been contending is central to the proof of the principle of the Second Analogy. The question thus arises as to how the understanding makes the representation of objects possible.

Kant indicates that this occurs through the order that has to be given to time being part of the condition of the existence of "objects" in so far as this existence is something we can cognize at all. All "objects" of experience have determinate positions within time but these positions cannot have arisen from perception of time itself, as there is no perception of time itself. So it must rather be the case that the provision of temporal order within experience arises as a condition for how the objects that are perceived in time are given at all. The series of appearances, that is, "produces and makes necessary the same order and continuous connection in the series of possible perceptions as is met with *a priori* in time" (A200/B245). The order that has to attach to temporality is one of succession such that each moment produces the next, as was specified in the discussion of the Axioms of Intuition. This order has however to also be met with in the series of perceptions or rather cognition has to *produce* it which is why Kant described the principle of the Second Analogy in the first edition as a principle of *production*. This *production* of appearances is the setting out of them according to a rule "under which an event invariably and necessarily follows" that which preceded it. This is the schematization of the principle of sufficient reason, the principle that Kant in the *New Elucidation* already thought of as a "determining" principle. At the next stage of his argument Kant presents the basic proof of the view that this determining principle is "the ground of possible experience" (A201/B246).

The proof of the principle (A201–2/B246–7)

The next section of the discussion is a product of the whole account as we have reconstructed it so far. There is, as was found to be the central contention of the argument of the Transcendental Deduction, no empirical knowledge without transcendental synthesis, the key form of which is that of imagination. Imagination is the means by which we represent to ourselves that which is not present and is hence the means by which temporally discrete moments are brought together. The elements of time have been shown however to have a formal principle, which is that they do not merely succeed each other but do so according to a necessary rule. The provision of this rule requires a determination of the temporal manifold so that the succession in it is ordered. This order indicates to us something more than the process of imaginative combination of parts since imaginative connection is indifferent to necessary order. Production of an "object" in experience is perception of it in accordance with the judgment that must be at work in all experience to the effect that each state is a consequence of the one previous to it. Unless each state is comprehended in this fashion as a product of its predecessors then the order of events will be purely subjective.

> Thus the relation of appearances (as possible perceptions) according to which the subsequent event, that which happens, is, as to its existence, necessarily determined in time by something preceding in conformity with a rule—in other words, the relation of cause to effect—is the condition of the objective validity of our empirical judgments, in respect of the series of perceptions, and so of their empirical truth; that is to say, it is the condition of experience. The principle of the causal relation in the sequence of appearances is therefore also valid of all objects of experience ([in so far as they are] under the conditions of succession), as being itself the ground of the possibility of such experience. (A202/B247)

If something is a possible perception it stands in relation to the states of what preceded it as something produced by these previous states. Unless it possesses this characteristic of necessity it does not belong to the realm of perception at all but merely to a purely subjective combination as occurs in dreams and fantasies, the order of which can vary either at will (in the case of fantasies) or according to rules of association that whilst being beyond me lack necessity of connection (as in dreams). The order of experiences in dynamical connection is the order of perceptions as determined by the order of time. This order of time does not merely show the necessary relations between qualitative points of connection but it also determines these latter so that they can be cognized as "objects". Without the rule of necessary connection there would be no experience of "objects" at all, merely an experience of dreams and fantasies.

The justification of the principle of the Second Analogy is a description according to how anything has to begin, as was described in the formulation of the first edition. Nothing can begin from nothing is a principle that resulted from the consideration of the First Analogy and so anything that begins must do so from a previous state having been given. But if the reference of any beginning is always to a previous state then the production of any state is always a consequence of the preceding ones. This necessity is what Kant is describing as the relation of cause and effect, a relation that enables us to describe "objects" of experience as being precisely "objects" at all. This law guarantees the continuity of objective connection by showing that all succession has to conform to a rule and cannot be merely arbitrary.

Prior to moving to the concluding discussion in which Kant derives from his treatment a connection between substances and causality that shows the relationship between the First Analogy and the Second he includes a brief discussion of simultaneity of cause and effect as the general discussion has seemed to depend upon the view that the appearance of something in a causal connection with something else is a description always of a succession of states. However the heat in a room and the heat in a stove in the room are co-existent with each other so that the relationship between them is one of simultaneity of presence and it is not only not difficult to find a multitude of other examples it is even, as Kant puts it, the normal situation that causes are simultaneous with their effects. This brings us back to the point that what has been Kant's real concern is not the necessity of lapses in time but the necessity of time as a set of perceptions that have *order*. Only certain types of order are possible as for example the heating of the stove is co-determinative of the heating of the room but the relation does not work in reverse if there is nothing else in the room to produce heat. So it is this necessity of one state being the producer of the other that follows from the necessary of temporal objects always being given in definite orders.

Substance and causality: The second proof (A204–11/B249–56)

Kant now proceeds to bring the discussion of the Second Analogy to a conclusion and in doing so provides a second and lengthier proof of its principle that simultaneously connects it to an elucidation of the First Analogy that supplies us with the "empirical criterion" of substances that we found was wanting from the statement of the latter's proof. These closing sections are thus of serious importance for understanding the inter-connection of the analogies. Kant opens this last part of the discussion by stating that the concept of causality leads us to the notion of action and that this latter is connected to force. Forces would be, to put this briefly, what was being manifested in any action through the relation between attractive and repulsive elements. These elements are however expressive of something that they are determinations *of* or, to put this in other terms, if there are forces then they are produced by, and are states of, substances.

The question now turns again to why we take substances to be permanent and Kant responds in accord with the proof of the First Analogy by stating that since the production of effects is the production of something transitory that is given to us under the mode of succession that the ultimate subject of all such changeable determinations must be that which guarantees their unity and this is what we term "substance". Since each change that is brought about involves causal connections these changes require being based on something that does not itself change as without this latter there would be no possibility of awareness of change at all as there would be no distinction *between* things. So if there is action then this points us to the "empirical criterion" of substance as referring to that, which produces the actions in question. The proof of this statement is what brings together the first two analogies in a dense and key paragraph towards the conclusion of the Second.

Kant refers us back to the question of how one state produces another that is successor to the first. We are aware that the production of the change in question requires time and we are aware from the arguments of the Axioms and the Anticipations that all parts of appearances are magnitudes. So transition from one state of things to another is an alteration of the magnitude of the appearances over time. "Now every alteration has a cause which evinces its causality in the whole time in which the alteration takes place" (A208/B253). The alteration in question does not suddenly begin, as it is rather an expression of the constancy we found to be required in the principle of the Anticipations for anything to be experienced at all. So alteration is "a continuous action of the causality" and this continuity of alteration is in fact the fundamental law of nature. All particular "causes" are thus part and parcel of the substantial natures of what is interacting, a point that points us forward to the Third Analogy. The reason given here though for taking it that there is such a fundamental law of nature as that of continuity of action is that neither time nor the appearances in time are reducible to simples. We know that the appearances in time can never be reduced to simples due to the proof of the Anticipations and we can see that since all time is filled with the sensa in question that neither can time itself be reducible to simples. This continuity of action is here clearly expressed as a link between the causal principle and the account of the real given in the Anticipations of Perception.

As Kant concludes the discussion: "every transition in perception to something which follows in time is a determination of time through the generation of this perception, and since time is always and in all its parts a magnitude, is likewise the generation of a perception as a magnitude through all degrees of which no one is the smallest, from zero up to its determinate degree" (A210/B255).

The nature of these proofs

Now that we have stated what the proofs of the principle of the Second Analogy consist in and how Kant arrived at them it is time to review their nature. They are what Steven Bayne has termed "transcendental proofs", that is, proofs based on the possibility of experience. Bayne states that in such cases a proof of necessity is given as the basis on which an experience can occur at all.[29] To understand further this type of proof it is useful to revisit Kant's treatment of the highest principle of synthetic judgments, a treatment given between the chapter on schematism and the Axioms of Intuition. Kant wrote in this section that the explanation of synthetic judgments is the most important question of transcendental logic adding if we not merely look at the possibility of synthetic *a priori* judgments but also "take account of the conditions and scope of their validity" then this gives us the "only question" with which transcendental logic need be concerned (A155/B193). For a synthetic judgment to be given we recall is for a combination to occur between two concepts through the medium of a third something and, following the demonstrations of the Transcendental Deduction and the chapter on schematism, Kant describes this third something as the *a priori* form of inner sense, time. "The synthesis of representations rests on imagination; and their synthetic unity, which is required for judgment, on the unity of apperception" (A155/B194). Imagination is the precondition of all combination as it allows reference to that which is not present. Without reference to that which is not present we could only have comprehension of the unity of a given moment and, whilst even this requires complexity as we demonstrated at length in Chapter 2, the form of judgment points necessarily beyond the particular moment even in attempting to grasp the particularities of that moment. If the form of judgment does this then the combination that is required for judgment to take place has to be connected to that which allows the unitary representation of time and this is the basis of the *symmetry thesis* expressed in the Metaphysical Deduction.

Kant goes on to make clear that cognition can have no object unless any objects that are cognized meet the conditions under which they can be given. For an object to be given however requires it to be thought in relation to the conditions of experience and even space and time have to be connected to the *matter* of such experience if they are to present any object to us. So what transcendental logic has to show is that the conditions of our having any experience in general are that this experience is produced by *a priori* synthesis, which Kant refers to as requiring "universal rules of unity" (A157/B196).

To understand how these rules of unity describe a *dynamical* connection as they are required to do in the proof of the principle of the Second Analogy requires connecting the discussion of the nature of synthetic principles to the division between mathematical and dynamical principles and thus reprising this distinction in order to justify the nature of Kant's proof and doing this will require replying to an objection Paul Guyer makes to the characterization of the dynamical principles.

The distinction between mathematical and dynamical principles revisited

Kant describes dynamical principles, by contrast to mathematical principles, as describing the "existence of the objects of a possible empirical intuition" so that the *a priori* necessity they express is only given "under the condition of empirical thought in some experience" (A160/B200). Kant adds to this account of the dynamical principles the point that they are not, like the mathematical principles, *constitutive* but only regulative, as we cannot construct existence. What is meant by the use of regulative is the provision of a rule that applies to the relations of existence. This point is supported by reference to the philosophical, rather than mathematical, understanding of analogies with Kant stating that if: "a perception is given in a time-relation to some other perception, then even although this latter is indeterminate, and we consequently cannot decide *what* it is, or what its *magnitude* may be, we may none the less assert that in its existence it is necessarily connected with the former in the mode of time" (A179/B222).

Paul Guyer objects to this characterization of dynamical principles, partly due to his failure to attend well to the description of mathematical principles. The nature of the latter, by contrast to the former, is that they describe conditions that enable us to construct the *form* of intuition and the *matter* of empirical intuition. An example that Kant gives here of the construction of the *degree* of sensations of sunlight is described as including a set quantitative magnitude of illuminations of the moon. Guyer objects to this example and in the process to the distinction between these principles writing: "The principle tells me that I can assign *some* definite degree to the intensity of my sensation of sunlight, and thus to the real which it represents, namely sunlight itself, by measuring it with *some* unit based on *some* . . . sensation of light" (Guyer, 1987, p. 188). The point of this is to state that the application of mathematical principles to empirical objects is always indeterminate and, since he takes the difference Kant has described between mathematical and dynamical principles to be that the former are supposedly determinate and the latter not, he proceeds to deny that there is a difference in kind between constitutive and dynamical principles stating: "To the extent that any of these principles are valid, they are all certainly regulative in the sense defined" (Guyer, 1987, p. 189).

To respond to this criticism is important, as the distinction between mathematical and dynamical principles is central to the type of proof being offered of the Second Analogy. Guyer's account depends on viewing Kant's distinction as one between determinate mathematical principles and indeterminate dynamical principles, a distinction Guyer believes is not substantiated by the examples Kant gives of the operation of these principles. The passages from which Guyer takes these characterizations and on which his interpretation is based are from the proof of the general principle of the analogies. Kant has here indicated that the analogies rest on the necessary unity of apperception in respect of possible empirical consciousness of perception "*at every [instant of] time*" (B220). Kant then goes on to state that these rules of universal time-determination tell us not about the synthesis of empirical intuitions but the relation of the appearances within these intuitions in their existence. It is the *existence* of these appearances that cannot be produced *a priori* and *even were existence to be open to inferential demonstration*, it could not be cognized in any determinate fashion. The denial of determination to the dynamical principles is a denial of determination of *what* could exist but Kant subsequently adds it is also a denial of determination of the *magnitude* of what could exist.

This differs from the procedure of mathematics, as what can only occur in mathematics is a procedure of combination whereby a *degree* of sensation *can be constructed* from information concerning illumination. The example here is meant to show that the *matter* of the sensation can be anticipated *given* that an equation is set up between distinct quantities such as the description of the nature of the illumination and the effect of this quantity on another given quantity. The result of the equation arises from the equality of the related quantities and the result is thus *determinate*. The description of the dynamical principles by contrast includes the necessity, given the existence of two states of *determinate order* between them.

Due to the fact that Guyer has not attended to this difference in determination of the mathematical and dynamical principles he expects the principle of the Second Analogy to justify something quite different to what it does. Thus Guyer describes the justification of this principle via emphasis on the contrast between the ship and the house, the contrast we took to be part of the build-up to Kant's proof, not to be the proof itself. Guyer interprets the contrast between the house and the ship as providing Kant's proof by the following explanation of what is shown by this contrast:

> Kant's theory is precisely that it is only if we are *in possession* of causal laws which dictate that in the relevant circumstances—that is, not in general, but in the particular circumstances of wind, tide, setting of the sails, and so forth, which are assumed to obtain—the ship could *only* sail downstream that we actually have sufficient evidence to interpret our representations of it to mean that it *is* sailing downstream.[30]

This description of "Kant's theory" is precisely wrong as it suggests that the grasp of these laws has to precede the awareness of the event as being the event that it is and it also builds into the laws in question the reference to determinate individual particulars that results from a conflation of the dynamical principles with the mathematical ones. Guyer's statement of this view was introduced as a reply to an account of Kant's principle provided by Graham Bird. Bird in fact characterizes part of Kant's point here better than Guyer as Bird correctly *denies* that Kant's principle requires reference to *particular* causes but Bird derives from this point the view that the causal law "expresses a conceptual truth which is a precondition of the formulation or discovery of particular causal laws".[31] If the causal law merely stated a *conceptual truth* then it would not be synthetic *a priori* and thus Bird assimilates the dynamical principles here to analytic truths, a mistake attributable to neglect of Kant's conception of *transcendental* logic.[32]

Transcendental logic, as we have unearthed from Kant's account of the principle of synthetic judgments, is concerned neither with the justification of *particular* empirical judgments as Guyer suggests nor with revealing conditions of purely conceptual dependence as Bird suggests. It is rather concerned with the justification of synthetic *a priori* judgments, judgments that reveal to us the conditions of possibility of experience. Thus what changes is a mode of determination of substance and this mode of determination is also what allows us to state that *there are objects at all.* What, though, is the condition of there being any objects? It is expressed in what Kant terms the "highest principle of all synthetic judgments", a principle that he gives in the following form: "every object stands under the necessary conditions of synthetic unity of the manifold of intuition in a possible experience" (A158/B197).

The necessary conditions of synthetic unity of the manifold of intuition were given in the mathematical principles. The Axioms describe for us the universal condition of all intuitions, which is that they are combined by the transcendental synthesis of imagination. This guarantees pure mathematics and at the same time describes the necessary form of empirical intuition. Kant indicated that the result of this was to show that what is constructed in pure mathematics is "necessarily valid" of the objects apprehended in empirical intuition so that space is necessarily in conformity with geometry. After defending this principle Kant outlined the other mathematical principle as showing us that the nature of all the *matter* of intuition was such that it must have a *degree*, something that applied even to *quale* and that showed all *quale* must be subject to a rule of continuity. However if it therefore follows from the defence of these mathematical principles that the *form* of intuition and its *matter* require "progression in time" (A170/B211) then the condition of any *object* that is given to us in experience is that it must *fall under* these principles even though we cannot anticipate anything more about its particularity than was given in the material principle of the Anticipations.

The demonstration of the mathematical principles has thus already shown us a great deal as on the basis of these principles we can state that if there are any "objects" they have to possess *continuity of degree* and hence be given according to the conditions of temporality, that is, as *flowing.* This brings out why Kant spends so much time in the discussion of the Second Analogy with the notion of succession. If there is continuity in apprehension as its necessary condition then any "objects" have to follow the rule of this continuity As Kant went on to write after stating the supreme principle of synthetic judgments: "the conditions of the *possibility of experience* in general are likewise conditions of the *possibility of the objects of experience*" (A158/B197). We can now see that what this is stating is that there could be no experience of objects at all if objects did not meet the conditions of possibility of experience in general so that the arrival at the conviction that there *are* objects is, considered from the standpoint of transcendental philosophy, *the result of the description of the conditions under which they could possibly exist*. The condition that is shown to be *necessary* for the *existence* of objects is thus that they must conform to the conditions of successive apprehension but that such conditions require that there are *determinate* orders of apprehension and these determinate orders are *productive of the objects themselves*. This is the sense in which the transcendental synthesis of imagination is a *productive synthesis* as it, in combining percepts together by means of an *a priori* rule of succession, provides the condition under which all sensa can possibly be given as objective.

The description at the close of the B-Deduction of the synthesis of apprehension is thus now one that we can see to provide a foretaste of the defence of the schematized category of causality in the Second Analogy. Kant there described the apprehension of the house as occurring in conformity with the synthetic unity of the manifold in space and thus as something presented in accord with the principle of the Axioms of Intuition. Having stated this Kant went on to describe the perception of the freezing of water, a perception that is one of successive states being perceived *in an object*. Thus there is here reference to temporal order, which is determined, and the combination of this order here occurs by the category of cause being applied to sensibility, which states that the order is governed by a universal rule (B163–4).

Kant's conception of "Hume's problem" and the difficulty of the Herz letter

Having described what the proof consists in and the connection of it to Kant's notion of dynamical principles I have almost completed my account of the Second Analogy. The Second Analogy was justified, in accord with a long pattern of interpretations of it, as Kant's response to "Hume's problem" but, distinctively, I took Kant's conception of this problem to be based on the difficulty he expressed in his celebrated letter to Herz. In what sense then does the proof Kant provides of the principle of the Second Analogy constitute a response to what he took "Hume's problem" to be?

We found that the characterization Kant gave of "Hume's problem" in the "Preface" to the *Prolegomena* concerned what reason we have to think that the positing of the existence of one thing leads to the positing of the existence of another. What we have found to be Kant's reply is that the positing of the existence of anything at all is under the condition of succession and that for succession to be *of objects* is for the latter to conform to the conditions of the *matter* of intuition. The *objects are generated from the matter of intuition as flowing* and the nature of this flowing is that it must, in the first place, be *objective*. The rationale for this assertion is provided in the concluding considerations of the Second Analogy, considerations I presented above as the second proof of its principle.[33] These concluding considerations bring the discussion of the Second Analogy into connection with those of the First and point forward to the Third. What Kant states here is that permanent substances are the ground of the production of forces and that all change, in conformity with the demonstrations of the mathematical principles, is an alteration of magnitudes. The alteration of magnitudes was demonstrated in the description of the Anticipations of Perception to require continuity of action and showed us that there are no simples. So, if experience is *of objects* these objects have to conform to the conditions we found applied to sensibilia.

The concluding argument thus connected the principle of the Second Analogy to the principle of the First and showed that experience of objects must be experience of *quanta continua*. The reason for taking it that what experience is of cannot merely be sensa but must point also to "objects" is that, as was shown in the First Analogy, all alteration is alteration of something that does not alter so what experience of forces is experience *of* is the *action of substances*. The first argument for the Second Analogy already showed that empirical knowledge must be dependent on the transcendental synthesis of imagination which unifies time and, when we connect this to the argument of the First Analogy, what we can state is that unity of temporality is dependent on the unity of temporal objects. So, given the combination of the First Analogy with the argument of the Anticipations, we get as a result the fact that there must be succession of objective apprehension or, otherwise put, *substances must be productive of the flows of forces in experience.* When we make judgments of experience we *produce* the objects we are judging by placing them under the conditions of pure concepts, as these pure concepts of substance and causality are *the* concepts that unite the elements of our judgment by combining the elements of time together in a necessary order. This is Kant's argument and his reply to his construal of "Hume's problem".

The reply to the difficulty Kant raised in the Herz letter is to state that pure concepts bring the object they describe into being so that the possibility of intentionality, that is, of making objects that are *about* something is based on the combination of concepts together in a necessary manner through the *a priori* combination of synthesis in accordance with the *a priori* forms of sensibility. The principles of pure understanding are required to show that representations are of objects as without use of these principles according to the necessary forms of sensibility we could have no experience except through arbitrary combination of figures and thus imagination would be alone the basis of experience. The *a priori* combination of imaginative elements is what leads the combination to have an order that is invariant and this shows that the relational categories are necessary for objects of experience. This brings together the criteria we argued would be necessary for the argument of the Second Analogy and shows that this argument thus conforms to the requirements set by the preceding parts of the *Critique* just as Kant's account of the supreme principle of synthetic judgments would lead one to think it should. Marginalization of the mathematical principles thus has the effect of obscuring Kant's transcendental description of experience as does taking the point of these principles to be the justification of the application of mathematics or to be only concerned with the justification of it. In showing the necessary nature of the *form* and *matter* of experience Kant has prepared the way for showing what *relation to an object* must be concerned with and in his proof of the principle of the Second Analogy has demonstrated that this relation must be governed by an *a priori* rule that regulates all appearances.

The principle of the Third Analogy

As with the first two analogies Kant alters both the title and the formulation of the principle of the Third Analogy between the two editions of the *Critique*. In the first edition the title of the principle described it as being of community, which refers us to the third of the categories of relation. The formulation of the principle in the first edition states: "All substances, so far as they coexist, stand in throughgoing community, that is, in mutual interaction" (A211). This principle follows from that of the first two analogies in showing that the existence of different substances requires their interconnection. The title of the principle in the second edition is "a principle of coexistence in accordance with the law of reciprocity or community" and it is now formulated in the following way: "All substances, in so far as they can be perceived to coexist in space, are in throughgoing reciprocity" (B256). The second edition formulation, like the first, states a universal condition but its title now clearly describes this condition as one that is a law and the second edition formulation has the clear advantage of referring to the condition of the reciprocity of substances to be that they are *perceived* to co-exist *in space*. The reference to perception connects the principle of the Third Analogy to the Anticipations of Perception and the reference to space also refers us to the Axioms of Intuition. These twin backward references to the mathematical principles show that the Third Analogy, like the Second, is clearly intended to build on the demonstrations of them in accordance with Kant's declared procedure.

The argument for the Third Analogy

The proof of the principle of the Second Analogy focused on the conditions of successive apprehension being objective. The proof of the principle of the Third Analogy has a related objective, namely to show that the simultaneous apprehension of two distinct states is apprehension of two distinct objects. Since the Second Analogy has demonstrated to us that the *production* of objects themselves is dependent upon the synthetic *a priori* combination of perceptions by means of pure concepts of understanding we will naturally expect the proof of this principle to build upon that of the Second Analogy.

In experience we take two things to be simultaneously existent when it is possible to view them in any order. Since time is not itself an object of perception the question is what, in the nature of empirical intuition, leads us to correctly judge that this is the case? The synthesis of imagination is again insufficient to show this alone as the presentation of the respective objects could be varied by imagination without us therefore being able to say that the different things were both existent at the same time. So, as was the case with the Second Analogy, we need recourse to a pure concept in order to be able to describe the two simultaneously existent things to be in reciprocal relation with each other. What is required to describe simultaneous co-existence is that the distinct existences influence each other or are in reciprocal interaction. So if we experience two things as co-existent within the same space we need to be able to assert that the two things have an effect upon each other.

The reasoning that follows for this conclusion is that the substances could have no relation to each other at all if each was completely without effect on the other. So we would not be able to perceive co-existence of perceptions unless these perceptions were of things that affected each other. If the substances did not affect each other they would be separated by an empty space and then it would not be possible for the synthesis of perceptions to determine whether things were co-existent or successive. So they must affect each other and this implies that each substance "must therefore contain in itself the causality of certain determinations in the other substance, and at the same time the effects of the causality of that other" (A212/B259). This mutuality of connection between the substances is necessary for the co-existence of them as without this mutuality there would either not be *community* between the substances or one of them would simply not *be* a substance. If there are distinct forces, as we have had reason to think since we looked at the demonstrations of the *New Elucidation* that there are, forces such as attraction and repulsion, then there must be distinct substances that are the *bearers* of these forces. Unless there were *distinct substances* there would be no ground for claiming that the forces were also distinct. Further, unless these substances were in *community* with each other there would be no way of justifying the view that these forces belonged together to one world. Thus dynamical community of forces is the ground of the possibility of the forces belonging together to the same world-whole.

If the basis of the co-existence of different objects is thus revealed to reside in the necessity of the dynamical community of substances then the possibility of the objects of experience is hereby revealed to require this community. What this points to with regard to empirical judgments is the "continuous influences in all parts of space" that are required for us to perceive any element of what is given within this unitary space. So it is not merely the case that unity of space is required for us to perceive anything as this unity of space is dependent itself on the unity of the *matter* of sensation as we would expect from the proof of the Anticipations of Perception. This demonstrates that the way Kant has retrieved his description of position in the 1768 essay on directions of space that all parts of it require reference to a whole is by now stating that this whole is not merely mathematical as the Newtonian view requires but rather dynamical, that is, a principle of the *matter* of space: "We cannot empirically change our position, and perceive the change, unless matter in all parts of space makes perception of our position possible to us" (A213/B260).

The parts of matter are related not mereologically through space but rather through reciprocal influence, a reciprocity that makes the mereological connection of spaces itself coherently dependent upon the matter of what is presented *through* it. This community of all matter is the basis of the continuity of perception as belonging to a dynamical world-whole as without this perceptions would be broken at every moment and would stand in no relation to time. This requires that objects of experience exert *real influence* upon one another and without this real influence we could not, in experience, find perceptions to actually be of co-existent things.

Our perception of co-existent things is perception of them as belonging together to a unitary space but this perception of the unitary space is further dependent on the combination of all parts of space together with the parts of time. The unity of space indicates that co-existence of objects is an expression of the *quanta continua* of the *matter* of perception and if this matter reveals to us different forces then these forces have to be connected to discrete substances. These discrete substances thus *interact* with each other and must do so continuously for the spatial perception of co-existence to be possible. So the unity of space as dependent upon the unity of time shows that the substances that are required to unite the latter must be continuously engaged with each other. Kant in fact expresses this clearly in a letter to Johann Schultz dated 17 February 1784 where he writes: "the fact that determinations of one substance can be produced by another substance is an idea that one cannot absolutely presuppose; rather, the idea is one of the syntheses without which no reciprocal relation of objects in space, and consequently no outer experience, would be possible" (Ak. 10: 367). The continuity of connection of all substances is thus productive of space itself, which could not otherwise be given to us as a unity. Thus with the proof of the Third Analogy Kant demonstrates that the mathematical principles that described the nature of spatial connection are themselves connected to an *actual* world only through this dynamical principle.[34]

The Second and Third analogies and the *New Elucidation*

Before turning to an account of the inter-relationship of the three analogies I wish to reprise the connection of the principles of the Second and Third analogies with the Principles of Succession and Co-Existence described in the *New Elucidation*. The Principle of Succession in the *New Elucidation* described reciprocal dependence of substances upon each other as the condition of possibility of substances changing. This principle hence is the ancestor of the Third Analogy. In defending this principle Kant denied the Leibnizian notion of pre-established harmony, a notion that is clearly still his target in the discussion of the Third Analogy so that the defence of this principle constitutes Kant's reply to Leibniz. In the *New Elucidation* Kant's defence of his principle already pointed to the need for external relations to be connected to substances if substances were to be capable of change. In doing so Kant was on the brink here of arguing for the need for space to be given for succession of time to be capable of describing change. In a sense this defence, if so assayed, would have required the Second Analogy to be based upon the Third. What ruins this possibility in the *New Elucidation* is the defence of the succeeding Principle of Co-Existence. This principle argues that the condition of substances' interaction is by reference to a principle of the divine understanding. Given this dependence on the divine understanding Kant's account of his two principles in the *New Elucidation* has an arbitrary element in it. Its arbitrary character was noted also by Langton who confessed that on the basis of the *New Elucidation* Kant's denial of the reducibility of relational properties depended on his conception of them as being super-added by God, something that would make their connection with substances *accidental* (Langton, 1998, p. 121).

In the *Critique*, by contrast, the Second Analogy shows that the condition of representation of any object at all is that objects have to conform to the conditions of sensibility defended in the mathematical principles so that dynamical connection can be seen to be necessary in the world due to the fact that all *matter* in the world is continuous. This reference of the Second Analogy to the principle of the Anticipations of Perception shows that Kant has come to the view that material principles are essential for transcendental philosophy. These material principles define the form of a world as being one that is *experienced* not merely described in concepts and figures. The forces that are subsequently described in the Third Analogy are not *super-added* to the world, they are what make the world a *material* one, or a *dynamical* whole that has *mathematical* qualities built into its necessary conditions of being given. Thus in the *Critique* Kant has arrived at a conception of substance that is not dependent on accidental combinations, even ones produced by God. The world is not merely a whole of arbitrary combinations; it is rather one of necessary connections. The basis for this move is the rejection of the Cartesian conception that the primary qualities of bodies are defined as extensive as these qualities are rather the *formal* ones of intuition whilst the *material* ones of nature are intensive. The intensive primary qualities of bodies are the forces that are expressed to us through sensations and which enable us to be affected. The transcendental receptivity that is at the basis of our experience is hereby expressed, a position that Kant was incapable of stating in the *New*

Elucidation due to the absence throughout his "pre-Critical" period of the question he posed in the Herz letter. The arrival at this question forced Kant to think about the nature of the relation of cognition to its object, the fundamental question that enabled him to re-pose the difficulty of how substances are causally related.[35]

The connection of the three analogies

The inter-connection of the three analogies is that in each of them time is represented as the condition of *a priori* determination of representations in experience and yet the nature of this determination is, as was promised in the Aesthetic, described by analogy to space (A33/B50). The analogies to space are drawn out in the concluding discussion by Kant: "the relation to time itself as a magnitude (the magnitude of existence, that is, *duration*), the relation in time as a *successive* series, and finally the relation in time as a sum of all *simultaneous* existence" (A215/B262). In taking time to be a magnitude we are presenting it as *extensive* but the only way extensive magnitudes can actually be *dynamically* given, that is, attached to existence, is by revealing the condition of duration to be one that requires that there are substances. In taking time to describe a *series* we are representing it spatially, normally by drawing a line in thought. This representation is one whereby we subject all appearances to successive conditions. These conditions require a means of being given that is *determinate* if they are to describe objects at all as without this determination no state would be sufficiently stable to be descriptive of objects. This determination is one of necessary time-order. Finally, the representation of simultaneous existence is a clear way in which temporal relations are connected to spatial ones as only by means of positions being taken to belong to an equivalent whole can they be said to be simultaneous. If they were part of an equivalent whole this would be merely mathematical unless the parts thereof were mutually intertwined. This mutual connection of all the parts of experience together is the description of nature as a dynamical whole. So nature is "the connection of appearances as regards their existence according to necessary rules, that is, according to laws" (A216/B263). The original laws, which make experience itself possible at all, are the *a priori* rules revealed by transcendental inquiry. The connection of the three analogies together is described in the Third as it shows that the whole that is dynamical requires reference of all its parts to a principle of substantial inter-connection. On this basis we can state that all appearances "lie, and must lie, in *one* nature, because without this *a priori* unity of experience" no determination of objects would be possible at all.

The dynamical community of substances is a key principle of transcendental idealism and the nature of the arguments of the Analogies shows Kant to clearly be engaged in renovation of metaphysics. The burden of this chapter and this book has been to show how the *Critique* requires and elaborates an account of transcendental synthesis culminating in the description of the material theory of experience that we have described. The nature of Kant's subsequent investigations of this material theory of experience in the *Metaphysical Foundations of Natural Science*, later lectures on metaphysics and the *Opus Postumum* cannot be dealt with here but is essential to the consideration of the nature of Kant's contribution to metaphysics. Focus on the *Critique* leads to the need for consideration of Kant's own systematic understanding of metaphysics, one that the *Critique* was only intended to be a propaedeutic for.

Notes

1 Synthesis and intuition

1. Wilfrid Sellars (1968) *Science and Metaphysics: Variations on Kantian Themes*, London and New York: Routledge.
2. It is worth contrasting this characterization with that Sellars gives elsewhere of receptivity where he speaks of that "that peculiar brand of the passivity of sense and the spontaneity of the understanding which is 'receptivity'", a brand that enables representations of "this-φ" rather than full-fledged judgments. Wilfrid Sellars (1967) "Some Remarks on Kant's Theory of Experience" in W. Sellars (1974) *Essays on Philosophy and Its History*, Dordrecht and Boston: D. Reidel Publishing Company, p. 49. What this indicates is that the nature of the relationship between spontaneity and receptivity is the fundamental question in grasping Kant's account of experience. We will return to further reflections on this problem in Chapter 2.
3. Sellars introduces this notion in §39, p. 16 of Sellars (1968) and here credits Wittgenstein for introducing this "relevant concept". See Ludwig Wittgenstein (1945–9) *Philosophical Investigations*, translated by G. E. M. Anscombe, Oxford: Basil Blackwell, 1953, §§169–78.
4. John McDowell (1998) "Having the World in View: Sellars, Kant, and Intentionality", *The Journal of Philosophy*, Vol. XCV, No. 9, p. 456. McDowell's article is the printed version of the Woodbridge Lectures that he gave in 1997 at Columbia University. In support of this account by McDowell of the role of analogy in Sellars' view, see the following passage from *Science and Metaphysics*: "By overlooking the importance of analogical concepts—save in theological contexts—and hence by failing to note the analogical character of our concepts of the attributes and relations which sense impressions *must* have to perform their explanatory role, Kant reduces the concepts of receptivity and sensibility to empty abstractions" (Sellars, 1968, §77, p. 30).
5. The importance of this account is that it requires an understanding of the treatment of space in the Refutation of Idealism to be related to the notion of Aristotelian abstraction.
6. In footnote 23 to page 446 of the Woodbridge Lectures McDowell states that this involves a change of view from that he presented in his earlier book *Mind and World*. The argument of *Mind and World* was explicitly connected to an interpretation of Kant that was derived from Peter Strawson, via the intermediary of Gareth Evans. McDowell presented there a notion of a "transcendental framework" that basically fits the characterization of transcendental philosophy that he later came to reject: see for example John McDowell (1994) *Mind and World*, Cambridge, Mass. and London, Harvard University Press, p. 43. The rejection of this standpoint in the Woodbridge Lectures is accompanied by the suggestion that the adoption of this picture of transcendental philosophy was to do with the influence of Richard Rorty although it is worth noting that the vast majority of references to Rorty in *Mind and World* are critical.

The rejection of the earlier position also leads McDowell to now see a connection between Kant and Hegel as when he writes that: "the thought that Hegel tries to capture with the image of Reason as subject to no external constraint—the rejection of a sideways-on standpoint for philosophy—is already Kant's own thought" (McDowell, 1998, p. 490).

7. Patricia Kitcher (1986) "Connecting Intuitions and Concepts at B160n", *Southern Journal of Philosophy*, Vol. XXV, Supplement, p. 141.

8. Günter Zöeller (1987) "Comments on Professor Kitcher's 'Connecting Intuitions and Concepts at B160n'", *Southern Journal of Philosophy*, Vol. XXV, Supplement, p. 152. Zöeller goes on to point out the artificiality of the notion of "after the fact" awareness of the unity of the manifold.

9. Zöeller's positive reading of the note is given in the following passage: "Kant merely claims that the unity of the formal intuition '*belongs* (gehört) to space and time, and not to the concept of the understanding' (B161n; my emphasis). He nowhere claims that the unity in question *originates* in sensibility. There is no inconsistency in Kant's claiming that formal intuitions belong to sensibility and that they presuppose a synthesis if one considers formal intuitions as products originating through a synthesis exercised by the understanding upon the pure manifold of the senses. And there would be no need, then, for ascribing to Kant an equivocal use of the term 'formal intuition'" (Zöeller, 1987, p. 154).

Whilst this view is attractive in getting away from the notion that Kant is somehow suffering from a confusion due to a conflation of senses of a term, it ignores the statement of the sentence previous in the note where Kant states that the unity "precedes all concepts" even though it presupposes synthesis. Hence this synthetically produced unity that is prior to concepts does need accounting for and Zöeller does not do so.

10. The "Kant book" is of course Martin Heidegger (1929) *Kant and the Problem of Metaphysics*, translated by Richard Taft, Bloomington and Indianapolis: Indiana University Press, 1990. The lecture course that preceded its publication and in which Heidegger gave the first version of his interpretation was given in the winter semester of 1927–8 at the University of Marburg. This course has now been published and translated as Martin Heidegger (1927) *Phenomenological Interpretation of Kant's "Critique of Pure Reason"*, translated by Parvis Emad and Kenneth Maly, Bloomington and Indianapolis: Indiana University Press, 1997, and will be cited hereafter as Heidegger (1927–8).

11. This contrasts interestingly with Sellars' suggestion that the understanding has "its own mode of receptivity" (Sellars, 1968, p. 2).

12. For Heidegger by contrast it is geometry that is a formal intuition and this identification of formal intuition with geometry is what leads Heidegger to speak of a different unity, a "syndotical" one that is supposed to be the one prior to concepts but this mangles the text of the note very badly. For a similar complaint, see Martin Weatherston (2002) *Heidegger's Interpretation of Kant: Categories, Imagination and Temporality*, London and New York: Palgrave Macmillan, p. 54.

13. The basic problem with Heidegger's account is thus that on his reading if there is a pre-conceptual unity this can have nothing to do with synthesis of the understanding. This is the reason why he reaches for the notion of

"syndosis". If this notion is to be avoided in the interests of articulating the nature of Kant's view then it is as well to point out that what needs to be accounted for is this action of the understanding that is pre-conceptual. It is worth pointing out that Heidegger's account of this problem is only given in the lecture course and does not get repeated in *Kant and the Problem of Metaphysics*, a fact that ensures that the latter work scarcely mentions our problem at all. It is merely touched on in the latter work as in the following: "Pure intuition, then, very much has its 'something intuited', and indeed has it to the degree that it gives this intuited only in and through the intuiting itself" (Heidegger, 1929, p. 33).

14. Henry Allison (1983) *Kant's Transcendental Idealism: An Interpretation and Defense*, New Haven and London: Yale University Press, pp. 96–7. In the recent re-edition of his work Allison no longer words matters in quite the same way but he still is clear in stating that the difference between forms of intuition and formal intuition is one between conceptualization and its absence. See Henry Allison (2004) *Kant's Transcendental Idealism: An Interpretation and Defense*, Revised and Enlarged Edition, New Haven and London: Yale University Press, p. 115.

15. Wayne Waxman (1991) *Kant's Model of the Mind: A New Interpretation of Transcendental Idealism*, Oxford and New York: Oxford University Press, p. 95. Whilst Waxman does agree with Heidegger that it is the notion of forms of intuition that has to be explained this does not mean that he subscribes to Heidegger's conception of what a formal intuition consists in as whilst for Heidegger this refers us to geometry for Waxman by contrast it refers to the indeterminate unities of the Transcendental Aesthetic.

16. Jaakko Hintikka (1969) "On Kant's Notion of Intuition (Anschauung)" in T. Penelhum and J. J. MacIntosh (eds) *The First Critique: Reflections on Kant's Critique of Pure Reason*, Belmont: Wadsworth Publishing Company.

17. Manley Thompson (1972) "Singular Terms and Intuitions in Kant's Epistemology", *Review of Metaphysics*, Vol. 26, p. 319.

18. Thompson further argues that the distinction between empirical intuitions and pure intuitions is that whilst the former are unified by concepts the latter have a unity of their own, a point that harmonizes with the statement at B160n. This leads him to a very different account of Space to that of Sellars: "While Kant holds that we must intuit all 'outer' objects under the forms of space and time, he does not hold that we must represent them conceptually in any specific spatiotemporal relation to ourselves beyond that indicated by the word 'outer'. The specific relations we represent by demonstratives are conceptual determinations of what we intuit, just as much as any other relation to which we give a linguistic representation" (Thompson, 1972, p. 329).

19. Lorne Falkenstein (1991) "Kant's Account of Intuition", *Canadian Journal of Philosophy*, Vol. 21, No. 2. Falkenstein's argument can be construed on the general terms he gives on page 189 of this article as proceeding in the following way: "The pattern of argument, therefore, is that of inference from what is given in the intellectual representation back to what must have been present in the data originally given to intellect prior to processing."

20. Howard Caygill (1995) *A Kant Dictionary*, Oxford: Basil Blackwell, pp. 265–6.

2 Judgment and austerity

1. Dieter Henrich (1976) "Identity and Objectivity: An Inquiry into Kant's Transcendental Deduction" in D. Henrich (1994) *The Unity of Reason: Essays on Kant's Philosophy*, Cambridge, Mass. and London: Harvard University Press, p. 130. The essay in question is translated here by Jeffrey Edwards. The suggestion of this "data sensualism" is akin to Sellars' view as given in *Science and Metaphysics* Chapter 1 that intuition should, when considered in its immediacy, be construed on the model of Humean impressions.
2. As Henrich puts this: "The cognitive setting and the multiplicity of occurrences through which an object is presented to us can change to a great extent while the object of cognition remains the same" (Henrich, 1976, p. 131).
3. This way of framing the problem should remind one of what is stated in Chapter 1 of *Science and Metaphysics* concerning the nature of space as a form of outer sense.
4. This fact about judgments is what in fact led to the dispute concerning Bolzano's notion of "objectless presentations". For a description of this in connection to mereology, see G. Banham (2005a) "Mereology, Intentional Contents and Intentional Objects" in G. Banham (ed.) (2005b) *Husserl and the Logic of Experience*, London and New York: Palgrave Macmillan.
5. P. F. Strawson (1974a) *Subject and Predicate in Logic and Grammar*, London: Methuen & Co.: Ltd, pp. 14–15. Strawson goes on to remark that the statement as literally given here is an "exaggeration" as the judgments in question would be corrigible but this simply relocates the force of the statement as asserting isomorphic relation.
6. "To illustrate the notion of a range: the concepts of lion, tiger, panther, belong to one range, the feline animal-species range; the concept of yellow, red, blue, to another, that of colour or hue; of lying, standing, sitting, say, to another (physical attitude); of being completely surrounded by, being to the right of, being to the left of, being above, below, on a level with, to another (possible) range; of being square, circular, triangular, to another" (Strawson, 1974a, p. 18).
7. Henrich seems to also be of the view that this conclusion tells against the characterization of judgment that we cited above from the Metaphysical Deduction (A68–9/B93–4). The reason he thinks this is that in that citation Kant asserted that the arrival of a *higher* presentation than that of the pure simple of "sensation$_1$" was described by the presentation of the collective function of judging itself. It is clear from the examination of Strawson's argument that this cannot be adjudged to be the effect purely of combination itself but what can be said to follow from it is the arrangement of relations into a more complex pattern.
8. It will be necessary next to look at a number of distinct pieces by Sellars (and, as we shall soon see, others as well) and I will in treating these initially describe some lines of argument prior to citing the pieces in question. The point of this is to allow what is persuasive in the lines of argument set to emerge without having to track each stage of the articles in question which have many more agendas than it is necessary or desirable to pursue and critically analyse here.
9. Wilfrid Sellars (1949) "The Logic of Complex Particulars", *Mind* NS, Vol. 58, No. 231, p. 310.

10. This conclusion points, as Sellars notes, in the direction of the assumption that there is a further aspect to the judgment, namely that the *ingredient* in the judgment is a *case* or *instance*. This would support the view that such ingredients are instances of a certain sort of universal, a qualitative one. The argument to this effect requires a description of the nature of universals that would begin from the suggestion that particulars are indeed discreetly different in different instances and that qualitative universals are arrived at through a form of "distributive unity". For arguments to this effect, see the following articles by G. F. Stout (1930) "The Nature of Universals and Propositions", *Proceedings of the British Academy*; (1947) "Distributive Unity as a Category", *Australasian Journal of Philosophy*. It is to forestall this argument that Strawson argues that the capacity of a judgment to be truth-bearing does not reside in a quality of exemplification (Strawson, 1974a, p. 22). It is however noteworthy that Strawson's strictures here touch only on the "linguistic expression of the judgment" whereas Sellars' use of an argument that is akin to that of Stout is precisely not concerned with this.

11. Strawson's asymmetry between the properties of particulars and the properties of concepts that describe particulars already led in this direction but his commitment to thinking of the subject–predicate relationship as the "basic combination" of judgment naturally prevented him from analysing the possibility of judgments that concerned themselves with understanding the *otherness* rather than the *incompatibility* of statements concerning particulars.

12. This gives him the *atomic reduction* of statements as in the example: "Anger (Fido)=(Ey) I (y, Fido) & Anger (y)" or there exists a y such that y is an ingredient of Fido and this y is what is termed anger. This is what I would term an atomic judgment though Sellars is clear that it is not a necessary condition of the analysis that any such judgments ever actually take place.

13. Hence the problem with which Locke is apparently grappling, whether we take him to subscribe to the existence of such substrata or to be revealing the basic impossibility of them, would be effectively one against a notion that there is no logical reason to uphold.

14. The "obvious" source of arrival at this notion is that particulars are *misunderstood* to be facts. As will be seen shortly, despite the fact that Sellars' whole point is to suggest that *this* confusion is *not* the source of the central problem with the doctrine of "bare particulars", Alston assumes that this *is* precisely Sellars' point.

15. Despite the fact that Sellars adds here that each particular could be thought of also as an instance of one simple dyadic relation and that simple triadic relations can also be patterned on this notion (etc.). Carl Hempel seems to have missed this point and thought it possible to provide a riposte to Sellars' whole discussion on the basis of pointing to the possibility of such simple relational universals. See Carl Hempel (1958) "Review" of Sellars (1949 and 1952) with Alston (1954) *The Journal of Symbolic Logic*, Vol. 23, No. 4, pp. 441–2.

16. Wilfrid Sellars (1952) "Particulars" in Sellars (ed.) (1963) *Science, Perception and Reality*, London: Routledge & Kegan Paul and New York: Humanities Press, p. 286.

17. That bare particulars are thus in a sense not particulars at all but only facts is hereby demonstrated but as will be shown this alone is not sufficient to remove the notion from analytic ontology.

18. In Sellars (1949) four different types of such complexes are distinguished leading from the atomic judgment to judgments that describe characteristics of objects. To review these and their relation to the argument stated in Sellars (1952) would take us far from our objective here but that this would be necessary to think of a logic that would describe ontological relations clearly is a cardinal contention of Sellars. A comparison and clarification of the relation between this attempt and the construction of formal ontology in the work of Edmund Husserl would be a rich task to undertake elsewhere.

19. William P. Alston (1954) "Particulars—Bare and Qualified", *Philosophy and Phenomenological Research*, Vol. 15, No. 2, pp. 253–8.

20. Alston's reply to the point about why the bare particular *a* is not itself Greem but part of the complex-instancing-greem is likewise problematic as he here conflates the particular in classic fashion with a fact: "The substratum, *a*, is greem in the sense of underlying Greemness, while the complex *a-underlying-Greemness* is greem, in the sense of including Greemness" (Alston, 1954, p. 258).

21. It is worth specifying here what Strawson takes to fall under the general heading of such non-particulars: "non-particulars include qualities, properties, relations, species, numbers, sentences (types), etc.". P. F. Strawson (1957a) "Logical Subjects and Physical Objects", *Philosophy and Phenomenological Research*, Vol. 17, No. 4, p. 444.

22. The two classic examples Strawson mentions are those of Locke and Aristotle. Whereas the former seems to assume that whatever exists is particular the latter takes the account of substance in the *Categories* to require a reference to particulars in the first instance, a requirement fertile of difficulty in the study of the relation between this work and Book Zeta of the *Metaphysics*. It is worth adding to this list the curious example of Nietzsche who, here as often elsewhere, adopts a radical empiricist position that is almost Humean rather than Lockean.

23. Strawson in raising this problem refers to the historical precedents of Ramsey and Quine but without looking at the details of the difficulties these authors propose it is clear that the problem arises from the simple characterization of individuals that Strawson himself has given.

24. This is obviously the familiar Aristotelian point concerning subjects of predication being ultimate in that whilst all matters can be predicated of them they cannot be predicated of anything.

25. Wilfrid Sellars (1957) "Logical Subjects and Physical Objects", *Philosophy and Phenomenological Research*, Vol. 17, No. 4, p. 465.

26. "The symmetry of the dialectical distinction between subject and predicate has not the slightest tendency to support talk to the effect that *Socrates* and *wisdom* 'enter symmetrically' into *Socrates: wisdom*" (Sellars, 1957, p. 467).

27. The manner in which I have formulated my understanding of Sellars' argument should help to clarify the rationale for the laudatory references to Cook Wilson with which Sellars begins his response to Strawson.

28. P. F. Strawson (1957b) "A Reply to Mr. Sellars", *Philosophy and Phenomenological Research*, Vol. 17, No. 4, p. 474.

29. An interesting variation on this same point is often referred to as the "victory of particularity" as in J. P. Moreland's statement: "When a particular

exemplifies a universal, the resultant state of affairs—the particular having the universal—is itself particular." J. P. Moreland (2001) *Universals*, Chesham: Acumen, p. 14.

30. P. F. Strawson (1959) *Individuals: An Essay in Descriptive Metaphysics*, London: Methuen, p. 77.

31. This also demonstrates certain difficulties in Henrich's discussion of *quale*, difficulties that arise from sympathy with Alston's reply to Sellars. On Henrich's account qualia are "nothing but the instance of the character that is to be ascribed to them" and hence "actually have no properties whatever" (Henrich, 1976, p. 149). Effectively this is false in one of two ways: either qualia can be given in ranges in which cases classes of qualia are formable and these have characteristics that go beyond the strict particulars and in fact this supports Sellars' explicit use of them as types or universals that are not merely conceptual. Conversely, they are after all bare particulars but in this case they can be given no characterization at all without the supposition of substratum.

32. These formulations are taken from Paul Guyer (1982a) "Kant's Tactics in the Transcendental Deduction" in J. N. Mohanty and Robert W. Shahan (eds) *Essays on Kant's "Critique of Pure Reason"*, Norman: University of Oklahoma Press, pp. 162-3. It is worth comparing these formulations with those given in Paul Guyer (1987) *Kant and the Claims of Knowledge*, Cambridge and New York: Cambridge University Press, p. 85. In the latter work the second formulation is made tighter with Guyer there stating that on this strategy judgments about empirical objects do not merely imply but "presuppose" *a priori* knowledge of the categories. Similarly the first claim is tightened up from a suggestion that judgments about empirical objects merely assume some synthetic *a priori* knowledge to the suggestion that they "actually contain" some. In both cases Guyer has significantly increased the burden of the arguments being discussed without indicating either the change in formulation or giving any justification for it.

33. A different complaint launched in Guyer (1982a) concerns the question of what the *a priori* principles of geometry have to do with the categories. This presupposes that the passage in question was going to show us something about the categories but on my analysis of the passage it is simply *not* intended to do this. In some sense the categories *will* be shown to part of the principles necessary to cognize geometrical objects by being related to the transcendental synthesis of imagination but since the passage tells us nothing about the manner of the principles in question or how they are connected to any notion of imagination it would be vain to search it for a description of the relevance of the categories to cognition of geometrical objects. The relevance that is stated to be required for categories to yield such cognition will surely come elsewhere, namely in the Axioms of Intuition.

34. It is worth noting here Guyer's tendency to spend considerable time expounding Reflexion notes in order to set out a story about the development of Kant's discussion. The peculiarity of this story is that Guyer's hermeneutic approach to the Kantian text is not predicated (as was that of Norman Kemp Smith) on assuming that the divergent strands of Kant's thought point to discrete stages of development of that thought but only on the suggestion that logically divergent and incompatible arguments can be found in

passages that are closely connected in his work. It is thus strange that Guyer spends the amount of time he does expounding Reflexion notes. In any case the alleged "evidence" such notes supply should surely be subordinate to considerations taken from the text of the *Critique* itself. On this basis I will only be considering Guyer's account of published texts of Kant's, not his discussion of fragmentary notes.

35. There is also something odd about the way Guyer takes the account of the logical form of judgments to relate to the categories. He seems at times to adopt the view that we cannot use the former unless the latter have been justified as when he writes the following: "it is hard to see why we should be able to make hypothetical—that is, 'if . . . then——'—judgments only if we can detect *causal* connections among objects, and disjunctive judgments—that is, 'either . . . or——' judgments—only if objects *interact*" (Guyer, 1987, p. 99). Why Guyer believes that Kant thinks of the logical forms of judgment as only usable if the categories are is hard to imagine when Kant's argument seems rather to require that the categories can be derived from the forms of judgment so that the latter are clearly distinct from the former and can be used without them.

36. This already indicates a sharp departure from a Cartesian position. The nature and extent of this departure is not given full articulation here however, it has to await the arguments of the Fourth Paralogism and the Refutation of Idealism.

37. Evidence to this effect is not hard to seek as both Locke and Hume make the suggestion that comparison is the basis of judgments that yield a notion of "experience". For Locke, see the *Essay* Book IV, Chapter 1, §2 and Book II, Chapters 11 and 25. Even more important however is the case of Hume. Hume in Book 1, Part III, §2 of *A Treatise of Human Nature* writes the following: "All kinds of reasoning consist in nothing but a *comparison*, and a discovery of those relations, either constant or inconstant, which two or more objects bear to each other. This comparison we may make, either when both the objects are present to the senses, or when neither of them is present, or when only one. When both the perceptions are present to the sense along with the relation, we call *this* perception rather than reasoning." David Hume (1739) *A Treatise of Human Nature*, Oxford: Clarendon Press, 1967 reprint, p. 73. Here we see that for Hume "perception" is not conceived as involving a judgment whereas it is for Kant but the nature of the former's view that what is given in such perception is a relation between distinct objects requires a connection of conditions of identification of particulars according to relations of time and space but it is only when the further relation of causation is added to these that reasoning is said to take place. Hence Hume's movement from perception to reasoning is in close parallel with Kant's distinction between judgments of perception and judgments of experience with the significant difference that for Hume perception in itself is a purely passive process that does not require judgments, something that may make one wonder how for Hume conditions of identification can be thought to be given in a purely passive manifold.

38. Since this is so it does not seem to me accurate to state, as Guyer does, that the argument in the *Prolegomena* prescinds from reference to the conditions of self-consciousness (Guyer, 1987, p. 101).

39. To this point Guyer might reply by referring to the suggestion that conditional necessities are sufficient to supply us with the conception of the notepad (Guyer, 1982a, p. 172) but this is to substitute the problem of the condition of supplying a particular given empirical object's particular element of being given for what Kant is enquiring namely is the condition for *any* object to be given to us at all. Similar confusions bedevil the treatment at Guyer, 1987, pp. 107–8.
40. To this Guyer might add that this construction of the argument would ensure it was one that could not convince an empiricist (Guyer, 1987, p. 123). This does not seem to me obvious as if succession can be taken to be primary data in an account of experience and such succession can be shown to have elements that cannot be removed without succession itself disappearing then the burden is here on the empiricist to find any other way of describing this situation than as one that has been shown to be necessary to it.

3   Apperception and synthesis

1. I would emphasize that this description of arguments that do not require recourse to "transcendental psychology" was only part of Strawson's initial project of reconstruction of the central aspects of the *Critique* as, for reasons we will subsequently investigate, he was not able to maintain this position.
2. P. F. Strawson (1966) *The Bounds of Sense: An Essay on Kant's "Critique of Pure Reason"*, London and New York: Routledge, p. 72.
3. It is worth noting that Strawson himself concludes the chapter of his 1966 work in which this discussion is set out with an acknowledgement of the very high level of generality his reconstructed deduction argument has.
4. For an important recent critical reconstruction of Fichte's appeal to the notion of reflection in the context of tracing an Idealist trajectory that begins with an account of the transcendental deduction, see Kryiaki Goudeli (2002) *Challenges to German Idealism: Schelling, Fichte and Kant*, London and New York: Palgrave Macmillan, especially Chapter 3.
5. Notoriously, Kant issued a statement towards the end of his career repudiating connection with Fichte, albeit worded in a manner that many have found suspicious.
6. Dieter Henrich (1969) "The Proof-Structure of Kant's Transcendental Deduction", *The Review of Metaphysics*, Vol. 22, p. 642.
7. Importantly for our later considerations the "second conclusion" of the B-Deduction by contrast explicitly refers to the problematic of synthesis, explicitly re-phrasing the synthetic elements of the A-Deduction into an argument for justification of the categories.
8. The division implied here between "understanding" and "imagination" is one that we can in the first instance think of as being of Cartesian provenance given its echo of what is stated in the Sixth Meditation by Descartes. However the question of the proximity between a transcendental account of cognition and a Cartesian one should not be taken as being here predetermined as it is rather an issue of the utmost importance to us and one which we will be treating subsequently with some care.

9. Paul Guyer (1986) "The Failure of the B-Deduction", *Southern Journal of Philosophy*, Vol. XXV, Supplement, p. 73.

10. Guyer could of course reply that our view as given here involves a more complex chain of argument than Kant gives in §15 but to this it is possible simply to state that Kant's argument here has condensed the chain of considerations that we have adduced and that the point in any case is primarily to think of what the required premises of Kant's arguments are, not whether he in each case states them all. When we referred in the text above to "experience" in the standard empiricist sense we were of course thinking of the difficulty of capturing the two senses of "experience" that Lewis White Beck has well described in his distinction between "Lockean" and "Kantian" experience (or L and K experience). See Lewis White Beck (1975) "Did the Sage of Königsberg Have No Dreams?", *Essays on Kant and Hume*, New Haven and London: Yale University Press.

11. Henry Allison (2004), p. 171.

12. This should remind us of the definition of time that Aristotle gives in the *Physics*: "For this is what time is: a number of change in respect of before and after" (219a30).

13. James Van Cleve (1999) *Problems From Kant*, Oxford and New York: Oxford University Press, p. 79.

14. Howard Caygill hence nicely attempts to rescue Kant from this Fichtean notion of reflection when he states that "it is by no means clear whether reflection is an act of a subject or whether the subject is nothing but a mode of reflection" (Caygill, 1995, p. 352).

15. Patricia Kitcher (1990) *Kant's Transcendental Psychology*, Oxford and New York: Oxford University Press, p. 122. On these grounds she denies that what is described by the transcendental unity of apperception are, as Strawson thought, properties of "persons", stating that Kant's theory is one "of 'mental' rather than 'personal' unity" (p. 123).

16. There are two reasons why this point does not trouble Kitcher. First, she takes it that Kant's description of the processes of synthesis are "subpersonal" processes and, secondly, she takes it that Kant's primary question is not the epistemological one of describing how the subject can tell which states are *its* states. Kant does use the personal vocabulary that she eschews however and a rationale for his use of it needs to be given, particularly if it turns that the use of it is of substantive philosophical import. Thirdly, her distinction between "epistemological" and "metaphysical" questions is one in which she takes the latter to be central to the *Critique* and identifies them with questions about the relations states have to each other rather than how they stand in relation to me.

17. Patricia Kitcher (1999) "Kant on Self-Consciousness", *The Philosophical Review*, Vol. 108, No. 3, p. 381.

18. The distinction mentioned earlier from Beck between "Lockean" and "Kantian" experience could be said to have here its sharpest expressions since this conception of a singularity of "experience" itself goes precisely beyond any claims of "data-sensualism" that can find purchase in empiricist and phenomenalist reductions of the relationship of cognition to "objects". The transcendence of the level of such "data-sensualism" is precisely what therefore has to be regarded as the basic task of Kant's transcendental account.

19. Andrew Brook (1994) *Kant and the Mind*, Cambridge and New York: Cambridge University Press, pp. 55–6.

20. This is the first point at which I have given specific attention to the distinction between the distinct formulations of the transcendental deduction in the two editions of the *Critique*. This might be thought strange given, as Caygill puts it, that "expressing a preference for one or other of the deductions has become a shibboleth in Kant studies", something he connects to the division in contemporary philosophy between continental and Anglo-American traditions (Caygill, 1995, p. 153). However, just as Caygill's use of the term "shibboleth" here suggests a distancing from these types of preference, a distancing reinforced by his claim that in both versions "the overall conclusion remains unchanged", so I also wish to consider the degree to which reconstruction of the point of the argument can be abstracted from textual consideration of the different versions. In Brook's case however the distinction is important for drawing out aspects of his own reading so I will now follow him in moving between the versions.

21. Brook displays a great deal of confusion concerning this passage since he takes it that since Kant here has made clear the dependence of the analytic unity upon the synthetic one that the latter is not even *a priori* but only an empirical observation (Brook, 1994, p. 223). This does not however follow, it simply shifts the order of *a priori* dependence in a direction that Brook did not expect.

22. Pierre Keller (1998) *Kant and the Demands of Self-Consciousness*, Cambridge and New York: Cambridge University Press, pp. 22–3.

23. There is an intriguing parallel to this passage in Husserl who writes the following at one point: "If now we perform an act of cognition, or, as I prefer to express it, live in one, we are 'concerned with the object' that it, in its cognitive fashion, means and postulates. If this act is one of knowing in the strictest sense, i.e. if our judgement is inwardly evident, then its object is *given* in primal fashion (*originär*). The state of affairs comes before us, not merely putatively, but as *actually before our eyes*, and in it the object itself, *as the object that it is*, i.e. just as it is intended in this act of knowing and not otherwise, as bearer of such and such properties, as the term of such relations etc." Edmund Husserl (1900–1901) *Logical Investigations*, translated by J. N. Findlay (1970), partially modified by D. Moran, London and New York: Routledge, 2000, p. 145, my emphasis. Noticeably however here for Husserl it is the identity of the state of affairs that is presented in this way, not the identity of the act of presentation of it by a principle like the unity of apperception. That Husserl increasingly came to feel such a principle was however necessary led to his adoption of a position he termed "transcendental idealism" subsequently. Charting the relationship between this notion and Kant's and the relationship and difference between the two conceptions of apperception would be a major work which I hope to attempt elsewhere. Suffice it here to say however that when Husserl arrives at this principle in *Ideas I* he draws directly upon the discussion of apperception in §16 of the B-Deduction.

24. As Henrich nicely puts this: "This is knowledge in which self-consciousness makes reference to possible experience prior to all experience" (Henrich, 1976, p. 192).

25. This is suggested at pp. 202–3 of Henrich 1976.
26. This is clearly presented in Guyer (1982a, p. 183). Guyer does not derive from these considerations a need to attend to the synthesis of imagination as he takes it that there are other problems with the argument he discerns taking place at this point in the *Critique*.

4   Synthesis and imagination

1. Paul Guyer (1979) "Review" of Henrich (1976), *The Journal of Philosophy*, Vol. 76, No. 3, p. 166.
2. These problems relate fundamentally to Paul Guyer (1982b) "Kant on Apperception and *A Priori* Synthesis", *American Philosophical Quarterly*, Vol. 17, No. 3, particularly p. 211.
3. This is at any rate my reading of the account in Paul Guyer (1986) "The Failure of the B-Deduction", *The Southern Journal of Philosophy*, Vol. XXV, Supplement.
4. Paul Guyer (1989) "Psychology and the Transcendental Deduction" in Eckart Förster (ed.) (1989) *Kant's Transcendental Deductions: The Three "Critiques" and the "Opus Postumum"*, Stanford: Stanford University Press, p. 59.
5. Guyer (1989) is in fact consistent in its presentation of psychological "arguments" as stating empirical conditions and hence is in principle incapable of addressing the notion of transcendental psychology.
6. This description occurs for example at Strawson (1966, p. 32) and is connected to the following comment on the same page: "Belief in the occurrence of the process of synthesis as an antecedent condition of experience and belief in the antecedent occurrence of disconnected impressions as materials for the process to work on are beliefs which support each other and are necessary to each other. But, by hypothesis, experience can support neither belief; and since neither is necessary to the strictly analytical argument, the entire theory is best regarded as one of the aberrations into which Kant's explanatory model inevitably led him." The suggestion that "experience" cannot support these beliefs depends itself on a prior notion of what "experience" involves and, as we have already seen, a strictly analytical argument alone cannot provide us with a viable deduction strategy.
7. P. F. Strawson (1974b) "Preface" in Strawson (ed.) (1974c) *Freedom and Resentment and Other Essays*, London: Methuen & Co. Ltd, p. vii. I would like to thank Mike Garfield for bringing this volume, and particularly the essay on imagination in it which I will now be turning to, to my attention.
8. P. F. Strawson (1970) "Imagination and Perception" in Strawson (ed.) (1974c), p. 45.
9. Wilfrid Sellars (1978) "The Role of the Imagination in Kant's Theory of Experience" in H. W. Johnstone, Jr (ed.) *Categories: A Colloquium*, Penn. State: Pennsylvania State University. I am not here referring, however, to the published form of this article but to the hypertext copy of it transcribed by Andrew Chrucky as part of his invaluable website *Problems From Wilfrid Sellars*. The URL for this article is http://www.ditext.com/sellars/ikte.html and the version I downloaded was accessed on 10/04/02. Chrucky's transcription retains the paragraph numbers of the original and it is to these I will refer.

10. Unfortunately many of J. L. Austin's comments about the nature of plays and dramatic performance suggest this picture and are faulty because of it.

11. As we will see in due course there are a number of distinctions that need to be examined in order to relate imagination to understanding in the comprehension of perception. Kant points to the difference between concept, schema and image at A140/B179, a distinction we will proceed to examine in due course.

12. It is to be regretted however that he did not adopt a similar move with regard to the synthesis of apprehension which seems to me to have the same dual structure. It is initially introduced as a transcendental act (A99) but subsequently often characterized as merely empirical. Clearly the empirical level of apprehension, like the empirical level of imagination, needs to be distinguished from the transcendental level. Instead Kant often simply characterizes apprehension as merely empirical as such and when he does this he is, I take it, separating it from the synthesis of imagination with which it is inseparably bound up when considered transcendentally (A102).

13. The picture to which Sellars is objecting is well presented in the description of receptivity given by Rae Langton, a description correctly set out there as diametrically opposed to that of Sellars and, interestingly, couched in Strawsonian terms. See Rae Langton (1998) *Kantian Humility: Our Ignorance of Things In Themselves*, Oxford and New York: Oxford University Press, Chapter 2 *passim*.

14. Wilfrid Sellars (1967) "Some Remarks on Kant's Theory of Experience" in W. Sellars (1974) *Essays In Philosophy and Its History*, Dordrecht and Boston: D. Reidel Publishing Company, p. 54.

15. "Kant's *primary* use of the term 'concept' is to refer to general concepts, whether sortal or attributive, a priori or empirical" (Sellars, 1968, §6, p. 3).

16. At B430–1 Kant adds the point that in becoming aware of something that is only cognizable temporally but nonetheless is also that which gives form to all judgments we have an item of distinct awareness that relates to "a non-sensible intelligible world" (B431). This is precisely what is subsequently made available in practical philosophy as the notion of *agency*. It is only practically that any broad notion of this agency is available as purely theoretically no more can be said here than we have got to at this point but what has emerged is still, *pace* Allison, a "content".

17. Sellars (1968, §7, p. 3) states that intuitions are "representations of *thises*" and this makes them conceptual on the model of demonstratives without appealing here to the distinction between *a priori* and empirical intuitions.

18. Sellars (1968, §19, p. 8). This statement is connected to the view that what "sheer receptivity" is *of* is "impressions" whilst the receptivity that emerges from the transcendental synthesis of imagination, by contrast, is of "objects of intuition".

19. This points to a central difficulty with the notion of "sheer receptivity" which is that nothing could be cognized as having its form.

20. Allison (2004, pp. 187–8) argues for this problem but couples it with an argument to the effect that Strawson also has too "empiricist" an account of imagination due to his discussion of images. It is not clear that this objection chimes with the one about intellectualism or that it is correct. Allison

does however share our reservations about the Sellarsian notion of "sheer receptivity".

21. Edmund Husserl (1913, §62).

22. Edmund Husserl (1920–5) *Analyses Concerning Active and Passive Synthesis: Lectures on Transcendental Logic*, translated by Robert Steinbock, Dordrecht and London: Kluwer, 2001, p. 410. These lectures are central for the formation of Husserl's late notion of transcendental genesis, a notion that advances significantly on the early adoption of static analysis in the first formulations of phenomenology. The relationship between genetic methodology and transcendental thought in Husserl is one that requires considerable research, not least in relation to the development of Husserl's responses to Kant and the Neo-Kantianism prevalent in the early decades of the twentieth century.

23. This should remind us of Leibniz's notion of *petites perceptiones*, not least due to the fact that Husserl never hid his Leibnizian heritage.

24. The question of the extent to which Sellars' "sense-impression inference" and Husserl's transcendental conception of passive constitution and passive genesis harmonize in giving an account of a form of transcendental constitution that is precisely beyond the reach of apperception would be a rich field of research that I intend to explore elsewhere.

25. This much is already clear from Edmund Husserl (1900–1901) VIth Investigation, §23, but is set out in considerably more detail in the lectures on passive synthesis where an extensive account of *a priori* association is given.

26. Husserl (1900–1901) already contains criticism of the notion of transcendental psychology though it is not here made clear what specific problems it involves, a point which is connected to the considerable difficulty of thinking through the nature of what Husserl stigmatizes as "psychologism".

27. Edmund Husserl (1929) *Formal and Transcendental Logic*, translated by Dorion Cairns, The Hague: Martinus Nijhoff, 1969, §§99–100 states the thought adumbrated here that effectively Kant's failure to transcendentally investigate logic itself results in a confusion of the production of sense with the activities of certain "faculties".

28. Martin Heidegger (1927–8, §12, p. 103). This statement echoes one made in the pages of *Being and Time* where Heidegger states: "The first and only person who has gone any stretch of the way towards investigating the dimension of Temporality or has even let himself be drawn hither by the coercion of the phenomena themselves is Kant." Martin Heidegger (1927) *Being and Time*, translated by J. Macquarrie and E. Robinson, Oxford: Basil Blackwell, 1978, p. 45.

29. Heidegger (1927–8, p. 111) and Heidegger (1927, p. 45) both state this as the problem with the latter connecting Kant's treatment of this question to that of Descartes.

30. Heidegger (1927–8, §8, p. 89), where "pure spatial relations" are separated from the empirical intuition of spaces so that space and time are made available as "intuitions without things".

31. Here Heidegger repeats the classical objections of Husserl directly: cf. Heidegger (1927–8) §23 b) α) pp. 215–16 and §23 β) p. 219.

32. "In its original selfhood the subject is temporality itself, and only as ecstatic temporality does the subject release (in fact necessarily for itself as a self) time

in the sense of the pure sequence of nows" (Heidegger, 1927–8, §25 d, p. 267). The peculiarity of this conception with response to Kant is that Heidegger seems to assume that the Kantian presentation cannot admit that physical objectivity is given immediately with time for Kant. This is the nature of his response to Kant's "psychologism" as is made evident in *Being and Time* where Heidegger writes: "contrary to Kant's opinion, one comes across world-time *just as immediately* in the physical as in the psychical, and not just roundabout by way of the psychical" (Heidegger, 1927, p. 471). The fact that this basically states the argument of the Refutation of Idealism as if it could be turned *against* Kant indicates a fundamental problem with how the relation between time and apperception has been understood in Kant's argument, a problem connected with the status of transcendental psychology. See also Heidegger's response to the Refutation of Idealism at §43 *a* of Heidegger 1927, a response that takes the argument of the Refutation to be narrowly epistemological and does not see its ontological force. For a description of the Husserlian view of temporality that seems to underlie what Heidegger is articulating in the reading of Kant, see Gary Banham (2005c).

33. The suggestion of one author here will merit further consideration although it seems to us to short-circuit some of the problems with which we are concerned. The suggestion is as follows: "Since the unity of space and time as formal intuitions long precedes any concept of an object in space and time, and is effected by the categories alone, this synthetic unity belongs to space and time in a sense not true of any other sensible representation" (Martin Weatherston, 2002, pp. 64–5).

34. For an argument to this effect, see Dieter Henrich (1955) "On the Unity of Subjectivity" in Henrich (ed.) (1994).

35. Béatrice Longuenesse (1993, p. 116, note 29).

36. Allison (2004, pp. 179–82) argues that the two passages can be brought into alignment on the whole by thinking of judgments of perception as merely a rendition of a conception of judgment that is held by empiricists, particularly Hume. However this view of it is admitted by Allison to not fit the description of judgments of perception as being types of primary relation to manifolds that are subsequently superseded by judgments of experience.

37. So I do not here agree with Longuenesse who claims that the judgments of perception "are at first deprived of any claim to subjective universality, that is objective validity" (Longuenesse, 1993, p. 173, note 13) because it seems to me that subjective universality is something quite distinct from objective validity and that the latter requires, in addition to the logical universality that must underlie even a singular judgment the element that enables the conversion of such judgments into ones that have inter-subjective validity. This element would be the movement from the form of logical universality to that of categorial universality.

38. Longuenesse (1993, pp. 187–8) separates the distinction between types of judgment given in the *Prolegomena* from the distinction between judgments and associations in §19 by stating that in the latter case Kant is describing two possible origins of judgment and showing why the Humean notion of judgments originating in associative imagination will not do as an account of them. Whilst this reading is ingenious and results in a rationale for *not* assimilating the distinction in the deduction with that in the *Prolegomena*

the problem with it is that Longuenesse does not, by means of it, account for the fact that in §19 Kant does clearly describe the law of association as presenting a type of judgment, namely "It, the body, is heavy", a judgment clearly of a piece with judgments of perception. I would suggest by contrast that the associative combination set out here is one that is of a piece with the judgments of perception and that all Kant has done is give a different description of the same distinction. In both cases there is described the same basic elements and the difference between them is simply that in the *Critique* Kant has not presupposed the existence of bodies of synthetic *a priori* truths and provided a regressive argument that justifies them. Kant has instead shown that the formation of judgments that have the property of objective validity requires the utilization of categories as these latter are what describe objects and that the descriptions of objects that they give will involve the specification of sets of principles, principles that are not treated and given serious justification in the deduction but will be in the Analytic of Principles.

39. This element of "grasping" is I take it what Kant is referring to in his play on words between *Begriff* and *Bewusstein* (A103).

40. Kant writes that such consciousness "however indistinct, must always be present" as without it "concepts, and therewith knowledge of objects, are altogether impossible" (A104). This statement indicates that whilst the reflective act that would consist in becoming aware of apperception is not required for relationship to the manifold at any given empirical point that what is required for relationship of the manifold to count as awareness at all is that the conceptual ability that I have been describing through the concepts of reflection takes place. These elementary acts of combination, differentiation and identification seem to me necessary *even for dreams*.

41. Longuenesse (1993) refers to the categories as "rules for forming rules", a description that accords well with the description of the understanding as faculty of rules with which Kant closes the A-Deduction (A126) and this also points forward again to the Schematism since the nature of such meta-rules is described there.

42. This "speculative proposition" is one that perhaps indicates a certain short path from Kant to Hegel. It would though be one that would have the difficulty that the Hegelian movement, whilst beginning from a reflective comprehension of logic, has to relate such reflexivity to something that is modelled not on a Kantian limitative model but on a Fichtean expansive one, a movement that would require a great deal of philosophical work. For considerations of why it might not be a movement easy or worthwhile to make, see Karl Ameriks (2000) *Kant and the Fate of Autonomy: Problems in the Appropriation of the Critical Philosophy*, Cambridge and New York: Cambridge University Press.

5   Schematism and imagination

1. Paul Guyer (1987, p. 157) and Chapter 6 *passim*. This argument is based on Guyer's peculiar conception of the nature of a transcendental deduction.

2. "Time is pure original receptivity and original spontaneity. Original temporality is that in which the primal activity of the self and its *concern with the self* is grounded. And it is the same temporality which at any time makes possible a *self-identification* of the self" (Heidegger, 1927–8, p. 267).
3. Longuenesse (1993, p. 244). It is notable however that Longuenesse gives no detailed reading of the chapter on schematism preferring instead to devote considerable attention to the workings of schematism in the description of the Analytic of Principles. Whilst there are many good reasons for this focus it has the effect of failing to address the questions that have been raised about the coherence of the doctrine of schematism itself.
4. This was clearly intended by Kant to forestall the Leibnizian suggestion, that of an identification of the subject with its predicates.
5. Whilst this might have a Wittgensteinian ring I will shortly be explicating the nature of Kant's difference from a certain kind of Wittgensteinian model.
6. "It is what human beings *say* that is true and false; and they agree in the *language* they use. That is not agreement in opinions but in form of life." Ludwig Wittgenstein (1945–9, §241). Intriguingly this marks the effective conclusion of a series of pieces which directly precede the setting out of the famous "private language argument".
7. Geoffrey Warnock (1949) "Concepts and Schematism", *Analysis*, Vol. 8, p. 82. In arguing that this objection is Wittgensteinian I am only suggesting it has the same basic form as the problem with rules that Wittgenstein himself adduced.
8. Edmund Husserl (1894) "Psychological Studies in the Elements of Logic" in E. Husserl (1994) *Early Writings in the Philosophy of Logic and Mathematics*, translated by D. Willard, Dordrecht and London: Kluwer Academic Publishers, 1994, p. 154. Whilst Husserl is here speaking of arithmetic it is evident that his example can be extended easily to geometry.
9. There is evidence that Husserl does indeed think of Kantian pure intuition as a form of idea in E. Husserl (1913, Chapter 12), evidence I set out in Banham (2005c).
10. The obvious alternative empiricist way of characterizing the procedure of imagination would be in terms of rules of association. This is something whose possibility we will examine in our account of the Second Analogy below.
11. Howard Caygill (1989) *Art of Judgement*, Oxford: Basil Blackwell, p. 5.
12. Caygill (1989, p. 251).
13. Caygill's claim about an aporia of judgment has been subjected to a critical assessment by Paul Crowther (1998) "Judgment, Self-Consciousness and Imagination: Kant's Transcendental Deduction and Beyond" in Herman Parrett (ed.) (1998) *Kant's Aesthetics*, Walter De Gruyter: Berlin and New York, whose central claim seems to be the following: "Sensibility and the intellect are brought into alignment in judgement—not by some paradoxical more fundamental judgement, but rather by the reciprocity of subject and object of experience. Particular judgements can only be made insofar as they *exemplify* that general categorial framework whose use also defines unity of self" (p. 133).
14. Martin Heidegger (1929, p. 74).

15. Kant states that the pure schema of magnitude is number which he terms "simply the unity of the synthesis of the manifold of a homogeneous intuition in general" (A142–3/B182), a description of key importance for the ensuing Axioms of Intuition.

16. Martin Weatherston (2002, p. 171).

17. Heidegger attempts to prevent this problem from emerging when he writes: "pure space is no less rooted transcendentally in the transcendental power of imagination than 'time', insofar as this is understood merely as what is formed in pure intuition as the pure intuited, the pure succession of the sequence of nows. In fact, space in a certain sense is always and necessarily equivalent to time so understood" (Heidegger, 1929, pp. 139–40). The succeeding paragraph makes clear however that in fact time is understood by Heidegger to still be axially prior to space due to the fact that it makes possible self-affection. Hence Heidegger both attempts to eliminate this problem and then re-opens it, exactly as occurred with his attempt to eliminate the problem of transcendental judgment. For a classic statement of the view that space is insufficiently attended to in Kant's treatment of schematism, see Gregg E. Franzswa (1978) "Space and the Schematism", *Kant-Studien*, Vol. 69.

18. Somewhat remarkably this natural conclusion from Kant's description of his method is almost never drawn in the literature on the principles.

19. However whilst the mathematical principles themselves are not treated their possibility is in the Axioms of Intuition.

20. Thus he contrasts the judgment "a man who is unlearned is not learned" which does require reference to time as he who is not learned now could become so later with the statement "no unlearned man is learned" the opposite of which would involve the direct conflict between subject and predicate that is required for an analytic judgment (A153/B192–3). It is important to note that the temporal interpretation of the principle of contradiction that Kant earlier upheld, and in the *Critique* repudiates, has the authority of Aristotle's *Metaphysics* (1005 b 33).

21. As Howard Caygill remarks: "This means that the conditions for a coherent experience also determine the objects of such experience—marking a philosophically sophisticated attempt to align being and logic which is characteristic of the entire critical philosophy" (Caygill, 1995, p. 333).

6 Synthesis, intuition and mathematics

1. The connection between the singularity criteria for intuitions and the treatment of mathematics has been argued by Jaako Hintikka in particular, the classic treatment of which is provided in J. Hintikka (1967) "Kant on the Mathematical Method", *The Monist*, Vol. 51, reprinted in Carl J. Posy (ed.) (1992) *Kant's Philosophy of Mathematics: Modern Essays*, Dordrecht and London: Kluwer Academic Publishers. In this piece Hintikka connects his account of mathematical construction to a description of Euclid that draws on a description of the structure of Euclid's method in some detail.

2. See the treatment for example of *Thoughts on the True Estimation of Living Forces* in Michael Friedman (1992) *Kant and the Exact Sciences*, Cambridge, Mass. and London: Harvard University Press, "Introduction".

3. Explication of the conception of philosophy that the young Kant held has been given serious attention in Martin Schönfeld (2000) *The Philosophy of the Young Kant: The Precritical Project*, Oxford and New York: Oxford University Press. Since Kant's works of the 1790s however seem to return explicitly to the considerations set out in these early works it would be work well worth while to treat the nature of Kant's accounts of the material possibilities of metaphysics in connection with his understandings of science and nature across the Critical/Pre-Critical divide in order to open for renewed consideration the question of the "doctrine" of theoretical philosophy, a question buried in most contemporary treatments of Kant.

4. In the next chapter some of these works will be re-treated with explicit focus on one of the central metaphysical questions that Kant returned to throughout the 1750s and 1760s, the question of how to think substance in connection to force. The Leibnizian background to this question is obvious enough but the demarcation of it from the questions about mathematics and intuition that we are imposing here was less than obvious to the author of these works.

5. For a description and critical discussion of the "pluralizing parts principle", see Verity Harte (2002) *Plato on Parts and Wholes: The Metaphysics of Structure*, Oxford and New York: Oxford University Press, pp. 53–63.

6. Leibniz by contrast utilized the Cartesian conception of analytic geometry and this enabled him to separate divisibility from the Euclidean dependence on diagrams.

7. I obviously mean this only in terms of the restricted question here being posed as the Newtonians and Cartesians had many other reasons for disagreement as is well chronicled.

8. Kant's argument here thus implicitly reprises the one Leibniz gives in his fifth letter to Clarke. See H. G. Alexander (ed.) (1956) *The Leibniz-Clarke Correspondence*, Manchester and New York: Manchester University Press, pp. 69–72. For reasons that will be rehearsed in Chapter 7 below this interpretation of the account of space in the *Physical Monadology* is controversial but since the reasons for treating it as such have more to do with the understanding of substance and force than with intuition and mathematics I have left defence of this interpretation to the following chapter.

9. The proof Kant mobilizes had however been used by theorists of the period to show that matter must be divisible and this points to a physical interpretation of geometry that is in accordance with the Newtonian conception of infinitesimal calculus.

10. This distinction is not stated in these terms in the *Physical Monadology* but the difference between physical co-existence and distinction of forces is effectively equivalent to this.

11. We find here an early form of the Anticipations of Perception.

12. See the "Introduction" to Walford and Meerbote (1992) *Theoretical Philosophy 1755–1770*, Cambridge and New York: Cambridge University Press, pp. lxi–lxii

for reasons for thinking that the Prize Essay in fact pre-dates, at least in part, *Negative Magnitudes*.

13. In some respects this continues the move Kant made as early as the *New Elucidation* away from conceiving of the notion of contradiction as the cardinal principle of all thought. For details of this demonstration and some discussion of its importance, see Chapter 7.

14. Naturally as with the *Physical Monadology* this account leads again to a description of the opposition of forces.

15. Kant subsequently attempts a demonstration of the conservation of matter as a requirement for real opposition having enduring effect (Ak. 2: 194).

16. Kant does not clearly state this to be the consequence of his position here referring instead to space as something *"given"* to the geometer from "ordinary representation", a statement that almost suggests an analysis (Ak. 1: 278). I take it he means however that since mathematics is based on comparison and combination that this practice not merely requires spatial representation but in the process demonstrates the nature of what is involved in the spatial representation it has presupposed. In this way it *constructs* the space in question.

17. Whilst there is a contrast here between arithmetic and geometry it is clearly possible on the account of arithmetic presented in the Prize Essay to understand the figures of geometry as enumerable quantities which hence can, in Cartesian fashion, be entirely replaced by signs and thus presented in algebra. In this respect it appears to me that these texts of the 1760s allow in principle for replacement of the Newtonian conception of infinitesimal calculus with the Leibnizian conception.

18. This point is used by Hintikka in support of his claim for the primacy of singularity.

19. The key argument to this effect is made by Lorne Falkenstein (1991) "Kant's Account of Intuition", *Canadian Journal of Philosophy*, Vol. 21, No. 2.

20. This traditional pattern of reasoning clearly follows the Aristotelian account of metaphysics that we can see to be here underlying the School Philosophy that was based on codification of Leibniz.

21. The parallel here, and not merely in terms of name, is clearly with Locke's "concepts of reflection" which is why the account of these terms in the *Critique* is the Amphiboly which is where Kant demarcates his sense of them from Locke and uses them to reply to Leibniz.

22. If Kant had simply summarized the Transcendental Aesthetic as providing the first elements of a science of accidents he would have made absolutely central the revolutionary nature of his undertaking.

23. This statement, which is repeated in the account of time in the Transcendental Aesthetic, is directly contrary to Hume's view. See Book I, Section III of the *Treatise* for an argument to the effect that the concept of time derives from that of succession. The basis of this argument is that since time is itself not perceived directly but only through something that is taken to have successive conditions of apprehension so the concept is derivative from this observation of successive processes. Hence Hume takes off from the fact that time cannot itself be perceived to reach his conclusion. The very same observation is used against Hume in the central arguments for the Second Analogy as will be discussed in detail in Chapter 7.

24. See Falkenstein (1991, p. 178) for a lapidary presentation of this argument.
25. It is interesting to speculate why there is not a similar conclusion derived from the treatment of time. Perhaps the reason for the difference is that even time requires space to be represented whilst time does not provide a condition for the representation of space.
26. It is worth pointing out however that Bertrand Russell argues that mathematical judgments are synthetic in his earliest treatments of the subject only altering his view in the course of working on *Principia Mathematica*.
27. The crude view of Kant's account has been rectified in recent years to the point where many contemporary philosophers are prepared to suggest that Kant's philosophy of mathematics is practically equivalent to post-Fregean views. For the basic argument to this effect, see Gottfried Martin (1938) *Arithmetic and Combinatorics: Kant and His Contemporaries*, translated by J. Wubnig, Carbondale: Southern Illinois University Press. The acceptance of a view that, whilst less pronounced than this, goes nonetheless some ways towards it has been facilitated in recent years by the translation of Kant's philosophy of mathematics into logical formulae by Jaako Hintikka. For an elaborate demonstration of this, see J. Hintikka (1973) *Logic, Language-Games and Information: Kantian Themes in the Philosophy of Logic*, Oxford: Clarendon Press.
28. The difficulty post-Fregean philosophers tend to have with this is that the rules of commutation, association and distribution required for a mathematical system to be operative are thought of as requirements of formal consistency. Whilst Brouwer's reform of mathematics was based on a difficulty with the principles of such formalization of consistency Kant's point is rather that such consistency cannot be regarded as a product of rules of formal logic alone due to the need for equivalence operations to convert into homogeneous quantities what are themselves terms only given arbitrary combination.
29. For a treatment of the many senses that can be given to "affection" see Allison (2004), Chapter 3.
30. Noticeably the pure elements of intuition are thus conversant with Descartes' treatment of the pure notion of body, not with the Leibnizian insistence on the quality of force being added to geometrical notions. So Kant here seems to think of pure intuition only mathematically, not dynamically. Force is in fact even here aligned with a concept of the understanding and although impenetrability is taken to belong to sensation the notion of this is aligned with matter, not form.
31. Caygill (1995, pp. 265–6). It is notable however that the treatment given here focuses much more on the arguments of the Dissertation than on those of the Aesthetic even though there is no mention of immediacy in the former.
32. This notion that what the Axioms supply is only a "metric" is the basis of the account given in Gordon G. Brittan, Jr (1978) *Kant's Theory of Science*, Princeton: Princeton University Press, Chapter 4 and Brittan's view is endorsed by Paul Guyer (1987), Chapter 7.
33. Daniel Sutherland (2005) "The Point of Kant's Axioms of Intuition", *Pacific Philosophical Quarterly*, Vol. 86, p. 152. See also here for a view of much the same character Longuenesse (1993, p. 274).
34. So Norman Kemp Smith for example describes this definition of extensive magnitudes as involving "a view of space and time directly opposed to that

of the *Aesthetic*". Norman Kemp Smith (1918) *A Commentary to Kant's "Critique of Pure Reason"*, London and New York: Macmillan Press, p. 347. Robert Paul Wolff (1963) concurs with this verdict in *Kant's Theory of Mental Activity: A Commentary on the Transcendental Analytic of the "Critique of Pure Reason"* Cambridge, Mass.: Harvard University Press, p. 228. Wolff also professes considerable puzzlement as to why Kant should wish to treat in the Analytic mathematical principles at all, apparently oblivious to the difference in level between the account provided in the Aesthetic and that given in the Analytic of Principles.

35. Martin (1938) famously argues on the basis of this exchange and the resulting change in Schultz's manuscript which he studied that Kant's conception of arithmetic is axiomatic, a view clearly at odds however with the statement concerning the lack of axioms in arithmetic in our passage. Charles Parsons (1969) "Kant's Philosophy of Arithmetic" in Posy (ed.) (1992), pp. 53–4, is attentive to Kant's denial that arithmetic has axioms and derives from it a problem concerning how Kant would explain the commutative and associative principles that have long been recognized as cardinal for it. Parsons also presses a problem about the types of "objects" arithmetic is dealing with, which leads him to fault the notion that arithmetic is connected to intuition at all.

36. This confirms the view set out in Parsons (1969) that Kant does not allow there to be any "object" *specific* to arithmetic.

37. See Guyer (1987, pp. 190–5) for these critical comments.

38. Guyer writes that Kant presupposes a theory of empirical perception which "settles such questions merely by assuming that the properties of the *a priori* forms of intuition are necessarily and fully instantiated by empirical intuition as well" (Guyer, 1987, p. 196).

39. The dependence of Kant's description of geometry on Euclidean assumptions is clear in terms of his connection of geometrical demonstration to construction, a procedure that non-Euclidean geometries appear to render otiose. Hintikka's description of Euclidean procedures is now classic but see for a detailed treatment of the background assumptions of Euclid's system and its connections to the School Philosophy of Wolff Lisa A. Shabel (2003) *Mathematics in Kant's Critical Philosophy: Reflections on Mathematical Practice*, New York and London: Routledge, Parts 1 and 2. Unfortunately the third part of this book that concentrates on Kant has, as the author confesses in her preface, some serious problems in terms of its treatment of the nature of intuition. Michael Friedman (1992, Chapter 1) describes the historical backdrop to Kant's account of geometry in great detail although in so doing tends to a view of transcendental imagination that somewhat diminishes its transcendental character. Strawson (1966, Part 5) presents an attempt to rescue Kant's discussion of geometry by freeing it from the physical interpretation that was so important in the initial turn towards discussion of geometry by Kant in the *Physical Monadology*. Longuenesse (1993) indicates a more charitable interpretation: "Kant overstepped what he had actually deduced (but not the method of the geometry he knew) when he thought he could assert that the form of pure intuition, of which he had provided a transcendental genesis, necessarily possessed the features associated with the space of Euclidean geometry" (p. 291).

40. The classic statement to this effect is provided by Bertrand Russell (1897) *An Essay on the Foundations of Geometry*, Cambridge University Press: Cambridge, p. 63.

41. This summarizes the view of a large number of critics of Kant's view of geometry. Brittan (1978) cites a statement from Rudolf Carnap to this effect on pp. 68–9 but the view is, as Brittan states, held much more widely. Friedman (1992, Chapter 1) sharply defends this distinction between "pure" and "applied" correctly noting its difference to Kant's conception of the difference between pure and applied mathematics. Shabel (2003) is also clear on the Kantian difference between pure and applied mathematics being at clear variance to the distinction as formulated in this standard objection to Kant's view of geometry.

42. Stephen Barker (1985) "Kant's View of Geometry: A Partial Defense" in Posy (ed.) (1992), pp. 227–8, describes a number of ways of understanding the nature of "pure" geometry in contemporary accounts from viewing such geometry purely deductively, to seeing it as set of hypothetical propositions or as a scheme, much like Kant's view of arithmetic, as a scheme for rules for manipulating marks. The fact that the claimed "pure" geometry has no settled status in contemporary philosophy indicates that the nature of the disagreement between its proponents and the Kantian picture can in fact take discretely different forms and that if there is "pure" geometry in the sense claimed there is considerable room for dispute concerning its connection to contemporary logical systems.

43. Barker (1985) describes again three different forms of such interpretation of "straightness" in terms of light rays, measuring rods and taut cords. All in a sense presuppose straightness or simply accept something as a standard for it, much as the Paris metre rule is taken to be a standard for metres, raising the Wittgensteinian questions we mentioned in Chapter 5 about the nature of rules and application. It is thus far from clear to me that the notion of "applied" geometry has the sense its proponents interpret it as having.

44. A minimal defence of the claim that Euclidean geometry is the form of at least *our* visual space is provided by J. Hopkins (1973) "Visual Geometry", *Philosophical Review*, Vol. LXXXII but decisive objections to this very limited defence of the Kantian claim are made by Gordon Nagel (1983) *The Structure of Experience: Kant's System of Principles*, Chicago and London: The University of Chicago Press, pp. 33–9.

45. Barker adds to this point others concerning whether critics of the Euclidean conception can utilize principles of parsimony to rule out the notion of "straightness" having necessity connected to it. To do this would however be a clear metaphysical move requiring philosophical argument whilst the majority of these critics have attempted to view it as a question of empirical science. It would *at least* be a question of what Kant terms "pure natural science" however and this cannot be justified other than philosophically.

46. I owe this argument to Robert Hanna (2001) *Kant and the Foundations of Analytic Philosophy*, Oxford and New York: Oxford University Press, pp. 276–9 and see his account also of the problems with Helmholtz's objections to the Kantian thesis.

47. For some treatments of Kant's philosophy of arithmetic that relate it extensively to post-Fregean and post-Russellian notions of logic, see Wing-Chun

Wong (2000) "On a Semantic Interpretation of Kant's Concept of Number", *Synthese*, Vol. 121, Robert Hanna (2002) "Mathematics for Humans: Kant's Philosophy of Arithmetic Revisited", *European Journal of Philosophy*, Vol. 10, No. 3, Sun-Joo Shin (1997) "Kant's Syntheticity Revisited by Peirce", *Synthese*, Vol. 113 and Hector-Neri Castaneda (1960) " '7 + 5 = 12' as a Synthetic Proposition", *Philosophy and Phenomenological Research*, Vol. 21, No. 2.

48. Martin Heidegger (1935) *What is a Thing?*, translated by W. B. Barton and V. Deutsch, Chicago: Regnery, 1967, p. 219.

49. Caygill (1995, p. 74), where this point is made but the implication of it left carefully unstated.

50. Guyer (1987, p. 197), where Guyer in fact accentuates Heidegger's difficulty with the first edition formulation.

51. Kemp Smith (1918, p. 349) and H. J. Paton (1936) *Kant's Metaphysics of Experience: A Commentary on the First Half of the "Kritik der Reinen Vernunft"*, London: George Allen & Unwin and New York: Humanities Press, Vol. 2, p. 135.

52. Allison (2004) does not discuss any part of the mathematical principles and Strawson (1966) simply dismisses this section of the *Critique*. Wolff (1963) professes bewilderment about the anticipations. By contrast Caygill (1995) declares the anticipations "the most fundamental of all the principles" (p. 75) and Heidegger (1935) already bemoaned the lack of attention to it as indicative of a failure to grasp the import of Kant's critical philosophy. Guyer (1987) is unusual in both a having dismissive attitude towards them and yet giving them extended consideration.

53. Kemp Smith (1918, p. 349). To clarify this point: Kemp Smith takes both the formulation of the first edition principle and the *proof for the second edition principle* to share the "phenomenalist" view but thinks, like Heidegger, that the second edition formulation of the principle is free from this taint. This ensures however that Kemp Smith's conception of the second edition treatment of the principle is not only more complicated than Heidegger's but also one in which the source of the complaint cannot, as is usual with Kemp Smith, reside in the attribution of "patch-work" considerations.

54. In the chapter on schematism Kant described the real as pointing to "being (in time)" (A143/B182) indicating however what this meant was precisely the *filling* of time. As will be shown soon this corresponds entirely with the view presented in the description of the principle of the anticipations as indeed it should.

55. Intriguingly the argument Leibniz provides for *petite perceptiones* is precisely of the sort that there must at all times be apprehension of some form of sensation as otherwise there would not be experience given. It would be worth thinking of the connection between this argument and Kant's treatment of the principle of the anticipations on another occasion.

56. Wolff (1963, p. 235).

57. Paton (1936, Vol. 2, p. 148).

58. Nagel's challenge to these points of Kemp Smith's translation has been effective. It is stated in Nagel (1983, pp. 101–2) and followed in Abela (2002, pp. 137–9) and the translations of the *Critique* by Guyer and Wood and Pluhar conform here to the suggestions Nagel has made. Nagel also challenges Kemp Smith's translation of the opening paragraph that was added to the

Anticipations in the second edition but if his challenge to the first passage falls, as I will argue it does, this second challenge has rather less importance.

59. Nagel (1983, p. 101) and the subsequent amplification of the point over this page and the one following makes it clear that Nagel takes apprehension of the degree to involve awareness of particular quantitative measures.

60. See Paton (1936, Vol. 2, pp. 137–8), where Paton lists three possible meanings of sensation before selecting this one as Kant's.

61. Guyer (1987, pp. 203–4).

62. The place of material principles in theoretical philosophy awaits more detailed treatment and should awaken suspicion of Kant's attempt in the *Prolegomena* to declare his view that of "formal" idealism, a designation adopted to distance his position from that of Berkeley. For an argument for the centrality of material principles to the understanding of practical philosophy, see G. Banham (2003).

63. Guyer (1987, p. 187) where he states that it is difficult not to read the principle of the anticipations as involving a statement about "the *existence* of an empirical object", namely the "object" of sensation.

7 Substance, causality and community

1. Schönfeld (2000, Chapter 6 *passim*) shows that in intertwining ontological and epistemological principles Kant was both following and subverting procedures of School Philosophy. It is particularly notable that Baumgarten, following Aristotle, thinks of such principles as those of contradiction as *ontological*.

2. This leads Kant to formulate his version of a proof of the existence of God here namely that "nothing can be conceived of as possible unless whatever is real in every possible concept exists and indeed exists necessarily" (Ak. 1: 395). This argument is explicitly distinguished from the Cartesian ontological one in a manner which foreshadows the treatment in *The Only Possible Argument*. It would be work for another occasion to treat the genesis and structure of Kant's treatment of the arguments for the existence of God in the *Critique*, a treatment importantly intertwined with the consideration of how he arrives at and justifies the Postulates of Empirical Thought. I hope to undertake this enquiry on another occasion.

3. For an extensive treatment of these elements of the *New Elcudiation* and the subsequent Critical version of them in the Third Antinomy, see Banham (2003), Chapters 1 and 2.

4. The problem about that which remains constant and permits notice of change is centrally connected to the understanding of substance as the structure of Aristotle's *Metaphysics* shows concluding as it does with a discussion of the nature of change after having formally deduced the properties of substances.

5. In the *Monadology* Leibniz is clear that only internal change occurs to substances but thinks he can argue that such internal change does not require the interaction of substances.

6. Friedman (1992, p. 8). Langton is aware of this view and unsure as to whether it means that Friedman takes it that Kant is committed to the

doctrine that space is thus constituted by substances or by the dynamical properties of substances. The difference in scope between these points would be that if space is constituted only by dynamical properties of substances but that these latter are co-original with the substances then relational properties would still not be reducible to non-relational ones. See Langton (1998), pp. 108–9, n. 17.

7. Guyer (1987, p. 352), although the citation given here in support of this view from Ak. 1: 413 merely states that relations and their determining reasons cannot be said to be based directly upon the existence of a substance and hence is far from being a full argument to the effect that relations are not "real". Nonetheless the distinction of relational notions from substantial ones is one that Langton has to concede in some sense as we shall see.

8. Lorne Falkenstein (2001) "Debate: Langton on Things in Themselves", *Kantian Review*, Vol. 5, p. 58. John A. Reuscher (1977) "A Clarification and Critique of Kant's Principiorum Primorum Cognitionis Metaphysicae Nova Dilucidatio", *Kant-Studien*, Vol. 68, p. 30, argues more charitably that Kant is here providing a basis for physics and it is clearly the intent of the demonstration of the Principle of Co-Existence to show a ground for gravity.

9. Rae Langton (2001) "Reply to Lorne Falkenstein", *Kantian Review*, Vol. 5, p. 71.

10. Langton (1998) tries to deny this view due to the implication that relational properties are thereby shown to be dependent on non-relational ones, just as we have argued to be the case in the *New Elucidation* giving the following reason: "The requirement that substances must have some intrinsic nature is not the requirement that relations must supervene on intrinsic properties. It is a far weaker requirement. The requirement that substances must have some intrinsic nature follows simply from the independence requirement on substance. A substance may be independent whether or not relations are reducible to intrinsic properties" (p. 102). Here Langton elides *dependence* of relational properties on intrinsic ones with *reducibility* of relational properties to intrinsic ones but one does not follow from the other.

11. This interpretation is close to Friedman (1992). Friedman argues that Kant has here combined the Newtonian view of the *reality* of space with the Leibnizian conception of its relational character and with the latter having been safeguarded shown space to be derivative of external relations between monads (Friedman, 1992, p. 9, n. 12). Since the spatial relations are dependent on the external relations of the substance it only remains to ask whether these external relations are further dependent on intrinsic properties but since the external relations are precisely accepted by Kant to be extrinsic and extrinsic properties to be dependent upon intrinsic ones the answer seems to me to be clearly in the affirmative.

12. This earlier letter dated 7 June 1771 indicated that Kant was at work on something that would discuss "The Bounds of Sensibility and Reason" (Ak. 10: 123).

13. Kemp Smith (1918, p. 355), where he also objects to the first edition formulation as requiring the division of the principles into mathematical and dynamical, to which he also objects.

14. Paton (1936, Vol. 2, p. 160).

15. Wolff (1963, p. 240) and see Guyer (1987, p. 208) for a similar view.

16. Guyer (1987, p. 210).

17. Paton (1936, Vol. 2, pp. 207–9), where Paton provides some tentative reasons for rejecting the equation of this principle with Newton's. Strawson (1966) comments in lapidary fashion that "the arguments for the Principles can, in a number of cases, be reasonably viewed as fundamental assumptions of physical theory as it existed in Kant's day" subsequently making clear he means Newtonian assumptions (pp. 118–19). For an interpretation of the argument of the First Analogy in accord with this view, see Carl Friedrich V. Weizsäcker (1971) "Kant's 'First Analogy of Experience' and Conservation Principles of Physics", *Synthese*, Vol. 23. Kant treats Newton's three laws in the *Metaphysical Foundations of Natural Science* (Ak. 4: 542–7) and the connection between them and the Analogies would require lengthy treatment, not in my view on the lines suggested by Strawson and Weizsäcker.

18. Allison (2004, p. 237), where Allison makes clear that he does not think this is what Kant is doing and here Guyer (1987) is in agreement stating that the second edition formulation follows from the main arguments Kant gives for the First Analogy (p. 216).

19. Paton (1936, Vol. 2, p. 196): "Kant is asking how there can be any durations for us to measure." That duration is noticeable *at all* refers us to transcendental conditions not how one change is measured relatively to a different change but what it is that enables us to say that there is *any* change. The direct contrary of this view is stated by Arthur Melnick (1973) *Kant's Analogies of Experience*, Chicago and London: The University of Chicago Press, who writes: "The First Analogy is concerned with the determination of time magnitude; i.e., with determining (measuring) time intervals" (p. 60).

20. Longuenesse (1993, p. 344), where this point is explicitly presented in reply to Melnick (1973).

21. A separate argument Guyer tries to generate from this citation concerns whether the understanding of matter as permanent despite its transitory way of being given leads to the conception that the permanence of it is an inference (Guyer, 1987, p. 220). That it does not was however part of the argument of the Anticipations where the immediacy of sensation is shown to be the prime element of experience, an immediacy that points directly to the apprehension of magnitudes in experience.

22. Jonathan Bennett (1966) *Kant's Analytic*, Cambridge and New York: Cambridge University Press, pp. 182–4.

23. Wolff (1963, p. 255) where having stated this Wolff goes on to contend that this entails that the argument for the First Analogy is thereby contrary "to the trend of the general argument in the Analytic". It is not contrary to the argument for the Anticipations as it accords entirely with our presentation of this and we will show in due course that it is also not contrary to the argument for the other two analogies.

24. James Van Cleve (1999, p. 108). This argument is a variant of the view that only relative persistence is required for objects to be represented, not the permanence of nature that Kant's argument requires, a point stated by, for example, Strawson (1966, p. 129).

25. In the *Opus Postumum* Kant argues for the existence of an *ether* on grounds similar to those suggested by Van Cleve.

26. Kemp Smith (1918, p. 363) gives a description of the different arguments said to exist and Paton (1936, Vol. 2, p. 224) corresponds to this division.

On the basis of these accounts six distinct arguments are said to exist for the principle of the Second Analogy. This approach has fallen out of favour in more recent treatments with the emphasis instead shifting to providing a reconstruction of the single argument taken to be underlying the discussion. Without seeking here to entirely revive the earlier approach I will be giving reasons for thinking that the argument for the Second Analogy conforms to some degree to the division of it given by Paton although it is noticeable that the whole discussion from A204–11/B249–56 is neglected in his account.

27. In the *Treatise* Hume remarks: "Either we have no idea of necessity, or necessity is nothing but that determination of the thought to pass from causes to effects and from effects to causes, according to their experienc'd union" Hume (1739, Book I, Part 3, Section XIV, p. 166). Here and in this chapter Hume makes clear that for him causal connection can only be a subjective combination that arises from comparison and in the very next paragraph subsequent to this one draws the direct consequence that therefore causal relations are in essence equivalent to mathematical relations.

28. So I cannot here agree with Paton that this part of the discussion fails to add anything to what has been stated (Paton, 1936, Vol. 2, p. 252). With regard to the point about mathematical combination, it is worth pointing out that Kant describes the view that the causal law could arise from inductive generalization as a "construction" of its concept (A196/B241).

29. Steven M. Bayne (2004) *Kant on Causation: On the Fivefold Routes to the Principle of Causation*, Albany: State University of New York Press, p. 33.

30. Guyer (1987, p. 252, my emphasis). Guyer adds that the information concerning the particular circumstances is the reply to "Kant's question of just *how* we can identify the event" (p. 252).

31. Graham Bird (1962) *Kant's Theory of Knowledge: An Outline of One Central Argument in the "Critique of Pure Reason"*, London: Routledge & Kegan Paul and New York: Humanities Press, p. 165.

32. Bird's construal of Kant's argument is the one that is vulnerable to Strawson's infamous accusation of a "a *non sequitur* of numbing grossness" as this accusation rested on the assumption that Kant moved from conceptual necessity to causal necessity in his argument which is just what Bird attempts to do. See Strawson (1966, pp. 137–8).

33. This proof is rarely attended to in the secondary literature which focuses almost exclusively upon the argument from irreversibility that involves the contrast between house and ship. For a good example of this focus, see Bayne (2004) *passim* who shows it to underlie interpretations of quite different sorts and who continues to subscribe to it himself.

34. My view here is close to that of Margaret Morrison who, in her important article on the Third Analogy, states the following: "What the third analogy provides is the unified spatial structure that allows to locate matter (substance) in space and to experience motion through a continuous space. Each of the relational categories/principles is concerned with a specific kind of time determination; what makes the third analogy different is that the temporal feature (simultaneity and coexistence) cannot be achieved without the accompanying spatial component. In other words, we cannot conceive of two substances existing at the same time unless they are in different regions of space." Margaret Morrison (1998) "Community and Coexistence:

Kant's Third Analogy of Experience", *Kant-Studien*, Vol. 89, p. 272. What Morrison does not point out but which has been a point we have returned to again and again is the co-determination of time and space. Just as space is the only form in which time can be represented so is temporal order here shown to be necessary for the conception of spatial position.

35. Langton (1998, p. 166) effectively also states this point when she mentions that Kant makes *powers* or *forces* the primary properties of substances. This emphasis connects to the denial of a reducibility thesis in the *Critique* concerning relational properties. It should be clear however that this thesis is quite different from that of the *New Elucidation* as the latter's conception of relational properties prevents them from having the status of fundamental metaphysical principles in making them dependent on the accidental nature of God's action. In the *Critique* by contrast the reference to God is unnecessary to think the material necessity of relational properties and this indicates that these properties possess finally in the latter work the characteristic of true necessity in experience.

Bibliography

Primary sources

The standard German edition of Kant's works is that of the Prussian Academy of Sciences that was begun in 1902 and continued subsequently by the German Academy of Sciences. Citations are given from its pagination except when the *Critique* is itself being quoted as this is referred to according to standard A and B references. A number of translations of the *Critique* are now available but I have chosen here to cite Norman Kemp Smith's translation as I have become convinced that it is the clearest not only for teaching the *Critique* to students but also when engaging in serious reflection on the *Critique*. The reissuing of this translation by Palgrave Macmillan is an important corrective to the tendency to abandon it in recent years in favour of other translations. Cambridge University Press have been providing English readers in recent years with a large number of translations of Kant's works and the following have been used here:

Henry Allison and Peter Heath (eds) (2002) *Theoretical Philosophy after 1781.*
David Walford and Ralf Meerbote (eds and trans.) (1992) *Theoretical Philosophy 1755–1770.*
Karl Ameriks and Steve Naragon (eds and trans.) (1997) *Lectures on Metaphysics.*
Arnulf Zweig (ed. and trans.) (1999) *Correspondence.*
J. Michael Young (ed. and trans.) (1992) *Lectures on Logic.*

Secondary sources

Abela, Paul (2002) *Kant's Empirical Realism*, Oxford and New York: Oxford University Press.
Alexander, H. G. (ed.) (1956) *The Leibniz-Clarke Correspondence*, Manchester and New York: Manchester University Press.
Allison, Henry (1983) *Kant's Transcendental Idealism: An Interpretation and Defense*, New Haven and London: Yale University Press.
—— (2004) *Kant's Transcendental Idealism: An Interpretation and Defense: Revised and Enlarged Edition*, New Haven and London: Yale University Press.
Alston, William P. (1954) "Particulars—Bare and Qualified" in *Philosophy and Phenomenological Research*, Vol. 15, No. 2.
Ameriks, Karl (1992) "The Critique of Metaphysics: Kant and Traditional Ontology" in Karl Ameriks (ed.) (2003).
—— (2000) *Kant and the Fate of Autonomy: Problems in the Appropriation of the Critical Philosophy*, Cambridge and New York: Cambridge University Press.
—— (2003) *Interpreting Kant's Critiques*, Oxford and New York: Oxford University Press.
Banham, Gary (2000) *Kant and the Ends of Aesthetics*, London and New York: Macmillan.
—— (2002) "Kant's Critique of Right", *Kantian Review*, Vol. 6.

—— (2003) *Kant's Practical Philosophy: From Critique to Doctrine*, London and New York: Palgrave Macmillan.

—— (2005a) "Mereology, Intentional Contents and Intentional Objects" in Gary Banham (ed.) (2005b).

—— (ed.) (2005b) *Husserl and the Logic of Experience*, London and New York: Palgrave Macmillan.

—— (2005c) "Husserl, Derrida and Genetic Phenomenology", *Journal of the British Society for Phenomenology*, Vol. 36, No. 2, May 2005.

Barker, Stephen (1985) "Kant's View of Geometry: A Partial Defense" in Posy (ed.) (1992).

Barnes, Jonathan (ed.) (1984) *The Complete Works of Aristotle: The Revised Oxford Translation*, Princeton and Chichester: Princeton University Press.

Bayne, Steven M. (2004) *Kant on Causation: On the Fivefold Routes to the Principle of Causation*, Albany: State University of New York Press.

Beck, Lewis White (1975) "Did the Sage of Königsberg Have No Dreams?" *Essays on Kant and Hume*, New Haven and London: Yale University Press.

—— (1986) "Introduction" to L. W. Beck, Mary Gregor, R. Meerbote and J. A. Reuscher (eds) *Kant's Latin Writings: Translations, Commentaries and Notes*, New York: Peter Lang.

Beiser, Frederick C. (2002) *German Idealism: The Struggle Against Subjectivism 1781–1801*, Cambridge, Mass. and London: Harvard University Press.

Bennett, Jonathan (1966) *Kant's Analytic*, Cambridge and New York: Cambridge University Press.

Bird, Graham (1962) *Kant's Theory of Knowledge: An Outline of One of the Central Arguments of the "Critique of Pure Reason"*, London: Routledge & Kegan Paul, and New York: Humanities Press.

Brittan Jr, Gordon G. (1978) *Kant's Theory of Science*, Princeton: Princeton University Press.

Brook, Andrew (1994) *Kant and the Mind*, Cambridge and New York: Cambridge University Press.

Castaneda, Hector-Neri (1960) " '7 + 5 = 12' As a Synthetic Proposition", *Philosophy and Phenomenological Research*, Vol. 21, No. 2.

Caygill, Howard (1989) *Art of Judgement*, Oxford: Basil Blackwell.

—— (1995) *A Kant Dictionary*, Oxford: Basil Blackwell.

Crowther, Paul (1998) "Judgment, Self-Consciousness and Imagination: Kant's Transcendental Deduction and Beyond" in Herman Parrett (ed.) *Kant's Aesthetics*, Berlin and New York: Walter De Gruyter.

Falkenstein, Lorne (1991) "Kant's Account of Intuition", *Canadian Journal of Philosophy*, Vol. 21, No. 2.

—— (2001) "Debate: Langton on Things in Themselves", *Kantian Review*, Vol. 5.

Förster, Eckart (ed.) (1989) *Kant's Transcendental Deductions: The Three "Critiques" and the "Opus Postumum"*, Stanford: Stanford University Press.

Franzswa, Gregg E. (1978) "Space and the Schematism", *Kant-Studien*, Vol. 69.

Friedman, Michael (1992) *Kant and the Exact Sciences*, Cambridge, Mass. and London: Harvard University Press.

Goudeli, Kryiaki (2002) *Challenges to German Idealism: Schelling, Fichte and Kant*, London and New York: Palgrave Macmillan.

Guyer, Paul (1979) "Review" of Henrich (1976), *The Journal of Philosophy*, Vol. 76, No. 3.

—— (1980) "Kant on Apperception and *A Priori* Synthesis", *American Philosophical Quarterly*, Vol. 17, No. 3.

—— (1982a) "Kant's Tactics in the Transcendental Deduction" in J. N. Mohanty and Robert W. Shahan (eds) *Essays on Kant's "Critique of Pure Reason"*, Norman: University of Oklahoma Press.

—— (1982b) "Kant on Apperception and *A Priori* Synthesis", *American Philosophical Quarterly*, Vol. 17, No. 3.

—— (1986) "The Failure of the B-Deduction", *Southern Journal of Philosophy*, Vol. XXV, Supplement.

—— (1987) *Kant and the Claims of Knowledge*, Cambridge and New York: Cambridge University Press.

—— (1989) "Psychology and the Transcendental Deduction" in Eckart Förster (ed.).

Hanna, Robert (2001) *Kant and the Foundations of Analytic Philosophy*, Oxford and New York: Oxford University Press.

—— (2002) "Mathematics for Humans: Kant's Philosophy of Arithmetic Revisited", *European Journal of Philosophy*, Vol. 10, No. 3.

Harte, Verity (2002) *Plato on Parts and Wholes: The Metaphysics of Structure*, Oxford and New York: Clarendon Press.

Heidegger, Martin (1927) *Being and Time*, translated by J. Macquarrie and E. Robinson, Oxford: Basil Blackwell, 1978.

—— (1927–8) *Phenomenological Interpretation of Kant's "Critique of Pure Reason"*, translated by Parvis Emad and K. Maly, Bloomington and Indianapolis: Indiana University Press, 1997.

—— (1929) *Kant and the Problem of Metaphysics*, translated by Richard Taft, Bloomington and Indianapolis: Indiana University Press, 1990.

—— (1935) *What is a Thing?*, translated by W. B. Barton and V. Deutsch, Chicago: Regnery, 1967.

Hempel, Carl (1958) "Review" of Sellars (1949 and 1952) with Alston (1954), *The Journal of Symbolic Logic*, Vol. 23, No. 4.

Henrich, Dieter (1955) "On the Unity of Subjectivity" in D. Henrich (ed.) (1994) *The Unity of Reason: Essays on Kant's Philosophy*, Cambridge, Mass. and London: Harvard University Press.

—— (1969) "The Proof-Structure of Kant's Transcendental Deduction", *The Review of Metaphysics*, Vol. 22.

—— (1976) "Identity and Objectivity: An Inquiry into Kant's Transcendental Deduction" in D. Henrich (ed.) (1994).

Hintikka, Jaakko (1967) "Kant on the Mathematical Method", *The Monist*, Vol. 51, reprinted in Carl J. Posy (ed.) (1992) *Kant's Philosophy of Mathematics: Modern Essays*, Dordrecht and London: Kluwer Academic Publishers.

—— (1969) "On Kant's Notion of Intuition (*Anschauung*)" in T. Penelhum and J. J. MacIntosh (eds) *The First Critique: Reflections on Kant's Critique of Pure Reason*, Belmont: Wadsworth Publishing Company.

—— (1973) *Logic, Language-Games and Information: Kantian Themes in the Philosophy of Logic*, Oxford: Clarendon Press.

Hopkins, J. (1973) "Visual Geometry", *Philosophical Review*, Vol. LXXXII.

Hume, David (1739) *A Treatise of Human Nature*, Oxford: Clarendon Press, 1967.

Husserl, Edmund (1894) "Psychological Studies in the Elements of Logic" in E. Husserl (ed.) (1994) *Early Writings in the Philosophy of Logic and Mathematics*, translated by D. Willard, Dordrecht and London: Kluwer Academic Publishers, 1994.

—— (1900–1901) *Logical Investigations*, translated by J. N. Findlay (1970), partially modified by D. Moran, London and New York: Routledge, 2000.

—— (1913) *Ideas I: General Introduction to Pure Phenomenology*, translated by W. R. Boyce Gibson, New York: Collier Books, and London: Collier Macmillan, 1931.

—— (1920–5) *Analyses Concerning Active and Passive Synthesis: Lectures on Transcendental Logic*, translated by Robert Steinbock, Dordrecht and London: Kluwer, 2001.

—— (1929) *Formal and Transcendental Logic*, translated by Dorion Cairns, The Hague: Martinus Nijhoff, 1969.

Keller, Pierre (1998) *Kant and the Demands of Self-Consciousness*, Cambridge and New York: Cambridge University Press.

Kitcher, Patricia (1986) "Connecting Intuitions and Concepts at B160n", *Southern Journal of Philosophy*, Vol. XXV, Supplement.

—— (1990) *Kant's Transcendental Psychology*, Oxford and New York: Oxford University Press.

—— (1999) "Kant on Self-Consciousness", *The Philosophical Review*, Vol. 108, No. 3.

Langton, Rae (1998) *Kantian Humility: Our Ignorance of Things In Themselves*, Oxford and New York: Oxford University Press.

——(2001) "Reply to Falkenstein", *Kantian Review*, Vol. 5.

Leibniz, G. W. (ed.) (1714) "Monadology", *Philosophical Texts*, Oxford and New York: Oxford University Press, 1998.

Locke, John (1690) *Essay Concerning Human Understanding*, Penguin: London, 1997 edition.

Longuenesse, Béatrice (1993) *Kant and the Capacity to Judge: Sensibility and Discursivity in the Transcendental Analytic of the "Critique of Pure Reason"*, translated by Charles T. Wolfe, Princeton and Oxford: Princeton University Press, 1998.

—— (2001) "Kant's Deconstruction of the Principle of Sufficient Reason", *The Harvard Review of Philosophy*, Vol. IX.

Martin, Gottfried (1938) *Arithmetic and Combinatorics: Kant and His Contemporaries*, translated by J. Wubnig, Carbondale: Southern Illinois University Press, 1985.

McDowell, John (1994) *Mind and World*, Cambridge, Mass. and London: Harvard University Press.

—— (1998) "Having the World in View: Sellars, Kant, and Intentionality", *The Journal of Philosophy*, Vol. XCV, No. 9.

Meerbote, Ralf and Harper, W. H. (eds) (1984) *Kant on Causality, Freedom and Objectivity*, Minneapolis: University of Minnesota Press.

Melnick, Arthur (1973) *Kant's Analogies of Experience*, Chicago and London: The University of Chicago Press.

Moreland, J. P. (2001) *Universals*, Chesham: Acumen.

Morrison, Margaret (1998) "Community and Coexistence: Kant's Third Analogy of Experience", *Kant-Studien*, Vol. 89.

Nagel, Gordon (1983) *The Structure of Experience: Kant's System of Principles*, Chicago and London: University of Chicago Press.

Parsons, Charles (1969) "Kant's Philosophy of Arithmetic" in Posy (ed.) (1992).

Paton, H. J. (1936) *Kant's Metaphysics of Experience*, 2 volumes, London: George Allen & Unwin, and New York: Humanities Press.

Pippin, Robert B. (1997) *Idealism As Modernism: Hegelian Variations*, Cambridge and New York: Cambridge University Press.

Posy, Carl J. (ed.) (1992) *Kant's Philosophy of Mathematics: Modern Essays*, Dordrecht and Boston: Kluwer Academic Publishers.

Reuscher, J. A. (1977) "A Clarification and Critique of Kant's Principiorum", *Kant-Studien*, Vol. 68.

Russell, Bertrand (1897) *An Essay on the Foundations of Geometry*, Cambridge: Cambridge University Press.

Schönfeld, Martin (2000) *The Philosophy of the Young Kant: The Precritical Project*, Oxford and New York: Oxford University Press.

Sedgwick, S. (ed.) (2000) *The Reception of Kant's Critical Philosophy: Fichte, Schelling & Hegel*, Cambridge and New York: Cambridge University Press.

Sellars, Wilfrid (1949) "The Logic of Complex Particulars", *Mind* NS, Vol. 58, No. 231.

—— (1952) "Particulars" in W. Sellars (ed.) (1963).

—— (1957) "Logical Subjects and Physical Objects", *Philosophy and Phenomenological Research*, Vol. 17, No. 4.

—— (1963) *Science, Perception and Reality*, London: Routledge & Kegan Paul, and New York: Humanities Press.

—— (1967) "Some Remarks on Kant's Theory of Experience" in W. Sellars (ed.) (1974).

—— (1968) *Science and Metaphysics: Variations on Kantian Themes*, London and New York: Routledge & Kegan Paul.

—— (1974) *Essays on Philosophy and Its History*, Dordrecht and Boston: D. Reidel Publishing Company.

—— (1978) "The Role of the Imagination in Kant's Theory of Experience" in H. W. Johnstone, Jr (ed.) *Categories: A Colloquium*, University Park, PA: Penn. State University Press. (See also: Andrew Chrucky's website, *Problems From Wilfrid Sellars*, <http:/ /www.ditext.com/sellars/ikte.html> 10/04/02.)

Shabel, Lisa A. (2003) *Mathematics in Kant's Critical Philosophy: Reflections on Mathematical Practice*, New York and London: Routledge.

Shin, Sun-Joo (1997) "Kant's Syntheticity Revisited by Peirce", *Synthese*, Vol. 113.

Smith, Norman Kemp (1918) *A Commentary to Kant's "Critique of Pure Reason"*, London and New York: Macmillan Press.

Stout, G. F. (1930) "The Nature of Universals and Propositions", *Proceedings of the British Academy*.

—— (1947) "Distributive Unity as a Category", *Australasian Journal of Philosophy*, Vol. 25.

Strawson, P. F. (1957a) "Logical Subjects and Physical Objects", *Philosophy and Phenomenological Research*, Vol. 17, No. 4.

—— (1957b) "A Reply to Mr. Sellars", *Philosophy and Phenomenological Research*, Vol. 17, No. 4.

—— (1959) *Individuals: An Essay in Descriptive Metaphysics*, London: Methuen & Co. Ltd.

—— (1966) *The Bounds of Sense: An Essay on Kant's "Critique of Pure Reason"*, London and New York: Methuen & Co. Ltd.

—— (1970) "Imagination and Perception" in Strawson (ed.) (1974c).

—— (1974a) *Subject and Predicate in Logic and Grammar*, London: Methuen & Co. Ltd.

—— (1974b) "Preface" in Strawson (ed.) (1974c).

—— (1974c) *Freedom and Resentment and Other Essays*, London: Methuen & Co. Ltd.

Sutherland, Daniel (2005) "The Point of Kant's Axioms of Intuition", *Pacific Philosophical Quarterly*, Vol. 86.

Thompson, Manley (1972) "Singular Terms and Intuitions in Kant's Epistemology", *Review of Metaphysics*, Vol. 26.

Van Cleve, James (1999) *Problems From Kant*, Oxford and New York: Oxford University Press.

Walford, David and Meerbote, Ralf (1992) "Introduction" in *Theoretical Philosophy 1755–1770/Immanuel Kant*, translated and edited by David Walford and Ralf Meerbote, Cambridge and New York: Cambridge University Press.

Ward, Andrew (2001) "Kant's First Analogy of Experience", *Kant-Studien*, Vol. 92.

Warnock, Geoffrey (1949) "Concepts and Schematism", *Analysis*, Vol. 8.

Watkins, Eric (1997) "Kant's Third Analogy of Experience", *Kant-Studien*, Vol. 88.

Waxman, Wayne (1991) *Kant's Model of the Mind: A New Interpretation of Transcendental Idealism*, Oxford and New York: Oxford University Press.

Weatherston, Martin (2002) *Heidegger's Interpretation of Kant: Categories, Imagination and Temporality*, London and New York: Palgrave Macmillan.

Weizsäcker, Carl Friedrich V. (1971) "Kant's 'First Analogy of Experience' and Conservation Principles of Physics", *Synthese*, Vol. 23.

Wittgenstein, Ludwig (1945–9) *Philosophical Investigations*, translated by G. E. M. Anscombe, Oxford: Basil Blackwell, 1953.

Wolff, Robert Paul (1963) *Kant's Theory of Mental Activity: A Commentary on the Transcendental Analytic of the "Critique of Pure Reason"*, Cambridge, Mass.: Harvard University Press.

Wong, Wing-Chun (2000) "On A Semantic Interpretation of Kant's Concept of Number", *Synthese*, Vol. 121.

Zammito, John H. (1992) *The Genesis of Kant's Critique of Judgment*, Chicago and London: The University of Chicago Press.

Zöeller, Günter (1987) "Comments on Professor Kitcher's 'Connecting Intuitions and Concepts At B160n'", *Southern Journal of Philosophy*, Vol. XXV, Supplement.

—— (ed.) (2004) *Kant: Prolegomena to Any Future Metaphysics*, Oxford and New York: Oxford University Press.

Index